**Recent Titles in
Critical Responses in Arts and Letters**

The Critical Response to Mark Twain's *Huckleberry Finn*
Laurie Champion, editor

The Critical Response to Nathaniel Hawthorne's *The Scarlet Letter*
Gary Scharnhorst, editor

The Critical Response to Tom Wolfe
Doug Shomette, editor

The Critical Response to Ann Beattie
Jaye Berman Montresor, editor

The Critical Response to Eugene O'Neill

Edited by
John H. Houchin

Critical Responses in Arts and Letters, Number 5
Cameron Northouse, Series Adviser

Greenwood Press
Westport, Connecticut • London

Library of Congress Cataloging-in-Publication Data

The Critical response to Eugene O'Neill / edited by John H. Houchin.
    p. cm.—(Critical responses in arts and letters, ISSN
1057-0993 ; no. 5)
   Includes bibliographical references and index.
   ISBN 0-313-27617-X (alk. paper)
   1. O'Neill, Eugene, 1888-1953—Criticism and interpretation.
I. Houchin, John H. II. Series.
PS3529.N5Z62728 1993
812'.52—dc20   93-6562

British Library Cataloguing in Publication Data is available.

Copyright © 1993 by John H. Houchin

All rights reserved. No portion of this book may be
reproduced, by any process or technique, without the
express written consent of the publisher.

Library of Congress Catalog Card Number: 93-6562
ISBN: 0-313-27617-X
ISSN: 1057-0993

First published in 1993

Greenwood Press, 88 Post Road West, Westport, CT 06881
An imprint of Greenwood Publishing Group, Inc.

Printed in the United States of America

The paper used in this book complies with the
Permanent Paper Standard issued by the National
Information Standards Organization (Z39.48-1984).

10 9 8 7 6 5 4 3 2

Copyright Acknowledgments

The editor and publisher gratefully acknowledge permission for use of the following material:

"Seen on the Stage: The Provincetown Players," Anonymous, *Vogue*. Copyright © 1918, Condé Nast Publications.

"The Plays of Eugene O'Neill," Barrett H. Clark, *New York Sun*, 1919. From Molly Clark Day, reprinted by permission of the family of Barrett H. Clark.

"Second Thoughts on First Nights: The Provincetown Plays," by Alexander Woollcott, November 9, 1919, *The New York Times*. Copyright © 1919 by The New York Times Company. Reprinted by permission.

"The Drama: *Beyond the Horizon*," by J. Rankin Towse. Review of *Beyond the Horizon*, by Eugene O'Neill. Reprinted with permission from the *New York Post*. Copyright © New York Post Inc., 2/4/20.

"*Beyond the Horizon*," by Lola Ridge. *The New Republic*, January 5, 1921.

Kenneth Macgowan, "The New Season," *Theatre Arts Magazine*, January 1921. Used by permission of Peter Macgowan.

"*Emperor Jones* Revived," May 7, 1924, *The New York Times*. Copyright © 1924 by The New York Times Company. Reprinted by permission.

"The Play," by Alexander Woollcott, December 29, 1920, *The New York Times*. Copyright © 1920 by The New York Times Company. Reprinted by permission.

Ludwig Lewisohn, "*Gold*." Review of *Gold*, by Eugene O'Neill. *The Nation* magazine/The Nation Company, Inc., copyright 1921.

"Second Thoughts on First Nights," by Alexander Woollcott, November 13, 1921, *The New York Times*. Copyright © 1921 by The New York Times Company. Reprinted by permission.

"Chris and Poseidon: Man Versus God in *Anna Christie*," by Winifred L. Frazer, December 3, 1969. Reprinted by permission of *Modern Drama*.

"Theatre," by Harold Clurman, April 30, 1977. *The Nation* magazine/The Nation Co., Inc. © 1977.

"*The Hairy Ape*," by Stark Young. Review of *The Hairy Ape*, by Eugene O'Neill. *New Republic* 22 March, 1922: 112-113.

Hugo von Hofmannstahl, "Eugene O'Neill," *Freeman*, May 21, 1923 (translated by Barrett H. Clark). Reprinted by permission of the family of Barrett H. Clark.

"The Theatre: *Welded*," by George Jean Nathan. *American Mercury*, May 1924. A version of this article appears in Materia Critica, pp. 122-123. Reprinted by permission of Associated University Presses.

"New O'Neill Play and the Mayor," *New York Post*, May 16, 1924. From *The New York Post*. Reprinted with permission.

Edmund Wilson, "*All God's Chillun* and Others." Review of *All God's Chillun Got Wings*, by Eugene O'Neill. *New Republic* 28 May 1924: 22.

Peter J. Gillett, "O'Neill and the Racial Myths." *Twentieth Century Literature* XVIII (January-October 1972). Reprinted from *Twentieth Century Literature* XVIII (January-October 1972).

Douglas Watt, "O'Neill Rarity in Weak Revival." Reprinted by permission of *The Daily News*, © The Daily News, March 21, 1975.

Joseph Wood Krutch, "The God of Stumps." Review of *Desire Under the Elms*, by Eugene O'Neill. *Nation* 26 Nov. 1924: 578. *The Nation* magazine/The Nation Company, Inc., copyright 1924.

R.M.L. "*Desire Under the Elms*." Review of *Desire Under the Elms*, by Eugene O'Neill. *New Republic* 3 December 1924: 44.

Peter L. Hayes, "Biblical Perversion in *Desire Under the Elms*," *Modern Drama*, 11.4 (February 1969): 423-428. Reprinted by permission of *Modern Drama*.

Barrett H. Clark, "The New O'Neill Play and Some Others," *Drama*, February 1926. Used by permission of the family of Barrett H. Clark.

Richard Dana Skinner, "*The Great God Brown*." Review of *The Great God Brown*, by Eugene O'Neill. *Commonweal* 10 February 1926: 384. Copyright © Commonweal Foundation.

Stark Young, "*The Great God Brown*." Review of *The Great God Brown*, by Eugene O'Neill. *New Republic* 10 February 1926: 329-330.

Harold Clurman, "Theatre," January 1, 1973, p. 28, *The Nation* magazine/The Nation Co., Inc., © 1973.

Michael Hinden, "*The Birth of Tragedy* and *The Great God Brown*," *Modern Drama*, 15.2 (September 1973): 129-140. Reprinted by permission of *Modern Drama*.

"After the Battle," by Brooks Atkinson, January 22, 1928, *The New York Times*. Copyright © 1928 by The New York Times Company. Reprinted by permission.

Barrett H. Clark, "Eugene O'Neill and the Guild," *Drama*, March 1928. Used by permission of the family of Barrett H. Clark.

Doris M. Alexander, "*Strange Interlude* and Schopenhauer." Reprinted with permission of the publisher from *American Literature*, vol. 25/33. Copyright 1953/1961 by Duke University Press.

Richard Watts, Jr., "O'Neill's *Strange Interlude* Retains Its Dramatic Power." Review of *Strange Interlude*, by Eugene O'Neill, *New York Post* 12 March 1963. Reprinted with permission from the New York Post. Copyright © New York Post, Inc. 3/12/63.

Frederick C. Wilkens, *Strange Interlude* on Broadway, *The Eugene O'Neill Newsletter*, Spring 1985, p. 46. Reprinted by permission of Frederick C. Wilkens.

"*Lazarus Laughed* Produced on Coast," by George C. Warren, April 10, 1928, *The New York Times*. Copyright © 1928 by The New York Times Company. Reprinted by permission.

David Carb, "Seen on Stage: *Dynamo*," *Vogue*, March 30, 1929. Courtesy Vogue. Copyright © 1929 by The Condé Nast Publications, Inc.

Copyright Acknowledgments

"The Theatre: The American Dramatist," by George Jean Nathan, *American Mercury*, April 1929. Reprinted by permission of Associated University Presses.

"Tragedy Becomes O'Neill," by Brooks Atkinson, November 1, 1931, *The New York Times*. Copyright © 1931, by The New York Times Company. Reprinted by permission.

Robert Benchley, O'Neill's *Mourning Becomes Electra.*" *The New Yorker* (November 7, 1931): pages unknown. From *Benchley at the Theatre* (Ipswich Press). © 1931, 1959, Robert Benchley. Originally in *The New Yorker*. All rights reserved.

Joseph Wood Krutch, "Our Electra," Review of *Mourning Becomes Electra* by Eugene O'Neill. *Nation* 18 November, 1931: 551-552. The *Nation* magazine/The Nation Company Inc., copyright 1931.

Jack Kroll, "The Circle Moves Up," NEWSWEEK, 11/27/72, p. 78. From NEWSWEEK November 27, © 1972. All rights reserved. Reprinted by permission.

S. Georgia Nugent, "Masking Becomes Electra: O'Neill, Freud and the Feminine." *Comparative Drama* (Sprng 1988): 37-55. Reprinted by permission of the editors of *Comparative Drama* and S. Georgia Nugent.

Thomas F. Van Laan, "Singing in the Wilderness: A Dark Vision of Eugene O'Neill's Only Mature Comedy," *Modern Drama*, 22 (March 1979): 9-18. Reprinted by permission of *Modern Drama*.

John Simon, "Great Day for the Irish," *New York Magazine*. July 11, 1988, pp. 48-49. Review of *Ah, Wilderness!* and *Long Day's Journey Into Night*. Copyright © 1992 K-III Magazine Corporation. All rights reserved. Reprinted with the permission of New York Magazine.

George Jean Nathan, "The Theatre: L'amour et—Mon Dieu," *Vanity Fair*, March 1934. Reprinted by permission of Associated University Presses.

Fred Eastman, "O'Neill Discovers the Cross," Copyright 1934 Christian Century Foundation. Reprinted by permission from the February 7, 1934 issue of *The Christian Century*.

Lionel Trilling, "Eugene O'Neill," *The New Republic*, September, 1936.

Richard Watts, Jr., "Eugene O'Neill's New Play Is Powerful and Moving." Review of *The Iceman Cometh* by Eugene O'Neill, *New York Post* 10 Oct. 1946. Reprinted with permission, New York Post. Copyright © New York Post, Inc., 10/10/46.

"Iceman Returns," by Brooks Atkinson, May 20, 1956, *The New York Times*. Copyright © 1956 by The New York Times Company. Reprinted by permission.

Cyrus Day, "The Iceman and the Bridegroom: Some Observations on the Death of O'Neill's Salesman," *Modern Drama*. 1 (May): 3-9. Reprinted by permission of *Modern Drama*.

"Stage: 'Iceman Cometh' to Broadway," by Clive Barnes, December 14, 1973, *The New York Times*. Copyright © 1973 by The New York Times Company. Reprinted by permission.

Bette Mandl, "Absence as Presence: The Second Sex in *The Iceman Cometh*." *The Eugene O'Neill Newsletter*. (Summer/Fall 1982): 10-15.

Robert Brustein, "Robert Brustein on Theatre: Souls on Ice," *The New Republic*, October 28, 1985, pp. 41-43. Reprinted by permission of *The New Republic* © 1985, The New Republic, Inc.

Walter Kerr, "Long Day's Journey Into Night," © 1948, *The New York Herald Tribune*, November 8, 1948.

"Theatre: Tragic Journey," November 8, 1956 by Brooks Atkinson, *The New York Times*. Copyright © 1956, by The New York Times Company. Reprinted by permission.

Edith Oliver, "Off Broadway: Return Journey." *The New Yorker* (May 1, 1971): 94. Reprinted by permission, © 1971 The New Yorker Magazine, Inc. All rights reserved.

Jack Kroll, "Theatre: The Haunted Tyrones." From NEWSWEEK, 2/9/76 © 1976, Newsweek, Inc. All rights reserved. Reprinted by permission.

Clive Barnes, "Long Day's Worth the Journey." From the *New York Post*, March 4, 1981. Reprinted with permission.

John Henry Raleigh, "Communal, Familial, and Personal Memories in O'Neill's *Long Day's Journey Into Night*," *Modern Drama*, 31 (March 1988): 63-72. Reprinted by permission of *Modern Drama*.

Steven F. Bloom, *Long Day's Journey* in New York City, *The Eugene O'Neill Newsletter*, Summer/Fall 1986, p. 33.

Richard Hayes, "The Stage: The Image and the Search," *Commonweal*, August 30, 1957, 541-542. Copyright © Commonweal.

Anthony West, "*A Moon for the Misbegotten* and yet . . ." *Vogue*, Sept. 15, 1968. Courtesy Vogue. Copyright 1968 by the Condé Nast Publications, Inc.

Harold Clurman, "Theatre" (Review of *A Moon for the Misbegotten*). January 19, 1974. *The Nation* magazine/The Nation Co., Inc. © 1974.

John Simon, Review of "*A Moon for the Misbegotten*," *New York Magazine*. May 14, 1984. Copyright © 1992 K-III Magazine Corporation. All rights reserved. Reprinted with the permission of New York Magazine.

James A. Robinson, "The Metatheatrics of *A Moon for the Misbegotten*," in *Perspectives on O'Neill: New Essays*, Shyamal Bagchee, ed. Reprinted with permission of James A. Robinson, Associate Professor of English, University of Maryland.

John Chapman, "Portman, Hayes and Stanley Magnificent in *Touch of Poet*, *New York Daily News* (October 3, 1958): pages unknown. © 1990 New York News, Inc., Reprinted with permission.

Gore Vidal, "Theatre," Review of *A Touch of the Poet*, by Eugene O'Neill, *Nation* 25 Oct. 1958: 298-299. Gore Vidal, "Theatre," *The Nation* magazine/The Nation Company, Inc., copyright 1958.

T. E. Kalem, "Theatre: Dream Addict," TIME, 01/09/78. Copyright 1978 Time Warner, Inc. Reprinted by permission.

Laurin Porter, *A Touch of the Poet*: Memory and Creative Imagination, in *The Banished Prince: Time, Memory and Ritual in the Late Plays of Eugene O'Neill* (Ann Arbor: UMI Research Press, 1988) Chapter 2. Reprinted with the permission of Laurin Porter.

Wilfrid Sheed, "Late O'Neill." Review of *Hughie* by Eugene O'Neill. *Commonweal* 15 Jan. 1965: 518-519. Copyright © Commonweal Foundation.

"O'Neill's *More Stately Mansions* Opens," by Clive Barnes, November 1, 1967, *The New York Times*. Copyright © 1967 by The New York Times Company. Reprinted by permission.

John Simon, "Unfinished Mansions." Review of *More Stately Mansions*, by Eugene O'Neill. *Commonweal* 8 Dec. 1967: 335-336. Copyright © Commonweal Foundation.

Jere Real. "The Brothel in O'Neill's Mansions." *Modern Drama*, 11.4 (February 1970): 383-389. Reprinted by permission of *Modern Drama*.

Stephen L. Fluckiger. "The Idea of Puritanism in the Plays of Eugene O'Neill." *Renascence* (Spring 1978): 152-162.

Linda Ben-Zvi. "Freedom and Fixity in the Plays of O'Neill." *Modern Drama*, 31 (March 1988): 16-27. Reprinted by permission of *Modern Drama*.

"O'Neill's Many Mothers: Mary Tyrone, Josie Hogan, and Their Antecedents," in *Perspectives on O'Neill: New Essays*, Shyamal Bagchee, ed. This essay first appeared in *Perspectives on O'Neill: New Essays*, ed. Shyamal Bagchee, English Literary Studies, 1988.

Copyright Acknowledgments

Excerpts from Eugene O'Neill, *Long Day's Journey Into Night*, Copyright © 1955 by Carlotta Monterey O'Neill; Copyright 1956 by Yale University Press. Reprinted with permission of Yale University Press, Jonathan Cape Ltd., and the Estate of Eugene O'Neill.

Excerpts from Eugene O'Neill, *A Touch of the Poet*, Copyright © 1957 by Carlotta Monterey O'Neill. Reprinted with permission of Yale University Press, Jonathan Cape Ltd., and the Estate of Eugene O'Neill.

Excerpts from Eugene O'Neill, *More Stately Mansions*, Copyright © 1964 by Carlotta Monterey O'Neill. Reprinted with permission of Yale University Press.

Excerpts from Eugene O'Neill, *Anna Christie*, from PLAYS OF EUGENE O'NEILL. Copyright 1922 and renewed 1950 by Eugene O'Neill. Reprinted by permission of Random House, Inc., Jonathan Cape Ltd., and the Estate of Eugene O'Neill.

Excerpts from Eugene O'Neill, *Desire Under the Elms*, Copyright 1924 and renewed 1952 by Eugene O'Neill. Reprinted by permission of Random House, Inc., Jonathan Cape Ltd., and the Estate of Eugene O'Neill.

Excerpts from Eugene O'Neill, *Mourning Becomes Electra*, Copyright 1931 and renewed 1959 by Carlotta O'Neill. Reprinted by permission of Random House, Inc., Jonathan Cape Ltd., and the Estate of Eugene O'Neill.

Excerpts from Eugene O'Neill, *A Moon for the Misbegotten*, Copyright 1945, 1952 by Eugene O'Neill and renewed 1973 by Oona O'Neill Chaplin and Shane O'Neill. Reprinted by permission of Random House, Inc., Jonathan Cape Ltd., and the Estate of Eugene O'Neill.

Excerpts from Eugene O'Neill, *Strange Interlude*, Copyright 1928 and renewed 1956 by Carlotta O'Neill. Reprinted by permission of Random House, Inc., Jonathan Cape Ltd., and the Estate of Eugene O'Neill.

Excerpts from Eugene O'Neill, *Great God Brown*, Copyright 1926 and renewed 1954 by Carlotta Monterey O'Neill. Reprinted by permission of Random House, Inc., Jonathan Cape Ltd., and the Estate of Eugene O'Neill.

Excerpts from Eugene O'Neill, *The Iceman Cometh*, Copyright 1946 by Eugene O'Neill. Copyright renewed 1974 by Oona O'Neill and Shane O'Neill. Reprinted by permission of Random House, Inc., Jonathan Cape Ltd., and the Estate of Eugene O'Neill.

Excerpts from *The Philosophy of Schopenhauer* by Arthur Schopenhauer, edited by Irwin Edman. Copyright 1928 and renewed 1956 by The Modern Library, Inc. Reprinted by permission of Random House, Inc.

Every reasonable effort has been made to trace the owners of copyright materials in this book, but in some instances this has proven impossible. The editor and publisher will be glad to receive information leading to more complete acknowledgments in subsequent printings of the book and in the meantime extend their apologies for any omissions.

TO MY FAMILY,
JOHN AND VIRGINIA HOUCHIN,
ALICE HENDREX,
MARNI VAN DER LINDE,

AND TO
LYNN PIRANIO

Contents

Series Foreword by Cameron Northouse   xix
Preface   xxi

INTRODUCTION

The O'Neill Discourse   1
John H. Houchin

1. EARLY SUCCESS

Down an Alley on Drama Trail   9
Heywood Broun
Washington Square Players   10
Anonymous
The Play: New Bill at the Greenwich Village   10
Louis Sherwin
Seen on the Stage: The Provincetown Players   11
Anonymous
Theatre Arts Bookshelf   12
Anonymous
The Plays of Eugene O'Neill   12
Barrett H. Clark

Second Thoughts on First Nights: The Provincetown Plays   14
Alexander Woollcott
The Drama: *Beyond the Horizon*   15
J. Rankin Towse
Beyond the Horizon   16
Lola Ridge
Chris   19
Anonymous
Eugene O'Neill's Remarkable Play *The Emperor Jones*   19
O.W. Firkins
The New Season   22
Kenneth Macgowan
***Emperor Jones* Revived**   23
Anonymous

2. EXPERIMENTATION AND CONTROVERSY

The Play   25
Alexander Woollcott
Drama: *Gold*   26
Ludwig Lewisohn
Eugene O'Neill's *Anna Christie* **Is Thrilling Drama,
Perfectly Acted with a Bad Ending**   27
Maida Castellun
Second Thoughts on First Nights   29
Alexander Woollcott
Chris and Poseidon: Man Versus God in *Anna Christie*   30
Winifred L. Frazer
Theatre   36
Harold Clurman
Eugene O'Neill's *The Straw* **Is Gruesome Clinical Tale**   37
The Playgoer
First Man, **New O'Neill Play, Is Gloomy Suburban Story**   38
Lawrence Reamer
The New Play   40
Percy Hammond
The Hairy Ape   41
Stark Young
Eugene O'Neill's *Emperor Jones* **and** *The Hairy Ape*
as Mirror Plays   44
Emil Roy
The Theatre: Eugene O'Neill   53
Hugo von Hofmannstahl (translated by Barrett H. Clark)
The Theatre: *Welded*   57
George Jean Nathan

Contents

New O'Neill Play and the Mayor Anonymous	58
All God's Chillun and Others Edmund Wilson	60
O'Neill and Racial Myths Peter J. Gillett	61
O'Neill Rarity in Weak Revival Douglas Watt	71
Drama: The God of Stumps Joseph Wood Krutch	73
Desire Under the Elms R.M.L.	75
Biblical Perversion in *Desire Under the Elms* Peter L. Hayes	77
The New O'Neill Play and Some Others Barrett H. Clark	81
The Great God Brown Richard Dana Skinner	83
The Great God Brown Stark Young	85
Theatre Harold Clurman	87
The Birth of Tragedy and *The Great God Brown* Michael Hinden	88
After the Battle J. Brooks Atkinson	99
The Theatres: *Strange Interlude* Percy Hammond	100
Eugene O'Neill and the Guild Barrett H. Clark	102
Strange Interlude and Schopenhauer Doris M. Alexander	105
O'Neill's *Strange Interlude* **Retains Its Dramatic Power** Richard Watts, Jr.	117
Reviews of O'Neill Plays in Performance: *Strange Interlude* Frederick Wilkens	118
Lazarus Laughed **Produced on Coast** George C. Warren	120
Seen on Stage: *Dynamo* David Carb	122
The Theatre: The American Dramatist George Jean Nathan	125
Tragedy Becomes O'Neill J. Brooks Atkinson	126
The Theatre: Top Robert Benchley	129

Our Electra	131
Joseph Wood Krutch	
The Circle Moves Up	133
Jack Kroll	
Masking Becomes Electra: O'Neill, Freud, and the Feminine	134
S. Georgia Nugent	
A Great American Comedy	149
Euphemia Van Rensselaer Wyatt	
***Ah, Wilderness* Revived by Guild**	150
John Anderson	
Singing in the Wilderness: The Dark Vision in Eugene O'Neill's Only Mature Comedy	152
Thomas F. Van Laan	
Great Day for the Irish	160
John Simon	
The Theatre: L'amour et—Mon Dieu	161
George Jean Nathan	
O'Neill Discovers the Cross	162
Fred Eastman	
Eugene O'Neill	165
Lionel Trilling	

3. THE LATE PLAYS

Eugene O'Neill's New Play Is Powerful and Moving	171
Richard Watts, Jr.	
O'Neill—at Long Last	173
Howard Barnes	
***Iceman* Returns**	175
J. Brooks Atkinson	
The Iceman and the Bridegroom: Some Observations on the Death of O'Neill's Salesman	177
Cyrus Day	
Stage: *Iceman Cometh* to Broadway	183
Clive Barnes	
Absence as Presence: The Second Sex in *The Iceman Cometh*	184
Bette Mandl	
Robert Brustein on Theatre: Souls on Ice	191
Robert Brustein	
Theatre: *Long Day's Journey Into Night*	193
Walter Kerr	
Theatre: Tragic Journey	195
J. Brooks Atkinson	
Off Broadway: Return Journey	196
Edith Oliver	

Contents xvii

Theatre: The Haunted Tyrones 197
  Jack Kroll
***Long Day's* Worth the Journey** 199
  Clive Barnes
Reviews of O'Neill's Plays in Performance: *Long Day's Journey Into Night* 200
  Steven Bloom
Communal, Familial, and Personal Memories in O'Neill's *Long Day's Journey Into Night* 203
  John Henry Raleigh
Great Day for the Irish 212
  John Simon
O'Neill Opus Long but Fiercely Great 213
  John McClain
The Stage: The Image and the Search 214
  Richard Hayes
Theatre: *A Moon for the Misbegotten* "and yet..." 216
  Anthony West
Theatre 217
  Harold Clurman
A Moon for the Misbegotten 220
  John Simon
The Metatheatrics of *A Moon for the Misbegotten* 221
  James A. Robinson
Portman, Hayes and Stanley Magnificent in *Touch of Poet* 233
  John Chapman
Theatre 234
  Gore Vidal
Theatre: Dream Addict 236
  T.E. Kalem
***A Touch of the Poet*: Memory and the Creative Imagination** 238
  Laurin Porter
The Stage: Late O'Neill 250
  Wilfrid Sheed
Theatre: O'Neill's *More Stately Mansions* Opens 252
  Clive Barnes
The Stage: Unfinished Mansions 254
  John Simon
The Brothel in O'Neill's *Mansions* 256
  Jere Real

4. THEMATIC ANALYSIS

The Idea of Puritanism in the Plays of O'Neill   263
    Stephen Fluckiger
Freedom and Fixity in the Plays of Eugene O'Neill   273
    Linda Ben-Zvi
O'Neill's Many Mothers: Mary Tyrone, Josie Hogan, and Their Antecedents   283
    Judith E. Barlow

AN O'NEILL CHRONOLOGY   291
SELECTED BIBLIOGRAPHY   297
    Index   311

Series Foreword

Critical Responses in Arts and Letters is designed to present a documentary history of highlights in the critical reception to the body of work of writers and artists and to individual works that are generally considered to be of major importance. The focus of each volume in this series is basically historical. The introductions to each volume are themselves brief histories of the critical response an author, artist, or individual work has received. This response is then further illustrated by reprinting a strong representation of the major critical reviews and articles that collectively have produced the author's, artist's or work's critical reputation.

The scope of *Critical Responses in Arts and Letters* knows no chronological or geographical boundaries. Volumes under preparation include studies of individuals from around the world and in both contemporary and historical periods.

Each volume is the work of an individual editor, who surveys the entire body of criticism on a single author, artist, or work. The editor then selects the best material to depict the critical response received by an author or artist over his/her entire career. Documents produced by the author or artist may also be included when the editor finds that they are necessary to a full understanding of the materials at hand. In circumstances where previous, isolated volumes of criticism on a particular individual or work exist, the editor carefully selects material that better reflects the nature and directions of the critical response over time.

In addition to the introduction and the documentary section, the editor of each volume is free to solicit new essays on areas that may not have been adequately dealt with in previous criticism. For volumes on living writers and artists, new interviews may be included, again at the discretion of the volume's editor. The volumes also provide a supplementary bibliography and are fully indexed.

While each volume in *Critical Response to Arts and Letters* is unique, it is also hoped that in combination they will form a useful, documentary history of the critical response to the arts, and one that can be easily and profitably employed by students and scholars.

Cameron Northouse

Preface

The present volume attempts to present a comprehensive collection of critical opinions concerning Eugene O'Neill. It contains both reviews of productions and representative examples of scholarly research. This anthology is not an attempt to argue a specific thesis about O'Neill. Rather it is meant to illustrate to the reader the highly polarized opinions which O'Neill's dramas generated and the wide array of studies which they have inspired. The reviews and essays are arranged chronologically by play. That is, each play is treated in the order in which it was originally produced, and articles are arranged by play in the order of their publication date. Because of space limitations "minor plays" are limited to one review; major works are represented by at least two. Only New York productions have been included. Scholarly essays, rather than forming a discrete section, are arranged according to the preceding format. In this way the reader will be able to compare the attitudes of reviewers with those of academicians.

The essays have been written by a wide range of individuals. Some are authored by influential critics, others by anonymous observers. The main criterion for selection, however, was not the reputation of the author, but the uniqueness of the critical observation. The majority of this material has never been reprinted. A few essays, however, have appeared in other anthologies and have been included here because of their unquestioned worth.

The bibliographic entries represent only a fraction of the material which has been written about O'Neill. Books containing sections on O'Neill, or articles which appear in this or other anthologies have not been included. I have, however, listed the titles of these anthologies and marked them with an asterisk. Also omitted are the voluminous number of reviews and articles published in newspapers and popular periodicals. This awesome task has already been completed by Jordan Miller in *Eugene O'Neill and the American Critic* and Madeline Smith and Richard

Eaton in *Eugene O'Neill: An Annotated Bibliography*. Both books are absolutely necessary in order to conduct serious research.

    I would like to thank the following people for their kindness, patience and support throughout this process: Robert W. Corrigan, Robin Carbone, Laurie Champion, Kateri Cale, Cameron Northouse, Vicki Bullock, Sheila Blankenship, Henry Reed, Maureen Melino, Marilyn Brownstein, Gary Vena, Laurin Porter, Cathyann Fears, Ann LeStrange, Ed Walters, Jo Ellen Roach, Liz Leiba, Kelly Baggett and Tina McCallon.

The Critical Response to Eugene O'Neill

Introduction
The O'Neill Discourse
John H. Houchin

Eugene O'Neill has been the subject of more discussion than any other American in the history of theatre. During his lifetime literally hundreds of articles by gossip columnists, house and home journalists, religious writers, and drama critics were written about him. Since his death in 1953, scholars have studied his relationship to virtually every major literary figure in the Western world. Classicists, modernists, post-modernists and feminists have devoted acres of print and barrels of ink to the investigation and evaluation of his family, the sources of his plots and characters, his attitude toward women, his politics, his wives, his colleagues, his correspondence, and his unfinished plays. The reasons for this enduring fascination are nearly as divers as the areas of his art and life which have been investigated.

O'Neill was the first great playwright of the American theatre. He made his debut in 1915 into a theatrical arena which was littered with formulaic melodramas and mindless farces. They presented audiences with simplistic moral posturing and one dimensional characterizations. The dramatic revolution which swept Europe in the 1880's had not yet arrived in America. Although O'Neill did not necessarily set out to transform this theatrical landscape singlehandedly, he nonetheless succeeded in catapulting American drama into the vanguard of twentieth century art. During the first years of his career, he dignified the profession of playwright, elevating it from a purely technical role to that of a serious observer of the human condition. He expressed a general abhorrence of Victorian morality and especially the Protestant work ethic as it was expressed in middle class smugness, the adoration of technology and the addictive consumption of material goods. He attempted instead to create an indigenous American tragedy which embraced historical movements as well as individual subconscious pressures. For O'Neill, tragedy held the same significance it did for the Greeks, ennobling existence while releasing humans from the bondage of petty concerns. By attempting to create this type of theatre he hoped to illuminate the hopeless struggle for satisfaction which took place amidst the inescapable desperation of contemporary life.

Although O'Neill garnered considerable critical acclaim when he achieved his artistic goals, he became the subject of intense debate when his vision exceeded his skill. He was frequently excoriated for his lack of poetic ability and his failure to capture the elevated spirit of the Attic tragedies and those of Shakespeare and Racine. Other critics abused him for his heavy-handed treatment of situations and the unrelenting despair which permeated his narratives. Abysmal failures such as *Welded*, *Dynamo* and *Days Without End* provoked claims that O'Neill was indeed a hack whose reputation as a gifted artist was vastly overrated:

> Occasionally, its [*Dynamo*'s] wild raving is relieved by a pulsating dramatic scene in the author's fine early manner, but those occasions come so seldom that they fail to do more, either as illumination or as fire, than the sparks of a lighter that has no fuel....The unrest is stated, but no more. And the statement has been made in such an awkward manner and in terms so lugubrious, when not downright silly, that the impression comes early and persists throughout the evening that one is listening to the loud ululations of a schoolboy.[1]

These broadsides were countered, in turn, by equally aggressive defenses of his achievements. George Jean Nathan, who himself on occasion unleashed withering criticism of O'Neill, nonetheless defended his overall contributions:

> [He has] written a number of plays of very definite quality, a number of plays that outdistance any others thus far written by Americans and whether in his better work or poorer, shown an attitude and an integrity—to say nothing of a body of technical resource—far beyond those of any of his American rivals. There is something relatively distinguished about even his failures....[They contain] that peculiar thing that marks off even the dismal efforts of a first-rate man from those of a second-rate.[2]

This same controversy flared again in the late forties and early fifties, this time spurred by the premiere of *The Iceman Cometh*. Critics such as Mary McCarthy claimed that his language had the "wooden verisimilitude, the flat dead echoless sound of stale slang."[3] Eric Bentley asserted that O'Neill's fame was due to Broadway's "subintelligencia":

> They don't all like O'Neill, yet his "profound" art is inconceivable without them. O'Neill doesn't like *them*, but he needs them, and could never have dedicated himself to "big work" had their voices not been in his ears telling him he was big.[4]

The 1956 revival of *Iceman* and the premiere of *Long Day's Journey Into Night* prompted another revaluation which again enshrined O'Neill in the pantheon of twentieth century creative geniuses. Brooks Atkinson raved that the impact of *Long Day's Journey* transcended the story:

Introduction

> The characters are laid bare with pitiless candor. The scenes are big. The dialogue is blunt. Scene by scene the tragedy moves along with a remorseless beat that becomes hypnotic as though this were life lived on the brink of oblivion.[5]

Some years later John Gassner attempted to reconcile these widely differing opinions:

> It is true that O'Neill sometimes appears to be aiming too consciously at greatness. In the pursuit of magnitude he falls into some errors of taste and tact and tends to pile up his catastrophic situations and to schematize his dramatic conceptions....He is not a man for finesse; his temperament appears to have had little use for it. Whenever there is truth or depth of experience in the plays it is futile to wish that he had composed them less repetitively and insistently. Their emotional power is bound up with their massiveness.[6]

Robert Brustein reiterated this same observation in his 1985 review of a revival of *The Iceman Cometh*:

> Still one must recognize that the work consists not of one but of 13 plays, each with its own story; O'Neill has multiplied his antagonists in order to illuminate every possible aspect of his theme, and every rationalization, whether religious, racial, political, sexual, psychological, or philosophical, with which humankind labors to escape the truths of raw existence. And in some crazy inexplicable way, the very length of the play contributes to its impact, as if we had to be exposed to virtually every aspect of universal suffering in order to feel its full force.[7]

Aside from the controversy surrounding his artistic achievements, critics have also been fascinated by the autobiographical nature of his plays. Early champions such as Joseph Wood Krutch, Arthur Hobson Quinn and Barrett H.Clark frequently noted that his early sea plays were imbued with a reality which could have only been created by someone who had actually experienced the life he described. Also of great interest was the influence which his actor/father exercised over him as an artist. Even after James O'Neill had been dead for eight years and his son had won three Pulitzer Prizes, Robert Benchley credited the elder O'Neill for the success of *Mourning Becomes Electra*:

> Let us stop all this scowling talk about the "inevitability of Greek tragedy" and "O'Neill's masterly grasp of the eternal verities" and let us admit that the reason why we sat for six hours straining to hear each line...was because *Mourning Becomes Electra* is filled with good, old fashioned, spine-curling melodrama. It is his precious inheritance from his trouper-father....In this tremendous play he gives us not one thing that is new and he gives us nothing to think about...but he does thrill the bejeesus out of us, just as his father used to and that is why we go to the theatre.[8]

The noted scholar John Henry Raleigh develops this thesis even further. He claims that the theatre of his father's era, specifically *The Count of Monte Cristo*, influenced "the content, the technique, the rhetoric and the rhythm" of many of O'Neill's first plays. In addition he asserts that O'Neill's life-long preoccupation with the mystery of family and the ambiguities of paternity, maternity and son-ship likewise may have its roots in *Monte Cristo*.[9] This interest rapidly increased after

O'Neill's death. The appearance of *Long Day's Journey Into Night* and its spiritual sequel, *A Moon for the Misbegotten*, revealed the tragedies of the O'Neill family. Subsequent research disclosed that play after play had its conscious (and unconscious) genesis in O'Neill's "need to find a pattern of explanation by which his life could be understood."[10]

Throughout the previous discussion I have described some of the artistic and biographical factors which have kept O'Neill at the center of critical inquiry for seventy-five years. The precise nature of that inquiry is somewhat more convoluted. Basically, the life and work of O'Neill have been the focus of two related, but distinct groups of writers. The first, theatre critics, have been largely concerned with O'Neill the theatre practitioner. Consequently, the manner in which he dealt with the traditional elements of language, plot, characterization and scenography became issues of serious consideration. His experiments with formal elements such as masks, asides, soliloquies, and sound effects challenged accepted theatre practices and generated heated debates. Finally, controversial subject matter such as misogyny, incest, matricide, patricide, abortion, alcoholism, and drug addiction called into question the very nature and purpose of theatre.

The most contested of the above areas is O'Neill's ability (or inability) to construct language which illuminated his lofty ideas. O'Neill himself frequently acknowledged the difficulty he experienced constructing effective dramatic dialogue. He even made it the subject of a brief exchange between James and Edmund Tyrone in *Long Day's Journey*:

> TYRONE. Yes, there's the makings of a poet in you all right....
> EDMUND. The *makings* of a poet. No, I'm afraid I'm like the guy who is always panhandling for a smoke. He hasn't got the makings. He's only got the habit.[11]

Early critics, however, lauded the "mood and effectiveness" of the sea plays, and attributed them to the faithful "approximation" of the language of sailors.[12] Barrett H. Clark was even more lavish with his praise. He credited O'Neill with the ability to reveal the genuine feelings of his characters and for his sincere depiction of "that segment of life which he knows and with which he sympathizes....He makes you feel even in his feeblest work that he understands the secret springs in the men and women he sets before you."[13]

This enthusiasm continued until the production of *Gold* in June 1921. Poorly received, most critics voiced displeasure with the shallow, superficial realism of the dialogue. He was particularly berated for his inability to create a believable female role. Ludwig Lewisohn complained that "Mr. O'Neill's women are terrible lay figures who talk as shop-girls do not talk but as they imagine they would if it were their good fortune to be involved in a sad romantic situation."[14] Yet *Anna Christie* produced just five months later won a Pulitzer Prize and was roundly hailed for its language, which, like his characters "glows with life."[15] Alexander Woollcott, claiming that the play had sprung from the finest mind that had ever worked in American theatre, praised O'Neill as a "master of dramatic dialogue."[16]

What observers were beginning to experience, and what would become even more obvious, was the effectiveness of O'Neill's raw, emotionally charged characters versus those which sprang from intellectual or philosophical attitudes. As Edmund Wilson noted in his review of *All God's Chillun Got Wings*, "Mr. O'Neill's eloquence seems to diminish in direct proportion to his distance from the language of the people."[17] Even works which were acclaimed to be landmarks of American theatre received negative marks for language and dialogue—frequently in the same article. Robert Benchley labeled the asides in *Strange Interlude* "a lazy man's method of writing exposition."[18] Brooks Atkinson called the language "flagellation pursued for its own sake."[19] *Mourning Becomes Electra* also drew compromising opinions. Joseph Wood Krutch, after claiming that one had to compare it to *Hamlet* or *Macbeth* to find any flaw, went on to comment that the play lacked language—"words as thrilling as the action which accompanies them."[20]

Perhaps the most cogent explanation/defense of this O'Neillian quality has been offered by Jean Chothia. She asserts that O'Neill's keen displeasure with the condition of theatre compelled him to experiment with many types of dramatic expression. This explanation, in her opinion, accounts for the wide variety of scenic and costume elements as well as the wide array of verbal expression used in his plays. Moreover, she continues, O'Neill was committed to "supernaturalism" or "real realism," a concept he absorbed from Strindberg which expressed the true meaning and mystery of life:

> It [real realism] proclaims his dissatisfaction with mere presentation of the everyday incident...and his clear need to root his plays in a recognizable time and place and to create identifiably human characters. The adjectives—'super' and 'real'—suggest extraordinary intensity: looking at a man's face but seeing his psychological or metaphysical being; hearing his seemingly casual words and understanding their implications for himself....When we investigate O'Neill's experimentation with a succession of anti-realistic devices, then we need to recognize that, in part, the experimentation arises from the dramatist's search for ways of creating "real realism" on the stage.[21]

O'Neill eventually found the voice which could convey his vision of humanity, and he employed it in his final works. Moreover, significant revivals in the 1950's, 1970's and 1980's indicate that he created rich, multifaceted dramas which continue to have an impact on audiences. In Chothia's words, he extended the "limits [of expression] and did assimilate into his form means of exploring areas of human experience which continue to be of pressing interest to us today."[22]

O'Neill's commitment to the theatre as an artform and his unceasing experiments also account for the attention of the second group of critics—literary scholars. Originally motivated by his power as a theatre practitioner, their continued research now addresses his plays as literature rather than scripts to be performed. Although one area of research frequently overlaps into another, this scholarship can be roughly divided into four categories: interpretative studies, comparative explorations, historical analysis, and biographical and psychobiographical research. The first area is the oldest and largest body of criticism, and investigates topics such as Biblical interpretations, symbolism of certain scenic elements, examinations of racial portrayals and discourses on various philosophical attitudes.

Of significant interest is a subcategory of this area which treats O'Neill's female characters. Although it is impossible to exclude biographical observations when discussing this topic, the vast majority of this research has attempted to explicate to a contemporary audience the complicated, contradictory and largely denigrated position of women in the O'Neill canon. Among the outstanding scholars working in this area are Linda Ben-Zvi, Judith Barlow, Bette Mandl, Doris Nelson and Trudy Drucker.

The second area examines O'Neill's relationship to other writers comparing sources, attitudes, and influences. During his life O'Neill openly acknowledged his debt to Strindberg, Nietzsche, and the Attic tragedians. Yet his voluminous writings have revealed similarities between him and scores of dramatists, philosophers, and novelists. As a result his relationship to individuals such as Schopenhauer, Freud, Ibsen, Joyce, Anouilh, Dante, Beckett, Shakespeare, Blake, Hauptmann, Melville, Hemingway and Wilde has been actively explored.

Historical scholarship is a specialized area which traces the development of certain writing projects or documents the staging of certain productions. It also contains bibliographic research as well as collections of correspondence between O'Neill and his family, friends and business associates.[23]

Perhaps the most compelling of all O'Neill scholarship is the biographical and psychobiographical because it attempts to articulate how he translated his personal experiences into dramatic statements. The anguish of *Long Day's Journey* was immediately seized upon by critics. Walter Kerr called it a "savage examination of conscience" which was "deliberately, masochistically harrowing in the ferocity of its revelation."[24] Shortly thereafter, in 1958, Doris Falk published her important work, *Eugene O'Neill and the Tragic Tension*. An interpretative study, she nonetheless attempts to trace important psychological patterns in O'Neill's plays to his life. In 1962, Arthur and Barbara Gelb published their massive work, *O'Neill*, which very clearly links events in his life to his writing. This effort was followed by Louis Sheaffer's influential biographical analysis, *O'Neill: Son and Playwright* and *O'Neill: Son and Artist*, published in 1968 and 1973, respectively. In them he sets out to prove that "O'Neill defies fathoming in any depth...unless one comprehends his relations with his parents, his predominant feelings toward both of them."[25] In 1982 Michael Manheim asserted that all of the familial motifs present in O'Neill's plays "grow out of the memories which haunted O'Neill throughout his adult life."[26]

Thus O'Neill has remained one of the most closely scrutinized writers in the history of Western theatre. During his life his plays, whether successful or unsuccessful, provoked heated exchanges. After his death, the shrouded secrets of his family began to emerge, initially through his autobiographical plays and later through the diligent research of dedicated writers. What emerged was a portrait of an artist who used his creative gifts to purge his own psyche of guilt and anger. He hoped art could achieve what religion had failed to accomplish. Whether or not he finally managed to rid himself of his ghosts is uncertain, possibly unknowable. Yet his mystique, his vision, his passion and his suffering will continue to stimulate inquiry into this and every other area of his complex and contradictory life.

NOTES

1. David Carb, "Seen on Stage: *Dynamo*," *Vogue*, March 30, 1929.

2. George Jean Nathan, "The Theatre: The American Dramatist," *The American Mercury*, August 1929: 500.

3. Mary McCarthy, "Dry Ice," *Partisan Review*, November/December 1946: 578.

4. Eric Bentley, "Trying to Like O'Neill," *Kenyon Review*, July 1952: 488.

5. Brooks Atkinson, "Theatre: Tragic Journey," *New York Times*, November 8, 1956.

6. John Gassner, *Theatre at the Crossroads* (New York: Holt, Rinehart and Winston, 1960) 69-70.

7. Robert Brustein, "Souls on Ice," *New Republic*, October 28, 1985.

8. Robert Benchley, "The Theatre," *New Yorker*, November 7, 1931: 28.

9. John Henry Raleigh, "Eugene O'Neill and the Escape from the Château d'If," in *O'Neill*, John Gassner, ed. (Englewood Cliffs: Prentice Hall, 1965) 28.

10. Travis Bogard, *Contour in Time* (New York: Oxford University Press, 1972) xii.

11. Eugene O'Neill, *Long Day's Journey into Night* (New Haven: Yale University Press, 1955) 154.

12. Heywood Broun, "Down an Alley on Drama Trail," *New York Tribune*, January 17, 1917.

13. Barrett H. Clark, "The Plays of Eugene O'Neill," *New York Sun*, May 18, 1919.

14. Ludwig Lewisohn, "Drama: *Gold*," *Nation*, June 22, 1921: 902.

15. Maida Castellun, "Eugene O'Neill's *Anna Christie* Is Thrilling Drama, Perfectly Acted with a Bad Ending," *New York Call*, November 4, 1921.

16. Alexander Woollcott, "Second Thoughts on First Nights," *New York Times*, November 13, 1921.

17. Edmund Wilson, "All God's Chillun and Others," *New Republic*, May 28, 1924: 22.

18. Robert Benchley, "Drama," *Life*, February 16, 1928: 21.

19. Brooks Atkinson, "Put on by the Theatre Guild—March of the Wooden Asides," *New York Times*, February 5, 1928.

20. Joseph Wood Krutch, "Drama: Our Electra," *Nation*, November 18, 1931: 551.

21. Jean Chothia, *Forging a Language* (Cambridge: Cambridge University Press, 1979) 32-33.

22. Chothia, 188.

23. Because of the specialized nature of this research and its importance to continued scholarship, I have marked these works with a double asterisk in the bibliography.

24. Walter Kerr, "Long Day's Journey Into Night," *New York Herald Tribune*, November 8, 1956.

25. Louis Sheaffer, *O'Neill: Son and Playwright* (Boston: Little, Brown, 1968) vii.

26. Michael Manheim, *Eugene O'Neill's New Language of Kinship* (Syracuse: Syracuse University Press, 1982) 4.

1
Early Success

Down an Alley on Drama Trail

Heywood Broun

     Here is a play which owes more to the creation of mood and atmosphere than to any fundamentally interesting idea or sudden twist of plot. *Bound East for Cardiff* merely shows the death of a sailor in the forecastle of a British tramp on a foggy night. The appeal lies in the successful approximation of true talk in such a speech as the one where the dying sailor fretfully complains: "Why should it be a rotten night like this, with that damn whistle blowin' and people snorin' all around? I wish the stars was out and the moon, too; I c'd lie out on deck and look at them, and it'd make it easier to go— somehow."
     Approximation, rather then faithful reproduction, must be the aim of the dramatist who deals with the looser talking sort of folk. Obviously, it is impossible to set down the conversation of sailors word for word. And yet it is possible to make their talk sound real, as in the speech we have quoted, or unreal, as in the scene where Driscoll, "a red-haired giant, with battered features of a prizefighter," refers to one of his companions as a "divil-may care rake av a man." This is false, not so much because the phrase is obviously one which would not be heard from the mouth of a sailor, but because the spirit is false.
     Such slips are few in the play. Eugene O'Neill has written several short plays about the sea, and is probably familiar with that subject. At any rate, he strikes a rich vein, the old Kipling vein, in the bit where the dying man and his pal mull over the times they used to have. "The moving pictures in Barracas? Some class to them, d'yuh remember?"

And they talk of sounds in Paseo Colon, and smells in the La Plata, rows in Singapore and sprees in Port Said, to say nothing of the fight on a dock in Cape Town, when knives were drawn.

Appropriately enough, there is a touch of sentiment about the pleasant-spoken barmaid at the Red Stork, in Cardiff. Perhaps it is of her that Yank is thinking just before he dies, when he grabs the dipper of water and gasps: "I wish this was a pint of beer."

New York Tribune, January 30, 1917.

Washington Square Players

Anonymous

In a bill of four short plays, pleasingly contrasted, with which the Washington Square Players opened their fourth season, *In the Zone*, written by Eugene O'Neill, a young author whose previous identification rests with the Provincetown Players, was the one that will probably meet with the widest approval. As in *Bound East for Cardiff*, the best of Mr. O'Neill's former efforts, the local of *In the Zone* is the forecastle, but this time of a munition ship entering the submarine zone.

The drama that is enacted therein is as simple and appealing as it is rife with excitement and suspense. It will be realized that it takes adroit craftsmanship to build up a simple story into a distinct thriller without resorting to claptrap melodramatic methods, but here the author has heightened the excitement with subtle touches. The climax is constructed smoothly and with economy of dialogue.

The characters in the story are the motley crew of the tramp steamer. Half a dozen of them think they have discovered a German plotter in another member because he was overseen to act suspiciously with a little tin box, which meant to their overwrought minds nothing but a bomb. They bind and gag the man and gingerly open the box only to find a packet of letters from a girl, telling a story of love and the curse of drink which has separated the two.

New York Drama Mirror, November 10, 1917.

The Play: New Bill at the Greenwich Village

Louis Sherwin

The best that can be said for the latest program at the Greenwich Village Theatre is that it is much more interesting than the two that came before it. In fact, if it were not for the amateurish, slovenly performance of Schnitzler's *The Big Scene* one might even say that it was on the whole excellent. As it was, however, only one of the three divisions of the program was in every way worthy of praise. And that was Eugene O'Neill's *Ile*. Not only did it prove to be a playlet of a very high order, but the acting, the staging, and the atmosphere were quite admirable.

The man O'Neill arouses the keenest interest in me. I don't know of any young man writing for the stage today, either in Europe or America, who shows more promise. His sailors live as Joseph Conrad's Marlow and Lord Jim and the unforgettable crew of the *Narcissus* live. He knows life, at any rate the life of the sea. He knows the people of the sea and their women. He has a a feeling for irony, for the sardonic humor with which the gods plot the drama of human affairs. He knows not only how his people talk, but what they feel and what they hope and how destiny mocks their pathetic ambitions. Take, for instance, the captain of the whaler in this little play, driving his crew to despair and his wife to madness with his determination to go on and on and on until he has a shipload of "Ile." It is not for the money—he has plenty for his needs. It is not for fear of being jeered at by the folks at home—they would not dare jeer to his face. It is because he has always returned with a full shopload before and vanity won't let him sail home with less. Very simple and obvious psychology, isn't it? But it is true, it is real, and it is the sort of truth you seldom find in plays. And, above all, it is so well done, so powerfully, tersely, vividly written.

Mr. O'Neill's talent so far has been displayed in one-act pieces. I am really eager to see what he will do with a full three-act play. He has a rare gift—a gift to be envied. It is hoped that he is making the utmost of it.

The setting for *Ile*, designed by John Wenger, conveyed just the right atmosphere. And the acting of the captain's part by Joseph Macaulay was full of life and indomitable vigor. Harold Meltzer, too, was quite in the picture as the second mate. And Margaret Fareleigh as the captain's wife was vivid and lifelike.

New York Globe and Commercial Advertiser, April 19, 1918.

Seen on the Stage: The Provincetown Players

Anonymous

The latest bill of The Provincetown Players was made memorable by the production of two one-act plays which were far above the average. The better of the two was *The Rope*, by Eugene G. O'Neill,—a young author who is endowed with a talent for the theatre that is quite extraordinary. In this play, the author maintained until the very curtain-fall a surprise that had been cleverly withheld. The characters were true to life; the dialogue was racy and authentic; and the pattern of the piece was truly admirable in technique. Here, indeed, is an author of whom much may be expected in the future; and such organizations as the Provincetown Players may be congratulated on performing a genuinely useful function when they "discover" such gifted playwrights as Eugene O'Neill.

Vogue, June 15, 1918.

Theatre Arts Bookshelf

Anonymous

Of all the American playwrights of one-act plays none has succeeded better than Eugene O'Neill in telling a complete and convincing story, developed through character and action, suited to the size of his canvas and the time allotted to him for performance. No one, in other words, has more completely mastered the technique of the one-act play. Yet a good technique is the least of the virtues of these straight driving plays of the sea, which read as well as they act. *Bound East for Cardiff, The Long Way Home, Ile, In the Zone*, bring the smell of salt to the library as they do to the stage. They are a welcome addition to American dramatic literature. They are bread and wine to the Little Theatres in search of material.

Theatre Arts Magazine, January 20, 1919.

The Plays of Eugene O'Neill

Barrett H. Clark

When, a few weeks ago, John Galsworthy asked me to name our most promising native dramatist I was at first unable to do so. I tried to think of some new star on the theatrical horizon and mentioned the names of two or three playwrights whose work seemed to me above the average.

It was not, however, until after I had exhausted the Broadway group that I thought of the one logical man. The name of Eugene G. O'Neill had not occurred to me at once in connection with Broadway, where Mr. O'Neill is practically unknown. My mind wandered to the Comedy Theatre and the Greenwich Village Theatre, where I had seen three plays that stood out above all other American plays that have come to my notice in recent years: *In the Zone, Ile* and *The Rope*. I told Mr. Galsworthy that in Eugene G. O'Neill I felt there was something genuinely American, that he was not only "promising" (Heaven knows, Broadway is full of the "promising youngsters" of yesteryear) but that his actual achievement was considerable.

I have just sent Galsworthy *The Moon of the Caribbees, and Six Other Plays of the Sea*, and I am sure he will realize, as I do, that O'Neill's volume is a significant collection of one-act plays, the most significant that has been published in this country....

Wherein are Mr. O'Neill's fifteen-odd plays different from the average product native product? Why is Mr. O'Neill, if not our most versatile and "finished," so indisputably our most powerfully sincere dramatist?

The first reason, I believe, is that he is intent before all else upon depicting that segment of life which he knows and with which he sympathizes. He never seeks to construct an effective vehicle for a star; he never wastes a moment's time in effect for effect's sake. He makes you feel, even in his feeblest work, that he understands the secret springs in the men and women he sets before you: his simple sailors and farmers are thrillingly alive; his is the power to convince you at once of the authenticity of a situation primarily through the vitality of the characters involved.

The atmosphere with which his best plays are saturated is not factitious; it is not the result of a heaping up of the actual; he resorts to no Belasco tricks to beguile you into believing you are in the presence of life because a well copied suit of clothes or a stage full of "real" bric-a-brac is foisted upon you. A cheap set such as was used in his play *Ile* at the Greenwich Village Theatre was all that was necessary in the way of material equipment. To this day I feel the presence of mountains of ice outside that forecastle. O'Neill used his imagination where Belasco would have collaborated with the ice company.

Or take *In the Zone*, which was produced by the Washington Square Players. A group of sailors in a forecastle, the tragedy of a man's life revealed to them, a touch of pity on the part of a few rough men for a fellow being. And for background the fateful sea of the submarine zone. Atmosphere? All one could ask for, but not one atom of it dragged in for effect. The situation demanded the atmosphere.

Ile I have already referred to. It is a stark picture of human misery at the mercy of human obstinacy. Here again is atmosphere, with a haunting sense of impending doom, but as always an integral part of the drama of humanity.

The Moon of the Caribbees is rather less a play of character than the others. At first sight the atmosphere seems to exist for its own sake, but on rereading it I am struck by the extraordinary artistry of the canvas, *as a background*. Here, amid the heat of the tropics, on shipboard in the harbor, is a scene of mad revelry; figures of men and women flit back and forth. Dim and insignificant at first, they gradually emerge just in time to play their petty parts and disappear.

This play does not grip one in quite the same way as does *In the Zone*; it is a broader canvas, in which the purely dramatic element does not predominate.

The Long Voyage Home is a heartbreaking little play; a Swedish sailor has hoarded his savings for years with the intention of returning to his aged mother, buying a farm and leaving the sea. Each time during the past that he has tried to carry out his determination he has taken too much drink and been robbed. In this play we see him ashore refusing whisky but accepting a harmless "belly wash"—which is drugged. He is robbed and carried aboard an outward bound ship. An incident, scarcely more; but I can count on the fingers of one hand the full length plays I have seen during the past two seasons that are as truly dramatic.

Where the Cross Is Made is somewhat different from the plays I have just mentioned. Mr. O'Neill has seen fit to introduce a touch of the supernatural, and while he has succeeded in creating the desired effect I cannot help feeling that this play lacks the freshness of the others. It has not the direct power of *In the Zone* and *Bound East for Cardiff*—another stark specimen of the forecastle play.

The last play is *The Rope*, a painful and bitter drama, the scene of which is the barn of a New England farm on the sea coast. It is a tragedy of greed, hatred and madness. Money lies at the bottom of it all. The touch at the end of the play is one Balzac would have appreciated. The little maid Mary climbs up on a chair to swing from the rope hanging from the loft; it comes loose and she pulls down a bag full of gold pieces. Spreading the coins on the floor, "she picks up four or five of them and runs out to the edge of the cliff. She throws them one after another into the ocean as fast as she can and bends over to see them hit the water."

These plays are the expression of a man of powerful imagination. They are written because of the "urge" of which Mr. O'Neill has spoken. Sincerity itself is nothing in art, of course; yet without it there is no art. But Mr. O'Neill has by the very force of his sincerity been able to mold the one-act play form to the requirements of his temperament. His technique...is exactly suited to what he had to say, and what more can we ask of any artist? I have been privileged to see the manuscript of *Beyond the Horizon*, Mr. O'Neill's new three act play, the production of which is announced for the fall. While I am not at liberty to describe it, I may say that the author of *In the Zone* is well able to handle a striking theme and living characters in a long play.

Having demonstrated his skill in the one-act form and, to me and his manager at least, in the three act, I see no reason why O'Neill should fail to be recognized as our leading dramatist. O'Neill is not perfect, he is not free from defects of characterization and style, but he is better equipped than any other young American. He *promised* five years ago, with his *Thirst* and other plays; since then he has fulfilled his promise; he has now only to develop, to widen his vision of men and women and do his best....

New York Sun, May 18, 1919.

Second Thoughts on First Nights: The Provincetown Plays

Alexander Woollcott

It is a provocative and almost continuously interesting evening that is provided in Macdougal Street, where another week remains for the first bill of short plays staged this season by the Provincetown Players. In the cramped and dismal little theatre off Washington Square, where the dramatic pauses are sometimes rudely interrupted by the boisterous hubbub of nearby plumbing, the kind of fare is served which used to be looked for at the Bandbox in the palmy days of the Washington Square Players.

It is to the Macdougal Street group we must look now for any considerable exploitation of the one-act play....Their first bill includes an engrossing negro playlet called *The Dreamy Kid*, by the oncoming Eugene O'Neill....*The Dreamy Kid* is a sketch which has as its central figure a young, crap shooting, gang-leading, gun-toting darky who has just killed a white man in a scrap and who, with the police hot on his trail, has nevertheless crept to the deathbed of his grandmother, because he knows in his heart he will have no luck all the days of his life if he does not obey her final summons. It is interesting to see how, just as Dreiser does in *The Hand of Potter*, so here the author of *The Dreamy Kid* induces your complete sympathy and pity for a conventionally abhorrent character. The performance is by negroes—amateurs mostly. That is well enough this time, because, after all, the entire program is on the quasi-amateur level, and pretends no more.

New York Times, November 19, 1919.

The Drama: *Beyond the Horizon*

J. Rankin Towse

A very large audience of a somewhat unusual character assembled in the Morosco Theatre yesterday afternoon to witness the performance of *Beyond the Horizon* described as a new American tragedy in three acts by Eugene O'Neill and was unmistakably interested and impressed by it. This is the first long play of a young dramatist hitherto known only in the experimental theatre by a number of short pieces acted and unacted of which a collection was published not long ago. These were realistic sketches of unequal merit, but all more or less notable for a vigorous realism coupled with a vivid if occasionally crude and violent imagination. In this latest effort he has made a great stride forward. There can be no question that it is a work of uncommon merit and definite ability, distinguished by general superiority from the great bulk of contemporaneous productions....

The description upon the programme was fully justified. This is a genuine, reasonable, poignant domestic American tragedy, arising out of the conflict between circumstance and character, wholly unsensational but sufficiently dramatic, showing a sympathetic comprehension of elemental human nature and presenting a realistic study of actual life....The tone is somewhat dreary and fatalistic. There are ten personages in the group—nine adults and an infant—who are sketched with vitality and clear discrimination. The scene opens with a picture of domestic content and propriety. An old farmer, James Mayo, has two sons, one of whom, Robert is a student and ambitious dreamer, hopelessly cramped by his environment; the second, Andrew, a simple, generous, sturdy yeoman, delighting in the work of the farm, is his father's main reliance. Both the boys are in love with Ruth Atkins, but Robert, believing his brother to be the favored wooer, has concealed his own passion and accepted the offer of his uncle, Capt. Scott, a bluff old sea dog, to make a sailor of him. On the eve, however, of his departure for the sea, exulting in the expectation of knowledge to be gained, Ruth tells him that it is he with whom she has really been in love all the time and begs him to stay at home and marry her. In the first flush of happiness he flings aside ambition and consents, whereupon Andrew, grievously hurt, but never dreaming of becoming his brother's rival, determines after a furious quarrel with his disappointed father to go to sea in his place.

It is not necessary at this time—as the piece is only to have three representations—to rehearse the story in detail. Suffice it to say that the record of disaster and failure springs from what is shown to be Robert's fatal mistake in following the impulse of passion, instead of the cravings of natural genius. The girl proves shallow and fickle and her unhappy husband, utterly misplaced in life and slowly worn down by increasing anxieties, bitter disappointment, the thwarting of his tenderest affections and finest aspirations, falls into a decline and finally dies with his unsatisfied eyes straining toward the horizon which he was doomed never to cross. Nor is he alone in the shipwreck of happiness. The whole tale is one of progressive and general disaster. The chief merit of the play lies in the skill with which the characters and disposition of the different characters are made the mainsprings of the dramatic action. Nothing depends solely upon the use of convenient coincidences. In this respect it is the full sense of the word dramatic. But it is not quite a masterpiece. It is somewhat shambling in construction; it is too long and too uniformly and unnecessarily somber. But it is exceedingly promising juvenile work. Richard Bennett played the dreaming, susceptible and unpractical Robert with delicate intelligence but scanty animation, and Edward Arnold furnished a rough but pleasing sketch of the less imaginative but more virile and enterprising Andrew. Helen MacKeller was scarcely equal to the part of Ruth, but was sometimes very successful in suggesting her mood of frustrated passion and sullen discontent. Louise Closser Hale, as a garrulous, uncharitable, impatient paralytic, supplied a striking study of a type of character which she so long ago made her own. Erville Anderson gave a vigorous and truthful portraiture of the old farmer and Max Mitzel caused laughter by his explosive old mariner, but was too noisy.

New York Post, February 4, 1920.

Beyond the Horizon

Lola Ridge

The authentic drama in America, the drama of the valiant Little Theatres and the dusty first editions unsold on publishers' shelves, is developing two distinct tendencies toward realism, the one subjective, almost subconscious, as in some of Alfred Kreymborg's plays, the other objective and romantic as in the dramas of Eugene O'Neill.

Beyond the Horizon

It is the fashion to speak of romanticism as though it had been hatched by the early Victorians, had reached with them a respectable old age and been buried with fitting honors in Westminster Abbey. The truth is the Victorians were not romanticists but sentimentalists. The age of Victoria ushered in an age of intense commercial activity incompatible with romance, but as wistfully eager for a public alliance with sentiment as any wealthy grocer for a beautiful and aristocratic wife. Sentimentality and big business, like sentimentality and politics, mutually assist and sustain each other, and this is even more true of our own than the Victorian age. We Americans, master-merchants of the world, are an exceedingly sentimental people—witness our popular magazines and the noble appeals in the editorials of our daily newspapers. But as for the Romance of Big Business—that is one of the ready-made phrases we keep in the labeled jars of our minds.

Romanticism is the will to beauty without any retarding consideration. It is as ageless as death or love or avarice. It is the fertilizer of life as well as of art, the infusion without which creation becomes a sterile and brittle thing, lacking the virility to reproduce itself.

Eugene O'Neill is a romanticist who takes one by the scruff of the neck and holds one's nose to reality. His is a spirit stark, eager and alive. Even in his most photographically realistic plays, *Before Breakfast* and another one act drama where the crushed seaman dies in his reeking quarters, one feels he has not only a hold but an agonizing clinch on life. Yet it is not life as some of the great Scandinavians and Russians have given it—life that has not only passed through the senses but through the inmost essence of a single consciousness to emerge in a great and terrible art. For this it is too minutely reproduced in its physical and accidental manifestations, such as dialect. The life of the spirit alone will bear faithful reproduction without either becoming "lurid" or losing its impressiveness. And this is perhaps only because the in-vision of even the greatest artist is not strong enough to discover spiritual minutiae; unlike the camera it cannot see too much.

The theme of the three act drama, *Beyond the Horizon*, is the old unappeasable hunger of the wandering spirit that is always at odds with those who are content to burrow in some little patch of earth. The brothers, Andrew and Robert Mayo, typify these opposing forces. Andrew is the pioneer who attaches himself firmly to that which surrounds him and which he, having no comparison of a richer inner life, finds complete and satisfying. Unlike Robert, driven always toward some shifting and elusive grail, Andrew only pulls up roots with the definite hope of a more durable replanting. While Robert is the eternal poet-adventurer who rides after his own dreams, unaware that he himself projects before him like a lantern the gleam that he follows. "You have it or you don't," he says explaining his obsession to Ruth on the eve of a three years' trip on a tramp steamer to the Orient. It is the appeal of Ruth, loved by both brothers, and by all authority of nature a mate for Andrew, that induces Robert—hopelessly unfit for such a well-made socket of earth—to stay on the farm and marry her. Andrew, the loss of his first love souring home for him, goes off on the tramp steamer in his brother's place. For this he gets the curse of his father. The old man whose farm has become his religion and who owns no God but earth, is left like some angry priest who sees an acolyte's back turned on a sacred fire.

In the second act we see the slow withering of personalty. The old man Mayo is dead, and Robert, his gleam almost blackened out without the winds of the world to blow on it, struggles ineffectually with the ruin about him. After a scene of recrimination, Ruth, her vanity outraged by the failure of her man to win the community's approval for the only values she or it comprehends, makes an advance to Andrew who is unbelievably obtuse. Andrew, unsensitive, hardy as speargrass, is the only one of the disrupted human beings who has prospered. But at the last he too is denourished, no longer sturdy, firm-rooted, but run to the very stalk of enterprise—"gambling with the thing that he had created."

The study of Andrew is a new light on our financiers. In it we see them as a race of denatured farmers, perverting their motive and creative power from the clean usage of the earth to the manipulation of "wheat pits" in the stone canyons of cities.

Andrew is a harsh mechanism of a man with the stridency of steel. His reiteration of material values falls upon the ear like hammer blows. Yet such as he is, he dominates the play—very much as his prototype dominates America.

The drama draws to a close with the spiritual paralysis of Ruth, who has sunk to a monotonous voice muffled in a dirty towel, and the death of Robert, who crawls out the window in his last moments to die as he would have died had he had the courage of his faith "in a ditch by the open road, seeing the sun rise."

Mr. O'Neill is most successful with such primitive types as Ruth. When he approaches a complex nature like Robert's, his presentation is weaker. Even Ruth remains too consistently crushed in the last act. Character cannot be changed or destroyed, though its manifestations may be suspended. And her possessive instinct would have again asserted itself and given some promise of closing with and overcoming the hostility of Andrew, thrust toward her by the chivalry of the dying man.

Beyond the Horizon is a good drama. It might have been a great one but for two defects that create and sustain each other, namely the theatre consciousness of the playwright, and the fact that he is a too anxious father to his brood. Not one of his characters is projected far enough from the parent mind to create the impression of an entity independent of his guiding will. Each fits too snugly in his individual part. Thus we do not feel that vital continuation of personality after and beyond the spoken word that makes living forces of the great characters of literature.

But here is a dramatist in whom life the magnificent is riding with a loose rein. It will be of absorbing interest to follow his next leap.

New Republic, January 5, 1921.

Chris

Anonymous

At the Broad Street Theater, Philadelphia, Eugene O'Neill's new play *Chris* was given its first presentation. It is a rough sea-story divided into six scenes, yet with a surprisingly slim plot and very little action. Most of the credit goes to Emmett Corrigan, Lynn Fontanne, and Arthur Ashley for their excellent acting, and to Frederick Stanhope for his well directed staging.

Chris is an old sea-dog from Sweden, who had sunk from "bo'sun" to being captain on a dirty coal-barge. He has hated the sea for years—ever since it separated him from his wife, who died while he was away. His child, Anna, has been carefully brought up in England and is now coming to America to seek out her father. Anna arrives, is shocked at the ugliness of the old barge which is "home" for her father. However, she is so happy to be with her father again, Chris easily persuades her to take a trip on the barge which she does "for the fun of it." Gradually, she feels the call of the sea within her, and grows to love it.

They are run down in the fog by a tramp steamer, taken aboard, and carried to Buenos Aires, a four weeks trip. Anna falls in love with the handsome second mate and in spite of her father's warning, decides to marry her hero. At first Chris attempts to kill the second mate (in the one dramatic-action scene of the play) but eventually relents, and accepts the job of "bo'sun" on the tramp steamer.

The material is very slim, but the play carries itself along from sheer excellence of presentation. Emmett Corrigan, in a blonde wig, enacts Chris with considerable skill, and his Swedish accent is well assumed. Lynn Fontanne, as Anna, was pleasing, and her refinement did much to off-set the common coarseness of the coal-bargers. Arthur Ashley was the good-looking mate, and played with ease and quiet manliness the rather brief part. Mary Hampton as the drab old Marthy made much of the one scene in which she appeared. There were numerous other "bits," all well done, mostly the rough types of men with whom Chris associated. John Rogers as "Jonsey" was particularly good.

New York Drama Mirror, March 27, 1920.

Eugene O'Neill's Remarkable Play *The Emperor Jones*

O.W. Firkens

Mr. Eugene O'Neill has done a remarkable thing in *The Emperor Jones*, newly presented by the Provincetown Players at 183 Macdougal Street. It shows indeed the limitations which peered at us through the seams of that surprising experiment, *Beyond the Horizon*. Mr. O'Neill's faculty is theatrical and literary, not dramatic, at least as I understand drama. There is no need to battle over words. Give drama its lowest, roomiest, and laziest interpretation, define it grossly as the representable in speech and action, and Mr. O'Neill is a dramatist. The erring public is sage in this particular and its indorsement of Mr. O'Neill has been decisive. But if drama is to be set apart from other forms of literature by any merely literary characteristic, by anything else than its reaction to the footlights, properties, and painted canvas, then Mr. O'Neill's work is undramatic. If causality be vital to the drama, *Beyond the Horizon* is only half dramatic; if conflict be vital, drama for this successful play is simply beyond the horizon. What it furnishes is a series of scenes vividly felt and vividly painted, theatrically producible, imperfectly solidified, and proving nothing except that poets should not take to agriculture. In America we scarcely need any reenforcement of the motives which prevent poets from rushing into husbandry

In *Beyond the Horizon* Mr. O'Neill has put a wide space between himself and drama; in *The Emperor Jones* he proves that he can widen the interval. In *Beyond the Horizon* he dispensed with conflict; in *The Emperor Jones* he puts by that far older, simpler, and broader requisite of drama, interaction. The first and longest scene is an information or (shall we say?) a bulletin scene in which Mr. O'Neill with that want of virtuosity which his power cannot obscure, but which cannot obscure his power, allows a shrewd man to talk indefinitely in a situation where shrewdness would have held its tongue. So much for the first scene; the rest is brazen monologue. The amount of real drama derivable from a cast which consists of one principal, one or two dummies, and phantasms in grisly abundance may be inferred by the least critical reader. Nevertheless, not as drama, but as a bit of letters in picture, *The Emperor Jones* is a high, imaginative, even a profound, piece of work, nourishing the conscience and the intellect with the same food with which it lures and banquets the imagination. Let us look more narrowly at its motive.

An American negro, sleeping-car porter, criminal, and convict, the so-called "Emperor" of the superstitious blacks whom he dupes and bleeds in an unnamed island of the West Indies, faces revolt on the part of his despoiled and discontented subjects. The alarm is given. On a certain night he traverses the windings of the forest in which he has secreted his booty to reach a French steamboat ready to bear him to regions where fresher credulities will offer plumper purses to his insatiate greed. The play lasts but one night. At dawn, after vain wanderings, he is shot by the blacks. But during this night which the Provincetown Players have vivified to our imaginations by the art of their settings, during this lonely, famished, footsore, and racking night, he has seen vision after vision of his own past life; Africa has bared to him her primeval secrets, and past cycles in a murky continent have muttered in his ear. The intellectual, like the corporal, vesture of the man has been stripped away, and the powerful, resolute, formidable man has been uncoiled layer by layer till nothing is left but the hysterical and crouching savage.

Mr. O'Neill's play takes depth and dignity from the moral which he conveys with force and reticence. I protested a little at first against the unmixed brutality of his hero; there is a limit to our pleasure in watching a hound lick his chops. But Mr. O'Neill knew his path, and he was wise enough not to mulct us of one atom of that inestimable baseness. The crime rests in the penalty as in a socket. This negro charlatan corresponds to Edgar's imagined description of himself in the heath-scene in *King Lear*: "A servingman, proud in heart and mind...false of heart, light of ear, bloody of hand; hog in sloth, fox in stealth, wolf in greediness, dog in madness, lion in prey;" and it is just because Mr. O'Neill's hero holds nothing but riot and ravin in his soul that he is given over to Modo, Mahu, and Flibbertigibbet. Godless in fortune, he recurs, in adversity, to belief; but the only spiritual or spiritualistic power to whose help he can turn is a power shaped in the image of his own predacious and cannibal ideals. His greed has played upon other men's fears, and, in the hour of his destitution and necessity, the only divinity that he can body forth is a greed that plays upon his own. Fang and talon must arm their god with fang and talon, though the sheaths for these piercing and riving instruments be their own breasts. The universe is a bank in which we deposit our cruelties or humanities, as the case may be; and our returns are congruous with our deposits.

The lesson, of course, does not stop with an astute negro's robbery of brainless natives on an islet of the West-Indian archipelago. This negro, in his Pullman-car service, had come close to the puissances of Wall Street; he had flicked the dust from their coats, had inhaled their Havanas, had savored their discourse. His career follows haltingly in their steps, and his panic is an enlargement of their apprehensions. Mr. O'Neill rejoins Wordsworth in his unforgettable

> Riches are akin
> To fear, to change, to cowardice, and death.

The shadings of capital are many, but the dubious millions which find their protection in the fears or the scruples of the multitude find their nemesis in the owner's foreboding of the passage of these fears and scruples. Alarm must sentinel those possessions which depend for safety on the consent—the revocable consent—of millions eager to get more for themselves and increasingly skeptical of an order in which the inequality of rewards is far in excess of the inequality in exertions or even of the inequality of powers. Pure greed everywhere has these recurrent liabilities. A quick fancy might note with interest that the negro has convinced his followers that only a *silver* bullet can end his life, and might associate the fact with the shudder that traversed the heart of Wall Street when Bryanism startled the country in 1896.

How far Mr. O'Neill has analyzed his own picture is another matter which is obscure—and unimportant. Great imagination is great through its relation to a psychologic or philosophic background. The extent to which the author has forestalled the critic in the divination and elucidation of this background is a relatively secondary point. The stage interpretation is quite another thing, and the debt of the play to Mr. Charles S. Gilpin, the negro who undertook the leading, almost the solitary, part is unbounded. Mr. Gilpin is an actor of extraordinary alacrity, versatility, and resilience. We watched him lazily and gloatingly uncoil his sinuosities in the first scene with the stupefied recoil with which we might have watched the same process in the nodes of a boa-constrictor. After that he had many things of many kinds to do. My own sensitiveness to the intemperate or exaggerated in tone is extreme, not to say morbid; yet, through the entire compass of a part in which the demands for variety were many and the temptations to exaggeration frequent, I was scarcely conscious of a lapse. Mr. Gilpin can harmonize, can attemper, a transition; he imparts to an angle the delicacy of a curve. I am in no hurry to settle, or even to broach, the question of his greatness. Greatness, being a vague term with an ostentation of precision, affords to the vague mind the luxury of feeling itself to be precise. Perhaps also, in the exaltation of other men to greatness, we, the uncrowned, relish ourselves in the role of Warwicks or king-makers. We make gorges where Nature was content with fissures. If I cared to frame a test for greatness, it should lie, I think, in a reenforced, an intensified sincerity. Sincerity on the first plane is characteristic of the good actor; he *permits* at least the entrance of the spectator into the part. A sincerity which enjoined, which commanded, that entrance I should call great. I saw no clear evidence of the possession of this quality by Mr. Gilpin in his rendering of *The Emperor Jones*; his work was distinguished, nothing more; he needed nothing more to make us thankful.

Weekly Review, December 8, 1920.

The New Season

Kenneth Macgowan

In *The Emperor Jones* that remarkable organization, the Provincetown Players, which shows no fear whatever of producing ten very ordinary and ineffective plays for every single contribution to the advancement of American playwrighting, has opened up a new reach in American drama and in the talents of that fine young playwright of its discovery, Eugene O'Neill. The play itself is printed in this issue of *Theatre Arts Magazine*. There in its lines you will find the some strong and natural speech that has always set Mr. O'Neill apart from all of our playwrights except Edward Sheldon....[There] is genuine imagination both in the material and in the structure of the drama. These eight short scenes shake free from the traditional forms of our drama; they carry forward easily and honestly upon the track of discovery. We follow a path that gathers bit by bit the progressive steps in a study of personal and racial psychology of real imaginative truth.

Considering the record of the Provincetown Players for producing their real discoveries, such as the plays of Mr. O'Neill, Susan Glaspell and Edna St. Vincent Millay, with little more adequacy than they give to their experimental commonplaces, their production of *The Emperor Jones* is a surprise as well as a sensation. During the summer the Provincetown Players installed on the tiny stage of their makeshift theatre near Washington Square one of those plaster sky-domes or *Kuppelhorizont* with which so many German theatres have replaced the flat canvas of the cyclorama. It is a property of this curving plaster to catch and mix light so deftly that, in the diffused glow that reaches the spectator, it is impossible

The Emperor Jones

to focus the eye with any degree of assurance upon the actual surface of the dome. Well lighted as to color and intensity, the *Kuppelhorizont* can counterfeit the beauty and almost the reality of the sky. Again and again in the seven jungle scenes, which follow the flight of the Pullman porter from his brief but prosperous rule as emperor of "bush niggers," Director George Cram Cook and his scenic artist Cleon Throckmorton, have used this sky with such inspiring effect as has ever been achieved in New York before. For the first scenes of the Emperor's flight, there is hardly more than a dark suggestion of the shadowy night-sky behind the gaunt trees. It blazes out into beauty when we reach the edge of a clearing and see the magnificent naked body of the emperor silhouetted against it. The concluding scenes of darker and darker terrors call less upon the sky, but in them all—particularly in the vision of the old chain gang from which Jones escaped by murder—the director and the artist have handled the lighting of the stage and its people quite as well as the lighting of the *Kuppelhorizont*.

To the skill of its producers and the lesson of the sky-dome, the Provincetown Players have added in this production a magnificent piece of acting. From Harlem they have brought a colored player, Charles Gilpin, to impersonate the emperor....In *The Emperor Jones* he shows not only a great power and a great imagination, in addition to his fine voice, but he displays an extraordinary versatility. It is a genuine impersonation, a being of flesh and blood and brain utterly different from the actor's other work. He carries the long soliloquy of the six scenes in the forest with extraordinary ease, building up steadily from his fright at the first Little Formless Fears, through his terror at the recurring visions of his crimes, to the horror that overwhelms him as the dim, buried, racial fears rise to carry him back to the auction block, the slave ship, and the voodoo gods of the Congo. Mr. Gilpin's performance is the crown to a play that opens up the imagination of the American theatre, and builds beauty and emotion out of the spiritual realities of one corner of our life.

Theatre Arts Magazine, January 1921.

Emperor Jones Revived

Anonymous

In reviving *The Emperor Jones* for a half dozen performances at the Provincetown Playhouse, the directors thereof seem to have been actuated primarily by a desire to give Paul Robeson his first opportunity before a Broadway audience—if that generic word may be stretched to include Macdougal Street. The results amply justified the effort, for Mr. Paul Robeson gave a stirring and frequently exciting performance in the role of the negro Pullman porter who flies panic stricken through a West Indian wood.

It is, to be sure, a great role, and Mr. Robeson's triumph in it last night, following Charles S. Gilpin's striking performance of the part, cannot but lead to fleeting suspicions that it is the play rather than the player that so holds an audience.....At all events, it should not be interpreted as weakening in any degree the fact that Mr. Robeson's performance as Brutus Jones last night was a singularly fine one.

Paul Robeson is an actor of standing in the negro theatre—and one who has turned to the theatre only after marked achievements in other fields. He is a giant in stature and possessed of a magnificent voice—just such a voice as *The Emperor Jones* demands. It is not easy to recall at this date the details of Mr. Gilpin's performance; nor, for that matter, is any comparison necessary. The excellence of Mr. Gilpin's performance is a matter of record; suffice it to say that Mr. Robeson is gorgeous in the part. Certainly the cheers with which the first-night audience rewarded him were not undeserved.

New York Times, May 7, 1924.

2
Experimentation and Controversy

The Play

Alexander Woollcott

The new plays by Eugene O'Neill come thick and fast, and the latest one to be revealed in Macdougal Street illustrates as well as any why each as it comes along stands out as an event in the dramatic year. This is *Diff'rent*, a short piece in two acts, which is part of the second bill of the Provincetown Players, for which room has been made at their theatre by the transfer of *Emperor Jones* to the Selwyn.

Diff'rent is set in a New England parlor of some seaport village, its first scene visiting that room in the Spring of 1890 and the second returning to it just thirty years later. In the first you see an exacting young woman austerely breaking her promise to wed a shamed-faced Captain, who has returned blushing from a whaling voyage pursued by a facetious tale about some escapade of his with a native girl in some island where they had put in for some water.

This same woman reigns in the same parlor thirty years later—still a spinster, but one clutching frantically with her hair dye and her cosmetics to the squandered youth, and, through a scene of almost intolerable discomfort, you must watch her angling boldly, awkwardly, hopelessly for the attentions of a gad-about young soldier, who lounges about the pitifully refurbished parlor and regales her with hints of his gay life overseas. For the sake of this ironic and caustic contrast, the play was written, and that much attended to, O'Neill seems to have lost interest. At least, he lets the play stumble on to a dull and conventional conclusion.

But before his own interest has flagged, yours cannot, for no other American playwright can write dramatic dialogue as his.

Diff'rent is no easy piece to play and it is creditably managed in Macdougal Street, with excellent work being done by Mary Blair as the woman and Charles Ellis as the soldier.

New York Times, December 29, 1920.

Drama: *Gold*

Ludwig Lewisohn

There is something half-hearted about this late production of Mr. Eugene O'Neill's new play at the Frazee Theater. One has the impression that it was due to Mr. O'Neill's reputation rather than to any commanding merit in the work itself. That reputation, at all events, has outstripped Mr. O'Neill's development and has even, perhaps, retarded it. He reached the highest point in certain passages of *Beyond the Horizon*. *The Emperor Jones* owes its success to its imaginative and formal daring and the exotic elements in its admirable presentation more than to any inner completeness or perfection; *Diff'rent* is both structurally and psychologically violent rather than powerful. In *Gold* Mr. O'Neill returns to the sea and to seafaring people. We cannot rid ourselves of the feeling that we had heard all this before.

The crew of the Triton is stranded on an island in the Malay Archipelago. A treasure is found which the men bury. But not before Captain Isaiah Bartlett has condoned, though not commanded, the murder of the ship's cook who has denied the genuineness of the treasure and is half falsely, half sincerely suspected of wanting it all for himself. Such is the substance of the very interesting first act. From that point on the play drags heavily. By a rather sentimental and theatrical ruse Captain Bartlett is prevented from sailing to recover the treasure. It becomes an obsession with him; it ends by driving him mad. Like John Gabriel Borkman he paces eternally up and down—we hear his footsteps—waiting for the ship that will never return. At last he reveals the secret of his insane suspense to his son and shows him the one bit of treasure he has hidden and kept so long. The boy cries out, just as the ship's cook did: "It's damned brass!" And that echo gives us the only other strong and moving moment. But that moment does not come until Captain Bartlett's madness has caused a domestic tragedy which is no tragedy at all because Mr. O'Neill's women are terrible lay figures who talk as shop-girls do not talk but as imagine they would if it were their good fortune to be involved in a sad and romantic situation.

What is finely conceived is the symbolism. The treasure is brass. Illusion is illusion. Yet the man who seeks to bring his fellows into contact with reality is killed. They spend the rest of their lives chasing the false treasure, slaying for it, maddened by it. But it remains brass—cheap though gleaming. Only, the unpleasant doubt obtrudes itself that, perhaps Mr. O'Neill did not intend any such symbolical meaning at all. His dialogue is roughly and superficially realistic. The tone never deepens nor is anything felt that is not wholly spoken. The structure is jagged like that of a shaky and obvious scaffolding, not firm and true and hidden like that of a house.

There is something raw about Mr. O'Neill's work, as though he himself had not got to the souls of his people or touched the depths of his own fables; there is a lack of that inner grace which has nothing to do with beauty of aspect or worldly circumstance and is, in truth, found oftenest in books or plays that deal with the humblest and the least of men. It is as though we were listening to the work of an extraordinarily gifted boy who is keen and observant but does not yet share the passions and struggles of mankind sufficiently to see them from within. He remains outside his subjects, a little cold and hard and almost disdainful of a more intense preoccupation. No doubt this description is, as it stands, unjust to Mr. O'Neill. All such descriptions miss a final truth. But it may serve to convey the lack of creative intensity and of inner warmth and flexibility that we feel increasingly in his work. He remains, for all that, a remarkable figure, and second, probably, to Susan Glaspell alone among our recent dramatists. He invites criticism on the plane of his own ambitions. Viewing him there one cannot doubt that he must soften and sink far deeper his spiritual key, as well as tighten the inner economy of his fables, in order to pass from wavering promise to secure performance.

Nation, June 22, 1921.

Eugene O'Neill's *Anna Christie* Is Thrilling Drama, Perfectly Acted with a Bad Ending

Maida Castellun

Eugene O'Neill just missed writing a great play in *Anna Christie*, and then butchered it to make a happy ending. For three acts this tragedy of a woman and two men lost in life's fog and beaten by that "old Devil Sea," lays its spell upon one. It is gloomy, terrible, ugly and irresistible. Back of its sordid commonplace broods the spirit of a magnificent fatalism.

The author has his three characters defy every stage convention of "what the public wants" with splendid courage. They are poor, they are degraded, their language is unfit for ladies to hear—as the poor prostitute smilingly rebukes her lover. They are the despised flotsam and jetsam of humanity—but they are living, suffering humanity. There is much talk and some will say the action drags—but the play lives.

For three acts and a half the audience at the Vanderbilt Theater sat in silent fascination, while under O'Neill's magic, life seemed to wreak its dreary jest on Anna Christie, her father and her wild Irishman.

Then slowly, unbelievably, in 10 minutes the inevitable doom turned into farce.

The "old Devil Sea" and the fog had been conjured up merely to deceive one. The pistol which was dragged into the last act was merely a stage toy. The dirty coal barge of gloomy Chris turned into Kipling's *Three Decker*. The wild Irishman embraced Anna, they drank each others's health in beer, with father's blessing, and made jokes about the time when the little stranger should bless their home.

Such an ending to such a beginning is tragic beyond expression. It is worse than a blunder. It is a crime against artistic truth as well as against life. It matters little when two or three different endings are tried on the purely commercial plays that come and go for no better purpose than to pass the time and to enrich manager and author. But in *Anna Christie* O'Neill had predestined the fate of his play as inevitably as any Calvinistic god—and then blundered.

Mat Burke might have returned to Anna Christie after she had told him her story, but then the curtain should have fallen on a silent scene that told of a love greater than passion. But after the fog and the sea and the fierce struggle of the third act, the talk of beer and babies is inexcusably banal.

As one watched that incredible last *mauvais quart d'heure*, it almost seemed as though the author had said defiantly, "They told me I give them only suicide and death and damnation—well, here's happy marriage!" Or can it be that Mr. Arthur Hopkins, the producer, who has tinkered with *Daddy's Gone a Hunting*, has fallen into evil ways? If so, we implore him to produce all the happy plays—all the comedies of youth and old age and the years between, on the market—but not to tamper with plays that from the first act, before the author ever set the first word on paper, must follow their course as inevitably as the sun.

We hope none of our readers will be deterred from going to see *Anna Christie* by what we have said. For three acts and a half, immeasurably beyond any other new play in New York today, it has that elusive quality we call greatness. Something that Gorki caught in *The Lower Depths*, something of Synge's wild beauty and fatalism in *The Shadow of the Glen* and *The Riders to the Sea* has been captured by O'Neill and allowed to shed its glamour over *Anna Christie*.

An old Swedish Seaman, his daughter from St. Paul who has been a prostitute, and an Irish stoker, who swaggers and brags and sentimentalizes for all the world like a Playboy of the Western World in Provincetown, are the characters with which O'Neill achieves tragedy on a coal barge. As though he wished to disprove that he can write a play only of men he has created a woman so real, so pitiful, and so defiantly unsentimental that she is a living arraignment of the father and lover who have a woman in every port yet dare to berate her.

As always, O'Neill's dialogue, like his characters, glows with life. Chris and Anna talk and act life itself, but Mat Burke seems borrowed, in part, from literature, possibly because he speaks like a Synge hero with the picturesque phrases of the Celt.

Production and acting are worthy of the play. Miss Pauline Lord lends poignant sincerity to Anna Christie that has not been equalled on our stage since Mrs. Fiske played Salvation Nell. From the moment when she enters the waterfront saloon, and nervously twitching, drinks down her successive whiskeys, to her amazed surrender to the mystery of fog and sea she denotes every phase of this victim of farm and gutter. In the third act, when she tears herself free from her father and her lover, fighting over her, and tells them what she thinks of them, an electric thrill is passed through the audience. It was like an echo of Nora in *The Doll's House*—this cry that she, who had sold herself many times, at least would not be "owned" by any man.

George Marion's portrayal of "the old squarehead" is almost as perfect as Miss Lord's of the daughter. He makes this heavy, clumsy obstinate old man, hating yet fascinated by the sea, who could forget his daughter 15 years and yet be intensely fond of her, wholly credible.

Frank Shannon plays the wild, roaring stoker with a touch of poetry and Miss Eugenie Blair makes Marthy Owen, the waterfront charmer who parts with Chris with a smile and gives Anna sage advice, an endearing old sinner.

Robert Edmond Jones has hidden the coal barge and its characters in a fog so beautifully mystifying that a breathless audience sat through one practically dark set without even coughing once—a rare tribute to everyone concerned.

For living drama and vivid acting, put *Anna Christie* at the head of your list.

New York Call, November 4, 1921.

Second Thoughts on First Nights

Alexander Woollcott

All grown-up playgoers jot down the name *Anna Christie* as that of a play they really ought to see. This is the sordid waterfront tragedy, salty and alive which is lifted into beauty by the sheer truth of Pauline Lord's performance in its title role.

It is the work of Eugene O'Neill whose other tragedy, *The Straw*, was finally produced on Thursday night at the Greenwich Village Theatre. *Anna Christie* is a singularly engrossing play. More than any other piece of his we have seen, it is hardened with theatrical alloy. It is occasionally clumsy, with a boyish awkwardness. It has one or two moments of feeble violence. It is cluttered up with the rubbish of an earlier play from the wreckage of which O'Neill built this one. It's last act shilly-shallies. Yet, because it is crowded with life, because it has sprung from as fine an imagination as ever worked in our theatre, and because it has been wrought by a master of dramatic dialogue, it is worth seeing again and again. It comes to the chronic playgoer like a swig of strong, black coffee to one who has been sipping pink lemonade.

Anna Christie is the tragedy of an old Swedish bosun who has developed a great fear and hatred of the sea. It has killed the men and saddened the women of his tribe as far back as the tales of them run. When his own lonely wife dies, he packs his little daughter off to some farmer cousins in Minnesota, so that she may grow up inland and never know the spell and the curse of his old devil sea.

This caged child of the sea, perishing for it, grows up into a forlorn and bitter woman, and it is from a raided brothel in St. Paul, sick and disconsolate, that she finally comes East to meet her father—and the sea. How it welcomes her and cleanses her till she feels as though all her miseries had been the miseries of some gone and forgotten person; how, in spite of all her father's plans for her, it is a sentimental seaman she falls in love with; how this fellow goes wild, tearing drunk when her new-found character bids her tell him what she's been; and how he can't help crawling back to her just the same—all this is vividly told in the four acts of *Anna Christie*.

"Don't bawl about it," says Anna to her whimpering father. "There ain't nothing to forgive, anyway. It ain't your fault and it ain't mine and it ain't his neither. We're all poor nuts. And things happen. And we yust get mixed in wrong, that's all."

Which expresses more of O'Neill's outlook in fewer words than any other speech he ever wrote. The two lovers are interlocked as the final curtain falls. O'Neill seems to be suggesting to the departing playgoers that they can regard this as a happy ending if they are shortsighted enough to believe it and weak-minded enough to crave it. He, at least, has the satisfaction of intimating in his final words that, whereas everything seems cheerful enough at the moment, there is probably no end of misery for everybody hidden just ahead in the enfolding mists of the sea. It is a happy ending, with the author's fingers crossed.

Here, for once, is O'Neill irresolute in the matter of his final scene. Hitherto he has gone to it as unerringly and inevitably as a man goes to the ground who has jumped from the roof of the Woolworth Building. The last act of *Anna Christie*, however, is full of bogus things and even gives way to the weakness of brandishing a revolver for no other conceivable purpose than that of jouncing the nervous playgoer into a state of receptive agitation. We may yet live to see O'Neill write a play in which a crook turns out in the last act to be a detective.

New York Times, November 13, 1921.

Chris and Poseidon: Man Versus God in *Anna Christie*

Winifred L. Frazer

Eugene O'Neill, more than any other American playwright of his time, had a feeling for myth and its enactment in ritual and drama. Witness his use of masks, his recognition of the power of a syncopated drum beat, his understanding of Oedipal family relationships, his satirical outlook on man's worship of the machine rather than of his essential Dionysian or Appolonian nature, his intuitive feeling for choric responses, his clear portrayal of the life-God Eros and the death-God Thanatos in conflict and collusion, his worship of the earth mother, his awe of the primal father, his feeling for resurrection in both Biblical and pagan mythology, his sense of the timeless and the cyclic, and his comprehension of the rites of passage to manhood.

But perhaps Poseidon presided over his psyche more than any other God. As a young boy, in a widely reproduced photograph, he gazes winsomely to sea from his seat on a large rock near the O'Neill's New London waterfront home. And the last house the dying playwright owned was at Marblehead on the rocky Massachusetts coast, where the eye had a vast wide-angle view of the Atlantic Ocean and the ear was assaulted by the battering of the waves against the concrete sea wall below the house. In between, O'Neill lived on the sand dunes at the tip of Cape Cod in a remodeled Coast Guard Station which the waves eventually carried into the sea, and in a mansion-sized "cottage" on the Georgia coast at Sea Island, where the sea was murky and warm. His sea voyages in the years 1910 and 1911 to Argentina, Africa, and England affected him deeply. According to the Gelbs, he learned to stand watch on the highest yardarms and found it the most exalting experience of his life.[1] Also, the only physical activity he seems to have enjoyed was swimming—which he could do for long distances far from shore in icy water.

O'Neill's effusions about the ocean are among the most lyrical in his plays. Paddy in *The Hairy Ape* remembers with a holy joy the clipper ship days when men who were sons of the sea sailed the ships, until sons, sea, and ships became one. And in *Long Day's Journey Into Night*, written two decades later, Edmund can hardly find words to express his ecstacy: "I became drunk with the beauty and singing rhythm of it [the ship on the sea], and for a moment I lost myself—actually lost my life. I was set free! I dissolved in the sea...." Swimming in the sea was also a religious experience: "When I was swimming far out,...I had the same experience....Like a saint's vision of beatitude."[2] And O'Neill at one time had expected "the grand opus" of his life to be an autobiographical play called *Sea Mother's Son*.[3]

To the Greeks, Poseidon, the God of the Sea, and brother of Zeus, was second only in importance to this God of Gods. A sea-faring people honored Poseidon by a great temple at Sunion, the rocky cape at the tip of the coast, south of Athens. The Earth-Shaker could calm the waves by riding upon them in his golden car, and in his three-pronged trident lay the power to shatter cities. This Bull-God secretly fathered Theseus, who had a special feeling for coming earthquakes created by his God-father. Poseidon, at Theseus' command, destroyed the falsely accused Hippolytus as he drove his chariot along the rocky coast of Greece. God of salt waters and of fresh, Poseidon contended with other Gods for domains of earth, could send sea-monsters and tidal waves inland, and was a power to be reckoned with by all the peoples of the Aegean.

To a sea-faring man like Chris Christopherson, the God of the waters is the power that rules his life.[4] Believing it devilish, still he is unable to keep away from the sea. Claiming that carrying coal on a barge between New York and Boston is not a sea job, nevertheless he is upon the waters. And further emphasizing his paradoxical attitude, he extols life on the barge for its sun, fresh air, good food, moonlight, and beautiful sights of passing schooners under sail, while in almost the same breath cursing the sea. O'Neill himself, in "Ballard *[sic]* of the Seamy Side," written after his sea voyages, complains about the hardships of a sailor's life, but makes the refrain of each stanza: "They're part of the game and I loved it all."[5] And in *The Iceman Cometh* the derelicts are sunk in a Bottom-of-the-Sea Rathskellar, which is also a haven. The Gods change form also in *The Great God Brown*. The Dionysian part of Dion Anthony becomes continually more sneering and Mephistophelian, while the Christian part becomes more strained, tortured, and ascetic.

But the fate which the Gods mete out is inevitable. Larry, the bartender, in the play's opening scene, listens skeptically to Chris's denunciation of the sea and his tale of protecting his daughter from its malevolent influence through her inland upbringing. "This girl, now," he prophesies, " 'll be marryin' a sailor herself, likely. It's in the blood." Generations of sea-faring men cannot produce a daughter who is not attracted to it. As surely as the Mannons are cursed by their Fate as New England Puritans, so are the Christopersons by the Sea. Chris's ardent hope that Anna will marry some "good, steady land fallar here in East" is obviously not in the cards. In fact Chris himself belies the wish by singing in expectation of that happy event. "My Yosephine, come board the ship,"—a most unlikely song for a "land fallar."

When Anna enters, she intimates that the open sea is the world for her by revealing that she "never could stand being caged up nowheres." The fate of the characters is thus exposed in the opening scene and as in Greek Tragedy the play consists of its unfolding. Old Marthy, in spite of her admiration for Chris, does agree that he is nutty on the one point of avoiding the sea and bursts into "hoarse, ironical laugher" when she learns that it is living on a farm that has made Anna a prostitute. But when Chris later learns the truth, far from seeing the irony, *he* attributes her fall in some mysterious way to the old devil sea. And he is perhaps not far wrong, for although she first exclaims, "Me? On a dirty coal barge! What do you think I am?" and Larry also exclaims, "On a coal barge! She'll not like that, I'm thinkin' "still it turns out that Anna experiences a magical transformation under the Sea God's spell.

> It's like I'd come home after a long visit away some place. It all seems like I'd been here before lots of times—on boats....Feel so—so—like I'd found something I'd missed and been looking for—'s if this was the right place for me to fit in....I feel clean....And I feel happy for once. (II)[6]

Chris has forebodings, but Anna chides him for his fear that he is a fool for having brought her on the voyage and comments satirically that whatever happens is God's will. Chris "starts to his feet with fierce protests," shouting, "dat ole davil sea, she ain't God."

But Chris is unavailing against Poseidon's potency, for at that moment, the full irony of Fate, an incarnation of the Sea God arises out of the fog to board the barge. Michelangelo couldn't have portrayed him better. Mat Burke, dressed in nothing but a pair of dungarees, is a powerful, broadchested six-footer,...in the full power of his heavy-muscled, immense strength." He is "handsome in a hard, rough, bold, defiant way," and "the muscles of his arms and shoulders are lumped in knots and bunches." Like Poseidon, he is not backward about proclaiming his strength. With scorn for the other sailors who went out of their minds with fear and weakness, he tells Anna that they would all be at the bottom of the sea except for "the great strength and guts is in me." When one storm after another raked the seas over the leaking ship from bow to stern he alone prevented mutiny in the stokehole. By a "kick to wan and a clout to another," which they feared more than the sea itself, he kept the men going beyond human endurance. Now, in spite of going without food and water for two days and two nights and rowing continuously with the others lying in the lifeboat, Mat boasts, "I can lick all hands on this tub, wan by wan, tired as I am!" (II) Mortal man could hardly fit the role of the Earth-Shaker better than Mat Burke.

Anna, he first thinks, is "some mermaid out of the sea," and later a Goddess, whose "fine yellow hair is like a golden crown on your head," but in either case, he was destined to find her: "I'm telling you there's the will of God in it that brought me safe through the storm and fog to the wan spot in the world where you was!" In spite of having been placed in the wilderness to die, Oedipus meets Laius at the appointed crossroads. Anna's inland upbringing does not thwart her predestined encounter with Mat. Admitting to a "bit of the sea" in her blood, which Mat senses, Anna announces with some pride that all the men in her family have been sailors and that all the women have married sailors too. Mat's response is fervent: "It's only on the sea you'd find rale men with guts is fit to wed with fine high-tempered girls like yourself." Chris hears words of courtship with open-mouthed desperation. Then recognizing his old antagonist, he shakes his fist with hatred at the sea, and illustrating the dramatic irony of man pitted against the gods, swears, "Damn your dirty trick, damn ole davil, you! But py God, you don't do dat! Not while Ay'm living!" (II) Anna, fathered by generations of sea men, cannot be reclaimed by the land. "Digging spuds in the muck from dawn to dark," Mat and Anna agree, is for the sodden in spirit. It is not a fruits-of-the-vineyard God they worship, but the uncontrolled, violent, yet clean, God Poseidon. The same is true of Chris in reality. He had become sick in a land job and had to go back to the "open air" of the sea to regain his health.

Criticism of the play has been that it is Chris's play through the first two and a half acts and Anna's and Mat's play thereafter, that Mat Burke is a somewhat comic Irishman, and that the ending is a happy one, which distorts the theme of the inevitable fate of those who live on and by the sea, which Synge so well shows in *Riders to the Sea*. But in spite of its critics, *Anna Christie* survives as a popular play (and musical and movie). Perhaps, looked at in the light of Greek myth, it has a unity which it seems to lack if viewed merely as a naturalistic American drama.

Acts II, III and IV take place on the barge at sea, where actors and audience feel surrounded by this salty medium in the breeze, the fog, and the sounds of steamers and fog-horns. Mat emerges from the sea itself, and if he is seen as an Irish Poseidon, he holds together the theme of the old devil sea as fate and the theme of Anna's rejuvenation by sea and love. And after all, there is a good bit that is comic about the Gods—at least Aristophanes thought so—and many a playwright has regaled us with the tale of Zeus and Amphitryon. So the fact that

O'Neill's God speaks with an Irish lilt—"Isn't it myself the sea has nearly drowned...and never a groan out of me till the sea gave up and it seeing the great strength and guts of a man was in me" (III) should not mean he is not to be taken seriously. Like Zeus in the form of Amphitryon, or Poseidon when he came to Theseus' mother in a sea cove, Mat is determined to father heroes. What you are "needing in your family," he tells Chris, is a man like himself, "so that you'll not be having grandchildren that would be fearful cowards and jackasses the like of yourself." (III) Anna does become the central figure in the second half of the play, fought over "like a piece of furniture" by Chris and Mat and there is considerable humor in Mat's dismay that she, "wan of the others," has taken an oath upon his sacred Catholic crucifix. Emphasis on the young characters, however, does not lessen the importance of Chris, whose happiness depends upon his daughter's welfare. Chris suffers the tragic effect of her revelation that she has been a prostitute. It is he who comes to a self-understanding (admittedly not of the soul-shaking proportions of the Greek hero) that he has not avoided the fate of the Christophersons.

As for the happy ending—Act IV closes, like Acts II and III, with Chris cursing that "ole davil, sea." And his foreboding words, with which Mat agrees, "I'm fearing maybe you have the right of it for once, divil take you" seem more like the "comma" with which O'Neill said he intended to close than a period declaring a happy marriage for Anna and Mat.[7] Anna has so confounded her father and suitor by the story of her past that they have stumbled ashore for a two-day orgy with the God Dionysus. She has been tempted to leave for New York, but the sea has pulled her back—its power and cleansing effect an antidote to her misery. It has also had its effect on the men: Chris, having decided that he is a no-good "Yonah" has offered himself as a propitiating sacrifice by signing on as bosun of the *Londonderry*,[8] a steamer sailing next day for Cape Town, half a world away, whereas Mat had unknowingly signed on the same ship as stoker—thus leaving Anna alone again.

Added to the presentiment of the play's last lines—"Fog, fog, fog, all bloody time. You can't see where you vas going, no. Only dat ole davil, sea[9]—she knows!"—is the muffled, mournful wail of steamers' whistles." (IV) It is a somber mood on which the curtain falls. The fact that Mat and Anna seem momentarily destined for happiness does not make them less dependent on whatever fate the God Poseidon metes out to them. O'Neill knew that Driscoll, the stoker on whom he had modeled Mat and Yank in *The Hairy Ape*, had drowned himself at sea. And the original Chris had drowned by falling between the piles of the dock one night on his way to the barge. Just as Poseidon sent his sea-son Mat Burke out of the depths into Anna's life, so he will remove him and Chris from it according to his will. As in the Greek dramatic trilogies, no more than a comma is needed at the end to indicate the inevitably tragic continuation of the story of a House.

In *Anna Christie* it makes no difference whether one is Swedish or Irish, Lutheran or Catholic, if he goes to the sea in ships, Poseidon controls his life. Since the early version called *Chris* was on a road tryout in early 1920, at the same time that *Beyond the Horizon* was on trial in New York, O'Neill must have concluded that neither the land, which ruins Robert Mayo, nor the sea, which ruins

Chris, bestows favors on human kind and Anna seems destined for destruction by both. In plays like *Bound East for Cardiff*, *The Long Voyage Home*, *Ile*, and *The Hairy Ape*, the characters, although buffeted or ruined by the sea, do not blame their fate upon it. And it has been claimed that Chris uses the sea as a scapegoat for his own responsibility. But if, as Thomas Mann says, myth is the "pious formula" into which human traits flow from the unconscious,[10] then Poseidon is as real as the psyche in determining man's fate. Whatever defect *Anna Christie* may seem to have because of Mat's overpowering presence in the last part of it is countered by his being an agent of the same powerful God who rules the Christophersons.[11]

NOTES

1. Arthur and Barbara Gelb, O'Neill (New York, 1950), p. 151.

2. (Yale University Press, New Haven and London, 1956), p. 153.

3. Gelbs, p. 671.

4. In an early version of the play, the windjammer on which Chris had been bosun was named *Neptune*, the Roman name for Poseidon. See Travis Bogard, "*Anna Christie*: Her Fall and Rise," *O'Neill*, ed. John Gassner (Englewood Cliffs, New Jersey, 1964), p. 64.

5. *A Bibliography of the Works of Eugene O'Neill Together with the Collected Poems of Eugene O'Neill*, eds. Ralph Sanborn and Barrett H. Clark (Benjamin Blom, London, 1965), p. 157.

6. *Anna Christie*, intro. Lionel Trilling (The Modern Library, New York, 1937) is the edition used. The Act is indicated by the Roman numeral following the quotation.

7. Barrett H. Clark, *Eugene O'Neill The Man and His Plays* (New York, 1929), pp. 110-117. Clark notes that O'Neill thought at one time of calling his play *Chris* or *Chris Christopherson* or *De Old Davil Sea* or *Comma*.

8. It is significant that the ship on which Mat and Chris are to sail is named the *Londonderrry*, for a skeleton graces the Coat of Arms of this Northern Irish County in memory of the siege by the British three centuries ago. The great Shane O'Neill, called Shane the Proud, a century earlier had ruled all of Ulster, including Londonderry and Tyrone. But when this young "meteor of Irish Independence" was stabbed in 1567 at the age of 35, his head was sent to rot on the battlements of Dublin Castle. O'Neill no doubt had Irish history in mind when he was writing *Chris* and *Anna Christie*, for his son, whom he named Shane, was born in October, 1919, and his father, who had given him the name of the Irish hero Eaghan (Eugene) Ruadh and had imbued him with Irish patriotism died in August 1920. Since his father was buried in New *London* and since *London* was added to the Irish name Derry when the British moved in and took over Ulster, it might have seemed to O'Neill that the Irish were fated to be subject to the British as Chris was subject to the sea. The *Londonderry* was not a propitious ship for Mat and Chris to sail on. See Christopher Trent, *Motoring on British Byways* (London, 1965), p. 20 and Roger Chauvire, *A Short History of Ireland* (New York, 1965), pp. 55, 56.

9. As John H. Raleigh points out in *The Plays of Eugene O'Neill* (Southern Illinois Press, Carbondale and Edwardsville, 1965), p. 176, Chris uses the phrase, "dat ole davil sea," as a kind

of incantation. O'Neill illustrates the primitive belief in repetitive words as a kind of magic which somehow help to tame the terrors of existence.

10. Joseph Campbell, *The Masks of God: Primitive Mythology* (New York, 1959), p. 18.

11. The mixed critical reaction to the play may reflect O'Neill's own anomalous felling about the sea and the play. According to the Gelbs (p. 630 and pp. 481, 482), he despised the play and tried at one time to exclude it from his published works. But at the same time he recognized that it was good enough to win a Pulitzer Prize and that it had merit. At the time of its production he had given the name of Anna Christie to a black cat which had strayed out to Peaked Hill and had felt that the fate of the play depended on the fate of the cat. Later in Ridgefield, he called a belligerent Irish terrier Mat Burke (Gelbs, p. 474 and p. 590). So the play was not far from his thoughts no matter how paradoxically he regarded it.

Modern Drama, 12 (December 1969): 279-285.

Theatre

Harold Clurman

"None of us can help the things life has done to us. They're done before you realize it, and once they're done they make you do other things until at last everything comes between you and what you'd like to be...." Mary Tyrone says this in *Long Day's Journey Into Night*. It is the feeling which sets the tone and creates the pervasive atmosphere of O'Neill's writing. It defines the fate which weighs down and imprisons most of his characters.

In *Anna Christie*, O'Neill associates this fate with the sea. The play's last lines, spoken by Anna's father, Chris Christopherson, a Swedish-born captain of a barge anchored in a New England harbor, are "Fog, fog, fog. All bloody time. You can't see where you vas going, no. Only dat old davil sea—she knows." It is the impenetrable mastery, the essential tragic force which Chris (through O'Neill) perceives in all occasions. In the evocation of the mood which results from that soul-burdening perception we recognize the O'Neill signature.

In his best plays the dramatic material suits his "music." In *Anna Christie* (Imperial Theatre) the plot is banal, as in fact are most of the characters: Anna, the blameless sinner; the Irish steamship stoker, muscular, loose-living, bragging, guileless, decent, superstitiously Catholic, and the confused, hard-drinking regretful father. In 1921-22 those who found fault with the play, that season's Pulitzer Prize winner, did so only on the ground of its "happy ending." Others, "the discriminating playgoers," to quote a prominent reviewer of the time, "who had learned what to expect of O'Neill were enthusiastic in their endorsement. It is a rough play....Much of its dialogue may prove offensive to super-fine sensibilities. [The characters] do not speak the language of the drawing room. But it is also one of the big dramas of the day, soundly human..."; etc., etc.

It requires no particular acumen at present to dismiss the play as corny, but it is important to understand that in 1921 it proved effective because crucial to it is the O'Neill spirit, that low-keyed but inescapable inner intensity which lends even his weakest plays an impressiveness that very nearly overrides many of our objections. In 1921 that spirit was embodied in the person of Pauline Lord, one of the most moving American actresses of the past fifty years or more. From Pauline Lord, who was by no means a pretty woman, there emanated a sense of a hurt and sorrowful consciousness, the counterpart of the persistent fatality that hangs over O'Neill's plays. She was not dramatically "exciting": hers was a seemingly mute presence, ineffably touching because it contained all the unshed tears in the common heartbreak of existence.

Liv Ullmann, who now plays Anna, is beautiful and remarkably resembles O'Neill's description of the character: "She is a tall, blonde, fully developed girl, handsome after a large, Viking-daughter fashion...." There is a muffled pain and yearning in Ullmann's voice, a kind of northland bewilderment in her blue eyes, as though her gaze had been forever fixed on a far-off but not quite discernable horizon. She also acts the part, line by line, scene by scene, quite well. Yet she does not express the quintessential Anna. As she enters the stage, she indicates the ill health Anna has suffered, but it is only a temporary indisposition. Anna's sickness is the ache of a soul, an unromantic existential pain which is exemplary and not only due to the accident of present circumstances. Ullmann, whatever her immediate ailment and trouble, strikes one as healthy at the core. Only with an Anna such as I have suggested through the image of Pauline Lord can the play affect us.

The rest of the cast, like Liv Ullmann, may be set down as "good." John Lithgow is certainly engaging as the boastful Irish swain, but somewhat callow in the torment of his discovery that Anna has been a prostitute. Robert Donley is descriptively right as Anna's father, but he is impeded by the nature of the production as whole. It is faithful to the action and the events of the play; it does not evoke the underlying sources from which the play must draw its power, and without which all O'Neill's work may appear shoddy. José Quintero's intelligent direction is in line with the play's overt course; it is external, which makes it vehement, professionally sound and, at bottom, ordinary. Good settings (especially that of the barge) by Ben Edwards and other assets do not overcome the basic deficiency. The production does not speak with the inner voice which alone could save it.

Nation, April 30, 1977.

Eugene O'Neill's *The Straw* Is Gruesome Clinical Tale

The Playgoer

If there is tuberculosis in your family do not go to see Eugene O'Neill's *The Straw*, which opened at the Greenwich Village Theatre last evening. If the White

Scourge has robbed you of a dear friend, keep away from this play. It will harrow your feelings and upset your nerves. A sanitarium on the stage may help its patients, but the sight of a sanitarium for consumptives in full operation for three acts of a play will not act as a tonic on an audience. This particular sanitarium may cure a patient when there is the straw of love and hope to cling to, but it is likely to kill the audience.

It is a gruesome, clinical tale that Mr. O'Neill narrates that is brightened but not redeemed by a very fine ending. If *The Straw* were an importation from Germany instead of a native product, everybody would remark that here is an example of morbid Teutonic drama. We wish Mr. O'Neill would stick to the sea as his background. His salt water dramas never make us seasick, but this play sort of makes us landsick, as it were.

The lady who went to the premiere with us coughed all the way home. Her parting words were that she was going to gargle with listerine before going to bed. So we cannot say the play was not effective, but its effect, generally, was very bad. And we do feel that Mr. O'Neill might have found a happier means than an intensive study of a tubercular
patient in a sanitarium for expressing his thesis that hope may be a more powerful curative than the whole materia medica.

Miss Margalo Gillmore acted Eileen Carmody, the chief consumptive of the play, who comes to the sanitarium in the second act handicapped by the halfhearted sympathy of a hard drinking, ignorant father and of a poltroon fiance who fears tuberculosis like poison. There she falls desperately in love with another patient, a newspaper man named Stephen Murray, whom she inspires to write marketable short stories. When Stephen goes away cured, carefree and heart free, Eileen steadily declines until in the last act she is desperately ill. Stephen returns to let her know he has at last fallen in love with her, and love and the desire to live are the hopeful signs at the final curtain that eventually she may get well.

Miss Gillmore was admirable, not only in her big scene in the fourth act when she declares her love to Stephen but also throughout the rest of the play, as she looked as charming as such a disagreeably sickly part permitted her to look. Not less convincing was Otto Kruger as Stephen Murray, and he, too, carried off his own big scene in the last act in stirring fashion. Miss Katherine Grey was a sympathetic head nurse and Harry Harwood played well Eileen's father. Most of the acting, however, fell to Miss Gillmore and Mr. Kruger, and their work hardly could be improved.

New York Sun, November 11, 1921.

First Man, New O'Neill Play, Is Gloomy Suburban Story

Lawrence Reamer

It is not fortunate for the reputation of Eugene O'Neill that his present vogue

The First Man

assures the production in one way or another of any drama he may write. There is of course no means for the commentator to know the experience of *The First Man*, which was acted at the Neighborhood Playhouse on Saturday, in the commercial theater. Whether it was ever offered there or not, it found its first performance in one of the more or less private theatres that have done so much to encourage the talents of the playwright. It would have been very much better for Mr. O'Neill's reputation if *The First Man* had never been played anywhere.

There is in the dialogue much of the author's vigorous and natural writing. Occasionally the observation of character is searchingly true to life. Yet it is not directed in a novel channel. The play deals with the narrowness of view which maintains in small communities and its eventually evil effect on the innocent. There is nothing new in this theme, which has been the inspiration of the dramatist in every age. So the critics of Bridgetown, Conn., who are so uncompromising in their views as to the conduct of the wife of a member family, are old friends. Their appearances in the drama, it might be said, are not skillfully arranged by the playwright. They enter the scene and depart with the mechanical awkwardness of an operatic chorus.

The horror of the explorer that his wife is to have a child, which will prevent her presence on his journey to China, since she is his best aid in his scientific pursuits, is in no way affected by the scandal of his family, which insists that the father of the unborn infant is one of the wife's friends, a widower whose children she has cared for. Her husband wants her help and society. The child is born, and after her cries of agony alternate with the gossip of his relatives the mother gives up her life. Yet the criticism of her husband's family, trying as it has been to the woman, has not affected her husband's faith. He even forgives the child, which he has held responsible for her death and professes his loyalty to her by driving out the malicious relatives who make their insinuations so pointed that the husband can no longer misunderstand what they mean. He protests his devotion to the boy, whom he will rear lovingly out of his affection for the dead woman. So not only are the slanderers rebuked, but *The First Man*, unlike most of those in the theater of its author, ends on an opportunistic note.

Mr. O'Neill has not told the story of the villagers with distinction. The task has been performed in better style by earlier dramatists, with the limitations, of course, of the prevailing dramatic models of their day, which are no longer to be regarded as models in our own time. The long conversations are in at least one case repetitious. There is an occasional cloudiness of motive. No characteristic of the work so reflects the author as his dialogue.

Augustin Duncan is a skillful producer of these dramas, and in some of the dialogues there was an admirable simulation of nature. There is likely to be a monotony of the naturalness, which does not always rise and fall with the emotion of the scene. The most slavish imitator of life would have to recognize an occasional change in rhythm under the impulse of emotion. Mr. Duncan is likely to continue, however, at one tempo.

The role of the explorer was not suited to him. The values of the drama demanded more impetuosity and fervor than he could impart. Margaret Mower,

Frederic Burt, Marjorie Vonnegut, Eva Condon and Eugene Powers were some of the intelligent actors engaged in the generally satisfying interpretation of *The First Man.*

New York Herald, March 6, 1922.

The New Play

Percy Hammond

It is a rotten world, Eugene O'Neill thinks, for the hairy apes. By hairy apes he means the ridiculous strong men who serve the furnaces in steamships or in steel mills where are forged the toilers' prison bars. The futile fellow with big disregard for everything but his own muscles. To bring it down to the particular hairy ape who is the topic of Mr. O'Neill's newest drama—the large, blustering, pugnacious employee who, endeavoring blindly to discover what it is all about, finds himself in a fatal *cul-de-sac.*

The above probably does not in the least resemble what O'Neill thinks about hairy apes. But it may serve to begin a report of last night's thoroughly interesting fantasy at the Provincetown Theatre. The Hairy Ape, known to his fellow stokers as "Yank" is having a good time in the first scene, domineering over his companions in the firemen's forecastle, with a pint of liquor at hand and a vast vocabulary of epithets.

He is proud of the great strength that manifests itself in coal shoveling, and of the fact that it is his skill and power that make the wheels go round. Everything else is "tripe." His comfort in that pride, however, is disturbed by the appearance of a lady passenger calling him a filthy beast. Thereafter he embarks upon the long and precarious pleasures of hatred, trying to find the young woman so that he may do her harm.

This lady is the daughter of the president of the Nazareth Steel Company, and as an uplifter, has enjoyed the "morbid thrills of East Side social work." Her grandfather, it may be, was also a hairy ape, but a successful one, for he was a puddler in his youth. Her grandmother smoked a clay pipe. The avenger first seeks her on Fifth Avenue on a Sunday after church, and he is arrested for interfering with a worshipper who is signalling a bus. Sent to the island, he learns from the prisoners there of the I.W.W., and he determines that organization shall be the instrument of his enmity. But he is thrown out of the I.W.W. headquarters when he applies for membership, being suspected as a spy; and at length he finds himself in front of a cage at the Zoo, trying to make friends with a gorilla. He ends there, not ignobly, in the unbrotherly embrace of the beast, and his last words are: "Where do I go from here?"

The Hairy Ape is played explicitly and with every indication of the role's characteristics by Louis Wolheim. It is an admirable performance, though monotonous at times with an endless reiteration of such expletives as "Get me!"

The eight scenes into which the play is divided are illusive pictures of a steamship's stokehole, its promenade deck, the island prison and other points in the allegory. The most effective, it seemed, is that of Fifth Avenue, where the pious, rich coming from worship, are represented as manikins with sinister false faces. *The Hairy Ape* comes under the classification of "interesting things," and it is no doubt the best of the O'Neill plays after *Anna Christie*.

New York Tribune, March 10, 1922.

The Hairy Ape

Stark Young

To say anything about Eugene O'Neill's new play we must begin at the very start and say over again that the art of the theatre is a separate and distinct art in itself. It is not easy to define; but it can at least be said to consist of movement, a rhythm, a pattern of elements that are distinctly its own characteristics. And other points about it can at least be indicated: that dialogue in literature, for example, is not the same as dialogue in the art of the theatre, words heard with the accompaniment of visual experience change; repetition gets a different effect; the cumulative result of things alters too; and so on. But all arts obscured in their essential character with borrowings from other arts and with things which, however delightful and even desirable, are inessential nevertheless to the art taken of itself. Sculpture, for one example, may borrow from painting; its fundamental sculptural basis may be confused, covered up, or the lack of it hidden, with the attractions of these added details. But the final test for any sculpture is the extent to which it can be stripped down to its own fundamentals. And the finest achievement in any art always rests on the success of its employment of those elements that determine its essential and individual nature. All of which needs to be said before we say that *The Hairy Ape* is a fine example of the art of the theatre. Not of fine writing, which it is not always, nor of subtle analysis or engrossing plot and enthralling spectacle; all these may be delightful enough but they are not the essentials. But a fine example of dramatic rhythm, of a pattern of movement. The progress and development of this play's fundamental structure is so simple and inevitable that by the casual it might be easily taken for granted. The line of the pattern is so simple and so rightly seen that it might escape consideration. The medium is in the main so rightly discovered and employed that the spectator's eye will be apt to turn entirely, with pleasure or with resentment, to the subject matter. But it is just this that makes *The Hairy Ape* such solid theatre, that it delivers its content with such unescapable finality of design. And it is just this that makes *The Hairy Ape* more significant as theatre than many other plays that are more delightful or even more powerful or more profoundly psychological if you like, in their general appeal.

    The story of the play moves so clearly and so straight as to seem almost obvious, which, as a matter of course, it becomes only through the simplifying unity of the control that has been exerted on it. In the first scene a crowd of stokers and sailors are drinking in the firemen's forecastle of an ocean liner an hour out from New York. Yank, the leader of them all, boasts and bullies, he makes the world go round, he is steel, he is twenty-five knots an hour, he belongs. Two days later the steel king's daughter on her way to new possibilities of sensation in the London slums completes her pose by coming with two officers to see the stokehole. At the sight of Yank's face there in the darkness and lurid light, something beyond anything that her slums have shown her, she faints. The next scene is the forecastle again; the men drink and jeer at Yank, who sits trying to think. She has called him a beast, she has looked at him as if he were a hairy ape, she has broken his nerve; he'll get her yet, he'll fix her white face. And three weeks later on Fifth Avenue he waits for her kind as they come out of church, bumps into them, tries to insult them, without making a single dent, and gets himself beaten up and carried off by the police. And then Yank awakes in a cell, with the prison howling about him and thinks himself in the zoo. He tells his wrongs and his fellows advise him to join the I.W.W. Which in the next scene he comes to do, but under the delusion that the society works with dynamite. They take him for a secret agent and throw him out. Then in front of their door he sits, wondering where he belongs, where he shall go; and an officer hustles him along; he may go "to hell." And finally next day at twilight you see him in the zoo before the gorilla's cage. He wants to see what the hairy ape is like. He talks with the gorilla, he says that the beast has it on the man this time. For the ape knows that he does not belong in the crowd; but the man who is talking to him knows his place is neither here nor there. He tears off the lock and lets the gorilla out. The beast crushes him to death in his arms, and so at last he belongs.

Compared to *The Emperor Jones* of last year *The Hairy Ape* seems less entertaining but more imaginative. Compared to the plot-design of *The Emperor Jones* or any other of Eugene O'Neill's plays, *The Hairy Ape* is a long step ahead. Its dénouement is inseparable from the whole idea; what happens and what is signified are one; the pattern is complete only with the last moment of the play.

Considering the limitations of the stage the production was remarkably successful, the stokehole especially and the scenes on deck and in front of the I.W.W. door. The fantastic setting for the Fifth Avenue episode had its cruelty and its burlesque comment on the idea; but the masks for the congregation's faces were, I think, carried too far from the mere impregnable fatuity intended by the author. The distorted lines of the bunks in the scene where Yank sits trying to make headway through his own wrongs and plans, seemed to me silly, the kind of thing that is wretchedly obvious once you get the point of it; and, in spite of its rather newer variety, just as much an intrusion as the older and more familiar fripperies, and in its way just as much a prettifying of the solid elements in the scene.

The acting was on the whole fair enough; though to me scarcely ever convincing. The truth is we have not decided yet what acting is exactly; how much it can be directly imitative, how much stylized, or how much the actual visible presence of the human beings that convey it interrupts and complicates this art as compared to others, the art of the play, for instance, or of the settings. *The Hairy Ape* is created with a certain simplification, a removal of the plane of it from mere actuality, in the Fifth Avenue scene of course and more subtly but as surely in the others. The acting has not been conceived very often in the same plane as the play itself. But that is a good deal to ask. Mr. Wolheim, certainly, has much for his particular part, the build, the voice—which he uses rather too monotonously through the play—and the steadiness and immobility of mere mass. His line and pose as he entered and stood the in I.W.W. office was very good indeed. In the scene where he sat in the street, thrown out, calling on whatever there is that will show him his way, and in the last scene, he struck the right pathos, confusion and tragedy. And better than Mr. Wolheim is the management of the gorilla at the very last, as he got more distinct and came so fearfully out of the cage. It was fine, extraordinary, out of class with any animal motive I have ever known on the stage.

And what a scene the last is, with that heavy, lost body stealing in there in the twilight; the darkness and the noises like those of the prison; and through the dim light the beast's figure looming up in the cage, more terrible and more beastly because half seen! The imagination behind the invention here is magnificent and unique; it exhibits a kind of dark and passionate warmth of life that is to be found nowhere else; it sums up and sweeps together into one grotesque and poignant moment all the life of that groping and wounded creature who comes there: his glimpses into thought; his impatient defeats and reticences, only half admitted and covered up with oaths; and the great inflexible bulk of this body, mind and soul that make such a tragic unity. But the most important thing about *The Hairy Ape* is in another direction.

In *Anna Christie* the first act gave me a conviction of something felt by the author, something raised from its ordinary tracks into a high vitality and excitement. But as the play went on I felt a blur. There seemed to be a movement toward an externality of incident or toward the necessity of making an end. The first act of *Diff'rent* had the same romantic depths of realism. But the rest of it never came through at all; the people were killed off and the play ended with a sort of impersonality. In *The Hairy Ape* I feel for the first time that the whole work expresses Eugene O'Neill. The play may be depressing, may be pessimistic as social criticism, lacking in culture, laid on sometimes with a trowel, as in the aunt and niece scene. Or it may be none of these things. That is not the point. The point is that there has been no impediment of event or convention to stand in the way, the conclusion in all its implications is true to the author. He has been able to carry himself through.

Eugene O'Neill has been greatly overpraised, partly, perhaps, for lack of a rival; certainly he has been praised without discrimination. But the instinct to praise him is entirely justified by reason of this tendency that he has always had to put himself, to be free as only in art of one kind or another the human soul can be free. And it is this, mainly, that makes *The Hairy Ape* the most important play of the year.

New Republic, March 22, 1922.

Eugene O'Neill's *Emperor Jones* and *The Hairy Ape* as Mirror Plays

Emil Roy

The Emperor Jones (1920) and *The Hairy Ape* (1921-22), are Eugene O'Neill's most successful experiments in expressionism. Considering the similarities in their cyclical structures, mock-heroic protagonists and archetypal symbolism, they are mirror plays whose aspects parallel or complement one another's correspondences. In *Emperor*, Jones is forced to flee his erstwhile subjects in a quest through a nightmarish, menacing dark night of the soul *(Walpurgisnacht)*. Once he has exhausted the *mana* or vital force attached to his silver bullet, he is forced to return to the sun-lit world of death. *The Hairy Ape* duplicates this order of events while inverting the symbolic content. Yank Smith, the protagonist, is almost immediately deprived of his persona through female duplicity. Emerging from his ship's womblike stokehold, he searches for rebirth through the labyrinthine bowels of the City. Repeatedly eluded by his lost identity, he finally enters the deathly embrace of his alter ego, the gorilla in the zoo. Both plays demonically parody the tragic ritual pattern which has been defined as a "transition by which—through the processes of separation, regeneration and return on a higher level—both the individual and the community are assured their victory over the forces of chaos which are thereby kept under control."[1] Although Yank Smith has some claims to tragic stature, being described by O'Neill as "a symbol in a sort of modern Morality play,"[2] and both protagonists engage in conflicts which probe the mysteries of the corrupted human will, the society of neither play is changed. Yank refuses to return at all, and the victory over chaos which "society" achieves through Jones assassination re-establishes a cabal of Calibans, a mindless gang of Yahoos. Nor do Jones and Smith achieve significant recognitions. Moreover, the expressionistic devices take effect less through the access to the unconscious supposedly provided by allegorical characters, anti-realistic staging, and unexpected transformations than through esthetic distancing. As in tragicomedy, which both plays closely resemble, the audience remains at a distance, yet within immediate call—impersonal, yet strangely involved.[3]

Both protagonists, we quickly notice, are messianic types whose unremarkable origins parody the characteristics which Otto Rank and Lord Raglan assign to the hero myth. Although Jones's parentage and childhood are unknown, Yank had run away from his drunken, quarrelsome parents—"Dat was where I loined to take punishment."[4] The most important fact about Jones is his escape from a chain gang, where he had been sent for murdering a guard who symbolically represented the cruel parent of folklore. As in the Moses and Jonas stories, Jones had safely arrived at the island after a sea journey. There he had been reborn. The "Emperor" which Jones has become, like Fitzgerald's "Great" Gatsby, then "sprang from his platonic conception of himself."[5] It is ironic, in retrospect, how closely Jones's regime had resembled a practical joke. Having shot down an assassin sent by Lem, his antagonist, he was suddenly inspired, as Smithers recalls: "You was so strong only a silver bullet could kill yer, you told 'em" (178). Jones foisted himself off as a god incarnate on a band of superstitious savages, relying only on his wits and bravado: "I knows I kin fool'em—I *knows* it—and dat's backin' enough fo' my game" (179), he boasts. Once he has milked his subjects dry, he plans to make a clandestine escape and have the last laugh in safety. W. H. Auden has observed the same phenomenon in a larger context:

> Unlike the ordinary ambitious man who strives for a dominant position in public and enjoys giving orders and seeing others obey them, the practical joker desires to make others obey him without being aware of his existence until the moment of his theophany.[6]

In O'Neill's play it is almost farcical that Jones's subjects accept him at his own fraudulent self-estimate: by being taken too seriously, he is hoist with his own petard. Yank Smith, on the other hand, is a vainglorious, truculent *alazon* or imposter lifted to heights of pride by a horde of semi-human mediocrities. He commands loyalty because he is egocentric enough to represent the collective ego of his followers: "I'm de end! I'm de start! I start somep'n and de woild moves! It—dat's me!—de new dat's moiderin' de old" (216)! Like the archetypal Prospero and Robinson Crusoe, both Jones and Smith have fled a highly competitive, more typical outside world because they "cannot accept men as they are. Rejection of that world is combined with an urge to dominate, an urge which is infantile in origin and which social adaptation has failed to discipline."[7]

The blazing sunlight, the "dazzling eye-smitting scarlet" (173) with which Jones's throne is painted, and even his red pants lending "something not altogether ridiculous about his grandeur" (175) implicitly link him with suffering heroes like Prometheus and disguised gods like Apollo, the sun-deity. Yank Smith takes on similar attributes through his association with noise, smoke and power, especially fire. Furthermore, both men endow precious or extremely hard metals with magical qualities they in turn identify with their own essences. "I'm de ting in gold dat makes it money! and I'm what makes iron into steel!" (216), Yank boasts, and even the tricky, skeptical Jones is "strangely fascinated" (179) with his silver bullet. Like the hero of romance, both are obliged to seek a magic weapon with which to slay the dragon. Ironically, however, Yank quests in vain for the dynamite whose equivalent, the silver bullet in *Emperor Jones*, has already lost its efficacy, unknown to Jones, through the taint of wealth. "I cook um money," Lem will explain at the end of the play, "make um silver bullet, make um strong charm, too" (203).

At the same time, the attempts of O'Neill's almost comically inadequate heroes to realize a messianic ideal of heroism in their worlds are displaced towards irony. In *Emperor Jones*, on the one hand, O'Neill uses Jones' naive, though shrewdly effective projections of self-aggrandizement to expose a debased, vulgarized present—as in George Bernard Shaw's *Saint Joan* and Arthur Miller's *Death of a Salesman*. Yank Smith on the other hand, is a likable, pure but incompetent idiot—as in *Don Quixote* or *Gulliver's Travels*. His totally inadequate attempts to reason, as parodied by his Rodin "Thinker" poses, are exposed as shams by his ludicrous failures. While O'Neill uses the more literally romantic action of *Emperor Jones* to comment on the heroic ideal, the inverted structure of *The Hairy*

Ape illuminates the kind of world in which heroism struggles and fails to be reborn.

Moreover, O'Neill's use of heroic archetypes is partly serious and partly ironic, never neglecting the crucial disparity between what his protagonists say and what they do. Immediately after Yank claims "Slaves, hell! We run the whole woiks!" a bell sounds and both he and his companions fall into a "prisoners' lockstep." And in *Emperor*, conversely, when Jones fully realizes the effectiveness of his deposition, he announces, "I resigns." Irony used in this way, as Empson has commented, "gives an impression of dealing with life completely...not to parody the heroes but to stop you from doing so."[8]

As is typical in O'Neill, both protagonists are flanked by complementary advisor-competitors who together project the crippled or struggling personality of the hero. They embody the left and right turns in the forked road traversed by the knightly questor. Lem in *Emperor* and Paddy in *Ape* are spokesmen for the dark gods of the underworld, nostalgic for a return to the womb of nature. As Paddy recalls the past, "'Twas them days a ship was part of the sea, and a man was part of a ship, and the sea joined all together and made it one" (214). And it is Lem in *Emperor Jones* who, taking Jones's joke in dead seriousness, taps chaotic sources of energy. Jones, like Ulysses' sailors who mistakenly released the winds from Aeolus's bag, is incapable of understanding these mysterious forces, let alone controlling them. Paddy and Lem long for fallen man's lost Eden, a state of innocence providing man with the instinctual security of belonging so completely that the question of being wanted or of being necessary cannot even arise. On the other side are the trader Smithers and the socialist Long, both articulate, cynical spokesmen for the reality principle, the ideology of success. Both are described as more refined, civilized and quick-witted than their animalistic counterparts, Paddy and Lem. Again, one play mirrors another even here. The revolution Long has failed to start is directed at a capitalistic system in which Smithers has never really succeeded, and the Edenic state Lem restores through "magic" is available to Paddy only through alcoholic withdrawal.

In myth the hero must undertake a night-sea journey into an ambiguous region either in the dark interior of the earth or below the waters. As Mircea Eliade has perceived, this initiatory pattern "is only a repetition of the first gestation and of carnal birth from the mother; it is also a temporary return to the virtual, precosmic mode (symbolized by night and darkness), followed by a rebirth that can be homologized with a 'creation of the world'."[9] He undergoes there a symbolic death that he may overcome the dragon of death, experience the peace of paradise, and bring his special truth back to a fallen world in order to redeem mankind.

But Brutus Jones and Yank Smith are not so much summoned to adventure as they are ejected from paradise into a fallen world, although neither Jones' throne room nor Yank's stokehold much resemble our conception of paradise. The crisis, when it comes in *Hairy Ape*, is directly induced by the appearance of Mildred Jordan in the stokehold. Within the tradition of American fiction, Mildred Jordan is a spoiled neurotic, the daughter of a steel millionaire whose imagination, stifled by overwhelming wealth, is piqued only by fear and sexuality. Blonde, possessed of "neither vitality nor integrity," and dressed in white, the color of ambiguous purity, she is a version of the archetypal sexual temptress appearing as Duessa in Spenser or Eve in *Paradise Lost*. Other of her faces can be seen in Fitzgerald's Daisy in *Great Gatsby*, Hemingway's Lady Brett in *The Sun Also Rises*, and Williams's Blanche Du Bois in *A Streetcar Named Desire*. By turns, she is stridently self-assertive and painfully tormented by inadequacies: "When a leopard complains of its spots, it must sound rather grotesque" (220). Further, she is brazenly dishonest and coyly seductive in visiting the stokehold, referring to an escorting engineer as "an oaf—but a handsome, virile oaf" (222). Her encounter with Yank Smith recapitulates the archetype of a monster tamed and controlled by a virgin. Yank's reaction to her screaming attack—"Oh, the filthy beast!" (226)—is delayed, but violent, a symbolic equivalent of rape. As Joseph Campbell puts it, "When it suddenly dawns on us, or is necessarily tainted with the odor of the flesh, then, not uncommonly, there is experienced a moment of revulsion."[10] Yank flings his shovel at a steel bulkhead, the sheer excess of his rage reflecting the depths of his own self-contempt and his inability to tolerate withheld affection. Mildred's "dark" counterpart in *Emperor Jones*, the stealthy, thieving native woman, performs a vestigial but equivalent function, announcing for the first time in the play Jones's loss of power and authority.

Although each *agon* has its own completeness, the sequential patterns of encounters involve a total scene or "topocosm," a concentric geometric spatial design. This "symbolic geography" of the plays reflects an image of space and time shaped by O'Neill from his tradition, experiences, and fantasies. The action in both plays involves not only cyclical quests (Jones literally running in a circle) but attempts to either ascend or resist falling. Thus the symbolic world in both implies levels of existence whose moral content is highly ambiguous and misleading. The outer, upper limits of both worlds are defined by empty sea, sky, and forest, which Jones mistakenly assumes are inhabited by a benevolent, protective spirit. At the edge of the sea is a French gunboat guaranteeing him safe passage, like his cache of food at the edge of the sinister Great Forest. Overhead floats the God of "De Baptist Church [which] done pertect me and land dem all in hell" (185). But Jones never reaches the boat, the white stone under which his food is hidden maliciously multiplies, and the emptiness of the sky above is confirmed by the rushing moon. Its advance positions in each scene mark Jones's progress towards lunacy, helplessness, and death. Jones's curse, like that of seers such as Teiresias, Cassandra, and Coleridge's Ancient Mariner, is his "glittering eye," an unwanted access of insight into the unknown: "Dey's some tings I ain't got to be tole," he claims. "I kin see 'em in folks' eyes" (177). Yank's curse, unlike Jones's is the pitiless gaze of a near-deific malevolence, present everywhere but visible nowhere. The top level of his universe is dominated by a force of inhuman necessity personified in Yank's mind as Mildred Jordan's father, head and owner of Nazareth Steel Mills. His *bête noir*, manifested in the action by protean embodiments of his will, squats spider-like at the pinnacle of experience, repeatedly entangling Yank in skeins of steel: "Cages, cells, locks, bolts, bars—dat's what it means!—holdin' me down wit him at de top!" (244), Yank complains.

Just beneath and within this cosmic round lies the level of ordinary human experience, with its anomalies and injustices. The realm of social interaction is never very palpably imagined by O'Neill, as Lionel Trilling has commented: "For O'Neill, since as far back as *The Hairy Ape*, there has been only the individual and the universe. The social organism has meant nothing."[11] What passes for society is a ring of immobilized mannequins shutting Jones in just as they shut Yank out. The group in *The Emperor Jones* is as malevolent as it is indifferent in *The Hairy Ape*, but both are equally mindless. The social elite in *Emperor*, when it finally appears, consists of a squad of soldiers in "different degrees of rag-concealed nakedness" led by Lem, "a heavy-set, ape faced old savage of the extreme African type" (202). In *Hairy Ape*, the social group is composed either of mindless Neanderthal stokers, on the one hand, or ghoulish marionettes "with something of the relentless horror of Frankensteins in their detached, mechanical unawareness" (236).

Below, concealed under the historical layers of civilization, is the buried original form of society. It appears only fleetingly in *Hairy Ape* and never in *Emperor Jones*. It may emerge in imagery of morning freshness, clean air and sun, a general mood of rejuvenation, as in Paddy's reminiscences of the days of sailing clippers or in Yank's naive *aubade* in the zoo:

> Sure. I seen the sun come up. Dat was pretty too—all red and pink and green. I was lookin' at de skyscrapers—steel—and all de ships comin' in, sailin' out, all over de oith—and dey was steel, too. De sun was warm, dey wasn't no clouds, and dere was a breeze blowin'. Sure it was great stuff. I got it aw right—what Paddy said about dat bein' de right dope—on'y I couldn't get *in* it, see? (252).

When a paradisaical motif appears, it sharpens our sense of a speaker's alienation, is juxtaposed with images of crass commercialism, or is placed in the irretrievable past.

On the lowest level appears a world which corresponds to the traditional hell or world of death, but which may also serve as a fructifying reservoir of power or life. Both Great Forest in *Emperor Jones* and brightly lit City in *Hairy Ape* are labyrinthine hells through which Jones and Smith are forced to wander, although the Forest ambiguously represents man's fallen state under a curse, the constant irrational cycle of history, and the interior landscape of the soul. Ironically, Yank's obsessed identification with "fire—under de heap—fire dat never gets out—hot as hell—breakin' out in de night" (244) links him with Mildred Jordan's grandfather, another champion of process, as well as with Jones's magical fire-arm. Moreover, the mythic role of Jones as sea monster who has become the source of his people's sterility—"Look at the taxes you've put on 'em!" Smithers exclaims. "Blimey! You've squeezed 'em dry!" (178)—has its symbolic counterpart in *Hairy Ape*. For that society which appears utopian to Yank strikes his cowed fellows as an unharrowed hell, traditionally represented by the archetypal dragon which has swallowed a whole society alive. "Yank 'ere is right," announces Long. "E says this 'ere stinkin' ship is our 'ome....We lives in 'ell, Comrades—and right enough we'll die in it" (211). Paradoxically, the ship which appears cell-like and oppressive in *The Hairy Ape* has its liberating, maternally protective counterpart in *The Emperor Jones*. It awaits Jones womb-like on the other side of the Great Forest where, he believes, "She picks me up, takes me to Martinique when she go dar, and dere I is safe...." (183). Yet as Jones is drawn from the one terrifying cavity to another, the ship-like nourishing womb is demonically transformed near the end into the devouring maw which initially appears in *Hairy Ape*, Jones at last stumbles into a simulacrum of the hold of a slavers' ship.

With their forced withdrawals from human society, both Brutus Jones and Yank Smith embark on adventures into the unknown, their quests exemplifying man's fate in an irrational world. Both lines of action combine traditional descent themes with the archetypal hero's attempt to kill or pacify a dragon who guards a secret hoard of wealth or wisdom. However, their roles and functions have been radically inverted: Jones has fallen from charismatic redeemer to rejected tyrant, while Smith has been cast down from unquestioned tyrant to lonely redeemer. What both of these mock-heroes seek is a communal identity to replace their directionless egos, a sense of being human in an indifferent nature. Hitherto untried, both of them undergo a series of ordeals whose character, translating internal memories of the past (both individual and communal) into external referents, reveals the as-yet nascent spirit of the protagonists.

Brutus Jones experiences many elements of the ritual adventure, compressing his previous exploits together with a reverse chronology of a fallen world, all within the imagined episodes of a single night. At the outset a free agent, he is gradually caught up in a chain of causality in the Great Forest, a region where the unconscious may project its fantasies without the hindrance of time and space. Jones's downward, circular flight within a "ring" of malevolent avengers is shaped by a sequence of demonically repeated ordeals, each of which he fails. As in the solar myths, he travels perilously through a dark labyrinthine underworld full of monsters between sunset and sunrise.

While the content of his visions has a straight-line inevitability, their character is dialectical and paranoid. One after another he encounters enemies, from the Nameless Fears to Jeff, a dead one-time dicing partner, to the murdered chain gang guard, an antebellum auctioneer and planter, a ships's hold full of slaves, and finally a witch doctor and his alligator-totem. The sheer repetitiveness of his trials accentuate Jones's excess, in turn revealing his insufficient knowledge of the evil to be combatted. In *Emperor Jones*, as in *Hairy Ape*, each episode sets in motion an oscillation between an initial lapse into a self-defensive stupor and a furious revolt against all restraints, resembling the pendulating extremes of the manic depressive: "Rest! Don't talk! Rest!" (193), Jones frantically tells himself.

Just as Jones cannot adjust to the fallen human world, neither can he bridge the gap between the logical simple identity he has created for himself and the dark world of the unknown. He is not a whole man, a creature who realizes that both guilt and innocence, corruption and purity, are inevitably mixed in the human sphere. Both sense experience and intellect are useless, despite his repeated but weakening self-assurances: "Ha'nts! You fool nigger dey ain't no such things! Don't de Baptist parson tell you dat many time! Is you civilized, or is you like dese ign'rent black niggers heah! Sho'! Dat was all in yo own head" (193). Like Lear, he and Yank Smith have tremendous souls geared to puerile intellects. Moreover, Jones's visions, like Leer's storm, project psychic tempests onto the cosmos. At the same time, the progressive stripping away of Jones's uniform, like Lear's symbolic disrobing, reveals the "poor forked animal" beneath the egotistical, self-gratifying clothing. "Majesty!" he comments self-mockingly. "Der ain't much majesty 'bout dis baby now" (191).

Jones is undone not so much by his fear of isolation as he is by his terror of hostile impingement upon that solitude. Moreover, his fear of Lem and his band is gradually supplanted by his terror of the supernatural: "I ain't skeered o' real men. Let dem come. But dem odders—" (196). Failure in self control under an ordeal is felt to be particularly ignominious when all the questor "can do is create new problems for himself and await the gradual approach of his disintegration."[12]

The hero usually regresses to a state of servitude, symbolized by physical blindness in *Sampson Agonistes* and by an "antic disposition" in *Hamlet*, for example. In the last episode, with only his silver bullet remaining, Jones has become an automaton: "The expression of his face is fixed and stony, his eyes have an obsessed glare, he moves with a strange deliberation like a sleepwalker or one in a trance" (200).

Not only the dead-end finality of the episodes as a whole, but the similarity between incidents imply that history is the story of man's unsuccessful attempts to cope with his fallen state. O'Neill's reconstruction of mankind's social evolution confirms Herbert Marcuse's perception that prehistory "does not lead back to the image of a paradise which man had forfeited by his sin against God, but to the domination of man by man, established by a very earthly father-despot and perpetuated by the unsuccessful or uncompleted rebellion against him."[13] In the name of security, man has replaced one imperfection by another equally imperfect.

Unlike Jones, who is obsessed with change, with the mutability of corruptible mankind, Yank had engaged on a quest for a world of immutable values, of permanence. And while Jones becomes uncomfortably aware of being responsible for his own difficulties, Smith's wish to *be* serious and to be *taken* seriously stems from his aggrieved sense that he is *not* serious and that people do *not* take him seriously. He has becomes painfully aware that while he had supposedly acted on his own initiative, he had actually been the puppet of another's will: "She grinds the organ and I'm on de string, Huh? I'll fix her" (232)! Whereas all attempts to transfer guilt to Jones give him something of a the dignity of innocence, Yank Smith is the perfectly innocent victim excluded from human society. Motivated by an anguished desire for revenge on Mildred, whose "evil eye" had rendered him symbolically impotent, Yank's oedipal attack on her father is a confused variant of his earlier championship of "de new dat's moiderin' de old."

Once Yank embarks on his Promethean quest for dynamite to destroy the Nazareth Steel Mills, he both circles and tries to ascend. But his progress is balked by a series of threshold guards—realistic counterparts of Cerberus—whose opposite numbers in *Emperor Jones* are, rather, devilish tempters, incubi. He is enticed, like Jones, into hollow, womblike caverns where he is devoured rather than reborn. In his successive defeats by the social elite, the police forces of a repressive government, and even by his natural allies the union workers, Yank's fruitless attacks underline the play's assumption that lust for sadistic power on the part of the ruling class is strong enough to last forever. Thus Yank's giant-killing aims are placed in a bizarre light. When, for example, Yank is enraged by the mincing churchgoers, he tilts at them Quixote-like, "bumping viciously into them but not jarring them the least bit. Rather it is he who recoils after each collision" (238). Although the society against which Yank vents his aggression is revealed to be full of anomalies, injustices, and crimes, it is seen by O'Neill as permanent and undisplaceable. Even if Yank were, by some fluke, to blow up Jordan's mill, he would accomplish nothing, O'Neill revealed in a suggested film version of the play: "All his attempt does is to blow down a section of wall—and immediately an army of workers rebuilds the wall up before his eyes (an expressionistic touch)."[14] On the one hand, then, we have in Jones the man who denies his commitment, his responsibility to an ideal; on the other, Yank Smith as the man of action who, while protesting his own innocence or at least ignorance, does act to fulfill his responsibility.

While Jones's death by gunshot resembles the failure of the mythic hero to return from the supernatural to the real world without his magic amulet, Yank's surrender to the gorilla's crushing embrace involves the hero's refusal to return to the troubled life he has left. But for both, the constant menace of personal disintegration has been met futilely by violence. Conflict between the conscious and unconscious life has been resolved, although the terrorized Jones meets his end with as much resistance and incomprehension as Yank displays passive, accepting endurance. Denied his faith in an external order as Yank quests vainly for an identity, Jones death is as much a suicide symbolically as Yank's is literally. For the green-eyed alligator god is a projection of the monster Jones's subjects take him for. Jones's shot, fired simultaneously with that of Lem's soldiers, fulfills his self-prophesied suicide:

> Dis baby plays out his string to de end and when he quits, he quits wid a bang de way he ought. Silver bullet ain't none too good for him when he go, dat's a fac'! (184)

The alligator, like Yank's gorilla, embodies what has been called "the power that would destroy one's egocentric system,...the divine being that is the image of the living self within the locked labyrinth of one's own disoriented psyche."[15] Yank's soul escapes from his body with the gorilla's assistance just as the gorilla escapes with Yank's help, from his cage. Together the gorilla and Yank Smith, like body and soul, externalize the total personality for which Yank was searching when at the end, "perhaps the *Hairy Ape* at last belongs" (254).

Yet the vision of reconciliation between conflicting selves, at least in this life, remains only a pipe dream. In O'Neill it appears as it does in much serious contemporary drama. "Both alternatives of the choice imposed are absurd, irrelevant, or compromising....What once was tragedy," as Jan Kott says, "today is grotesque."[16] In *Emperor Jones* where society is depicted as a condition of savagery, comedy consists of inflicting pain on a helpless victim and tragedy of enduring it. In *Hairy Ape*, where society is depicted as a condition of over-refined rigidity, tragedy consists of the denial of identity to an ignorant victim, and comedy in his fruitless, painful attempts to achieve it forcefully. Jones is guilty in the sense that he had deliberately provoked the reaction which overtakes him. He is innocent, however, in the sense that his mental aguish is far greater than anything he has done deserves. Yank Smith is guilty in the sense that he lives in world where injustices are an inescapable part of existence. He is innocent in the sense that his isolation from his society is imposed on, rather than invoked by, him. At the end of *Emperor Jones*, which is ironic comedy, we recognize the absurdity of society's attempt to define the enemy of society as person outside that society.

O'Neill's sense of modern man as both criminal and prosecutor, victor and victim, emerges through the calculated ambiguities both within and between these two plays. Whatever his restless, unending strivings for religious certainty might have been, he manages at his best to compensate for his and his audience's loss of the primitive's secure belief based on a religious world view by finding an equivalent, though not a substitute, order in artistry and form.

NOTES

1. Herbert Weisinger, "The Myth and Ritual Approach to Shakespearean Tragedy," in *Myth and Literature*, ed., John B. Vickery (Lincoln, Neb., 1966), p. 151.

2. Letter to Robert Sisk, March 15, 1935, Beinecke Library Collection, Yale University.

3. See J. L. Styan, *The Dark Comedy* (Cambridge, 1962), p. 249.

4. *The Hairy Ape* in *The Plays of Eugene O'Neill* (New York, 1954). All further page references to both *The Hairy Ape* and *The Emperor Jones* will be taken from the same edition.

5. F. Scott Fitzgerald, *The Great Gatsby* (New York, 1925), p. 99.

6. *The Dyer's Hand* (New York, 1958), p. 36.

7. Othar Manoni, *Prospero and Caliban*, trans. Pamela Powesland (New York, 1956), p. 180.

8. William Empson, *Some Versions of Pastoral* (Norfolk, Conn., n.d.), pp. 29, 30.

9. Mircea Eliade, *Rites and Symbols of Initiation* (New York, 1958), p. 36.

10. *The Hero with a Thousand Faces* (New York, 1949), p. 122.

11. Lionel Trilling, "The Genius of O'Neill," *O'Neill and His Plays*, ed. O. Cargill (New York, 1961), p. 299.

12. Campbell, p. 59.

13. *Eros and Civilization* (New York, 1955), p. 54.

14. Letter to Sisk, *op. cit.*

15. Campbell, p. 60.

16. Jan Kott, *Shakespeare Our Contemporary*, trans., Boleslaw Taborski (Garden City, N.J., 1966), p. 135.

Comparative Drama, 2 (Spring 1968): 21-31

The Theatre: Eugene O'Neill

Hugo von Hofmannstahl (translated by Barrett H. Clark)

It was at the Salzburg Festival last summer that I first heard the name of Eugene O'Neill. Max Reinhardt was producing one of my plays there; a sort of mystery, a synthetic handling of allegorical material mounted in a church. There were a few Americans in our audience, who aroused my curiosity by relating merely the plots of *The Emperor Jones* and *The Hairy Ape*.

Some time after, I read both these plays; also *Anna Christie* and *The First Man*.... Judging from those of his plays with which I am familiar, his work is throughout essentially of the theatre. Each play is clear-cut and sharp in outline, solidly constructed from beginning to end; *Anna Christie* and *The First Man* as well as the more original and striking *Emperor Jones* and *The Hairy Ape*. The structural power and pre-eminent simplicity of these works are intensified by the use of certain technical expedients and processes which seem dear to the heart of this dramatist and, I may presume, to the heart of the American theatre-goer as well; for instance, the oft-used device of the repetition of a word, a situation, or a motive. In *The Hairy Ape*, the motive of repetition progresses uninterruptedly from scene to scene; the effect becomes more and more tense as the action hurries on to the end. Mr. O'Neill appears to have a decided predilection for striking contrasts, like that for instance, between the life of the sea and the life of the land, in *Anna Christie* or between the dull narrowness of middle class existence and unhampered morality, in *The First Man*. The essential dramatic plot—the "fable," that is—is invariably linked to and revealed by that visual element which the theatre, and above all, I believe, the modern theatre, demands. The dialogue is powerful, often direct, and frequently endowed with a brutal though picturesque lyricism.

In an American weekly publication I find the following judgment on Mr. O'Neill, written by an intelligent and very able native critic: "He has a current of thought and feeling that is essentially theatrical. Taken off the stage it might often seem exaggerated, out of taste or monotonous." To this just praise—for it is intended as praise—I can heartily subscribe. But the same writer goes on to say, however, that the manner in which Mr. O'Neill handles his dialogue offers an opportunity for some interesting speculations of a general character on the whole question of dramatic dialogue.

In my opinion, granting the primary importance of the dramatic fable, or plot, the creative dramatist is revealed through his handling of dialogue. By this be it understood, I do not mean the lyrical quality or rhetorical power; these elements are in themselves of little importance in determining the value of dialogue. Let us assume a distinction between literature and drama, and say that the best dialogue is that which, including the purely stylistic or literary qualities, possesses at the same time what is perhaps the most important of all: the quality of movement, of suggestive mimetic action. The best dramatic dialogue reveals not only the motives that determine what a character is to do—as well as what he tries to conceal—but suggests his very appearance, his metaphysical being as well as the grosser material figure. How this is done remains one of the unanswerable riddles of artistic creation. This suggestion of the "metaphysical" enables us to determine in an instant, the moment a person enters the room, whether his is sympathetic or abhorrent, whether he brings agitation or peace; he affects the atmosphere about us, making it solemn or trivial, as the case may be.

The best dialogue is that which charges the atmosphere with this sort of tension; the more powerful it is the less dependent does it become upon the mechanical details of stage-presentation.

We ought not too often to invoke the name of Shakespeare—in whose presence we all become pygmies—but for a moment let us call to mind that Shakespeare has given us practically no stage-directions; everything he has to say is said in the dialogue; and yet we receive pure visual impressions of persons and movement; we *know* that King Lear is tall and old, that Falstaff is fat.

Masterly dialogue resembles the movements of a high-spirited horse: there is not a single unnecessary movement, everything tends towards a predetermined goal; but at the same time each movement unconsciously betrays a richness and variety of vital energy that seems directed to no special end; it appears rather like the prodigality of an inexhaustible abundance.

In the best works of Strindberg we find dialogue of this sort, occasionally in Ibsen, and always in Shakespeare; as fecund and strong in the low comedy give-and-take scenes with clowns and fools as in the horror stricken words of Macbeth.

Measured by this high ideal, the characters in Mr. O'Neill's plays seem to me a little too direct; they utter the precise words demanded of them by the logic of the situation; they seem to stand rooted in the situation where for the time being they happen to be placed; they are not sufficiently drenched in the atmosphere of their own individual past. Paradoxically, Mr. O'Neill's characters are not sufficiently fixed in the present because they are not sufficiently fixed in the past. Much of what they say seems too openly and frankly sincere, and consequently lacking in the element of wonder or surprise; for the ultimate sincerity that comes from the lips of man is always surprising. Their silence, too, does not always convince me; often it falls short of eloquence, and the way in which the characters go from one theme to another and return to the central theme is lacking in that seemingly inevitable abandon that creates vitality. Besides, they are too prodigal with their shouting and cursing, and the result is that they leave me a little cold towards the other things they have to say. The habit of repetition, which is given free rein in the plot itself as well as in the dialogue, becomes so insistent as to overstep the border of the dramatically effective and actually to become a dramatic weakness.

The essence of drama is movement, but that movement must be held in check, firmly controlled.

I shall not venture to decide which is the more important in drama, the driving motive-element of action, or the retarding or "static" element; at any rate, it is the combination, the interpenetration of the two that makes great drama. In Shakespeare's plays there is not a line that does not serve the ultimate end, but when one goes through the text to discover this for oneself, one perceives that the relation between means and end is by no means evident; the means seem tortuously indirect, often diametrically opposed to the end. Nineteen lines out of twenty in a comedy or tragedy of Shakespeare are (seemingly) a digression, an interpolative obstruction thrown across the path of the direct rays; retarding motives of every sort impede the onward march of events. But it is precisely these obstacles that reveal the plasticity, the vitality, of the story and characters; it is these that cast the necessary atmosphere about the central idea of the work. As a matter of fact, the unity of the play lies in these diversified and apparently aimless "digressions."

If one goes through *Antony and Cleopatra* looking only for the chain of physical events, the hard outlines of the plot, and neglects the indescribable atmosphere of pomp and circumstance, the spectacle of the downfall of pride and fulfillment of destiny, the contrasting colours of Orient and Occident, all of which is made manifest through the dialogue, what is left? Nothing more than the confusion and incoherence of nine out of every ten motion-picture dramas. Or if one consider the best pieces of Gerhart Hauptmann merely as samples of superficial naturalism, one would find them pedantic and weak in characterization. Or again, take the productions of the doctrinaire naturalists: a good example is the dramatizations of the Edmond and Jules Goncourt novels. Thirty years ago these played a role of considerable importance, so far as theatrical history is concerned; but there is no life in them, nor was there when they were first produced; they suffer from lack of fresh air. Hauptmann's best plays, on the other hand, are bathed in it; it unifies and breathes vitality into them because it is the breath of life itself, transfused by that secret process which makes all great art, be it drama or canvas, giving it richness, variety and contrast. This is what the painters call "*le rapport des valeurs*." The plays of Strindberg are unified in this wise, not because of the bare plot on which they are built, but through the medium of an indescribable atmosphere that hovers somewhere between the realm of the actual and the dreamworld.

The European drama is an old institution, laden with the experience of years, but as suspicious and watchful as a venerable though not yet impotent human being.

We know that the dynamic element in drama is a vigorous element, eternally striving for ascendancy. But we also know that great drama is and always has been—from the time of Aeschylus down to the present—an amalgamation of the dynamic and (shall we say?) "static" elements, and we are therefore a trifle suspicious of every effort towards the predominance of one element over another. The nineteenth century witnessed many such efforts, and each time great drama disappeared during the process. There is a constant danger that action—whether it masquerade as thesis-play or play of ideas, problem-play or drama of intrigue, or simply as the vehicle of a virtuoso playing with an anecdote—may prevail over the subtle and difficult but indispensable combination of dynamic and "static," the inseparable oneness of plastic form and action.

Sardou, the heir of Scribe, created a type of play the ingredients of which were entirely dynamic; action took the place of all else, and for twenty years Sardou dominated the stages of Europe, while his followers—the Sudermanns, the Bernsteins, the Pineros—have continued to dominate it to the admiration of the middle classes of all nations and the abomination of the artists! This was the type of play in which the personages were never guilty of any "irrational" exhibition of character: they were the fixed units in a sharply outlined plot, manipulated by the skilled hand of the playwright; and they passed their lives in rooms hermetically sealed against the breath of mortals.

Sardou coined an expression for his style of play: "Life through movement," which was turned against him by his critics, who retorted: "Movement through life." The critics were all true artists: Zola, Villiers de l'Isle-Adam and their followers, among whom was the young Strindberg; but the most influential was Antoine, a man of the theatre. But the pendulum swung back, and for the time being, perhaps, the European drama has gone too far in the opposite direction. It may be that this is the reason why the plays of Hauptmann are not popular outside Germany; for a large part of the German public is ready and able to listen to plays in which the "static" element is predominant, dramas in which psychological characterization and lyricism are of more importance than plot. Possibly this tendency is even a little overdeveloped.

Judged from this point of view, Hauptmann's plays are the exact antitheses of the plays of Eugene O'Neill. Where Mr. O'Neill reveals the first burst of his emotions in powerful, clean-cut pictures that seem almost like simple ballads in our complex world, Hauptmann supplies himself to making his characters plastic; he does this by throwing a half-light over his men and women and allowing the values to appear slowly, to emerge in new and true and wonderful aspects, gradually shown through an accumulation of tiny and seemingly unimportant incidents of everyday life. As a result, Hauptmann's plots do not progress with directness or force; and at first sight his scenes appear to possess neither dynamic nor even truly "static" elements; they seem somewhat confused. But what ultimately strengthens these scenes and gives them the rhythm of life is a steady and unremitting infusion of the essence of life, which is soul. Hauptmann's method is that of Rembrandt the etcher, who works with a fine steel needle. Since Hauptmann continues to work in this fashion, he must necessarily give little thought to his audience; and indeed he is in actual danger of losing sight of them altogether. Meantime, he manages to accumulate so much of the spiritual life of his characters that his last acts are filled with an almost explosive force, so that there is no need for the introduction of any mechanical tension. Henrik Ibsen has done the same sort of thing in the last act of *The Wild Duck* and Ibsen is the master from whom Hauptmann has learned most.

In the case of Mr. O'Neill, however, his first acts impress me as being the strongest; while the last, I shall not say go to pieces, but undoubtedly, are very much weaker than the others. The close of *The Hairy Ape*, as well as that of *The Emperor Jones*, seems to me to be too direct, too simple, too expected; it is a little disappointing to a European with his complex background, to see the arrow stride the target toward which he has watched it speeding all the while. The last acts of *Anna Christie* and *The First Man* seem somewhat evasive, undecided. The reason for this general weakness is, I think, that the dramatist, unable to make his dialogue a complete expression of human motives, is forced at the end simply to squeeze it out like a wet sponge.

I have no intention of giving advice to a man of Mr. O'Neill's achievements; what I have said is not said by way of adverse criticism; it is rather the putting together of dramaturgical reflections inspired by a consideration of his plays. His qualities as a dramatist are already very great, and I have no doubt that he will make progress when, in the course of time, which is necessary to each man who creates, he shall have acquired better control over his materials, and above all over his own considerable talents.

Freeman, March 23, 1923.

The Theatre: *Welded*

George Jean Nathan

In the case of *Welded*, O'Neill has tried on Strindberg's whiskers with the same unfortunate result as in the instance of an earlier play called *The First Man*. Following the technic of the late lamented August, he has set himself so to intensify and even hyperbolize a theme as to evolve the dramatic effect from the theme's overtones rather than, as is the more general manner, from its undertones. The attempt, in a word, is to duplicate the technic of such a drama as *The Father*, the power of which is derived not by suggestion and implication, but from the sparks that fly upward from a prodigious and deafening pounding on the anvil. The attempt, as I have said, is a failure, for all one gets in O'Neill's play is the prodigious and deafening pounding. The sparks simply will not come out. Now and again one discerns something that looks vaguely like a spark, but on closer inspection it turns out to be only an imitation lightning-bug that has been cunningly concealed in the actors' sleeves.

What O'Neill had in mind in the writing of *Welded* was unquestionably, a realistic analysis of love after the manner of Strindberg's *Dance of Death*. What he planned to show was that a deep love is but hate in silks and satin, that suspicion, cruelty, torture, self-flagellation and voluptuous misery and torment are part and parcel of it, that it constantly murders itself and that its corpse comes to life again after each murder with an increased vitality, and that once a man and woman have become sealed in this bond of hateful love they are, for all their tugging and pulling, caught irrevocably in the trap of their exalted degradation. What actually shows, however, is only vaguely what he set out to show. His intent and achievement are miles apart. He goes aground on the rocks of exaggeration. His philosophical melodrama is so full of psychological revolver shots, jumps off the Brooklyn Bridge, incendiary Chinamen, galloping hose-carts, forest fires, wild locomotives, saw mills, dynamite kegs, time fuses, mechanical infernal machines, battles under the sea, mine explosions, Italian blackhanders, last minute pardons, sinking ocean liners and fights to the death on rafts that the effect is akin to trying to read a treatise on the theme on a bump-the-bumps. O'Neill rolls up his sleeves and piles on the agony with the assiduity of a longshoreman. He has misjudged, it seems to me completely, the Strindberg method. That method is the intensification of a theme from within. O'Neill has intensified his theme from without. He has piled psychological and physical situation on situation until the structure topples over with a burlesque clatter. Strindberg magnified the psyche of his characters. O'Neill magnifies their actions.

Welded...has a terrible time with itself. It is forever climbing up the sides of steep mountains with ear-rending grunts and groans and with excruciating pains in its middle when all the while there lies a smooth, easy valley path to the other side of the mountain in plain view. It is constantly bawling at the top of its lungs when there is need for nothing but a whisper. It is always sitting down on its own hat.

The simple truth about the play is that its characters are intrinsically nothing but hams. O'Neill has intensified his human beings to the point where they are no longer human beings, or symbols of human beings, but just actors. And to pile Pelion on Ossa, he has made one of these characters an actress and another a Broadway theatrical manager! Further to add to the joviality of the occasion, the producers engaged Jacob Ben-Ami,...an actor intensified to such a degree that he seems always in danger of biting himself, brought to the already highly actorized role an artillery of histrionic nonsense that made it doubly unreal and absurd....Miss Doris Keane managed the woman's role with a fair share of skill. The staging of the manuscript by Stark Young was satisfactory save in the matter of lighting. Unless my eyes deceived me on the opening night, it was high noon outside the window of the room in Act II although the time was two o'clock in the morning. Again, the dawn of the last act was of a peculiar pea-green shade, as of Maeterlinck full of Chartreuse. Still again, although the room of Act I was illuminated only by a small and arty table lamp at the extreme left of the stage, the center of the stage—the battleground of the actors—was whimsically bathed in a dazzling radiance by a powerful balcony spotlight. After all, one can at times forgive Belasco many things, even his Catholic collar, Presbyterian coat and Methodist breeches.

American Mercury, May 1924.

New O'Neill Play and the Mayor

Anonymous

It developed in the Provincetown Theatre last night that not only have all God's chillun got wings, but that some of God's chillun got votes.

All God's Chillun Got Wings

This peculiar political fact was indicated when the director of the production explained the absence of Scene I from Mr. O'Neill's muchly debated play of miscegenation. He said that the Mayor had refused to approve the usual license permitting children to take part.

As the first scene was intended merely to show that "the color line does not cross childhood," it was read and the rest of the play enacted with it as a premise.

Macdougal Street was filled with talk about the Mayor and yards of it seemed very unkind. It is only half fair to give credit where credit is due, and it appears that City Hall has been sheltering all these years something of a dramatic critic.

Perhaps this was the opening gun in the third term campaign. Perhaps his Honor may be able to build an organization out of all those who object to child performers, and have himself swept again into office on the slogan "Children's place is in the home."

But if Mr. Hylan denied the God-given wings to the child actors, Mr. O'Neill's play seemed to get along very well without them.

Only it is a pity that our colleague in criticism couldn't have withheld some of the other scenes as well. By collaborating judiciously with Mr. O'Neill he might have pared the piece down to the one-act play that it really is, dramatically, and made of it a brief but profoundly moving tragedy.

As it stands it certainly does not rank with O'Neill's best work, and it is a scarcely passable piece of play writing. Much of it is dull and irrelevant. Yet at the climax of the second act the sheer conflict of it seizes you by the throat and forces from you a reluctant cheer—reluctant because you suspect all the time that Mr. O'Neill has juggled with you, that he has wheedled you into accepting these characters with their racial prejudices but with his own sensitiveness, their problems, but his own estimate of them.

It is the O'Neill of *Emperor Jones*, hypnotic and inscrutable, working his incantations before your eyes and making you believe in his magic. It is the same arbitrary O'Neill, single track, who goes straight to the center of a situation and tears its heart out. Such procedure leaves the landscape a wreckage, but it is breathtaking.

The play has been printed, and the controversy has been based on the published text. It's quite a different matter on the stage, as any one might have known it would be. Its few big moments are made highly effective by Mr. Robeson and Miss Mary Blair, who played the thing to the limit with the terrific and intense sincerity of their acting.

Mr. Robeson is a negro, and for the benefit of the morbid sillies who dote on racial jingoism it may be stated as a matter of record that his hand is still unkissed, unless he kissed it himself.

New York Post, May 16, 1924.

All God's Chillun and Others

Edmund Wilson

We are getting the backwash of the naturalistic movement—as we have of many other movements—when Europe is leaving it behind. What is called expressionism represents an attempt to get away from the literal methods of realism—as the cubism of Picasso and Braque represents an attempt to get away from the photography of nineteenth century painting. The expressionistic method, as Mr. Stark Young has said, is "merely the poetic method." But it is an attempt to write poetically on the part of people who have been brought up on the science of naturalism. It was easy for Shakespeare to disregard literal realism and to make people speak their inmost minds in the non-colloquial language of the imagination, because he had no John Galsworthy and Gerhart Hauptmann to unlearn. But the poet today has to take his original conception, which is almost always in terms of naturalism and impose poetry upon it—just as the modern painter has to take conventional still-life and by main force hack it to pieces and try to shuffle them anew....

All God's Chillun Got Wings by Eugene O'Neill, also shows signs of an attempt to impose subjective fancies upon an idea objectively conceived. The Provincetown Players, in producing the play, have disregarded the idea, which appears in the author's text, of having the walls and ceiling of the room contract as the situation becomes more oppressive, but they have made him a present of a curious church with a waist like a human being and flying buttresses of brick which seem to be streaming away to the wind. Both these devices strike one as rather mechanical, as not belonging with the rest of the play; but, in any case, they are unimportant and are not typical of treatment of the whole. O'Neill has made a more effective departure from the cumbersome naturalism of the "transcript from life"...by throwing overboard most of its detail. He has sheared away everything except the relation between his two central characters, and in doing so, he has gained intensity, one of the things that American realism needs most.

For the rest, *All God's Chillun Got Wings* is one of the best things yet written about the race problem and among the best of O'Neill's plays. Two of O'Neill's chief assets as a dramatist seem to be, first, a nervous driving force which carries the audience inescapably along, and second, a gift for writing eloquently the various forms of the American vernacular. Both of these *All God's Chillun* has. It is not quite so consistently well-written or attractive as *The Hairy Ape* or *The Emperor Jones*; it has its harsh notes and raw expanses. But then it is perhaps more satisfactory in showing two equally solid characters in collision instead of only one character wrestling with himself.

Another thing about O'Neill—which sets him apart from the other American dramatists, who tend merely to modify the conventional American comedy in the direction of Shaw or Sinclair Lewis—is that he nearly always, with whatever crudeness, has something real, something derived directly from life, at the bottom of his plays. The scene and the characters are sometimes bleak enough—as in the latter part of *All God's Chillun*—but at any moment they are likely to establish a violent electric contact between the audience and themselves by taking on the awfulness and the power of naked natural forces. This was true even of *Welded*—which failed, it seems to me, largely through not being well enough written. Mr. O'Neill, in cases of this sort, I believe, does not pay enough attention to style. A play, like anything else that is built of words, is primarily a work of literature, and even the sincerest and most vigorous dramatic idea cannot be trusted to make its effect without the proper words to convey it. All but the very greatest actors are capable of betraying a carelessly written text, but an eloquent and accurate text will speak for itself in spite of all but the very worst. Mr. O'Neill's eloquence seems to diminish in direct proportion to his distance from the language of the people. At one pole, you have *The Hairy Ape*, his best written play; at the other *Welded*, perhaps his worst. In *All God's Chillun Got Wings*, you see the barometer rising and falling—between the conventional language of melodrama, and the racy, the vivid, and the true.

New Republic, May 28, 1924.

O'Neill and Racial Myths

Peter J. Gillett

Until about 1940, various crushing handicaps prevented black authors from presenting the black experience cogently to a suitable public, and so the task of creating developed and truly representative black characters in works of sufficient literary merit to compel an audience fell chiefly upon white writers. Among the distinguished whites who accepted the challenge were Melville, Mark Twain, Conrad, Faulkner, and Eugene O'Neill. The challenge was a severe one for them partly because their own experience was perforce very remote from the black experience—color being a far greater barrier than, say, sex or social class—and partly becausse of a fact just as galling to black writers, that in America and Europe a black character cannot serve as vehicle for a universal theme: Everyman, in the West, is a white man. But their greatest difficulty, probably, lay in a set of received "truths" about black people, notions which we nowadays include among the racial myths but which, we must remember, were hard to transcend since blacks as well as whites at least partially accepted them.

In his response to this challenge O'Neill may perhaps be the most interesting of all white authors. It would have been quite understandable in the circumstances had he uncritically incorporated the racial myths in his work. For in the period spanned by his five so-called "negro plays," from 1914 to 1924, anthropology and psychology tended to give weight to some of the myths; moreover the last two of these five, *The Emperor Jones* and *All God's Chillun Got Wings*, coincided with the early days of the "Harlem Renaissance," in which black writers themselves often treated the black man as a primitive. Despite this—and herein, I believe, lies the interest of his treatment of the black American—in these five plays and in *The*

Iceman Cometh (1946) O'Neill met the various difficulties of presenting black characters with ever greater assurance, awareness, and success. As we move from *Thirst* through *The Iceman* we can watch America's most influential playwright more and more understanding blackness as part of the black man's humanity, and in the process sloughing off the influence of the traditional American racial myths.

The remarks of some critics on *All God's Chillun* might, however, lead one to believe almost the opposite, and before examining all the plays in turn we would do well to look at this one rather closely, scrutinizing especially its controversial ending. Jim Harris, its black protagonist, is repeatedly foiled in his ambition to succeed in the white world. This feeling becomes explicit on several occasions, but especially when he proposes to the white girl, Ella, with whom he fell in love in his early teens. "I don't want nothing," he protests in romantic ardor, "—only...to serve you...to preserve and protect and shield you...to become your slave!—yes, be your slave—your black slave that adores you as sacred!" The passage, as has been recognized, is an adaptation of Alfred Adler's psychological theory, according to which frustration of the innate "will to power" produced neurosis which might show itself in self-submission and self-humiliation; it also embodies the contemporary notion that a man's behavior was conditioned by his racial heritage;[1] it is also, much more importantly, an instance of O'Neill's talent for transmuting the abstractions of psychology into vital characters and significant art. It beautifully merges the hard fact of black slavery with a sentimental stock metaphor of romantic love to produce a disturbing and resonant ambiguity, and it foreshadows, and helps explain, the ending.

Two years after their marriage, Jim and Ella return from France disillusioned. They have failed to drown their difference of color, and the conflict between Ella's conscious love for Jim's humanity and her unconscious hatred of the blackness is driving her into insanity and into enmity with his academically successful sister-in-law, Hattie. At one moment, she encourages Jim in his studies, at the next she is a little child who wants only to play games with "old Uncle Jim who's been with us for years and years," at the next a homicidal monster with a carving knife, screaming "You dirty nigger!" at her husband. In the last scene she finds the source of all their miseries in the grotesque Congo mask hanging on the parlor wall: "It's you who're to blame for this! But why'd you want to do this to us?...I married you, didn't I? Why don't you let Jim alone?...He's white, isn't he—the whitest man that ever lived? Why do you come in to interfere? Black! Black! Black is dirt!" When Jim returns with the news of his latest failure in the law examinations, she openly rejoices, apparently thinking he ought to rejoice too. In her joy she "grabs the mask from its place, sets it in the middle of the table and plunging the knife down through it pins it to the table." She has killed her devil, she thinks. But as the Emperor Jones can only kill his devil by virtually killing himself, as the boys in *Lord of the Flies* have to kill "the Beast" over and over and still live in terror of it, so Ella's devil still lives. After a moment of rage in which he calls her a "white devil woman," Jim subsides. He will never aspire again. His metaphor of slavery has become truth. As Ella says, "brightly," "Well, it's all over now."

The ending which follows, in its bitter, ironic, twentieth-century way, is masterly. Some critics, indeed, have seen in Jim's self-abasement a mere escape. According to one, he "lacks not only the courage to face his problems, and the heroism to fight against them, but also the self-knowledge to understand them....The spiritual 'wings' which 'exalt' Jim Harris are not those of a tragic understanding and self-transcendence; they are those of pathetic defeat and self-delusion."[2] Another calls the last scene an anti-climax, which evades the tragedy of Jim and Ella by letting them revert to childishness while representing Jim's closing words as an enlightenment.[3] T.S. Eliot, in his brief review, was right: "Mr. O'Neill has got hold of a 'strong plot'; he not only understands one aspect of the 'negro problem,' but he succeeds in giving this problem universality in implying...the universal problem of differences which create a mixture of admiration, love, and contempt, with the consequent tension....The close is magnificent."[4]

From the moment when Jim cuts short his talk of how and why he wanted to become a lawyer—the moment, presumably, when he realizes that the time for futile aspiration is over and the time for something new has come—from this moment Ella, "chattering along," sketches out their future. Sometimes they will play at being the little boy and girl who fell in love in Act I Scene i. Sometimes, in a kind of racial transvestism, she will black her face while he chalks his—in the first scene Jim envied "Painty Face's" complexion, and she wished she were black. Sometimes he will be her "old kind Uncle Jim who's been with us for years and years." And he must "never, never, never, never" leave her. With utter ingenuousness, she speaks of her total dependence on him, her love for him. And suddenly, with "shining eyes" and transfigured face," Jim drops to his knees and prays, beginning as he prays to "weep in an ecstasy of religious humility." "Let this fire of burning suffering," he begs God, "purify me of selfishness and make me worthy of the child You send me for the woman You took away!" This approaches the very brink of maudlin religiosity—the two are as close, and as polar, as are "Hearts and Flowers" and the slow movement of Beethoven's Ninth, or far-left and far-right politics.

To understand this remarkable ending at all, we must see the whole play in two ways at once—both as a story of love and marriage perverted by destiny, by an ineradicable and ever-visible difference between the protagonists, and as an image of relations between the races in America. It is, beyond dispute, both of these, yet reviewers and critics have often chosen to look upon it as only one or the other. Much of the criticism is vague to the point of meaninglessness, perhaps because of the well-intentioned urge of liberal whites to get rid of the "negro problem" by simply not seeing it. In Act I Scene ii Joe taunts Jim with his white aspirations: "What's all dis schoolin' you doin'? What's all dis dressin' up and graduatin' and sayin' you gwine study be a lawyer?...What's all dis denyin' you's a nigger...? Is you a nigger or isn't you? Is you a nigger, Nigger? Nigger, is you a nigger?" And Jim replies, quietly, deflating Joe's rage, "Yes. I'm a nigger. We're both niggers." Eliot, of course, was right in saying that the play points through and beyond the question of race to all those differences which thwart and pervert human affections; but a critic who can see in such dialogue *only* a universal drama of souls, or who can see the play *only* as a drama of marriage, is surely both white and half-blind. The inevitable result of such one-eyed views is the complaint that Act I Scene i is unnecessary for the play's thematic development while the last scene is melodramatic and bathetic evasion.[5] Such criticism assumes that the theme is the conflict between a man's work and his wife, or love thwarted by social ostracism, and makes this assumption in defiance not only of the first scene but of the presence of Hattie, the stark black-and-white symbolism of Act I Scene iv, and many other features of the play. If O'Neill had desired to use the difference of race merely as motivation for a story of marriage, he, with his theatrical experience and his expressionistic proclivity, would certainly have realized that all other indications of the difference were rendered superfluous by the mere color of the actors' faces.

Looking at the play as a story of a crippled marriage, and suspending for a time our judgment as to the relevance of, for instance, the opening scene, we see that in the moment after Ella has stabbed the mask Jim has three, or perhaps four, choices. He can break up the marriage by divorcing Ella or committing her to an asylum, as Hattie advised. This course might have enabled him to contribute, like Hattie, to the liberation of his people; but probably, in view of his performance in examinations before he married Ella, he would have failed again—and while, of course, no one could justly blame him for breaking his bondage to a schizophrenic and dangerous woman, the course he actually takes is nobler. He can, alternatively, kill her—a finely symbolic action but a poor way to reconcile the claims to happiness of two people tied to each other. He can choose to live like Mr. Rochester with an imprisoned Gothic madwoman. Or he can do what he does.

A marriage—to perpetrate a platitude—is a compromise between two creatures who, being human, are unique. If the partners can, nevertheless, find happiness in conventionally approved ways, the marriage has a good chance of succeeding. But if just one of them is incurably "different" in mentality, incurably unconventional (the word "perverted" is unsuitably loaded for this context)—if, in other words, one of them can only find happiness in some way of which society disapproves, then either the marriage must end in separation, divorce, even murder, or the other partner must deliberately and radically change himself so as to find his own happiness in the same way, and thus secure for his mate that chance of happiness, which, ideally, is every human being's due. This, or something like it, is the resolution to which, between Ella's assault on the mask and the beginning of his prayer, between calling her a "devil woman" and calling her "the child You send me," Jim forces himself round, and by the last line—"Honey, Honey, I'll play right up to the gates of Heaven with you!"—the resolution has hardened. "Self-delusion" this is, no doubt, but a deliberately chosen, a willed, a hard-nosed and heroic self-delusion.

But this marriage which Jim preserves by his sacrifice symbolizes, too, the relations of the black and white races. Just as the "marriage" of blacks and whites in America was forced by the whites for their own profit and comfort, so Ella seeks Jim out as a husband to secure her own happiness. It is on this level of course, that the evident symbols do their work: the stage-setting for the marriage scene; the flatiron corner, black on one side and white on the other, at the opening; the portrait of the dear Mr. Harris in his lodge regalia; and above all, the Congo mask, an object "inspiring obscure, dim connotations...but beautifully done, conceived in a true religious spirit," yet acquiring, in the bourgeois, white-American setting of Jim's mother's house, a dominating, "diabolical quality."

What then are these "obscure, dim connotations"? O'Neill wrote several short pieces on the importance of masks to him as a dramatist.[6] He talks of "the soul-stifling daily struggle" of people in general "to exist as masks among the masks of living." "In *All God's Chillun Got Wings*, all save the seven leading characters should be masked; for all the secondary figures are part and parcel of the Expressionistic background of the play, a world at first indifferent, then cruelly hostile, against which the tragedy of Jim Harris is outlined." O'Neill further regarded it as "unquestionable" that the new insight into "human cause and effect" provided by psychology had "uncovered the mask,...impressed the idea of mask as a symbol of inner reality upon all intelligent people of today." And, significantly, he included the Congo mask in a list of symbolic masks he had used in his plays. The Congo mask, then, appears to connote—or to be connoted for O'Neill—many things. Obviously, in its setting, it suggests something about the racial past of the Harris family—or the twentieth-century American conception of that past, it makes no difference which. Hattie, defiantly proud of her African heritage, regards the mask as "beautiful" and perhaps also as embodying "a true religious spirit." She stresses its value as a work of art and the "reality" of its creator as an artist. Jim is prepared, for Ella's happiness, to put this reminder of his race out of sight. And she, fascinated by it from the start, loathes it. She talks to it, saying she is not afraid of it, threatening to "give it the laugh." The mixed fascination and hatred it arouses in Ella, and the stress placed on its religious meaning, suggest that it symbolizes more than just the black past. We first encounter it as a thing whose beauty has been perverted into menace by its transplantation into a twentieth-century white-bourgeois setting. As Jim wallows deeper in failure and Ella's madness grows, the mask more and more dominates the scene. So the mask means Jim's "inner reality"—his sense of failure, his blackness, and (like the Congo River in Vachel Lindsay's poem) the real primitiveness underlying the civilized aspiration and threatening the white; and it means, like the Congo River in Joseph Conrad's *Heart of Darkness*, Ella's unconscious mind, her *id*, the front of her irrational hate; and simultaneously it means the "soul-stifling struggle" of both "to exist as masks among the masks of living." And it suggests that these various referents make up a complex, a syndrome—that any one of them will at least probably accompany the others.

None of the characters is more aware of the mask as a symbol than Ella; when we view the play as an image of race relations, it is Ella's reactions to the mask that chiefly help us interpret the ending. She has, throughout Act II, been both fascinated and repelled by her own notion of her husband's racial past. That black might be beautiful, as it is for Hattie, Ella cannot and will not see—which explains why, whenever she wishes to praise Jim's kindness, honesty, or loyalty, she calls him white. She hates the notion of primitiveness which her husband's black skin and the mask both thrust upon her, and hates, in consequence, her own hateful self, the primitive *id* of which they keep reminding her. She stabs the mask because Jim's aspirations have died—because what she sees as an attempt of the black, the primitive, the *id*, to outdo and dominate her has failed. The devil is dead, and to keep him dead Jim must be kept a slave. He may serve her by living out the myth of the happy slave as her "old kind Uncle Jim." He may serve her by playing transvestive games in which she takes over from him the primitive power of blackness, that mythic power which whites have so often tried to appropriate through black-face shows, the jazz craze, slumming in Harlem, and dancing black dances. Or he may ferry her back to the innocence of her childhood, the time before she knew hatred or hated herself for knowing it.

Jim's heroic choice of self-delusion at the end of the play therefore means that the happiness of the white race in America can only be secured if the black race will deliberately seek its own happiness in serving a set of myths. It implies that there can be no settled love between whites and blacks except a perverted love purchased by the one partner's abrogation of his freedom and human dignity. It implies that the white race, in its attitudes to black people, is insane beyond cure, schizophrenic—wanting on principle to permit their advancement toward freedom, forced by its own sick nature to stifle them. If this is so, the play is indeed pessimistic; but there is one tiny note of hope at the end. Jumping excitedly to her feet as Jim prays, Ella says, "Don't cry, Jim!...I've only got a little time left and I want to play." Which Ella is it, one wonders, that only has "a little time left": the literal Ella; or the embodiment of race hatred as a primitive and inevitable attribute of man; or the Ella who cherishes, and imposes on the black man, the old racial myths; or simply Ella as the symbol of white dominance? In any case, there is a little hope here for all the Jim Harrises, all the Uncle Toms.

For Jim Harris is indeed an Uncle Tom. His final choice, heroic though it may be, establishes him as a Tom. Only a Tom could have used with such blindness and such ironic effect the romantic lover's metaphor of slavery to his beloved. But there surely never was a more sympathetic and provocative portrayal of the Uncle Tom than this. Jim, to be sure, is a traitor to the cause of his people, and Hattie is his foil. But Jim's words at the end of his quarrel with Hattie not only have an air of conviction but convey a keen awareness of his situation, a sense of purpose: "I have no own good. I only got a good together with her...Let her call me nigger! Let her call me the whitest of the white! I'm all she's got in the world, ain't I ?...You with your fool talk of the black race and the white race! Where does the human race get a chance to come in? I suppose that's simple for you. You lock it up in asylums and throw away the key!" The tragedy of Jim Harris is that he is an Uncle Tom not out of fear or desire for comfort, but out of love even more catholic than Hattie's, and that his love inescapably drags him into willing on himself a lifelong humiliation.

From *Thirst* (1914) through *The Moon of the Caribbees*, *The Dreamy Kid*, and *The Emperor Jones* to *All God's Chillun Got Wings* we can trace a gradual change in O'Neill's treatment of the black American. The Negro Sailor in that implausible play *Thirst* is a savage who, once civilization is out of sight, will cheerfully cannibalize a dead body. Of course he is also a noble savage who patiently bears the slanders of his white companions and spurns with quiet dignity not only their threats but also their bribes and the woman's tawdry enticements. He is also not very bright. If there were any black people in the audience at the play's first night at Provincetown in 1916 they might well have seen it as a stupid insult to themselves, a contribution to a set of dangerous stereotypes.[7]

The Moon of the Caribbees is much more subtle, and its sublety has encouraged white critics to play down its racial meaning. Barrett Clark calls it "a fairly successful attempt to suggest certain sensations through the use of rhythmical prose—not alone the spirit of the sea, but of man's lonliness in the presence of nature....There is practically no story in it."[8] And in general it has been interpreted as an atmosphere piece. Yet it has quite as much story as atmosphere, and more story than many one-act plays. Under the irrational moon, to the sound of a primitive death-chant, some sailors representative of modern Western civilization are visited by a group of women from the land whence the chant emanates. Like Pan and Dionysus, the black women bring sex and liquor, under whose influence the civilizations of the sailors is stripped away. They quarrel in the moonlight, they fight like satyrs, and a man is nearly sacrificed. Clearly the play states, in small compass but powerfully, an idea of man's nature which had been plausible since Darwin, Freud, Frazer, and the early works of Jung. But by using black characters and a black artefact—the song—to represent the primitive it becomes ambiguous in an unfortunate way. At the same time, *The Moon* modifies the view of O'Neill that *Thirst* may have given us; at any rate it makes *Thirst* look a little less like anti-black propaganda.

Of *The Dreamy Kid* (1919) Clark says, "This play about negroes is not one of his best: it is too obvious, too direct and melodramatic to be wholly convincing. It is the story of a murderer pursued by the police, who returns to see his dying mother and gets caught."[9] And that is all: the play contains nothing about race and superstition, apparently, and the totemic figure of the grandmother, the dread of whose curse makes the Kid, an urban black, pass up a chance of escape and stay at her deathbed to fight a gun-battle with the police, has even, by a Freudian slip, become the American mom. *The Dreamy Kid* is, in fact, a touchy play. Perhaps it portrays the residue of primitive superstition in civilized man; but perhaps its statement is only about the *black* man, perhaps it is a restatement of a popular racial myth. In any case, it well illustrates the impossibility of conveying a universal statement through a black character.

A well-known Anglo-Jewish writer once remarked that, as a Jew, he sometimes felt sick after hearing a Wagner music-drama, not because the music had seemed ugly but because it had intoxicated him, sucked him in, stirred in him a complex of emotions he would rather not have known himself capable of. The effect of *The Emperor Jones* is perhaps something like this, though whether the spectator feels any disgust afterwards, and how great the disgust is, will depend probably on his race, his upbringing, and the reality and depth of certain of his professed beliefs. The play foreshadows the complexities of *All God's Chillun* and at the same time presents again, more starkly, the ambivalence of *The Moon* and *The Dreamy Kid*. Is Brutus Jones an image of all mankind? Is he made black only because, in the days when Darwin and Jung smelt headier than they do now, any black man might seem, whatever his early environment and experiences, closer than the white to the common ancestry of both? Or is he an image only of his race? The comments of many white critics, even the best-intentioned of them, show how unfortunate is this ambivalence. "*The Emperor Jones* is a magnificent presentment of panic fear in the breast of a half-civilized negro." "It is a kind of unfolding, in reverse order, of the tragical epic of the American negro." The moon "casts its doubtful light on scenes of re-enacted memory—partly from the actual past of Jones's life, and partly from the racial past of the Negro people." Jones is "reclaimed by the primitive ancestral savagery that had spawned and doomed him." In the operatic version, Lawrence Tibbett as Jones "dominated the proceedings from the moment that he appeared, blustering, insolent, preposterous...until, an abject and ghostridden savage, praying, pleading, whimpering, and hysterical, shorn of his thin caking of sophistication, he shot himself..., an atavistic sacrifice."[10] That Darwinian-Jungian word "atavistic" pounds through the reviews as monotonously as the tom-tom in the play: one critic burbled of "the rhythmic frenzy of his atavistic terrors, as he stumbles through the jungle night back to the darkness of his ancestral savagery." "Regression" and "reversion," too, appear with tiring frequency.[11] Richard D. Skinner tries to argue that Jones is a symbol of mankind: he is made black only in order to indicate the nature of the individual soul's struggle with pride: "it is not a question of superiority or inferiority of race, but of the historical symbol which the negro has become through centuries of bondage."[12] But Skinner's is a lonely voice: people's recorded reactions do not bear him out. The equivocal nature of this impressive play is beautifully illustrated in a comment by Oscar Cargill, who call it "a study of the involuntary regression of an individual consciousness through the stages of its own history to the racial or collective unconscious."[13] Racial, or collective? If we only knew, we could feel more comfortable in applauding *The Emperor Jones*.

The same ambiguity, then, runs through all the "negro plays" up to *The Emperor Jones*, but as their meanings become more important, their technique more sure, their characters more credible, the ambiguity becomes more teasing and the possibility of interpreting them as propagandistic or myth-serving plays grows less. In *All God's Chillun*, not only did O'Neill succeed in creating more credible black characters still; he almost succeeded in so presenting his themes—primitivism, race prejudice, superstition, and so forth—that the kind of uncomfortable ambiguity we have seen in the earlier plays should exist only in the eye of the beholder. Or rather, Jim and Hattie are so human that the reader, refusing to see them as stereotypes out of a racist myth, is inclined to attribute to Ella's diseased mind the notion of ineradicable primitiveness conveyed in the symbolism.

The last stage in the progression is *The Iceman Cometh* (1946), a play with only one black character, and he merely one of the eighteen down-and-out habitues of Harry Hope's "End of the Line Cafe." Joe Mott's blackness contributes nothing to the play's thematic development. He objects, certainly, to being called a nigger, and declares himself essentially white; but these utterances have to be seen only as indications, the one of Mott's remaining pride in himself, the other of the particular kind of impotence and blindness which have helped bring him to Hope's limbo for the blind and impotent. But as the black critic John Lovell, Jr., wrote soon after the play came out, Joe Mott suddenly seems an important character—important not only in this play, but in O'Neill's whole output, in American drama, indeed in American history—when we look at him as the last of the series of portraits that began with the Sailor in *Thirst*.[14] Lovell underestimates *All God's Chillun* as a stage in O'Neill's development as a creator of black characters, seeing it as an advance only in that its author was the first white American dramatist to present "the lowliest American aspiring to the loftiest American ideals." But on the significance, in this development, of *The Iceman Cometh* Lovell is resoundingly right. Joe Mott's significance, he says, is not in the psychological accuracy of his portrayal. One theme of *The Iceman* is aspiration and failure: like the other dead-beats, Joe has aspired; like theirs, his soul has died because "his aspiration was not good enough." "Thus Joe Mott is given equality of struggle, aspiration, and failure, according to his constitutional rights. None of the equalities is more terribly important...The macabre stage at the end...has greater meaning than usual because here, for once in America...a Negro has aspired and died on terms of equality."

Mary Welch, the actress, once drew O'Neill into conversation on his "negro plays." "He had felt deeply about them, and his face grew bitter and forceful as he recalled how some of the New York theatre crowd had accepted these works." In his own words, "They didn't really understand what I was writing. They merely said to themselves, 'Oh look, the ape can talk!'"[15] But there are several causes for the misunderstanding, two of them attributable to O'Neill himself.

One cause, of course, was a prevalent attitude among white Americans toward black Americans—not the Ku Klux Klan attitude, nor even that of the *avant-garde* of the jazz age, but that of the ordinary, well-meaning "liberal" white, who tended, as we have seen, to be caught with his super-ego down by plays like *The Emperor Jones* and to try to read *All God's Chillun* as a tragedy of love and marriage. Another cause, though a lesser one, was the spirit of the black movements of the day. Blacks reacted just as vehemently to *All God's Chillun* as whites did, feeling that it reflected unfavorably on their race, and the black reaction to the "negro plays" in general was hostile because they presented the black man as an unfortunate creature in sordid circumstances. Four months after the first night of *All God's Chillun*, William Stanley Braithwaite, a black critic not normally given to vehement condemnations, published an article attacking O'Neill, among others, for giving a defamatory picture of black Americans, for dramatizing "the sordid aspects of life and undesirable types of character." Though Braithwaite was right, probably, in finding O'Neill and other white writers incapable of presenting "the immense paradox of racial life" because their culture limited them to a conception of the black American as "inferior, superstitious, half-ignorant," still, when he objects to O'Neill's and Ernest Culbertson's plays that "the best and highest class of racial life has not yet been discovered for literary treatment by white American authors," he betrays an attitude to literature comparable to that of Lenin or the more moralistic Victorian critics.[16] One wonders how Braithwaite would have responded to *The Iceman Cometh* twenty-two years later—or, for that matter, to Richard Wright's *Native Son*.

To add to the misunderstanding, O'Neill himself was not especially coherent in talking about his own plays: the plays may be fundamentally equivocal, but O'Neill's intellect was apparently less capable than his imagination of framing clear statements about racial issues. He repeatedly tried, in response to the muddled and misdirected criticism of *All God's Chillun*, to represent the racial issues in the play as merely incidental, and Jim and Ella as symbolizing nothing beyond themselves—a hopelessly untenable position, of course, since no reader or spectator could be expected to do such violence to his own response-system as O'Neill seems to demand.[17]

The most important cause of misunderstanding, however, lies in the plays themselves. It is the notion, distilled from an atmosphere full of Darwin, Frazer, and Jung—full of "atavism," "regression," and "the racial unconscious"—that the black American carried in his heredity a deeper shade of the Congo jungle, louder echoes of the witch-doctor's rattle, a livelier response to totems and funeral chants, than his white neighbors. To this suggestion white readers and spectators responded, generally, with glee. Their black counterparts, unable to change the prevalent intellectual scheme, either sidestepped the idea or, as did the Harlem Renaissance writers, adapted it to different ends. They had to wait until 1940, when Richard Wright supplied, in Bigger Thomas, a motivation for the crime and defiance of the Dreamy Kid, for the Negro Sailor's access of life at the death of the white woman, for the flight of Jones—a motivation more credible and, uncomfortably, closer to home.

Nonetheless, O'Neill achieved much in these plays. Only in one very early and trifling play—one which, in fairness to him, should probably be left in the obscurity he consigned it to—did he ever succumb to any of the crudest racial myths. The predominant myth in the plays up to *The Emperor Jones*, the myth of the black man as primitive, was not merely popular but had after all much scientific sanction. O'Neill wrote no *Leopard's Spots*, no *Birth of a Nation*, but instead worked his way gradually towards a sympathetic and imaginative presentation of the black American's blackness, towards presenting blackness as a subjective phenomenon. Having reached, or nearly reached, this goal in *All God's Chillun Got Wings*, he admittedly failed to go a step further; he might reasonably, for instance, have explored further the predicament which made an Uncle Tom of Jim Harris, or have examined more closely the social and psychological barriers to black equality. Instead, discouraged apparently by the perversity of his audiences, he abandoned black characters for twenty years. But at least, by 1924, he had developed the courage and insight to represent the white American response to blackness as diseased and degraded, and further than that no white writer of the time could probably be expected to have advanced.

NOTES

1. Edwin A. Engel, *The Haunted Heroes of Eugene O'Neill* (Cambridge, Mass., 1953), pp. 117-20.

2. Frederic I. Carpenter, *Eugene O'Neill* (Twayne Series, New York, 1964), p. 104.

3. Francis Fergusson, "Eugene O'Neill," *Hound and Horn* (Jan., 1930), repr. under the title "Melodramatist" in Oscar Cargill, N. Bryllion Fagin, and William J. Fisher, eds., *O'Neill and His Plays: Four Decades of Criticism* (New York 1961), p. 275.

4. *New Criterion* 4 (Apr., 1926), 395-96, repr. in Cargill *et al.*, p. 169. Eliot's words on

All God's Chillun Got Wings

"universality" chime quite well with O'Neill's own, quoted by Arthur and Barbara Gelb, *O'Neill* (New York 1960), pp. 535-36. Engel (pp. 121-26) is with the angels too.

5. Ferguson (Cargill *et al.*, pp. 274-75).

6. Three pieces which first appeared in *American Spectator* (Nov. 1932, Dec. 1932, Jan. 1933) are conveniently assembled in Cargill *et al.*, pp. 116-22.

7. The play was only once published, in *Thirst and Other One-Act Plays* (American Dramatists' Series, Boston, 1914), a collection which O'Neill later repudiated entirely. Barrett H. Clark, *Eugene O'Neill: The Man and His Plays* (New York, 1929), pp. 66-67.

8. Clark, pp. 83-84.

9. Clark, p. 92.

10. Clark, p. 105; ibid., p. 104; review by Lawrence Gilman in *New York Herald Tribune* (Jan. 8, 1933), in Carpenter, p. 90.

11. Gilman; and see, e.g., the excerpts from Isaac Goldberg and Andrew E. Malone in Cargill *et al.* (pp. 236, 240, 259) and Maida Castellun's *New York Call* (Nov. 10, 1920) repr. in Jordan Y. Miller, ed., *Playwright's Progress: O'Neill and the Critics* (Chicago, 1965), p. 23.

12. *Eugene O'Neill: A Poet's Quest* (New York, 1964), p. 86.

13. "Fusion-Point of Jones and Nietzsche," in Cargill *et al.*, p. 408, n. Noteworthy too is Malone's remark: "whereas the primitiveness of Jones is spiritual, that of Yank [in *The Hairy Ape*] is entirely physical." (Cargill *et al.*, p. 261).

14. "Eugene O'Neill's Darker Brother," *Theatre Arts* 32 (Feb., 1948), 45-48.

15. "Softer Tones for Mr. O'Neill's Portrait," *Theatre Arts* 41 (May, 1957), p. 82.

16. "The Negro in Literature," *Crisis* 28 (Sept., 1924), 204-10.

17. See, e.g., the quotation in Arthur and Barbara Gelb, pp. 535-36.

Twentieth Century Literature, 18 (October 1972): 111-119.

O'Neill Rarity in Weak Revival

Douglas Watt

I'm afraid that *All God's Chillun Got Wings* provides a desultory evening at the uptown Circle in the Square, where this fairly short and sketchy O'Neill drama was revived last night. The performance, under George C. Scott's direction, lacks tension and rhythm, and the play itself is unsuccessful. The evening almost becomes ludicrous, but not quite.

Writing in 1924, O'Neill considered the plight of a white woman and black man, friends since childhood on the streets of lower Manhattan, who marry in an alien society and find only misery in their love. There is, then, this heartfelt and refreshing concern on the part of a playwright maturing and feeling his way in a frivolous theater world. And it is reinforced and deepened, though at the same time confused, by his anguished memories of his own early family life. Like his parents, this pair are named Jim and Ella, and the analogies are many, the most striking being the pathetic decline of the wife though this Ella is truly insane rather than under the influence of drugs.

What weakens the impact of the play most severely is the fact that Ella, basically as contemptuous of blacks as the white associates of her youth, marries him only when she has been tossed aside by the boxer Mickey, lost the child she was bearing by him, and become a social outcast. Jim's love is the stronger, and he is inevitably the more appealing of the two.

So once again, as in other failed works of his, it is O'Neill's vision and fervor that hold our attention rather than workmanship. *All God's Chillun* is as crude in outline and clumsy in speech (even though the slang has been dressed up a bit) as anything he ever wrote. But we attend it, right up to the end.

What makes this a dead play is the fact that it is a contrivance with labels instead of characters. These are not real people, any of them, with the exception of the street bums. The actor accorded the most enthusiastic response last night was the drunken walk-on, the tattered Wino played by Chuck Patterson, who sang a few choruses of "Sometimes I Feel Like a Motherless Child" while he rummaged through ashcans.

And besides the fact that Jim and Ella, as well as Jim's mother and sister and the others are there to represent ideas rather than living, breathing people, O'Neill didn't even begin to penetrate the black consciousness in this play. When, for example, he has a voice raised in "She Was Only a Bird in a Gilded Cage" to represent the musical tastes of the white block, he has somebody along the black street singing "Waitin' for the Robert E. Lee" for contrast.

Though George C. Scott has staged the piece, which in seven scenes covers the years from childhood to maturity, with a decent enough eye for detail in the open playing area, he has been woefully unsuccessful in getting genuine performances from his actors. Even granting the absurdities of the dialogue, Trish Van Devere contributes little other than attractive features and a forlorn look to the part of Ella. Robert Christian tries, with occasional success, to pump some life into Jim, and Vickie Thomas makes a good stab at the thankless part of the sister. Minnie Gentry fusses around in her one brief scene as the mother, but can't summon up any conviction in the role. Though corny, the dead-end street types come off best.

Ming Cho Lee has designed a street setting that is both realistic and nicely atmospheric for the first four scenes. And somehow, after the intermission, we find the shabby sidewalks and cobblestone street between covered over with a linoleum floor for the three final scenes in the Harris' flat. Patricia Zipprodt's costumes are also admirable, and Thomas Skelton has provided effective lighting.

Speaking for myself, I was glad to have the opportunity to see this O'Neill rarity, minor as it is and even in this lame performance. And I hope, in its avowed intention to keep doing O'Neill, that the Circle in the Square brings us other neglected works.

New York Daily News, March 21, 1975.

Drama: The God of Stumps

Joseph Wood Krutch

In this age of intellectualized art there is an inevitable but unfortunate tendency to assume of Eugene O'Neill, as of every other arresting artist, that his greatness must lie somehow in the greatness or in the clarity of his thought; to seek in *All God's Chillun Got Wings* some solution of the problem of race or in the *Hairy Ape* some attitude toward society; and then, not finding them, to fail in the fullest appreciation of the greatness which is his. It was not thought which drove him, as a young man, to seek adventure among the roughest men he could find, and it was not thought which he brought back from this and other experiments in life. Something tempestuous in his nature made him a brother of tempests, and he has sought wherever he could find them the fiercest passions, less anxious to clarify their causes for the benefit of those who love peace than eager to share them, and happy if he could only be exultantly a part of their destructive fury. It is a strange taste, this, to wish to be perpetually racked and tortured, to proceed from violence to violence, and to make of human torture not so much the occasion of other things as the *raison d' etre* of drama; but such is his temperament. The meaning and unity of his work lies not in any controlling intellectual idea and certainly not in a "message," but merely in the fact that each play is an experience of extraordinary intensity.

Young-man-like, O'Neill first assumed that the fiercest passions were to be found where the outward circumstances of life were wildest and most uncontrolled. He sought among men of the sea, ignorant of convention and wholly without inhibitions, powerful appetites and bare tragedies, embodying his observation in the group of little plays now performed for the first time as a whole (and performed well) at the Provincetown Theatre, under the title of *S. S. Glencairn*; but maturity has taught him the paradox that where there is most smoke there is not necessarily most fire. He has learned that souls confined in a nut-shell may yet be lords of infinite space; that spirits cabined and confined by very virtue of the fact that they have no outlet explode finally with the greatest spiritual violence. As though to signalize the discovery of this truth he has, in his latest play, *Desire Under the Elms* (Greenwich Village Theatre), limited the horizon of his characters, physically and spiritually, to the tiny New England farm upon which the action passes, and has made their intensity spring from the limitations of their experience. Whether he or Robert Edmond Jones conceived the idea of setting the stage with a single house, and of removing sections of the wall when it becomes necessary to expose one or more of the rooms inside, I do not know; but this method of staging is admirably calculated to draw attention to the controlling circumstances of the play. It is a story of human relationships become intolerably tense because intolerably close and limited, of the possessive instinct grown inhumanly powerful because the opportunities for its gratification are so small, and of physical passion terribly destructive in the end because so long restrained by the sense of sin. To its young hero the stony farm is all the wealth of the world, the young wife of his father all the lust of the flesh. In that tiny corner each character finds enough to stimulate passions which fill, for him, the universe.

By half a century of unremitting labor Ephraim Cabot has turned a few barren hillsides into a farm, killing two wives in the process but growing himself only harder in body and mind and more fanatical in his possessive passion for single object which has absorbed his life. Two of his sons, rebelling against the hopelessness of their life, leave him for the gold-fields; the third, who remains with him in dogged determination to inherit the farm, he hates; and so he marries once more in the hope of begetting in his old age a son to whom, as part of himself, he can leave his property without ceasing to own it. But he has reckoned without considering the possessive instinct of the wife herself, and so between the three, and in an atmosphere charged with hate, is fought out the three-cornered battle for what has come to be the symbol of earthly possessions. Love springs up between the wife and her foster son, but in such a battle the directest win, and love, confusing the aims of these two, dooms them to tragedy, while to the old man is left the barrenness of lonely triumph. Unlike the others, he has a god, the hard God who hates the easy gold of California or the easy crops of the West, the God who loves stumps and stones and looks with His stern favor upon such as wring a dour life without softness and without love from a soil barren like their souls. And this God comforts him. "I am hard," he says, when he learns that the baby, murdered by its mother, is not his but his son's: "I am a hard man and I am alone—but so is God."

It may with some show of reason be objected that O'Neill's plays are too crowded with incident, that the imagination of the spectator refuses sometimes to leap with the author so quickly from tense moment to tense moment, or to accept violence piled so unremittingly upon violence, and his latest play is not wholly closed to such objection; but impetuosity is an essential part of his nature and not likely ever to be subdued. To those who, like the present writer, can overlook it, it brings great compensation. *Desire Under the Elms* will be, with one exception, the most moving play seen during the current season. It is competently acted and Mary Morris and Walter Huston deserve special mention.

Nation, November 26, 1924.

Desire Under the Elms

R.M.L.

The curtain goes up on Mr. Eugene O'Neill's *Desire Under the Elms* at the Greenwich Village Theatre, revealing the rear end of a two-story New England farmhouse, white clapboards, with four windows marked by dilapidated green blinds. The windows open into four rooms which are further revealed in various succession by dropping sections of the confronting wall. Obviously this is a treatment of the stage which has great advantages especially in a linear narrative play such as Mr. O'Neill's. Mr. Jones has made four, or counting the space at the foot of the house wall, five little stages grow where one grew before; and the action of the play slips easily from room to room without delay for changes of scene. Again, the wall arouses a high sense of expectancy. One can never tell at what point, or on what level, the action will break out next. Unfortunately it must be admitted that the device is better suited to the spaces of the Hippodrome than of a little theatre....Drawn to scale the actors should be about three feet tall. The effect is particularly ambiguous in the upper rooms, under the slanting roof which emphasizes the comedy of three burly farmers in or on the bed in Part I, while it dwarfs the tragedy of the connubial relations in the chamber on the other side of the wall. It must be said that Mr. Jones has used his perpendicular stage with great skill, to minimize its difficulties and enhance its possibilities. The ensemble scene in Part III, in which a dozen or more people are gathered to make merry in the living room and actually give the perspective of a Virginia reel, is a marvel of economy of space, and should be carefully studied by housing experts of congested districts. Again in the scene referred to between husband and wife, the exposure of the adjacent room with the figure of the listening boy enlarges the scene almost to tragic dimensions, and gives a poignant revelation of simultaneous life which counteracts the narrowing effect of the crowding walls. It is in such moments that the value of Mr. Jones's arrangements is greatest and the power of the play most enhanced. Mr. Jones treats his stage as an orchestra. Now the glimpses of action within are a pizzicato accompaniment to the action outside, and again a face at a window is the enunciation of the theme in the clear notes of a flute or oboe. In the former scenes he sometimes recalls the effect of the house of Agamemnon on Von Hofmannstahl's *Elecktra*, with its hurrying movements, flitting lights, and tragic faces looking out. His stark whitewashed exterior with its sinister openings is tragic; his interior, mean and circumscribed, reflects, and, quite without ironical intention, emphasizes the limitations of tragedy in New England.

So much is to be said of the setting because it is thoroughly characteristic of the play in its success and its shortcomings. Mr. O'Neill has placed the Greek motive of incest in New England setting. Ephraim Cabot at seventy-six brings his third wife, Abbie Putnam, to the farm which he has worked by the slave labor of his three sons. The two older decamp for California, after selling their rights to inheritance to their younger half brother, Eben, who has discovered and stolen their father's hoard of gold pieces. There has been a dispute as to the ownership of the farm between Ephraim and his second wife, and her son stays to defend her dead right. The new wife is strong in the possessive instinct. When she sees that to bear a child is her way of securing the inheritance she tries to seduce Eben. The boy, already awakened, turns from her with loathing, but led by the spirit of his mother he yields to a woman who promises him mother love as well as lover's joy. The neighbors, when they gather to celebrate the advent of the new born, are full of suspicion and innuendo, with a penetration which rather surpasses even the New England sense of scandal. Eben can take no part in the merry making, and provokes his father to boast that he has begotten this son to deprive him of his inheritance. Once more his love of his step-mother turns to loathing. She now loves Eben, and seeing no other way to convince him, misled by his vague words of killing which he means to apply to his father, she smothers the baby which Eben loves for his own. The stolen gold plot is revived when the old man discovers his loss. And Eben is convinced, and goes with Abby to take his part in the punishment for their common crime.

Clearly we have here many motives—paternal jealousy, stolen gold, ghostly mother love, filial and paternal hate, the desire of possession, sexual passion. There are too many to lie evenly within the frame, much less to grow and develop. As Mr. Jones tries to do too much with a small stage, so Mr. O'Neill tries to do too much in a brief play. As the action is cramped, so is the psychology. Abby has revealed her mercenary hand too clearly for Eben to fall to her even with the ghostly assistance of his mother. Ephraim's revelation of Abby's motive lacks sufficient introduction, even with the old man's drunkenness. And the break-down of Abby's strong commonsense seems arbitrary, even with her recent experience of childbirth. That we have to pause to think of these extenuating circumstances puts the drama under a partial eclipse. But at the edges there are flashes of intolerable light. By moments there is great and unique dramatic power. The exterior of Mr. O'Neill's play, like the exterior of Mr. Jones's setting, is stark and simple tragedy. The interior, the mind in which these human interests and emotions live and work, is huddled and confused.

Another question arises in connection with this revelation of a Greek tragic theme in New England—that is, in the matter of language. The New England dialect is not a noble form of human speech. Unlike certain variants of English, notably the Irish, the Scotch, the South England dialects, it has no resources of eloquence within itself, it is sparse, mean, homely, and its associations comic. Gerhart Hauptmann was confronted by this difference in the native quality of speech; he used the dialect of Silesian peasants in the tragedy of *Die Weber*; that of Berlin, in the comedies of *Biberpelz*, and *Der Rote Hahn*. Again, the natural inaptitude of American actors for dialect is to be considered. Mr. Huston as Ephraim Cabot is the only member of the company whose mastery of his tongue is easy and assured, and his lines, often possessing the dignity of scripture quotation, are finely delivered. In other portions of the cast the dialect wore pretty thin. Miss Mary Morris, indeed, does not need to speak to send her personality over to the audience. The look of her is all sufficient, especially in Part III where her blighted face and ravaged eyes make a portrait not easily forgotten.

New Republic, December 3, 1924.

Biblical Perversion in *Desire Under the Elms*

Peter L. Hayes

While O'Neill's plays are noted primarily for the dramatic force with which they express his tragic view of life, many of them—*The Hairy Ape, All God's Chillun Got Wings, Marco Millions, The Iceman Cometh*, and others—contain a great deal of social criticism. So does his early tragedy *Desire Under the Elms*, which has been critically examined for its use of the Hippolytus and Medea myths, its Freudian elements, its relation to O'Neill's early plays (e.g., *The Rope*) and own biography,[1] but there has been little close attention to the way in which religious references inform the play, and the way religion both causes the tragedy and comments upon it.

Eben's first word in the play is "God!" His first line of dialogue is "Honor thy father!"—his sarcastic reply to his brothers' statement that they must wait for their father's death before they can hope to own the farm—which Eben follows with, "I pray he's died."[2] This ironic use of the Biblical commandment and the perverse form of Eben's prayer set the tone of the play and forewarn us to note how almost all expressions of religious origin are similarly twisted. In fact, they help us appreciate the harsh and equally twisted religion practiced on this farm, a loveless religion largely responsible for the play's tragedy. The reaction of Eben's brothers to his wish that Ephraim Cabot, their father, were dead is typical of the hypocrisy in religious and other matters:

> SIMEON. ...Looky here! Ye'd oughtn't t' said that, Eben.
> PETER. Twa'n't righteous.
> EBEN. What?
> SIMEON. Ye prayed he'd died.
> EBEN. Waal—don't yew pray it? (p. 206)

For it is Simeon himself who says that they must wait for the farm until Ephraim dies. Their denunciation of Eben is perfunctory and conventional rather than an expression either of filial or Christian piety. Later in the play even this sanctimonious facade is dropped, though the dialogue still is couched in canonical terms. Speaking of their new stepmother, Simeon says:

> Waal—I hope she's a she—devil that'll make him wish he was dead an' livin' in the pit o' hell fur comfort.
> PETER. *(fervently)* Amen! (p. 215)

Similarly, the townspeople in Part III, Scene I, suspecting that the baby is Eben's and not Ephraim's, express themselves in terms of ribaldry, concealed envy, or mockery for Ephraim, whose physical strength they respect too much for them to ridicule to his face, but whose cuckoldry makes them feel superior to him. They come to eat, drink, and have fun behind the Cabots' backs:

> MAN. Listen, Abbie—if ye ever git tired o' Eben, remember me. (p.248)
> CABOT. ...[Eben] kin do a day's work a' most up t' what I kin....
> FIDDLER. An' he kin do a good night's work, too! *(A roar of laughter.)* (p. 249)
> FIDDLER. ...Let's celebrate the old skunk gittin fooled! We kin have some fun now he's went. (p. 253)

No one sympathizes or expresses genuine moral concern. And they too pervert scripture for their own ends. The fiddler says that Eben is in church offering prayers of thanksgiving, " 'Cause unto him a-—*(He hesitates just long enough)* brother is born!" (p. 248). It is Ephraim, though, more than any other character in the play who makes religious statements apply to irreligious acts. He tells Simeon: "I been hearin' the hens cluckin' an' the roosters crowin' all the durn day. I been listenin' t' the cows lowin' an' everythin' else kickin' up till I can't stand it no more. It's spring an' I feel damned....An' now I'm ridin' out t' learn God's message t' me in the spring, like the prophet's done." (p. 210) Then he drives off in the buggy singing a hymn. In spite of his seventy-five years, what Ephraim feels is need—for a woman, almost any woman. And as Simeon says when he hears that the elder Cabot has remarried for the third time:

> "I'm ridin' out t' learn God's message t' me in the spring like the prophets done," he says. I'll bet right then an' thar he knew plumb well he was going whorin', the stinkin' old hypocrite! (p. 215)

But Ephraim is not a hypocrite if we insist that hypocrisy be conscious dissembling. Ephraim is cruel, harsh, and devoid of charity, but knows himself to be so, desires to be so, and feels that he has Divine sanction for his ruthlessness. He practices a harsh and loveless Puritanical religion that worships toil, scorns ease and sentiment or even the expression of honest sentiment. As he says to Abbie in a rare burst of self expression which she does not hear like the soliloquies of Chekhov's characters, spoken at but rarely to a listener:

> ....Stones. I picked 'em up an' piled 'em into walls. Ye kin read the years of my life in them walls, every day a hefted stone,...fencin' in the fields that was mine, whar I made thin's grow out of nothin'—-like the will o' God, like the servant o' His hand. It wa'n't easy. It was hard an' He made me hard fur it. (pp. 236-237)

The whole rambling passage emphasizes possession, hardness, the sinfulness of easy wealth, the equation of virtue with hard work, and Ephraim's loneliness. The "objective correlative" of the passage is *stone*:[3] hard, unyielding, impenetrable. Piled one on top of another, they wall the farm like a prison, as Ephraim's values imprison him, his successive wives, and his sons, creating their mutual lack of contact; for stones piled to make a wall are individual objects, not a unit, without some sort of bond or mortar. And on the Cabot farm there is no such agent until Abbie and Eben realize their love late in the play. Instead there are the worst distortions of the Protestant ethic: greed, vengeance, incessant toil, and individual isolation. Even Ephraim, so insensitive to the real feelings of Eben's mother, Eben, or Abbie, feels this chill sense of loneliness-—"It's cold in this house [though at midsummer]. It's oneasy. They's thin's pokin' about in the dark-—in the corners."

Desire Under the Elms 79

(p. 238) And so for comfort, Ephraim goes down to the barn where it is warm and peaceful, largely because the animals do not covet one another's possessions, and because their behavior doesn't suffer from the restrictions and inhibitions of Ephraim's Christianity. Edward Arlington Robinson summed up the situation well in his famous sonnet "New England":

> Passion is here a soilure of the wits
> We're told, and Love a cross for them to bear;
> Joy shivers in the corner where she knits
> And conscience always has the rocking chair....(II. 9-12)

Thus, though each of the characters has his own desires, each pharisaically condemns the others' as lusts. Abbie, who has married Ephraim for the security of a home, tries to seduce Eben, and when she fails, when Eben goes off to see the town whore instead, screams, "Git out o' my sight! Go on t' yer slut—disgracin' yer Paw 'n' me! (p. 230) Though her motive is jealousy, not piety, she denounces Eben to his father in these terms: "[Eben's gone] t' see that harlot, Min !...Disgracin' yew an' me-—on the Sabbath, too! (p. 233) As if the day mattered to Abbie. And Cabot replies, "*(rather guiltily)* He's a sinner—nateral-born. It's lust eatin' his heart." (p. 233) Ephraim's guilt is two-fold, for Min was his mistress long before she was Eben's, and he has his own lusts; the one which drove him away from the farm months before to seek a wife, the same one for which he "stares at her [Abbie] desirously" and addresses her in terms of that ancient fertility chant, The Song of Songs; and the lust for a new son, proof of his virility, and worthy heir to the farm. Though Ephraim condemns Eben for lust, he himself calls Abbie his "Rose o' Sharon! Behold, yew air fair; yer eyes air doves; yer lips air like scarlet; yer two breasts air like two fawns....*(He covers her hand with kisses....)*" (p. 232) Though he denounces Simeon and Peter's desire to visit the California goldfields as "Lust fur gold—fur the sinful, easy gold o' California" (p. 223), he desperately covets a son as an extension of his own right of ownership: "...A son is me—my blood—mine. Mine ought t' git mine. An' then it's still mine—even though I be six foot under. (p. 234)[4] For good or for bad, Ephraim and even Abbie use prayer. When Abbie sees that her only real security lies in providing Cabot a son, she suggests to him that "mebbe the Lord'll give *us* a son" (p. 234); she emphasizes "us" because a new son will disinherit Eben, even though Eben is his father—which is what we, at this point in the play, suspect, and what Abbie plans. She says to Ephraim, "...I been prayin' it'd happen...," and he responds, "It'd be the blessin' o,' God, Abbie—the blessin' o' God A'mighty on me—-in my old age—-in my lonesomeness!...Pray t' the Lord agen, Abbie. It's the Sabbath!..."(p. 234) God does not hear the prayer, for the son Abbie bears is Eben's, even though Ephraim thinks it is his, and when Abbie suffocates the infant and is jailed for the crime with Eben, Cabot is even more alone—without any wife or son. And so this "good" prayer, for a son, is frustrated. But Ephraim prays for evil, too. When Simeon and Peter desert the farm, his farm, he prays to God to curse them:

> CABOT. ...Lord God o' Hosts, smite the undutiful sons with Thy wust cuss!
> EBEN. ...Yew'n'yewr God! Allus cussin' folks-allus naggin' 'em!...

Cabot's God is indeed the God of the old—He is the harsh, avenging God of the Old Testament, as popularly conceived of, distinct from the more loving, more forgiving and charitable God of the New Testament. But of course, this is not so—the God of the Old Testament, the same God, is merciful, forgiving, and loving; but Ephraim's perverse belief in Him as a hard and lonesome God (pp. 227, 268) has caused Cabot to value hardness and isolation, to work his first two wives to death, to drive off his two elder sons, to instill as values in his sons craftiness, vengeance, and suspicion instead of love, and to wall himself up and prevent any warm, personal, truly communicative relationship with any of his wives or sons. And so Eben seeks vengeance for himself and his mother's death through Abbie; Ephraim seeks to dispossess Eben and hand the farm on to a still younger son; and Abbie—at first—seeks to cheat them both, loving neither. Whatever tendencies of character Ephraim may have inherited that caused him to be as he is, undoubtedly his harsh religion—the same religion as Hawthorne's John Endicott and O'Neill's own Mannons—has developed and confirmed these traits. And by purposeful use of Biblical language or quotations in debased contexts, O'Neill has underscored this perversion of religion for us. He has also provided, by allusion, an analogue for comment and contrast.

For if one believes that Ephraim Cabot does ride from the farm to learn God's message as the prophets did, then one must assume that the message was to marry. And, indeed, God did instruct the first of the so-called Minor Prophets, Hosea, to marry—to marry, in fact, a harlot, which is what Eben calls Abbie for marrying Cabot in order to have a home. Hosea is commanded to wed a prostitute, and, even though she is unfaithful to him and deserts him, he is told to buy her back and to reaffirm his devotion—all as an allegory of the Lord's relation to Israel, which had broken its covenant with God and was prostituting itself both figuratively, with false gods, and literally: "the prophet's personal life is an incarnation of God's redeeming love."[4] And significantly, Hosea addresses Israel, the nation's eponymous name after Jacob, by the name of Joseph's younger son, eponymous founder of one of the twelve tribes (Gen. 48), Ephraim. And like Ephraim Cabot,

> E'phraim is oppressed, cursed in judgment, because he was determined to go after vanity. (Hos. 5:11)
>
> ...'Ephraim has hired lovers. (8:9)
>
> E'phraim has said, "Ah, but I am rich, I have gained wealth for myself:" but all his riches can never offset the guilt he has incurred. (12:8)

By denying Hosea's message of love and forgiveness, by perverting the message of the Bible, Ephraim Cabot has taught "Bloody instructions, which, being taught, return to plague the inventor." He has freed his animals before he learns that Eben has taken his savings, and all his relations are gone—"It's a-goin' t' be lonesomer now than ever it war afore—an' I'm gittin' old, Lord—ripe on the bough." (p. 268) In the words of Hosea, he has sown the wind and reaped the whirlwind. (8:7)

In his review of *Desire Under the Elms*,[5] Joseph Wood Krutch said that "the meaning and unity of his work lies not in any controlling intellectual idea and certainly not in a 'message,' but merely in the fact that each play is an experience of extraordinary intensity." Certainly this is as true for *Desire* as it is for O'Neill's other plays, but it is no less true that *Desire* is, if not controlled, then at least shaped, by an intellectual idea and a message: that the harsh, loveless, and covetous Puritanical religion practiced by Ephraim Cabot is a perversion of religion that cripples love and destroys men.

NOTES

1. Cf. Arthur and Barbara Gelb, *O'Neill* (New York, 1960, 1962), pp. 378, 538-541.

2. *The Plays of Eugene O'Neill* (New York: Random House, n.d.), I, 203, 205. All subsequent quotations will be from this edition and paginated in my text.

3. It is not without significance that not only does Peter's name mean stone, but so does Eben, in Greek and Hebrew, respectively.

4. That a man's bloodline descends through his sons is, of course, a common folk belief that finds expression in the Bible, Gen. 48:16 and Deut. 25:6.

5. *The Oxford Annotated Bible with Apocrypha* (New York, 1965), p. 1088.

6. *The Nation*, CXIX (Nov. 26, 1924), 578; quoted by the Gelbs, p. 571.

Modern Drama, 11 (Spring 1969): 423-428.

The New O'Neill Play and Some Others

Barrett H. Clark

The most important theatrical event of the month was the long-awaited production of *The Fountain*, the Eugene O'Neill play that was written four years ago and announced on several occasions by various managers. It ran just two weeks at the Greenwich Village Theatre, and was pretty generally condemned by the press and the small part of the public that went to see it. The production, directed by Robert Edmond Jones, who also furnished the lovely settings and costumes, was somehow not up to the play. This, however, is not entirely Mr. Jones' fault. To begin with, *The Fountain* requires acting of a kind that is practically non-existent in this country. The *Comedie Francaise* could perhaps furnish two or three players, and the Moscow Art Theatre almost a whole cast competent to carry through the difficult roles written by Mr. O'Neill. Style there must be, and a certain mixture of tradition and untrammeled ecstasy. Then there were the long waits between scenes that Americans still stand for. These only serve to accentuate the slowness of the performance. The manuscript is surprisingly short, and in reading it I saw far more clearly what the author intended. Where the poet passes lightly from scene to scene, the producer pauses with heavy emphasis....By the time the O'Neill play began to move toward its exquisite culmination, the audience didn't care what happened.

The Fountain—which is cast in the conventional romantic form of *Cyrano*—came as a surprise to the public which has never yet realized that O'Neill is, and has from the beginning always been, an idealist and a poet. It is concerned with the almost wholly imaginary story of the quest of the Fountain of Youth by Ponce de Leon, and his ultimate realization that such quests as his are and must be doomed to failure when rationally or materialistically conceived, but become shining and glorious events when identified with the quest for life, love and beauty. "One must accept, "says Juan, "absorb, give back, become oneself a symbol...Juan Ponce de Leon is past! He is resolved into the thousand moods of beauty that make up happiness—color of that sunset, of tomorrow's dawn, breath of the great Trade Wind—sunlight on the grass, an insect's song, the rustle of leaves, an ant's ambitions. I shall know eternal becoming—eternal youth!"

The chant that runs through the play as a motif is a lyrical choric comment on the theme:

> Love is a flower forever blooming,
> Beauty a fountain forever flowing
> Upward into the source of sunshine,
> Upward into the azure heaven;
> One with God but
> Ever returning
> To kiss the earth that the flower may live.

The Fountain is a dramatic poem of exaltation—the reflection of the poet's never-ending aspiration toward life, love, and beauty. Except for the form, which with O'Neill is always changing, this play is fundamentally a logical development of the art of the same man who wrote *The Moon of the Caribbees* and *The Hairy Ape*. O'Neill has never been simply a naturalist. It is therefore the more amusing to read his note on the program, the last sentence of which should silence those who declare that man to be devoid of a sense of humor. He says, "Therefore, I wish to take a solemn oath right here and now, that *The Fountain* is not morbid realism." As if he had ever been a morbid realist!

In spite of its conception, and in spite of the beauty of individual scenes, *The Fountain* is not wholly successful as a work of art. I feel that O'Neill, as always, is seeking a new means of expression, in this case a rather conventional romantic form that is not familiar to him. Of course, he knows the form, but I suspect he disdains it. In *The Fountain* he went to great pains to do the job as neatly as possible. While the conception was sincere (could it be otherwise with him?) the technical means employed were not wholly so. To be successful a play of this type must be written a little naively: it must master the poet. The trouble here is that the poet knew his form so well that *he* mastered *it*. Then there is the matter of language. There are scenes toward the end of the play that cry aloud not for fine writing or mere literature but for poetry. I mean formal verse. The poetic urge, the heat of the poet's passion, seems to burst the bonds of the prose—good as it is—and demand the formal freedom of inspired verse.

But in the final analysis I prefer such plays as this in book form. There is too much left to the mechanics of the theatre and to the individual temperaments of human actors.

Drama, February 1926.

The Great God Brown

Richard Dana Skinner

Three things emerge clearly from the puzzle of Eugene O'Neill's latest play, *The Great God Brown*. In his use of realistic masks—as distinct from the representative masks of old Greek tragedy—he has plunged into a new and fascinating mode of extending the scope of emotion and spiritual contrast on the stage. His courage and vision in this respect are not yet matched by ability to use the new medium. It engages him in a task that frequently proves too difficult for his technical resources. Lastly, and most important of all, O'Neill gives unmistakable signs of emerging, himself, from the sensual cloud in which he has been groping for many years. The new play has high moments of rich spiritual insight, of abiding faith, and understanding of the mystic vale of tears.

We all know the meaning of masks—from the impassive "poker face" of the card player to the defensive attitude or pose assumed by many sensitive souls as an armor against the cruel and misunderstanding eyes of neighbors. How often your apparently cynical or conceited man hides in the recesses of his nature a tortured, uncertain self—a truth which he reveals only to those whom he knows, intuitively, to be rich with understanding. These are commonplaces of experience. But O'Neill has put them on the stage. His characters wear masks when talking to certain people—discard them when talking with others. As their speech and attitude change, their faces change as well. It is a method of heightening, more completely than the facial muscles of actors can achieve, the gamut of emotions through which his characters charge and recoil.

This new method, as the first two acts of the play establish, would bring no insuperable difficulties, if the author were content to rest in the realm of objective drama. But *The Great God Brown* is far more than a play of many separate characters. It borders on the realm of the old morality play, in which characters represent aspects of the soul—as where Everyman talks with his own approaching Death, or with his Good Deeds. William Brown, the mask of popular success, and Dion Anthony, the poet and artist, become (whatever the conscious intentions of O'Neill may have been) conflicting aspects of one man. When Anthony dies, Brown assumes his mask, and the world, including Anthony's wife, does not know that Anthony is dead.

This idea is not hard to convey. In spite of the bewilderment of many of the critics, I cannot see why this is more difficult to understand than its counterpart in the folk-lore of nearly every country and time. In the old Norse legends, Siegfried, wearing the magic cap, assumes the form of Guenther in order to subdue Brunhilde and win her as Guenther's bride. Unfortunately, O'Neill allows himself to complicate the action of the play—the entrances and exits—to such an extent, that the exchange of masks becomes a technical bewilderment for the audience, no matter how clear its intention and meaning may remain. If you want your poetic vision to reach beyond a very limited group, it is wise not to ask too much of a mixed audience. O'Neill has created what I think is an unnecessary clash between reality and fantasy. Realism frequently obscures the authentic flow of imagery and inward fire.

The greatest achievement of this play, however, lies in discovery which O'Neill has made—or partly made—and which most of the critics have ignored. He has begun to fathom the meaning of earthly suffering. Probably no poet of the theatre in recent times has been more intensely aware of suffering than O'Neill. It has been his veritable obsession. Evil and its resulting catastrophe have been the central theme of most of his plays—evil in manifold forms, as pride, as sensuality, as cowardice, as avarice. But he has never seen beyond catastrophe to possible resurrection. Like Ibsen, he has dived into a swamp and his head has stuck there. He reached the lowest strata in *Desire Under the Elms*. Now there is an astonishing change. He tells us in this new play that from the tears of earth is born the eternal laughter of Heaven—that resurrection lies beyond death—that man should keep himself forever as a pilgrim on this earth—(using Thomas à Kempis as his text)—and that God is.

There is still confusion in his thought, for O'Neill feels more acutely than he thinks. But he has definitely come forth from the great shadow which fell forbiddingly over his recent work. He is approaching that ecstatic moment when tragedy transmutes itself, through song, into spiritual comedy. He can now, if he will, attain proportions of beauty and dramatic truth, to which Ibsen turned unseeing eyes.

For the rest, Robert Edmond Jones has never directed a piece with greater intuitive understanding, nor, perhaps, had finer actor material at his disposal. The Brown of William Harrigan, especially in the later episodes and the very earliest ones, has both power and depth. He succeeds less well in that period when he is supposed to bloom with self-satisfaction. Robert Keith's Dion Anthony carries, I should think, the full poetic pathos O'Neill has indicated—and that is a high compliment. Leona Hogarth as the unseeing wife also sweeps you beyond the realm of simple realism. But many of the finest moments are left to Anne Shoemaker as Cybel, the understanding one, the voice of O'Neill's comment on the meaning of suffering. In all, a most notable play—not for the occasionally perverse and confused dregs of an older O'Neill it contains—but for its latent promise and momentary attainment of a lofty notion.

Commonweal, February 10, 1923.

The Great God Brown

Stark Young

I had the curious experience with *The Great God Brown* of being moved with something that I felt behind the play, but almost always untouched by the play itself. It may be that such an observation makes no sense, that the only way in which such an impression could be received would be through the play, where else should we get it? Let it go at that, then, and say at any rate that I felt a torment of spirit, a groping love of life, a bitter pity and goodness, a warm and courageous desire, that make me like so many other people in America, wish Eugene O'Neill well, wish that it may be granted to him to fulfil his talent and devotion. I admired the passion for fresh and powerful dramatic form in Eugene O'Neill, and I felt like lining myself up in defense of the audacious integrity of his mood. But by the play itself as it went on I was entertained only now and then....

The writing in *The Great God Brown* is unequal, sometimes beautiful and keen, often well chastened toward the dramatic point to be expressed, often obvious, sometimes flat, poor poetry, third-rate taste. Now and again the idea is poignant and carrying, now and again commonplace or worse. Sometimes a beautiful speech like that of the intolerable chalice of life fails to stop and runs off into mediocrity. I confess to embarrassment sometimes, even, as for instance when the officer standing over the dead Brown-Dion asks what his name is and the all-wise prostitute says MAN—that seems only second rate Andreyev in his symbolic vein, and Andreyev can be bad enough.

The part of this new play that has the most immediate interest, of course, is the use of masks. Each of the leading characters is shown with two faces, his own, which represents what he is, and the mask that expresses only the distortion of himself that some may see. The surety with which this device has been employed and has been made necessary to the play's meaning and very existence indeed, the direct economy of the mask's application, appear when we try to tell in words the story. Any such account of it must be a mere travesty.

There are two sets of parents in business together. One of them has a son who is poetic and gifted. The son of the other is matter-of-fact, honest, persistent and practical. Both youths are close friends, both love the same girl, Margaret. The girl loves Dion, though she knows nothing of his real self. She marries him. They sell his share of the business to Brown, and go abroad. There are three children born. Brown, still loving Margaret, has never married. Dion has squandered his estate, has been a painter, a failure, an uncertain husband. Through Margaret's intercessions he is employed in Brown's office, his designs convert the architecture of the firm into imagination and art. There is a prostitute who gives to Dion an understanding that he has never had from his wife, however devoted she may be to him. Brown takes over the prostitute and supports her richly, in order to keep Dion faithful to his wife. Time passes; Dion, under the strain of life and the pain of hard reality against his sensitive dreams degenerates further and further. He has, nevertheless, what Brown can never have, the gift of life. He dies; his mask is put on by Brown, who, unknown to her, takes Dion's place with Margaret and gives her back the old happiness of the first days with Dion. Meanwhile Dion is supposed to be secluding himself by day at Brown's office, working at the designs. Margaret comes for him. In this crisis Brown declares that Dion has suddenly died. There is a cry of murder, the officers pursue, Brown is shot, he and Dion, now merged into one, die. In the epilogue Margaret, an old woman, masked to her three sons, speaks to them of their father.

The settings by Mr. Robert Edmond Jones are as courageous as the play. With extraordinary insight they achieve the dramatic point of the scenes they translate into stage decor. The high, overwhelming panel of the filing cabinet in Brown's profitable and laborious office, the walls of the prostitute's room bursting into red blossoms when Brown has set her up in luxury, these scenes are theatrical in the deepest sense. Mr. Jones directing is equally close to the play's method. He cannot put acting into the players, and their performance remains only adequate and never compelling. But the lay-out of the stage movement, of the positions, of the emphasis of individuals and groups is distinct and telling. Miss Leona Hogarth as Margaret and Mr. Robert Keith as Dion have at least a sympathetic relation to their roles. Miss Anne Shoemaker's prostitute, sure to be admired in many quarters, seemed to me an unctuous and rather tiresome performance, full of important missions to perform, not translucent in spirit, but conscious of meanings, and subtly lacking somehow in taste. Mr. William Harrigan, with the fat role of Brown was never tragic, ironical or poignant, though he has naturally perhaps a certain soldier-boy pathos in a small way. But he gave the sense of a good professional security, a kind of inherited dispatch and competency, of a sincere mind and a fine obligation to the play, and he never missed a point.

Of such a technical device as this use of masks, which is kept up all through *The Great God Brown* from the first line to the last curtain, two points are to be made. The first is that the unfamiliarity or rarity of such a device, the more or less innovative side of it, will make the play more admirable and exciting to some people and to others will be a hindrance, an annoyance or a confusion that hurts the play's effect. This condition is a matter of time only and acquaintance, a further use of masks in plays would more or less dispose of it. The second point is that when once a device is adopted in a drama and the expressive meaning of it has become clear, the continued significance or suggestiveness of its use will depend on the artist's imagination. You could take a knife and fork to represent a man and wife. But to achieve anything important there must then be imagination exercised in the use of these symbols, otherwise you have only the regular story, plus the knife and fork instead of man and wife, and have achieved nothing beyond the first device, the initial metaphor. In *The Great God Brown* the masks are used well. Coming on and off as they do when these human beings confront one another, they say quickly and clearly certain things that need to be said. They are made immensely economical; they say what nothing else in the play says or could quite say. On the whole, too, they manage not to be confusing or even very difficult, unless it be toward the last, when Brown puts on Dion's mask. By this time the masks are used not only to express the real character and the character sometimes shown the world, but also to express the transfer of one man's personalty to another, to carry perhaps one soul into another body. In this part of the play the idea is harder to state, though it is more or less felt. As to a profoundly imaginative use of the masks, points at which their use became a radiant necessity and a great leaping image full of creative life, I should have less to say. For me there were only two such places, though they were extraordinary. The moment when the prostitute, out of her understanding and love, hands the wretched Dion his mask to put on, like a shelter that her heart knows, startles and moves you. At the last when we see Dion's wife talking to the mask of the dead man whom she has loved but never known as he was, holding him now like a child in the bosom of her love, when we see that and realize that it is still only his mask that she kneels to there, the motive becomes suddenly luminous and revealing.

New Republic, February 10, 1926.

Theatre

Harold Clurman

Even when he had money and fame, his friends used to speak of Eugene O'Neill as "poor Gene." They were right for the wrong reasons. Part of O'Neill's merit results from the abiding torment in him. This torment gives *The Great God Brown* a certain amount of staying power. It is, to begin with, a personal torment, but it also acquires an extension in social meaning. Both these elements explain its success with the public in 1926, even though very few people "understood" it. And no wonder, it is a rather confused and confusing play (Lyceum Theatre).

At present we need not enter into the detail of its dramatic argument or its symbolism. Dion Anthony and his friend Billy Brown are two aspects of O'Neill's persona. The first is the self-lacerating artist, discontented with and even uncertain of his talent, as well as tortured by his rebellion against the faith of his forbears, which he suspects is the betrayal of something which alone might have sustained a sense of the wholeness (or holiness) of life. The artist in Dion-O'Neill envies the presumed equanimity that the "position" Brown was destined to achieve would give him. But Brown is no less jealous of the imagination and raging freedom of the artist Dion. Each is half of the other, each destroys the other. In this inner dichotomy and conflict lurks the *American* tragedy. It constitutes a theme of which several of O'Neill's plays offer variations.

It is a mistake to consider Dion a "hero"; it is an even greater mistake to view Brown as paltry. Brown is the center of the play: the innerly dissatisfied businessman, the big executive with a hole in his heart, is more typically American than the frustrated artist. It is to O'Neill's great credit that he recognizes Brown's hurt, his growing awareness of his inadequacy; for he, too, would be an "artist." Of the two men Brown is perhaps the more pathetic. The very construction of *The Great God Brown*—Dion dies in the second act, Brown in the third—is a clue to O'Neill's intention in this regard.

The chief fault of the new Phoenix Repertory Company's production, directed by Harold Prince, is that Brown's centrality in the play has not been realized. Or if realized, it is not embodied in the casting. John Glover's Brown is a callow boy, totally incapable of growth. He lacks tragic dimension. The play thus becomes a contrast between Dion, a "deep" person, and Brown, a hollow man, which makes it "clearer" to some, but basically trite.

The characterizations throughout are of a thin, conventional quality. John McMartin works hard as Dion but he is not naturally endowed for the embodiment of O'Neill's ache. He struck me as a light comedian hoping to achieve Hamlet....

In brief, then, the present production reduces the play's stature. Its salient faults—for instance, the adolescent "poetics" of its final scenes—are enhanced; its virtues—a genuine soulfulness, an intense striving to articulate passionate intuitions—flattened. Still, if you have not seen *The Great God Brown* you should see it now: O'Neill's voice is not entirely silenced in this production.

Nation, January 1, 1973.

The Birth of Tragedy and *The Great God Brown*

Michael Hinden

Eugene O'Neill's debt to the philosophy of Nietzsche, particularly his enthusiasm for *Thus Spoke Zarathustra*, by now is a matter of record.[1] O'Neill discovered Nietzsche's writings in the spring of 1907.[2] Later, in a letter to Benjamin De Casseres dated June 22, 1927, he wrote:

> 'Zarathustra,' although my work may appear like a pitiable contradiction to this statement and my life add an exclamation point to this contradiction, has influenced me more than any other book I've ever read. I ran into it, through the bookshop of Benjamin Tucker, the old philosophical anarchist, when I was eighteen and I've always possessed a copy since then and every year or so I reread it and am never disappointed, which is more than I can say of almost any other book.[3]

A copious note-taker, O'Neill eventually copied passages from some fifty of the book's eighty chapters;[4] at Harvard in 1914 he even struggled through a copy in the original German with the help of a German grammar and a dictionary.[5] O'Neill's acknowledgement of Nietzsche's influence continued throughout his life. In his 1936 Nobel Prize acceptance speech he paid homage to Nietzsche as his mentor, acknowledging the importance of his influence as well as that of Sweden's own son, August Strindberg: "For me, he remains, as Nietzsche remains, in his sphere, the master, still to this day more modern than any of us, still our leader."[6]

But if O'Neill's debt to *Zarathustra* is well known, the specific influence of *The Birth of Tragedy* on his plays has not yet been adequately studied. It is to be said first that documentation of O'Neill's earliest encounter with Nietzsche's exegesis on the origin of tragedy is rather difficult to assemble. Cyrus Day believes that O'Neill read the book along with *Zarathustra* during his New London days before the first world war,[7] a perfectly reasonable assumption. Oscar Cargill, on the other hand, feels that O'Neill did not "adequately digest" *The Birth of Tragedy* until after he had written *The Great God Brown*.[8] Yet this view apparently is contradicted by Barrett Clark's account of meeting O'Neill at the Hotel Lafayette in New York in 1926 and watching him stuff "a worn copy of Nietzsche's *Birth of Tragedy* into his pocket" before hurrying over to the Greenwich Village Theater to watch a rehearsal of that very play.[9] One thing certain is that in the playbill of *The Great God Brown*, produced later that year, there were two considerable quotations from *The Birth of Tragedy*.[10] The remaining question, it would seem, concerns the year in which O'Neill first read the book or when it was that he first read it carefully. As noted earlier, specific evidence for the date of a first reading is unavailable. Yet it is difficult to believe that the young O'Neill, a confirmed Nietzsche enthusiast and already determined in 1914 to become "an artist or nothing,"[11] would wait more than a decade before consulting his favorite philosopher on the subject of tragedy and art.

It now seems clear that what most fascinated O'Neill in *The Birth of Tragedy* was Nietzsche's view of the origin and symbolic meaning of Greek tragedy which Nietzsche associated with a spirit of irrational ecstasy growing out of the performance of a chorus of satyrs celebrating the ritual destruction and reunification of their god, Dionysus. To Nietzsche the Dionysian rituals of the Greeks symbolized an intuitive apprehension of what Schopenhauer had described as the eternal struggle of the suffering "world will." The tragic art created by the Greeks, argued Nietzsche, succeeded in imposing Apollinian form upon the tumultuous struggle of the will in its perpetual cycle of fragmentation and return to unity, the Dionysian hero representing a personal embodiment of this struggle—an individual powerfully striving for self-realization who unconsciously is driven to reveal the true nature of his identity as the embodiment of an irrational force. "In light of this insight," Nietzsche wrote,

> we must understand Greek tragedy as the Dionysian chorus which ever anew discharges itself in an Apollinian world of images. Thus the choral parts with which tragedy is interlaced are, as it were, the womb that gave birth to the whole of the so-called dialogue, that is, the entire world of the stage, the real drama. In several successive discharges this primal ground of tragedy radiates this vision of the drama which is by all means a dream apparition and to that extent epic in nature; but, on the other hand, being the objectification of a Dionysian state, it represents not Apollinian redemption through mere appearance but on the contrary, the shattering of the individual and his fusion with primal being.[12]

There can be little doubt that O'Neill embraced this notion; indeed, the principal plays of the twenties (coinciding mainly with O'Neill's "expressionistic" period) seem rooted in the concept of a "primal ground of tragedy" radiating "dream apparitions" leading to the revelation of some hidden force akin to Nietzsche's Dionysian will. In *The Emperor Jones*, Jones encounters such a force through his symbolic dream apparitions in the forest; Jim Harris encounters a similar force through the medium of a Congo mask in *All God's Chillun Got Wings*. Yank appears to embody that force in *The Hairy Ape*, while Juan seeks union with it in

The Fountain. Abbie, Eben, and Ephraim acknowledge the omnipotence of the force in *Desire Under the Elms.* In *Marco Millions* Marco comically ignores the force, but in *Lazarus Laughed,* Lazarus is sustained by it.

Actually, suggestions of O'Neill's acquaintance with Nietzsche's Dionysian outlook may be found even in the very early sea plays in which the sea almost always serves as a symbolic backdrop for an "inscrutable" life force. That force later is associated more specifically with Nietzsche's Dionysus—in O'Neill's words, "Not the coarse, drunken Dionysus, nor the effeminate God, but Dionysus in his middle period, more comprehensive in his symbolism, the soul of the recurring seasons, of living and dying as processes in eternal growth, of the wine of life stirring forever in the sap and blood and loam of things."[13] Concerning *The Moon of the Caribbees* (1916-17), O'Neill could write: "*The Moon* [was] an attempt to achieve a higher plane of bigger, finer values... Perhaps I can explain the nature of my feeling for the impelling, inscrutable forces behind life which it is my ambition to at least faintly shadow at their work in my play."[14] Earlier still, in a stage direction for *The Web* (written in 1913-14), Rose Thomas is described as suddenly being "aware of something in the room which none of the others can see—perhaps the personification of the ironic life force that has crushed her."[15] Later, in *Desire Under the Elms,* all of O'Neill's characters will sense that "somethin'" in the room—"Ye kin feel it droppin' off the elums, climbin' up the roof, sneakin' down the chimney, pokin' in the corners!"[16] but this mysterious force makes its appearance at the very outset of O'Neill's career.

Many other O'Neill pronouncements and techniques find echoes in *The Birth of Tragedy.* In later plays, particularly *The Emperor Jones, The Hairy Ape, Desire Under the Elms, The Great God Brown, Lazarus Laughed,* and *Mourning Becomes Electra,* Nietzsche's essay undoubtedly was mined in depth. In these plays the ubiquitous use of music, dream images and Dionysian symbolism, the reliance upon unconscious drives to motivate the characters, the use of masks and choric groupings, the anti-rationalist bias of the content and the general exaltation of the primitive, may all be traced to sources in *The Birth of Tragedy.* Indeed, in some instances it is difficult to discern whether O'Neill is thinking consciously of Nietzsche or whether by some process of osmosis or affinity the perspectives of the two have naturally coalesced. Nietzsche's chief influence, for example, may be seen in O'Neill's attitude toward tragedy's function and his concept of characterization. On this subject O'Neill writes: "A comprehensive expression is demanded here, a chance for eloquent presentation, a new form of drama projected from a fresh insight, into the inner forces motivating the actions and reactions of men and women...a drama of souls, and the adventures of 'Free wills,' with the masks that govern them and constitute their fates."[17] Nietzsche's fundamental conception of Greek tragedy, one recalls, is predicated on the argument "that all the celebrated figures of the Greek stage—Prometheus, Oedipus, etc.—are mere masks of the original [inner force or] hero, Dionysus. That behind all these masks there is a deity, that is one essential reason for the typical 'ideality' of these famous figures which has caused so much astonishment."[18] Again, O'Neill: "And just here is where I am a most confirmed mystic, too, for I'm always, always trying to interpret Life in terms of lives, never just lives in terms of character. I'm always acutely conscious of the Force behind—Fate, God, our biological past creating our present, whatever one calls it—Mystery certainly—and of the one eternal tragedy of Man in his glorious, self-destructive struggle to make the Force express him instead of being, as an animal is, an infinitesimal incident in its expression."[19]

Throughout his life O'Neill remained enthralled by Nietzsche's concept in *The Birth of Tragedy* of a fundamental unity underlying all phenomena, even when in his later, darker years that vision seemed beyond his grasp, just one other Apollinian illusion, a "pipe dream," as Hickey might call it in *The Iceman Cometh*. Yet the disillusioned pessimism of *The Iceman* serves also as a foil for Edmund's poignant vision of lost rapture, a moment of mystical oneness which O'Neill recreates for us in the final act of *Long Day's Journey Into Night*. Recalling Nietzsche's metaphor in *The Birth of Tragedy* of Dionysian oneness shattering "the veil of Maya," Edmund rhapsodizes:

> I lay on the bowsprit, facing astern, with the water foaming into spume under me, the masts with every sail white in the moonlight, towering high above me. I became drunk with the beauty and singing rhythm of it, and for a moment I lost myself—actually lost my life. I was set free! I dissolved in the sea, became white sails and flying spray, became beauty and rhythm, became moonlight and the ship and the high dim-starred sky! I belonged, without past or future, within
> peace and unity and a wild joy, within something greater than my own life, or the life of Man, to Life itself!...Like a saint's vision of beatitude. Like the veil of things as they seem drawn back by an unseen hand.[20]

Even O'Neill's exploration of obviously Freudian themes owes something to Nietzschean metaphor. The recurring theme of separation from the mother, for example, is rooted in Nietzsche and Schopenhauer's principle that individuation is the source of suffering. As Simon Harford pleads in *More Stately Mansions*, "Come, mother! Let us leave this vile sty of lust and hatred and the wish to murder! Let us escape back into peace—while there is still time!...We shall have gone back beyond separations. We shall be one again."[21]

The youthful appeal of mysticism never really soured for O'Neill, although eventually it did to Nietzsche. This marks a major difference between the two. One of Zarathustra's maxims argues that, "one repays a teacher badly if one always remains nothing but a pupil,"[22] and O'Neill obliged his mentor by quarreling with him inwardly. The influence of *The Birth of Tragedy* may have been subtle and therefore more sustaining, but speaking of *Zarathustra* in 1927, O'Neill wrote, "spots of its teaching I no longer concede."[23]

Moving steadily away from Schopenhauer's disavowal of individuation and his supposition of a supra-personal word entity, Nietzsche in his later writing develops the perspective of the willing individual as the repository of all values; it is the individual creative will defiant of all metaphysical and communal constructs, the private will ("beyond good and evil") that Nietzsche celebrates in *Zarathustra*. But like Ibsen, whom he admired greatly, O'Neill in the end remained basically a moralist. As he developed as a dramatist he tested Zarathustra's celebration of the ego and found in it a tragic source of destruction of that which alone could assure self-harmony and "belonging": the idea of community. That the *uebermensch* must rise above communal values to forge his own concept of good and evil O'Neill could visualize but not accept without accepting also Ibsen's proposition that the egotist presides over a crippled soul.

This uncompromising moral vision is present clearly even in *Servitude,* O'Neill's first full-length play, written in 1913. The play concerns a "Nietzschean" dramatist named David Roylston (bearing resemblance to O'Neill) whose "modern" plays have inspired a certain Mrs. Frazer to abandon her husband and come running to his doorstep seeking "emancipation." (The echoes of Ibsen are readily audible.) But once in Roylston's parlor, Mrs. Frazer discovers that beneath the mask of this prophet of the superman lies the clouded visage of a cruel and lonely egotist.

> Last night I thought—you were on such a high pedestal—I thought of the superman, of the creator, the maker of the new values. This morning I saw merely an egotist whose hands are bloody with the human sacrifices he has made—to himself!²⁴[24]

Instead of liberating Mrs. Frazer, Roylston later is converted to her own conclusion that happiness is servitude. "Of course it is! Servitude in love, love in servitude! Logos in Pan, Pan in Logos! That is the great secret—and I never knew!"[25]

This brief snatch of dialogue affords a fascinating glimpse of O'Neill's complex attitude toward Nietzsche's Zarathustrian perspective, and indicates also that it was the Dionysian framework of *The Birth of Tragedy* that spoke most directly to his own emotional needs. The continuing object of O'Neill's dramatic quest remained the discovery of some mysterious equation that might restore for him the once glorious but now shattered harmony between the individual and the universe, a fusion between man and nature, man and man, the Life Force and the ego. And only with a rekindling of man's ancient sense of community, he believed, could such a fusion be achieved. Man's struggle used to be with the gods, he reasoned, but "now [it is] with himself, his own past, his attempt to "belong."[26] Thus O'Neill found himself embracing Robert Edmond Jones' view of the function of the poet in the modern theater—a view which, while taking note of Zarathustra's stance, reasserts the central vision of *The Birth of Tragedy.*

> The new poet of the theater...may see in time, not only how people unconsciously reveal their inmost secret selves to the world in every attitude and gesture and intonation, but how they unconsciously group and regroup themselves into crowds and communities under the guidance of an ever-shifting, invisible plan. He may come to understand at last, in an ecstasy of clear seeing, that the radiant heroic beings of which he has dreamed are not supermen, not men at all, not even *uebermarionettes,* but groups of men—group-beings—and that the hero of his drama is in truth the people.[27]

O'Neill himself perhaps best expressed his conception of the theater in this passage from "A Dramatist's Notebook," originally published in the January 1933 issue of *The American Spectator:*

> What do I mean by an 'imaginative' theatre?...I mean the one true theatre, a theatre of the Greeks and Elizabethans, a theatre that could dare to boast—without committing a farcical sacrilege—that it is a legitimate descendant of the first theatre that sprang, by virtue of

man's imaginative interpretation of Life, out of his worship of Dionysus. I mean a theatre returned to its highest and sole significant function as a Temple where the religion of a poetical interpretation and symbolical celebration of life is communicated to human beings, starved in spirit by their soul-stifling daily struggle to exist as masks among the masks of the living![28]

O'Neill's most elaborate use of *The Birth of Tragedy* may be documented in *The Great God Brown* (1925), the symbolic epic that crowns the early Nietzschean phase of his career. "I think it's grand stuff, much deeper and more poetical than anything I've ever done before," O'Neill told Kenneth Macgowan shortly after the play had been completed.[29] He had been moving toward a major symbolic effort of this nature since *The Hairy Ape*, contemplating a personal epic of the soul in the mode of William Blake's *Jerusalem* or Percy Shelley's *Prometheus Unbound*. Indeed, the mythic frame of *The Great God Brown* includes a revelation of the cause of evil in the world, explains the fall of man from paradisal unity, and even points the way toward his redemption and eventual transcendence. Structured in harmony with the patterns of ancient seasonal ritual (the action is initiated in the spring and spans each successive season until spring returns in the final act), the play is a veritable ballet of masks symbolizing the ebb and flow of man's disunified psyche in the modern world. As the play suggests, the necessity of masking represents at the outset a violation of communal harmony, a freezing of the human spirit inimical to the life force which constantly demands a state of flux. When O'Neill's characters unmask, their genuine personalities are exposed; yet to survive at all they must torture their features into masks of "social selfhood" enforced upon them by a corrupt communal context. In the cosmology of *The Great God Brown* the origin of all suffering—the need for masking—lies in the fact that the individual self and the communal self have become separated. The play as a whole may be considered as an attempt to document the quest to reunite them.

Dion Anthony is the central representative of this conflict of divided souls. His name, according to O'Neill's account, derives from "Dionysus and St. Anthony—the creative pagan acceptance of life, fighting eternal war with the masochistic, life-denying spirit of Christianity as represented by St. Anthony—the whole struggle resulting in this modern day in mutual exhaustion—creative joy in life for life's sake frustrated, rendered abortive, distorted by morality from Pan into Satan, into a Mephistopheles mocking himself in order to feel alive...."[30] As the play opens Dion's quest for Dionysian wholeness is thwarted by the moral sense which increases his awareness of disharmony, guilt and individuation: "Now! Be born! Awake! Live! Dissolve into dew!—into silence—into night—into earth—into space—into peace—into meaning—into joy—into God—into the Great God Pan!...Cover your nakedness! Learn to Lie! Learn to keep step! Join the procession! Great Pan is dead! Be ashamed!"[31] In such a context Dionysus can no longer dance—"Why am I afraid to dance, I who love music and grace and song and laughter?" (Prologue, p.315)—and Dion (following Nietzsche's suggestion in *The Birth of Tragedy*) is forced to turn his poetic talents to the plastic, Apollinian arts. But Dion's Pan mask lacks its Apollinian complement and so is merely a distortion of Dionysus and a mockery of the aesthetic impulse. "Why was I born without a skin," Dion cries out, "O God, that I must wear armor in order to be touched?" (Prologue, p. 315). In this condition Nietzsche's inspired vision of the amoral, robust, artist-god degenerates once more to the cynical perspective of Silenus, Dionysus' companion in *The Birth of Tragedy*. Indeed, Dion's secret project as an employee of Brown's architectural firm is the construction of a cathedral dedicated to the life-negating satyr....

The impulse propelling O'Neill's play finds its objectification in Dion's quest to fabricate a "skin," an harmonious Apollinian mask to provide the form for his tortured creativity. But there exists no single counterpart for his divided nature. In addition to this internal conflict, the world can recognize only one aspect of Dion's external image. That is why Margaret fails him and why Dion eventually seeks death and rebirth again in the arms of Cybel, the mother of the gods. Margaret believes that she is willing to give birth again to Dionysus: "And I'll be Mrs. Dion—Dion's wife—and he'll be my Dion—my own Dion—my little boy—my baby." (Prologue, p. 314). And Dion thinks he has found peace: "She is warmly around me! She is my skin! She is my armor! Now I am born—I—the I—one and indivisible—I who love Margaret!" (Prologue, p. 316). But Margaret is able to accept Dion only in the guise of his corrupted mask, and when he reveals himself without it she rejects him.

Midway through the play this broken incarnation of the wine god drinks himself to death—and it is then that Brown takes up his mask. Symbolically, Brown ought to be the natural complement to Dion's incomplete persona; psychically, they are dual aspects of one personality. However, neither can perceive his image in the other's mask. Just as in Nietzsche's scheme Apollo is said to have appeared to the Greeks as the Olympian manifestation of Dionysian energy, so to the American community Brown appears as the visible god, while it is Dion's creative energy that sustains his enterprise. When Brown at last puts on the "skin" (the mask) of Dion, we might then expect apotheosis, but actually Brown gains only Dion's tortured mask of Pan which torments and eventually transfigures him. The significance of this development is best explained in O'Neill's words: "Brown is the visionless demi-god of our new materialistic myth—a Success—building his life of exterior things, inwardly empty and resourceless, an uncreative creature of superficial preordained social grooves, a by-product forced aside into slack waters by the deep main current of life-desire...When he steals Dion's mask of Mephistopheles he thinks he is gaining the power made self-destructive by complete frustration."[32] After stealing Dion's mask, Brown's only course is death and (hopefully) rebirth.

Moments before Dion's death we learn that it was Brown himself who was responsible for the creation of Dion's mask of suffering. Dion recreates the incident:

> Listen! One day when I was four years old, a boy sneaked up behind when I was drawing a picture in the sand he couldn't draw and hit me on the head with a stick and kicked out my picture and laughed when I cried. It wasn't what he'd done that made me cry, but him! I had loved and trusted him and suddenly the good God was disproved in his person and the evil and injustice of Man was born! Everyone called me cry-baby, so

> I became silent for life and designed a mask of the Bad Boy Pan in which to live and rebel against that other boy's God and protect myself from His cruelty. And that other boy, secretly he felt ashamed but he couldn't acknowledge it; so from that day he instinctively developed into the good boy, the good friend, the good man, William Brown! (III.ii, p. 346)

Billy's malicious attempt to stamp out Dion's creativity takes us back to the original violation of community upon which the plot depends. Narrowly interpreted, Dion is accusing Billy of having undermined his self-confidence so that when it came time for him to approach Margaret as a lover, he could do so only by adopting a false mask. But Dion's speech suggests an additional philosophical implication. He refers to his childhood victimization as a "snide neutralizing of the life force" (II.iii, p. 347); and in the cosmology of the play this comes very close to representing "original sin." "When Pan was forbidden the light and warmth of the sun," Dion continues, "he grew sensitive and self-conscious and proud and revengeful—and became the Prince of Darkness." (II.iii, p. 348). Traditionally, the sun is the symbol of Apollo; therefore, Dion's metaphor would seem to imply that sin (or man's awareness of sin) originated when Dionysian consciousness, deprived of its Apollinian complement, turned inward on itself and changed to guilt. That, of course, as Nietzsche might have said, was the origin of "bad conscience." D.H. Lawrence put the matter this way: "The old god Pan became the Christian devil, with the cloven hoofs and the thorns, the tail, and the laugh of derision. Old Nick, the Old Gentleman who is responsible for all our wickedness, but especially our sensual excesses—that is all that is left of the Great God Pan."[33]

With reference to the play's communal context, O'Neill seems to be asserting that the source of modern suffering is dualism and disharmony, the corruption of the natural process of self-realization in a desensualized, acquisitive culture. That process begins when the "Brown principle" instead of fusing with the "Dion principle" attempts perversely to exclude it, thus forcing the "Dion principle" to adopt a separate mask. Symbolically, with Dion's death that mask now is returned to its original giver. As Eugene M. Waith has pointed out: "When Billy inherits the demonical mask, it initiates him into Dion's sufferings, but the final result is not the same. In the last scene, where Billy is stripped bare and without the mask, he seems to have become the Dionysus which Dion potentially was. This dying god is the inner core of the composite character, whose complex reactions to environment have hitherto concealed the truth."[34] Perhaps it may be suggested that the real protagonist of the play, the "behind-life" force, is the original Dionysian unity which has divided into Dion and Brown, Nietzsche's "Primordial Oneness" undergoing the throes of individuation and moving once again toward its own redemption through pain and suffering.

Brown in the second cycle of the play's ritual progression becomes the vehicle of that apotheosis. As Dion suffers, so he suffers, his own face gradually becoming "tortured and distorted by the demon of Dion's Mask" (III.i, p. 357). Whereas Dion failed to possess and be possessed by Margaret on a level deeper than that afforded by the mask, so it is with Brown. He even adopts Dion's drinking habits and helps alter the plans for the new State Capitol they had been commissioned to build so as "to adroitly hide old Silenus on the cupola" (III.iii, p. 364). The climax of the masquerade occurs when Brown puts on his own mask again and in the presence of the city fathers tears up his and Dion's joint design. In so doing, Brown reenacts symbolically his original destruction of Dion's drawing in the sand. But he is acting now in a new context of self-conscious mockery: his suffering is increased doubly by self-awareness.

Having been brought to this ultimate point of recognition and understanding, Brown is ready to fulfill his destiny as an agent of ritual purgation. Putting Dion's mask back on again, he lays Brown's to rest, and then as Dion he is hunted down for "his own" murder. Comforted by Cybel at the close, he meets death standing in the garden in which Dion lies buried, crying: "Welcome, dumb worshippers! I am your Great God Brown! I have been advised to run from you but it is my almighty whim to dance into escape over your prostrate souls!" (IV.ii, p.373). Brown's sacrifice before Cybel parallels Attis' legendary castration as proof of his great love, and suggests that like Attis, Brown, or rather, Dion-Brown, may also be reborn. Speaking of the ancient myth, F.M. Cornford writes: "The Rising of the Earth-Mother with her new-born child involves a symbolism distinct from that of the contest, death, and resurrection of the God. But the two symbolisms can be combined; they are only, as it were, two acts in the drama of the divine life. The miraculous Birth of the wonder-child can be followed by his death at maturity."[35] To borrow T.S. Eliot's metaphor in *The Wasteland*, that corpse Brown planted in his garden last year has begun to sprout.

O'Neill later explained:

> It was far from my idea in writing *Brown* that this background pattern of conflicting tides in the soul of Man should ever overshadow and thus throw out of proportion the living drama of the recognizable human beings, Dion, Brown, Margaret, and Cybel. I meant it always to be mystically within and behind them, giving them a significance beyond themselves, forcing itself through them to expression in mysterious words, symbols, actions they do not themselves comprehend. And that is as clearly as I wish an audience to comprehend it. It is a Mystery....[36]

The Great God Brown, one may add, embodies a "Mystery" in the philosophic or religious sense of the word, shadowing forth what Friedrich Nietzsche described in *The Birth of Tragedy* as "*the mystery doctrine of tragedy*; the fundamental knowledge of the oneness of everything existent, the conception of individuation as the primal cause of evil, and of art as the joyous hope that the spell of individuation may be broken in augury of a restored oneness."[37] Brown's dying words may best be described only as an esoteric "parable of Dionysian wisdom": "The laughter of Heaven sows earth with a rain of tears, and out of Earth's transfigured birth-pain the laughter of Man returns to bless and play again in innumerable dancing gales of flame upon the knees of God!" (IV.ii, p.374).

In truth, Dion's death in the second act had interrupted the fitful rumblings of a laugh. Brown had begun to laugh at the beginning of the second act, proclaiming that "the streets are full of Lazaruses" (IV.i, p. 367). And in O'Neill's next play Lazarus himself rises from the grave, wracked with Zarathustrian laughter and prophesying the eternal recurrence of the dying god. If *The Great God Brown* ends with a return of Dionysus to the womb of the Great Mother, one may say that *Lazarus Laughed* attests to his rebirth.[38] It is, moreover, a rebirth in which the divisive St. Anthony aspect of the god's personality has been purged,[39] so that he has become once again the pure, ecstatic affirmer of the totality of life, the true embodiment of the higher man, the Dionysus once again welcomed by Zarathustra, who speaks thus: "How much is still possible! So *learn* to laugh away over yourselves! Lift up your hearts, you good dancers, high, higher! And do not forget good laughter. The crown of him who laughs, this rose-wreath crown: to you, my brothers, I throw this crown. Laughter I have pronounced holy; you higher men, *learn* to laugh!"[40]

With this dramatic resurrection the "Dionysian" phase of O'Neill's career attains its ultimate fruition.

NOTES

1. For a recent discussion of previous scholarship on this topic, see Egil Tornqvist, "Nietzsche and O'Neill: A Study in Affinity," *Orbis Litterarum*, XXIII, No. 2, 1968, pp. 97-126.

2. Arthur and Barbara Gelb, *O'Neill*, New York, 1960, p. 119.

3. Quoted in Tornqvist, pp. 97-98.

4. Ibid, p. 100. Tornqvist has discovered that it was Alexander Tille's translation of Zarathustra, brought out in 1896 and again in 1906, that O'Neill came across in Tucker's bookstore.

5. Barrett Clark, *Eugene O'Neill: The Man and His Plays*, rev. ed., New York, 1947, p. 25.

6. Quoted in Gelb, p. 814.

7. "*Amor Fati*: O'Neill's Lazarus as Superman and Saviour," *O'Neill: A Collection of Critical Essays*, ed. John Gassner, Englewood Cliffs, N.J., 1964, p. 74.

8. "Fusion-Point of Jung and Nietzsche, *"O'Neill and His Plays*, ed., Oscar Cargill, N. Bryllion Fagin, and William J. Fisher, New York, 1963, p. 413.

9. Clark, p. 5.

10. Cargill, pp. 412-13.

11. O'Neill in a letter to George Pierce Baker dated July 16, 1914. Quoted in *O'Neill and His Plays*, ed. Cargill, p. 19.

12. Friedrich Nietzsche, *The Birth of Tragedy*, trans. Walter Kaufmann, New York, 1967, section 8, pp. 64-65.

13. Excerpted from a stage direction in *Lazarus Laughed, Nine Plays by Eugene O'Neill*, New York, 1954, II.i, p. 415.

14. Quoted by Clark from a letter written to him by O'Neill, *Eugene O'Neill: The Man and His Plays*, p. 59.

15. Eugene O'Neill, *Ten "Lost Plays,"* New York, 1964, p. 53.

16. *Desire Under the Elms, Nine Plays*, III.i, p. 189.

17. Quoted in *O'Neill and His Plays*, ed. Cargill, p. 104.

18. *The Birth of Tragedy*, section 10, p. 73.

19. Quoted in *O'Neill and His Plays*, ed. Cargill, pp. 125-26.

20. *Long Day's Journey Into Night*, New Haven, 1956, IV, p. 153.

21. *More Stately Mansions*, ed. Donald Gallup, New Haven, 1964, III.ii, p. 185.

22. *Thus Spoke Zarathustra*, trans. Walter Kaufmann, New York, 1966, p. 78.

23. Quoted in Tornqvist, p. 98. On this point I am in agreement with William Brashear, "The Wisdom of Silenus in O'Neill's *Iceman*," *American Literature*, May, 1964, pp. 180-88, p. 188. Brashear discusses some aspects of *The Iceman Cometh* in relation to *The Birth of Tragedy*, but oddly enough concludes that it would be a serious mistake to maintain that Nietzsche is the theoretic key to O'Neill's work (p. 187). On that we disagree.

24. *Servitude, Ten "Lost Plays,"* III, pp. 280-81.

25. *Ibid.*, p. 294.

26. From an interview published in *The New York Herald Tribune*, March 16, 1924. Quoted in *O'Neill and His Plays*, ed. Cargill, p. 111.

27. Quoted in Kenneth Macgowan, *The Theatre of Tomorrow*, New York, 1921, pp. 273-74. O'Neill, Macgowan and Jones were associates in the management of the Greenwich Village Theatre from 1923-27.

28. Quoted in *O'Neill and His Plays*, ed. Cargill, pp. 121-22.

29. Quoted in Gelb, p. 578.

30. From a letter by O'Neill published in *The New York Evening Post*, February 13, 1926; reprinted in Toby Cole, *Playwrights on Playwriting*, New York, 1961, p. 237.

31. *The Great God Brown, Nine Plays by Eugene O'Neill*, "Prologue," p. 318. Subsequent references to *The Great God Brown* are drawn from this edition and will be cited parenthetically in the text.

32. Cole, p. 238.

33. D.H. Lawrence, "Pan in America," *Phoenix: The Posthumous Papers of D.H. Lawrence*, ed. Edward D. McDonald, London, 1961, p. 23.

34. Eugene M. Waith, "Eugene O'Neill: An Exercise in Unmasking," *O'Neill: A Collection of Critical Essays*, p. 37.

35. Francis M. Cornford, *The Origin of Attic Comedy*, Garden City, N.Y., 1961, p. 41.

36. Cole, p. 239.

37. *The Birth of Tragedy*, section 10, p. 74.

38. Edwin Engel, *The Haunted Heroes of Eugene O'Neill*, Cambridge, Mass., 1953, p. 177.

39. Sophus Keith Winther, *Eugene O'Neill A Critical Study*, New York, 1934, p. 96.

40. *Thus Spoke Zarathustra*, pp. 295-96.

Modern Drama, 15 (September 1973): 129-140.

After the Battle

J. Brooks Atkinson

Curiously enough, *Marco Millions*, in which Mr. O'Neill thumbs his nose at the modern American Babbitt, stands as the only play infected with the modish point of view. Into his character he has gathered all the bluff good humor, swank, cheap ethics, sentimentalities and mercantile crudities that have been freely knocked about ever since Sinclair Lewis set up his Babbitt several years ago.

To dismiss *Marco Millions* as hackneyed and unoriginal, however, is to be as obtuse as Babbitt himself and to ignore the more illuminating fact that Mr. O'Neill's treatment of the character exalts it above satire to tragedy. He does not interpret it in flat modern terms. By holding it in sharp focus against the rich wisdom of the great Kublai Kaan, the oriental splendor of Cathay and the gracious loveliness of Princess Kukachin, Mr. O'Neill transmutes it into the perennial tragedy of the greedy cheapjack in flippant contact with his betters. Marco's personal tragedy is implied in the tenders of affection he does not comprehend—in his "spiritual hump," his dull, mundane worldliness. But the tragedy of the self-seeker inevitably extends to his victims. And so Mr. O'Neill's Babbitt unwittingly kills the spirit of a Princess and breaks the heart of a wise pitying ruler. Receiving news of the despairing Princess, the Great Kaan muses sadly:

> My hideous suspicion is that God is only an infinite, insane energy which creates and destroys without other purpose than to pass eternity in avoiding thought. Then the stupid man becomes the perfect Incarnation of Omnipotence and the Polos are the true children of God! Ha! How long before we shall be permitted to die, my friend? I begin to resent life as the insult of an ignoble inferior with whom it is a degradation to fight!

Guzzling, gourmandizing, rattling his purse and clasping his fat, insensate wench to his bosom, Marco safe in Venice never suspects how fatally he has wounded the children of the East. Thus Mr. O'Neill employs the Babbitt motive to express profounder thought and more exquisite feeling than it has ever disclosed before.

If these qualities leave no impression on some who are now visiting the Guild Theatre, Mr. O'Neill cannot escape all the blame. He has not adorned his play with the many colored surface the theme deserves. Behind the succession of scenes and the dialogue of *Marco Millions* one feels the force, restlessness, perception, pity and anger of a poet and mystic—one who belongs among the great thinkers who are skeptical of experience and reason. For, like Thoreau, Mr. O'Neill is now concerned with the wonders that no intelligence can understand. To carry the playgoer with him to the imaginative world of his feeling he must speak in winged numbers. He must employ the magic of form, elegance, and coherence. Too much of *Marco* seems flat and perfunctory in verbal expression and too much of it presupposes a sensitivity equal to Mr. O'Neill's. Although he is writing satire he is no wit, and he is a humorist only in the mirthless sense of the word. One does not expect his dialogue to snap with the pop of smart remarks. But if he is to enrapture the casual playgoer with the beauties of his mystic ideas he must write with more grace and virtuosity; he must allure when he cannot explain. *Marco Millions* lacks the ultimate refinement of artistry. In comparison with *The Fountain*, which had a similar episodic form, *Marco Millions* represents Mr. O'Neill infinitely more lucid and poised and much more mature in his sense of values. The ruggedness, the passion the sincerity come through. The thinking is orderly. The Guild has blessed it with a gorgeous, versatile production and idiomatic acting. Costumes of refulgent splendor and bizarre variety, brilliantly composed groupings of Oriental figures, gongs, bells, chants, dirges, voices in chorus and mysterious declamation—stimulate the eye and ear and communicate the nuances of Mr. O'Neill's emotion....

New York Times, January 22, 1928.

The Theatres: *Strange Interlude*

Percy Hammond

One of the complaints about the Drama is that its stories stop but do not end. The final curtains fall in the midst of things, shutting us off from information concerning what happens to the characters after the playwrights have dropped them at 11 o'clock. Usually it is not a matter of importance, since two hours is enough of them, and in case we are interested in their future we can take it home with us and do as we like with it. In *Strange Interlude* Mr. O'Neill, having got us all wrought up about the people in his play, saves us the trouble involved in wondering what befalls them in later days. When *Strange Interlude* stops it is finished and you know that you have learned everything there is to learn about Nina Leeds and the men who have acted in the melodrama of her soul. They are all living corpses as the theater lights go out, excepting possibly Nina's son, who promises to become an aviating Babbitt. Nina, perhaps, is committing suicide at this very moment, but it is of little consequence. Mr. O'Neill has squeezed every

Strange Interlude

drop of life from her, as well as from the others, and their hereafter is as arid as a mummy's. Her husband dead, her pseudo-lover demolished, and her illegitimate son an ephemeral humming-bird, she slinks into the ashen arms of an aged suitor, there to extinguish her dying embers in his dusts.

The dénouement of *Strange Interlude* is thus less arbitrary than is usual, since its erring woman vanishes from our view without adopting the playwrights's customary expedient of sudden death or a violent, illogical and happy "ending." She fades away, ironically, and as she does so you feel satisfied if not satiated. You have peered into the open secrets of her interesting soul and body, and what you have seen is enough. In telling the tale of Nina Leeds and her strange interlude, Mr. O'Neill has broken the Drama's shackles and escaped from its person more successfully than other fugitives from its many walls. In the Theatre Guild, he has a friendly warder which permits him to be an undisciplined "trusty," knowing that, no matter how far he may stray, he will still retain a connection with the cells and iron bars of the Stage.

Although Mr. O'Neill had done everything he can to spare us the task of thinking, *Strange Interlude* is not a play for lazy drama lovers. His unlimited employment of "asides" to describe the unspoken thoughts of his character is more of a whip than a cushion to our imagination, and it keeps us busy. A five hour recital, with a hurried intermission for dinner, demands an alert and industrious audience. This it received on Monday night. Since the performance began in the afternoon, the Guilders attended the first part in day clothing and then made haste to change into evening dress for the second, which commenced at 9 p.m. And, as they went away from the John Golden Theater a 11 o'clock or thereabouts, they were a tired but happy band, having witnessed a complete and agitating drama, brilliantly acted and produced.

It is a tough job that Mr. O'Neill assigns to Miss Lynn Fontanne as the strange, irregular and rhythmic lady of his play. The daughter of a professor of dead languages in a New England university, she permits Gordon Shaw, her lover, to go to war without having given herself to him. He is killed in battle and thereafter she loathes herself, her body and her conservative father for their cowardice. Brooding over her failure, she decides morbidly to become a martyr, and as a nurse in a hospital for maimed soldiers she bestows herself upon this, that and the other crippled warrior. She explains her emotions and their frustration in a speech like this:

> I think I had some idea that Gordon wanted me to avenge him upon my body—sacrifice it on the altar of patriotism, as he did, or something silly like that. And as I hated it for its cowardice in not giving itself to him, I, too, wanted to punish it, to humiliate its purity....
> I knew it was a stupid, morbid business, that I was more maimed than they were, really, that the war had blown my heart and insides out! And I knew, too, that I was torturing these tortured men, morbidly supersensitive already, that they knew I was sick with pity for myself, that the body I gave them was as gutted of passion and joy and love as a violated grave, that they loathed the cruel mockery of my gift! Yet I kept on, from one to one, like a stupid, driven animal.

Then groping through Mr. O'Neill's dark blind-alleys, Nina, in her search for life, marries a likable weakling, a pal of her lover's, in the hope that she may have a child who will belong to her dead hero, to herself and to her husband. As that promise is about to be fulfilled her husband's mother tells her that it cannot be. The boy's ancestry is rotten with insanity and any babe of which he is the inspiration is liable to be a lunatic. Here is where *Strange Interlude* becomes abnormally majestic. Nina's mother-in-law (Miss Helen Westley) advises her that happiness is holiness, no difference how sharp and rough are the detours. She suggests that Nina have a baby by a wholesome outsider and give credit for that achievement to her vain and probably diseased husband. A handsome doctor (Mr. Glenn Anders) being near by, is explicably willing to be a guinea pig in the experiment, and so a healthy boy is born, the combined mental and physical product of several men.

Nina falls in love with the illegal father of her child, and he with her. Therefore there is the devil to pay, with Nina's neurotic soul and person madly tossed in nervous whirlpool of faithfulness and infidelity. Mr. O'Neill exposes her in all her nooks and crannies, and if he had searched the stage over from Bernhardt to Elsie Ferguson he could not have found an actress so competent to play Nina Leeds as Miss Fontanne is. There isn't a moment in the complex characterization that Miss Fontanne is not a miracle of illusion. She decants Mr. O'Neill's abnormal poetry into sane, believable and musical prose, and I think she is a greater figure than her author intended her to be. The scene, for instance, in which Miss Helen Westley, as her husband's mother, tells her that she must kill her unborn child because its father's blood is tainted with idiocy, is acted by Miss Fontanne so validly that you forget the accomplishments of all the other First Actresses, from Duse to Madge Kennedy. The associate actors are fine—as they have to be under the Guild's scrupulous baton, and if you are a semi-nervous patron of the theater, here is an opportunity for you to invest time, trouble, money and faith in a long, complete and agitating study of life as it is seen through Mr. O'Neill's brooding and acid eyes.

New York Herald, February 5, 1928.

Eugene O'Neill and the Guild

Barrett H. Clark

Let me begin my remarks on *Strange Interlude* by stating that the producers have spared nothing in doing ample justice to the play. There have been precious few plays that required more skill and a finer imagination than this ambitious and subtle play in nine acts. Philip Moeller has already a great deal to his credit as a director, but he never did anything that required greater intelligence and a more sympathetic understanding than *Strange Interlude*. His direction brought into relief as much as was humanly possible in a work that has so little of the theatrically conventional. You always know just what the players are doing; they interpret without appearing to do so. There is precious little of that "pointing," straining effect, that has often been apparent in the other Guild productions. One small objection I have, and one alone: all the actors speak a bastard sort of British English, an accent that sounds too much like Broadway trying to ape Piccadilly. O'Neill's characters are American, and no honest-to-God American says "bean" when he means "been" (bin).

What is this much-discussed *Strange Interlude*? It is many things, almost as many things as it has been called. The first important point to make is that from 5:30 p.m. until after eleven, except for intermission for supper, it holds the audience. Yet not through any sort of theatrical trickery. It is not the story, which could easily have been condensed into three acts; it is not the strangeness of the asides and monologues (that novelty wears off in five minutes); it is simply the triumph of O'Neill's art, his extraordinary gift for understanding and laying bare some of the complexities of the human mind and heart. He was clearly unwilling to make use of the conventional dramatic form which, in its latest manifestations does not admit the aside and the soliloquy, and refuse to allow the dramatist much more that two or two and a half hours' time.

He had, therefore, with a fine and characteristic disregard of current fashions, elaborated what would otherwise be a conventional plot into nine acts, with a total playing time almost twice as long as we are accustomed to. Why not? There is far more to hold the attention in *Strange Interlude* than there is in *Parsifal*. There is less literature but far more drama than there is in *Faust*. *Strange Interlude* carries four characters through their chief spiritual crises during some twenty-seven or -eight years. Nina Leeds, daughter of a college professor, loses her husband (someone coughed in front of me, and it may be that Gordon was only her fiancé) shortly after he goes away as an aviator. Her puritanical father has prevented the consummation of their union and this precipitates her decision to leave home, at first to become a nurse. She is actually in quest of satisfaction of her more or less imperfectly felt needs. From this point on she begins to develop into a sort of synthesis of the eternally feminine. She is a manifestation of the *Erdgeist*, the Cybel of *The Great God Brown*, mother, wife, mistress, prostitute, materialist idealist: in short, the artist's conception of Woman. Into her life are woven strands from the lives of many men: of Gordon (a romantic memory and an ideal); of the patient, mother-ridden Charles Marsden; of Sam, her husband; of Edmund Darrell, her lover; and later of her son, Gordon. For this woman no one man is enough. The marvelous creature, endowed with an inordinate thirst for life assumes the proportions of a superwoman and becomes a symbol of all humanity. With aspirations that can never be quite fulfilled, held in check by inhibitions driven onward by appetites, she is the incarnation of vitality, a creature that must meddle in the lives of others in order that her own life may be filled to overflowing. No one is a match for her; nothing arrests her progress, except time itself. At last she is overcome by time, and by that very spirit of youth (in the person of her son) that urged her on to rebel. The young Gordon and the girl he is determined to marry leave her, even as she had left her helpless father.

This, essentially, is the "story" of *Strange Interlude*. There are several plot incidents, absorbing in themselves, but utilized only in order to throw the character of Nina into higher relief. As I think back over the incidents of the play, I see in it no "moral," no "intention," indeed very little of any definite philosophy. It was O'Neill's aim to expose imaginatively, a chain of events in which a few people exhibit to us their thoughts and motives over a long period of years. Life begins; it offers us problems, joys, tragedies; it seems to take shape occasionally as a thing of beauty, but oftener as a senseless and cruel joke, yet it is a fascinating playground; the puppets are momentarily self-important with their little schemes for overcoming death and unhappiness and then toward the end they lose bit by bit their desires and the fierce impulses of youth, declining slowly into a sunset period in which peace alone seems worth having. Thus Nina seems to transcend her sex, to embody and be identified with the life instinct, as she dominates each situation in order not to be dominated it. Because she is first conceived as a woman, each situation in her life is symbolized by a man, possessing something that she needs, has needed, or will need. In the case of Marsden, we see her carefully appraising him in the first act. Marking him out for use at some future time; at the end of the ninth act, when everything else has passed, she falls into his protecting arms, there to end in peace the last days of her life. This last situation strangely reminded me of the end of *Faust*, but here Marsden is Gretchen and Nina Faust.

I have not yet touched on the essential element in *Strange Interlude*—the thing that makes it a masterly creation. This is no more nor less than the dramatist's divination of the motives of his people. As I have already said, he could easily have told his story in three acts, but he used nine in order that he might not be forced to say, "If I had had time, I might have told you everything essential about these people." He did have time, because he took it. Two years ago he told me in detail what he was at work on, and answered my conventional question "Why nine acts?" with "Why not? Dramatists allow their characters to tell *some* things, why shouldn't I make them tell more?"

We are almost at once let into the secrets of these characters; they tell us a great deal of what they think and feel. Not everything, of course, for that would be impossible, but surely enough for the purpose in hand. The thoughts expressed aloud cannot at most constitute more than a fraction of those half-thoughts, hints, shadowings that haunt the subconscious mind, but they are enough for O'Neill's purpose. Shakespeare did much the some thing and so did Goethe. O'Neill has gone a little farther and used the device somewhat more realistically. Simple and crude as it is, the device is surprisingly satisfactory. Hence there is no sort of surprise in the ordinary sense of the word: no suspense, and no curiosity of the sort aroused in conventional fiction. But I ask you, is there anything more surprising or more highly charged with the elements of suspense than a human being? Conrad knew this, and because Conrad knew a great deal about human beings, he often told his plot in the first two or three pages. O'Neill knows that *Strange Interlude* is heavy with suspense and for this reason he throws overboard all the devices by which dramatists usually stimulate it. He never for a moment releases the tension in his passionate pursuit of the mainsprings of human activity; this is his aim throughout. Like a surgeon he cuts deep, knowing always just what he is after.

While he has succeeded in exhibiting a remarkable series of events, each of which throws into relief some quintessential characteristic of one or more persons; while he has conceived largely and written nobly, I feel that *Strange Interlude* is not the perfect work it might have been. For one thing, I am convinced that the shade of Strindberg hovers a little too close over it all: there is something strained, a bit diagrammatic and intellectualized in the character of Nina. As presented, she is rather too special—too much the female of the species. If Nina is the *Erdgeist*, she is at the same the Earth Mother. Or rather, she ought to be. Woman, the beast of prey, is Strindberg's invention, and I don't think O'Neill's vision of the world is as narrow and warped as that of the Swedish poet.

And technically, what of the asides and the nine acts? Is it always necessary to express aloud what one thinks and feels? I believe that perhaps one-third of all the words that were not intended to be heard by the other characters might have been omitted without the loss of anything essential. O'Neill has overworked his device.

Finally, there is something lacking in the last two acts. They are somewhat repetitious, and could both have been either omitted or condensed into one.

Such are my impressions of a profound play. I must read it when it is printed for there is much that requires further thought.

Still O'Neill marches on. In New York we have *Marco* and *Strange Interlude*; Gilmore Brown is about to produce *Lazarus Laughed*. A new play, *Dynamo*, is reported to be nearly ready. There is a dramatic version of the *Book of Revelations*....And there are pessimists who bewail the decline of the drama!

Drama, March 1928.

Strange Interlude and Schopenhauer

Doris M. Alexander

Whether critics admire or deplore *Strange Interlude*, they rarely give it credit for a clear-cut intellectual design. Barrett Clark's statement "I see in the play no 'moral,' no 'intention,' indeed very little of any definite philosophy"[1] is, perhaps, typical. If critics do see an over-all intellectual design in *Strange Interlude*, they assume, as does Joseph Wood Krutch, that "the intellectual framework is supplied by Freudian psychology."[2] The purpose of this paper will be to demonstrate that O'Neill designed *Strange Interlude* according to a predominant intellectual pattern, and that this pattern expresses not Freud's psychology, but Schopenhauer's philosophy.

Dependable evidence that O'Neill was familiar with Schopenhauer's philosophy at the time he wrote *Strange Interlude* appears in his foreword to Benjamin De Casseres's *Anathema! Litanies of Negation*, which was published in 1928, the same year as the play. Here O'Neill writes of De Casseres's intellectual forebears: "If such genealogy counts for anything, he can be traced, among the philosophers, to Schopenhauer and Nietzsche, a hybrid product mixing despair and rhapsody."[3] It seems reasonable to assume that O'Neill must have been familiar with Schopenhauer in order to recognize his ideas in another man's work, and this assumption seems particularly plausible since his recognition of Nietzsche's ideas was certainly based on first-hand knowledge.[4] However, even if there were no external evidence that O'Neill knew Schopenhauer, such a knowledge is clearly indicated by the pervasive and consistent presence of the Schopenhauer *Weltanschauung* in *Strange Interlude*.

The whole treatment of love in *Strange Interlude*, specifically the love of Nina and Darrell, is entirely in line with Schopenhauer's view in *The Metaphysics of the Love of the Sexes*. There Schopenhauer points out that women "are principally won by the strength of the man, and the courage which is connected with this...." The physical qualities women desire in a mate are largely those that echo physical strength. "The woman is won especially by firmness of will, decision, and courage...." The one quality women are distinctly repelled by is a lack of virility: "women often love ugly men, but never an unmanly man...."[5] Nina confirms Schopenhauer entirely in her choice of a mate. In the first scenario for *Strange Interlude*, O'Neill gives a clear statement of Nina's basis for choosing Darrell as a mate. "She had got a feeling of strength from him, from mastery of life, of health and will and courage—the same feeling though different, she had got from Gordon."[6] In the published play Nina's attraction to Darrell's virility appears in her thoughts while she is shaking hands with him shortly before asking him to help her beget a healthy child. "Strong hands like Gordon's...take hold of you...not like Sam's...yielding fingers that let you fall back into yourself."[7] Just as her admiration for Gordon and Darrell is based on their strength, so her contempt for Sam is based on his weakness. This contempt is expressed more violently in other parts of the play, for instance, in her comment on Sam at the beginning of Act IV. "How weak he is!...he'll never do anything...never give me my desire."[8] Her contempt for Marsden, too, stems from a perception of his weakness. When Marsden takes her hand in his during Act VI, she thinks cruelly: "Pah!...how limp his hands are!...his eyes so shrinking!...is it possible he loves me?...like that?...what a sickening idea!"[9] Clearly Nina is attracted, as are all women according to Schopenhauer, by men of strength and courage.

Of course, the idea that women are attracted to men of strength and courage is too commonplace to serve, in itself, as evidence that *Strange Interlude* is based on Schopenhauer. Only in its relationship to the whole depiction of love in the play does it take on significance. Darrell's love for Nina follows Schopenhauer's theory as faithfully as does Nina's love for Darrell. According to Schopenhauer, the force that determines love is entirely beyond reason and totally indifferent to the temperamental and intellectual compatibility of the parties involved. Hence, "great passions," for Schopenhauer, "arise, as a rule, at the first glance."[10] Darrell's love for Nina, although not aroused in full force at first glance, is based, like love at first sight, entirely on physical attraction unqualified by temperamental or intellectual considerations. As he protests, when Nina urges him to marry her: "Be sensible, for God's sake! We're absolutely unsuited to each other! I don't admire your character! I don't respect you! I know too much about your past!"[11] Since Darrell's love for Nina is based on nothing in her character, its basis, apparently, is the sex urge. Just so, for Schopenhauer love is merely an expression of the sex impulse: "all love, however, ethereally it may bear itself, is rooted in the sexual impulse alone, nay, it absolutely is only a more definitely determined, specialized, and indeed in the strictest sense individualized sexual impulse."[12]

The course of Nina and Darrell's love illustrates perfectly the philosophical assumptions behind Schopenhauer's idea that love is simply a specialized form of the sex impulse. For Schopenhauer, the sex impulse itself is what man perceives, through ideas, of the *Ding an sich*, the reality beyond the world of phenomena, which Schopenhauer calls the "will" or "the will to live." The sex impulse in general is the phenomenal expression of the will to live, and love (the sex impulse directed to a specific individual) is the expression of the will to live in the form of the child who will be created by the mating of the lovers.[13] The will to live causes a man to love a woman in order to produce a specific type of offspring.[14] Man is serving the species, not himself, when he falls in love. Since the will to live cannot rely on man's consciousness to serve the needs of the species, it endows him with an instinctive illusion that he is serving himself, although actually he may be destroying all his personal goals in the service of the species:

> ...nature can only attain its ends by implanting a certain illusion in the individual, on account of which that which is only a good for the species appears to him as a good for himself, so that when he serves the species he imagines he is serving himself; in which process a mere chimera, which vanishes immediately afterwards, floats before him, and takes the place of a real thing as a motive.[15]

In the case of love, man is given the illusion that the consummation of his passion will bring him great happiness. "It is a voluptuous illusion which leads the man to believe he will find a greater pleasure in the arms of a woman whose beauty appeals to him than in those of any other; or which indeed...firmly convinces him that the possession of her will ensure him excessive happiness.[16] Just such an illusion takes hold of Darrell and Nina at the moment they have agreed, so that Nina may bear a child, to become lovers. Although the situation they are entering, a temporary, adulterous union for the purpose of producing a child, hardly seems to promise bliss, both are suddenly filled with the conviction that they will be happy. The words "happiness" and "happy" are repeated more and more frequently as Nina and Darrell approach the point of agreement to become lovers. When they have agreed, Act IV ends with a crescendo of repeated anticipations of joy.

> Darrell. (*suddenly falling on his knees and taking her hand in both of his and kissing it humbly—with a sob*) Yes—yes, Nina—yes—for your happiness—in that spirit! (*Thinking—fiercely triumphant*) I shall be happy for a while!...
> Nina. (*raising her head—thinking—proudly triumphant*) I shall be happy!...I shall make my husband happy!...[17]

Knowing Schopenhauer, one would not find it difficult to forecast the ultimate outcome of Nina and Darrell's extravagant expectations of happiness. The expectations, of course, are simply an illusion, a "chimera" that will vanish as soon as the will to live has achieved its objective, the production of another generation. It is not surprising, then, to learn that Nina and Darrell's "afternoons of happiness" are "paid for with years of pain."[18] For Schopenhauer, the fulfillment of desire cannot conceivably bring happiness because pleasure is negative, merely absence of pain, and pain, yearning, is the fundamental condition of life. "No attained object of desire can give lasting satisfaction, but merely a fleeting gratification; it is like the alms thrown to the beggar, that keeps him alive today that his misery may be prolonged till the morrow."[19] Certainly Nina and Darrell's love brings only a fleeting gratification that keeps them bound together through long years of mutual suffering. This suffering might have been predicted not only from Schopenhauer's assumption that no fulfilled desire can bring happiness, but also from his even more pessimistic idea that the satisfaction of love is actually most likely to bring unhappiness because the demands of the will to live are always indifferent and frequently hostile to the individual, rational goals of the lover. "Not only...has the unsatisfied passion of love sometimes a tragic issue, but the satisfied passion also leads oftener to unhappiness than to happiness. For its demands often conflict so much with the personal welfare of him who is concerned that they undermine it...."[20] In *Strange Interlude* the years of pain that follow the consummation of Nina's and Darrell's love are caused more by the way their love damages their personal welfare than by the fact that the satisfaction of the love cannot bring them happiness. Certainly Darrell's love for Nina is antithetical to his personal welfare, for it takes his son from him, keeps him from establishing a home and family of his own, and destroys his career.

Darrell's degeneration under the influence of love is one of the most extraordinary occurrences in *Strange Interlude*. Promptly and efficiently with the onset of love his career is destroyed. The remarkable thing about this degeneration is the fact that O'Neill gives no other cause for it than the love itself. As soon as he realizes that he loves Nina, Darrell senses the danger to his individual, rational goal, his career....For this reason, tinctured with a concern for Sam, he flees to Europe in order to "study!"....But he is already doomed. A year later he returns to Nina haggard and beaten, confessing openly, "I didn't study! I didn't live! I longed for you—and suffered!"[21] So his career begins to deteriorate from the moment he first feels love, and from this point on it steadily decomposes until finally he abandons his once brilliantly promising career in medicine to play a very minor role in biological research.

A reader of the play, innocent of the Schopenhauerian assumptions underlying much of its action, might question precisely why love is so destructive to Darrell's career. Of course, it may be argued that he is emotionally unable to work during the period he spends in Europe, away from Nina. But when he has returned and has become Nina's lover, no real reason appears for his inability to carry on a career. At no time does O'Neill present Darrell in a genuine conflict between love and work. Although Darrell leaves his research appointment at "the Institute" (which he considers his big opportunity)[22] in order to flee to Europe, no mention is made in the play of a damaging break with the Institute because of it, and O'Neill never makes clear why Darrell cannot resume his career, either at this institute or another, or why, since he receives a large inheritance at the time he becomes Nina's lover, he cannot at least set up his own research laboratory within easy walking distance of Nina. In view of his early devotion to work, Darrell's complete collapse at the first gust of love seems improbable. As the play is written, Darrell's degeneration takes place wholly because of his love for Nina, not even because of conflict arising from the particularly untidy role he is forced to play in love. It seems in this case as if O'Neill, entirely possessed with the Schopenhauerian view of love as most frequently destructive to individual, personal goals, neglected to show in concrete dramatic terms precisely why this is the case; the situation of an unreasoning love was, perhaps, self-evidently destructive for O'Neill, who was working on Schopenhauer's assumptions.

At any rate, the central incident of *Strange Interlude*, the love of Nina and Darrell, seems entirely illustrative of the Schopenhauer view of love in which individuals are swept into the love relationship in spite of their rational desires, their personal welfare, all individual considerations, and under the illusion that their love will bring them happiness, are destroyed. All their striving for joy is in vain, for "so long as our consciousness is filled by our will, so long as we are given up to the throng of desires with their constant hopes and fears, so long as we are the subject of willing, we can never have lasting happiness nor peace."[23]

During the same period that Nina and Darrell are preoccupied with "willing," with fruitless striving for happiness in love, Sam Evans, Nina's husband, is preoccupied with an equally meaningless form of striving, the pursuit of money. Through Sam's financial striving, O'Neill presents a critique of the American businessman and his values, a critique stated explicitly in Marsden's commentary on Sam: "What a fount of meaningless energy he's tapped!...always on the go...typical terrible child of the age...universal slogan, keep moving...."[24] From the over-all characterization of Sam, it is clear that these are O'Neill's views as well as Marsden's. Marsden's soliloquy stresses meaningless energy and a valueless striving as typical characteristics of the American businessman. Criticism of the bourgeoisie on these grounds was fairly common during the twenties. However, the idea of meaningless striving is also reminiscent of Schopenhauer's will to live. That O'Neill saw the meaningless striving of the American businessman as an expression of Schopenhauer's will to live seems evident from part of O'Neill's description of the stage set for Act V in the original longhand script of *Strange Interlude*. There O'Neill wrote of the Evans living room, the outer symbol of Sam's financial striving: "there is an atmosphere of vitality about this room, of a rank weedy life reproducing itself with the vulgar irresistibility of health. It is not sad, it has no past to think with, it is unreflectively loosely living and moving on—somewhere, because movement is the goal."[25] The concept of a life force "reproducing itself with the vulgar irresistibility of health" immediately brings to mind Schopenhauer's will to live, a force with no goal but perpetual striving, perpetual reproduction of itself. Of course, this description in itself is not sufficient evidence for assuming that O'Neill designed Sam's meaningless energy and goalless financial striving as an illustration of Schopenhauer's will to live. But a great deal of support is lent to this assumption by one of the speeches in *Marco*

Millions, O'Neill's full-length satire of bourgeois values, completed in 1925. In this play the wise Kubla Kaan, musing on the destruction of the Princess Kukachin, thinks: "My hideous suspicion is that God is only an infinite, insane energy which creates and destroys without other purpose than to pass eternity in avoiding thought. Then the stupid man becomes the Perfect Incarnation of Omnipotence and the Polos are the true children of God!"[26] The Kaan's "God" appears to be, from this description, Schopenhauer's will to live; the Polos, of course, represent the bourgeoisie. The businessman, then, is the true child of the will to live, the true expression of meaningless striving. If it is safe to assume that O'Neill described the American businessman in *Marco Millions* as an incarnation of Schopenhauer's will to live, it is certainly probable that he had the same concept in mind when he designed the meaningless striving of his businessman in *Strange Interlude*, a play that consistently reflects Schopenhauer's ideas. Sam Evans's financial striving, along with the love of Nina and Darrell, appears to be an illustration of the Schopenhauer *Weltanschauung*, in which human life is impelled by a will to live which is nothing but meaningless striving perpetually reproducing itself.

Meaningless striving, by its very nature, cannot reach a satisfactory goal. It is therefore not surprising that the characters in *Strange Interlude* reach no such goal. The conclusion of *Strange Interlude* has caused much commentary because, as John Gassner declared, it "reaches no climax except that of exhaustion."[27] Yet, in terms of Schopenhauer's philosophy, the ending O'Neill has given it represents far more than "exhaustion"—is, in fact, the most meaningful ending he could have given a play based on Schopenhauer's ideas. O'Neill could not have had his characters attain any earthly goal, for such an attainment would not be a climax, but one of the fleeting gratifications that serve as impulse to the perpetual striving; he could not have had his chief characters die, for death in Schopenhauer's terms, is reabsorption into the will to live, an eternity of meaningless striving.[28] For Schopenhauer there is only one way to escape from, one way to triumph over the meaningless striving of the will to live, and that is by a denial of the will to live. It is by a denial of the will to live on the part of his principal characters that O'Neill concludes *Strange Interlude*.

The conclusion of the play consists of Nina's final marriage to Charlie Marsden, the celibate novelist. This marriage demonstrates Nina's resignation from sex, love, passion, a resignation she begins to manifest at the age of thirty-five, when she is already looking forward to the menopause: "I'm thirty-five...five years more...at forty a woman has finished living...life passes by her...she rots away in peace!" Then she adds "intensely," "I want to rot away in peace!...I'm sick of the fight for happiness!"[29] Clearly Nina identifies life and "the struggle for happiness" with the sex life of the individual. The theory behind this identification certainly reflects Schopenhauer. According to Schopenhauer, the principal aim of the will to live is reproduction. Once it has accomplished this aim in a specific individual, it is, essentially, finished with him:

> The sexual impulse...proves itself the decided and strongest assertion of life by the fact that to man in a state of nature, as to the brutes, it is the final end, the highest goal of life...Nature also, the inner being of which is the will to live itself, impels with all her

power both man and the brute towards propagation. Then it has attained its end with the individual, and is quite indifferent to its death, for, as the will to live, it cares only for the preservation of the species, the individual is nothing to it.[30]

Nina's assumption that sex, and hence life, will be over promptly at the age of forty, astonishing to the unphilosophical mind, is perfectly in line with Schopenhauer's view of life. The menopause (which O'Neill seems to place exactly at forty) is the conclusion of the reproductive function in woman. Since the reproductive function is the main manifestation of the will to live, its disappearance naturally will be accompanied by a corresponding diminution of the will to live. For one who accepts Schopenhauer's premises, it follows that after forty Nina should desire nothing but to "rot away in peace."

It is extremely significant, moreover, that Nina consummates her desire to rot away in peace through marriage to Charlie Marsden. During her period of sexual life, Nina is revolted by the idea of marriage to Charlie, but as she nears the menopause, she thinks, "...dear Charlie, what a perfect lover he would make for one's old age!...what a perfect lover when one was past passion!"[31] Here she shows intuitive wisdom, for, in terms of Schopenhauer's philosophy, Charlie is the only character in the play who may be associated with true peace. No peace is possible, and hence no true well-being is possible for those acting in accordance with the will to live. Particularly in sexual love, the strongest assertion of the will to live, no peace is possible. For Schopenhauer the only possibility for peace in human life is the denial of the will to live.

> He...who has attained to the denial of the will to live, however, poor, joyless, and full or privation his condition may appear when looked at externally, is yet filled with inward joy and the true peace of heaven. It is not the restless strain of life, the jubilant delight which has keen suffering as its preceding or succeeding condition, in the experience of the man who loves life; but it is a peace that cannot be shaken, a deep rest and inward serenity, a state which we cannot behold without the greatest longing when it is brought before our eyes or our imagination....[32]

The most important step in denial of the will to live is, of course, sexual chastity, for the sexual impulse is direct expression of the will to live. "Voluntary and complete chastity is the first step in asceticism or the denial of the will to live."[33] Marsden, except for one adolescent experience with a "dollar tart," has lived a celibate life, and his complete sexlessness at the end of the play makes him a perfect companion for anyone interested in denying the will to live.

Marsden himself, as depicted by O'Neill, is clearly aware of his role as a source of the peace that comes from denial of the will to live. He has reached resignation, from which point he is able to view the struggles of the will to live with genuine indifference. Witnessing the love-making of Madeline and Gordon, shortly after Sam's funeral, Marsden thinks, as Schopenhauer might have, "...what have the living to do with the dead?...his duty is to love that life may keep on living." Marsden's recognition of the ultimate aim of the will to live expressed through this love-making is evident when he thinks, "But I'll have to interrupt their biological preparations." Whereas at one time Marsden would have been envious of this passionate loving, he now can look upon it with smiling indifference. "...but now I know that dear old Charlie...yes, poor dear old Charlie!—passed beyond desire, has all the luck at last!"[34] In very much the same manner, Schopenhauer depicts the man who has reached peace as looking back smilingly on the delusions of life: "He now looks back smiling and at rest on the delusions of this world, which once were able to move and agonise his spirit also...."[35] So complete is Marsden's consciousness of his role that he even recognizes Darrell as still concerned with willing and therefore unable to give Nina peace: "...why doesn't he go?...she doesn't love him any more...even now he's all heat and energy and the tormenting drive of noon... can't he see she is in love with evening?" Nina herself is consciously aware that it is Charlie who will bring her peace. "Peace!...yes...that is all I desire...I can no longer imagine happiness...Charlie has found peace."[36] The last words an audience of *Strange Interlude* hears are Marsden's: "God bless dear old Charlie...who, passed beyond desire, has all the luck at last!"[37]

The ending of *Strange Interlude* follows Schopenhauer's philosophy consistently to its ultimate conclusions. This consistent similarity could be accepted as decisive evidence that *Strange Interlude* expresses Schopenhauer, were it not that many of these ideas are not his exclusively. Much of the theory behind Nina's desire to rot away in peace appears not only in Schopenhauer, but also in Freud, and furthermore in a book by Freud, *Beyond the Pleasure Principle*, which O'Neill read.[38] In this book Freud identifies the life instincts with the sexual instincts, and connects these in turn with the "pleasure principle," or, in O'Neill's terms, "the struggle for happiness." Even Freud recognizes his close similarity to Schopenhauer in these ideas, for he remarks, almost with surprise, after formulating his theory: "...we cannot disguise...from ourselves, that we have steered unawares into the haven of Schopenhauer's philosophy...."[39] In so far as Schopenhauer's and Freud's ideas are alike in identifying life with sex and the struggle for happiness, O'Neill might have received these ideas from either one of them. Only the ways in which O'Neill departs from Freud's theory indicate that his primary source was Schopenhauer.

In his assumption that sex instincts and hence life instincts will cease promptly with the menopause, O'Neill is perfectly in line with Schopenhauer. However, Freud, who had a closer clinical contact with humanity than either Schopenhauer or O'Neill, considered the menopause not a termination of sexual desire, but a period of heightened sexual tension.[40] Surely Freud would not have believed that a woman could achieve peace by a sexless marriage at the age of forty-five after twenty years in which she had utilized both a husband and a lover to fulfil her needs. As a matter of fact, the whole concept of peace through denial of the will to live is entirely alien to psychoanalytic theory. One of the central conclusions to be drawn from Freudian theory is that mental health is predicated upon a satisfactory release of sexual tensions. It is in a blocking of the sexual instincts that Freud finds the causes of neurosis. The asceticism, the denial of the will to live in all its phases that Schopenhauer prescribes, and that O'Neill reflects in the conclusion of *Strange Interlude*, is wholly foreign to the Freudian concept of a healthy mode of adjustment. O'Neill may have been reinforced in some of his ideas by his reading of *Beyond the Pleasure Principle*, but he was certainly following the ideas as developed by Schopenhauer, not Freud, when he wrote *Strange Interlude*.

This is not, however, the only instance in *Strange Interlude* of ideas that are common to both Freud and Schopenhauer. Perhaps their major point of identity is their mutual assumption that human life is impelled by forces outside of man's reason. For Schopenhauer the impelling force behind human action is will. For Freud it is the id. The two concepts are very much alike.[41] Hence O'Neill's representation of his characters in *Strange Interlude* as helpless under the power of irrational forces might have been derived from either the philosopher or the psychologist. However, the conclusions O'Neill draws from this basic assumption about his characters depart widely from Freud, but remain in harmony with Schopenhauer. In *Strange Interlude* O'Neill emphatically rejects reason, particularly reason as expressed through science, as a means of guiding or understanding life. All of the characters are at the mercy of irrational forces, and the chief representative of the scientific approach to life, Darrell, is the most abject victim of irrational forces in the play. All his attempts to cope with life rationally and scientifically prove disastrous, so that at the end of the play he shows himself a complete convert to irrationalism in such remarks as: "Thinking doesn't matter a damn! Life is something in one cell that doesn't need to think!"[42] By the end of *Strange Interlude*, Darrell, and presumably the audience, are convinced that science is inadequate to cope with human life.

The basis on which O'Neill rejects science as a method of understanding and guiding life is very close to Schopenhauer's. Schopenhauer sees two ways of knowing, the world as idea and the world as will. The idea, perceived by the mind, is formed in terms of time, space, causality, the ways in which the mind perceives. The will is perceived by man as idea, and is also experienced directly by man, for his body is simply the "will become visible."[43] The will, for Schopenhauer, is the *Ding an sich*, the reality beyond the world as idea. The various branches of science deal only with the world as idea, only with phenomena.[44] Science cannot touch the content of phenomena, the basic reality which is the will. This conception of the role of science seems to have been O'Neill's also, if we can take it for granted, as I think we may, that he is expressing his own idea when he has Nina say: "Did you ever know a young scientist, Charlie? He believes if you pick a lie to pieces, the pieces are the truth!"[45] In Schopenhauer's terms, Nina's idea is that science deals only with manipulations of the phenomenal world, which is a "lie," for it is not the basic reality; science can only dissect phenomena, it can never arrive at truth.

The rejection of science and reason in general which O'Neill displays in *Strange Interlude* is comparable to Schopenhauer's view. Both O'Neill and Schopenhauer carry the idea that life is controlled by irrational forces to the conclusion that science is inadequate to understand and cope with life. Freud, on the other hand, carries his similar idea to no such conclusion. Although he sees irrational forces as controlling much of human life, he has firm faith in the possibility of gaining full rational control over these irrational forces. Through psychoanalysis he hopes to transfer the unconscious, the irrational, into the conscious, the rational.[46] Certainly Freud always asserts a full faith in science as a method of understanding and coping with life. Typical of his attitude is this statement made toward the end of his life. "Our best hope for the future is that the intellect—the scientific spirit, reason—should in time establish a dictatorship over the human mind."[47] Obviously, then, the intellectual framework of *Strange Interlude* which so emphatically rejects science and reason is not in accord with Freudian ideology.[48]

Altogether, then, the ideology of *Strange Interlude* differs too fundamentally from Freudian theory to be an expression of his psychology. Rather, the chief events of the play express in dramatic terms the major features of Schopenhauer's philosophy. The view of life as controlled by irrational forces which sweep individuals into personally destructive love affairs, the view of life as a perpetual striving from which there is no escape but denial of the will to live, in other words, the view of life in *Strange Interlude*, certainly tallies with Schopenhauer's outlook. Not only the major events in *Strange Interlude* follow Schopenhauer's *Weltanschauung*, but also occasional comments throughout the play reflect his ideology. For instance, in Act III, Marsden muses on why Nina has not announced her pregnancy: "...why do wives hide it from their husbands?... ancient shame...guilty of continuing life, of bringing fresh pain into the world."[49] Just so, Schopenhauer points out that with procreation "suffering and death, as belonging to the phenomenon of life, have also been asserted anew.... Here lies the profound reason of the shame connected with the process of generation."[50] On the whole, so pervasive and so consistent is the presence of Schopenhauer's ideology in *Strange Interlude* that it seems obvious that the play is an expression of Schopenhauer's philosophy.

The view of life presented in *Strange Interlude* has not been received favorably by most critics, whether they believe that the view represented no particular philosophy, or that it represented Freudian theory. As Krutch remarked, the play has "no satisfactory catastrophe, only a diminuendo, as the characters, who have neither solved their personal problems nor made defeat heroic, subside into the quiescence of age. They do not seem very important; they have failed to achieve tragic stature because neither intellectually nor emotionally are they convinced of their own importance either to themselves or to anything else."[51] This comment on the play demonstrates how faithfully O'Neill has communicated Schopenhauer's view of life through *Strange Interlude*, for as Schopenhauer himself has stated:

> The life of every individual, if we survey it as a whole and in general, and only lay stress upon its most significant features, is really always a tragedy, but gone through in detail, it has the character of a comedy. For the deeds and vexations of the day, the restless irritation of the moment, the desires and fears of the week, the mishaps of every hour, are all through chance, which is ever bent upon some jest, scenes of a comedy. But the never-satisfied wishes, the frustrated efforts, the hopes unmercifully crushed by fate, the unfortunate errors of the whole life, with increasing suffering and death at the end, are always a tragedy. Thus, as if fate would add derision to the misery of our existence, our life must contain all the woes of tragedy, and yet we cannot even assert the dignity of tragic characters, but in the broad detail of life must inevitably be the foolish characters of a comedy.[52]

Certainly O'Neill is to be congratulated on the success with which he conveyed Schopenhauer's view of life in *Strange Interlude*. The only question that remains is: Can great drama be constructed with such an outlook?

NOTES

1. *Eugene O'Neill: The Man and His Plays* (New York, 1947), p. 113.

2. "Introduction," *Nine Plays by Eugene O'Neill* (New York, 1941), p. xviii. See also Edmond Gagey, *Revolution in American Drama* (New York, 1947), p. 56; Lynton Hudson, *The Twentieth-Century Drama* (London, 1946), pp. 72-73.

3. (New York), p. ix.

4. Clark, *op. cit.*, p. 84.

5. *In The Philosophy of Schopenhauer*, ed. Irwin Edman (New York, 1928), pp. 354-355.

6. "Notebook 1920-1930, with Scenarios and Notes of *Marco Millions, The Great God Brown, Lazarus Laughed, Strange Interlude* and *Dynamo*," MS in the American Literature Collection of Yale University Library. I wish to thank Eugene O'Neill and the authorities of the Yale Library for permission to consult the O'Neill collection in the Yale Library.

7. Act IV, p. 79. All references to *Strange Interlude* are to *The Plays of Eugene O'Neill*, 3 vols. (New York, 1941), Vol. I.

8. p. 69.

9. p. 119.

10. *The Metaphysics of the Love of the Sexes*, p. 365

11. Act V, p. 103.

12. *The Metaphysics of the Love of the Sexes*, p. 340.

13. *Ibid.*, p. 342.

14. *Ibid.*, p. 343.

15. *Ibid.*, pp. 346-347.

16. *Ibid.*, p. 349.

17. p. 89.

18. Act VIII, p. 165.

19. *The World as Will and Idea*, in *The Philosophy of Schopenhauer*, p. 162.

20. *The Metaphysics of the Love of the Sexes*, p. 369.

21. Act V, p. 103; Act V, p. 105; Act VI, p. 130.

22. Act IV, p. 80.

23. Schopenhauer, *The World as Will and Idea*, p. 162.

24. Act VI, p. 122.

25. p. 67. In the American Literature Collection of Yale University Library.

26. In *The Plays of Eugene O'Neill*, II, p. 426.

27. "Eugene O'Neill and the American Scene," *Masters of the Drama* (New York, 1940), pp. 656-657.

28. *The World as Will and Idea*, p. 297.

29. Act VII, p. 138.

30. *The World as Will and Idea*, p. 273.

31. Act VII, p. 149.

32. *The World as Will and Idea*, p. 317.

33. *Ibid.*, p. 307.

34. Act IX, p. 187.

35. *The World as Will and Idea*, p. 318.

36. Act IX, pp. 196-197.

37. Act IX, p. 200.

38. In a letter to Martha Carolyn Sparrow, Oct. 13, 1929, O'Neill declared that he had read only two books by Freud, one of which was *Beyond the Pleasure Principle*. See Arthur H. Nethercot, "O'Neill on Freudianism," *Sat. Rev. of Lit.*, VIII, 759 (May 28, 1932).

39. Trans. C.J.M. Hubback (London, 1948), p. 63.

40. See, for instance, Sigmund Freud, *A General Introduction to Psychoanalysis*, trans. Joan Riviere (New York, 1949), p. 225.

41. Compare Schopenhauer, *The World as Will and Idea*, pp. 234-235, with Freud, *New Introductory Lectures on Psycho-analysis*, trans. W.J.H. Sprott (New York, 1933), p. 108.

42. Act VIII, p. 170.

43. *The World as Will and Idea*, p. 69.

44. *Ibid.*, pp. 154-155.

45. Act II, p. 41.

46. *New Introductory Lectures on Psycho-analysis*, p. 112.

47. *Ibid.*, p. 234.

48. For an account of the extent to which the psychological aspects of *Strange Interlude* are Freudian, see my unpublished dissertation "Freud and O'Neill: An Analysis of *Strange Interlude*," New York University, 1952.

49. p. 53.

50. *The World as Will and Idea*, p. 272.

51. "Eugene O'Neill, "*Literary History of the United States*, ed. Robert E. Spiller et al. (New York, 1948), II, 1247.

52. *The World as Will and Idea*, p. 265.

American Literature, 25(May 1953): 213-228.

O'Neill's *Strange Interlude* Retains Its Dramatic Power

Richard Watts, Jr.

Even enthusiasts for Eugene O'Neill have been pointing to the weaknesses of his *Strange Interlude* since it was first produced in 1928, and the flaws are not to be denied. But the Actors Studio Theater revival, which opened yesterday afternoon at the Hudson, brought out a fact of much greater importance. The intense and tortured study of a neurotic woman and her loves, which runs for nine acts and almost five hours, remains for all its overwrought extensiveness, an engrossing drama of enormous power and steady fascination.

This is not to dispute the accuracy of some of the charges against O'Neill. The play is unnecessarily long. The earthbound prose style and the essential humorlessness are a handicap and the growing knowledge of psychoanalysis makes some of the revelations of character seem a little naive. And the O'Neill version of "asides," by which the players express their unspoken thoughts, rarely contribute much that is revealingly significant, although José Quintero's expert staging has wisely removed most of the emphasis from them.

Yet, conceding O'Neill's defects in all of these matters, his towering talent for sheer theatrical power and emotional impact arises above them monumentally. It is no doubt ironic that he learned so much about stage effectiveness from the scorned melodramas in which his father acted, but there is a tremendous gift for impassioned drama in his story of Nina Leeds, tortured by memories of her idealized dead lover and never able to bring herself to the cruelty of telling her gentle adoring dolt of a husband that her child was not his.

Nor is it correct to say that O'Neill completely lacked grace of style or capacity for humor, since there are moving speeches and moments of genuine comedy in *Strange Interlude*. The desperation of Nina's life occasionally seems perhaps too much a dramatist's fabrication, but most of her story is enthrallingly believable, and the long, difficult and not always sympathetic role, which Lynn Fontanne created memorably, is beautifully played by Geraldine Page, who takes another important step forward as an actress of stunning talent. Ben Gazzara, always a dynamic actor, is brilliant as the actual father, who must keep his silence, and there are admirable performances by Pat Hingle as the child-like husband and William Prince as the undersexed old friend, so futile but eventually triumphant. These three roles were originally acted by Glenn Anders, Earle Larimore and Tom Powers. Geoffrey Horne has a good scene as the son, and Betty Field, Franchot Tone and Jane Fonda are excellent in important small roles. *Strange Interlude* is worthy of Eugene O'Neill's stature.

New York Post, March 12, 1963.

Reviews of O'Neill's Plays in Performance: *Strange Interlude*

Frederick Wilkens

Beyond the good news of its box office success, this transplantation of the 1984 London revival proved that *Strange Interlude* remains a theatrically viable entity and offered a production that is unlikely to be bettered in our time. Detractors of O'Neill's Freudian "woman play" may not have been converted; and a number of critics were disturbed at the amount of laughter it aroused (laughter as much at as with the characters and speeches); but the slightly trimmed performance with two intervals provided the fleetest 4 1/2 hours on broadway this season....

It's amazing what a fresh, even brash approach can do to resuscitate a play generally relegated to the dustbin of "interesting" failures and quaint antiquities. What director Keith Hack did, with the assistance of cast, composer and scenic designer, was scrape off the reverent barnacles that usually accompany the famous "spoken thoughts" and play it straight. No looming pauses; no change of position, tone or even volume; no freezing of the others as each blue bathed thinker reveals the feelings that contradict his public utterances. Such ponderous devices do more to elicit disbelief than aid its suspension. By eliminating them, Hack not only shortened the playing time; he also showed that O'Neill's theatrical instincts, even at their most untraditional, were right on the mark, thanks (in this case) largely to his canny decision to start the play with a character thinking *alone*. Marsden's opening monologue establishes the convention in a thoroughly traditional way; and when it is extended beyond his solo scene we continue to accept it when, as here, the actors treat it so "naturally." Discovering that we have been endowed with omniscience, we relish every revelation, especially when a character's thought is at war, not only with his spoken words, but with other, conflicting thoughts.

Granted, Hack's revisionist approach didn't reveal a flawless masterpiece; much of the aforementioned laughter would have horrified the playwright, who clearly took his characters' inner conflicts and attempts at analysis more seriously than the audience did. But even if O'Neill the psychologist didn't emerge unscathed, O'Neill the man of the theatre did: he triumphed. Many an uncluttered *Strange Interlude* will, I am sure, follow Hack's pioneering lead. If so, the major achievement will be less its own considerable success than its return to the standard repertory of a major dramatic work.

The set, designed by Vatic (the London designer) with Michael Levine, featured high walls of horizontal gray clapboard at rear and sides, towering over a slightly raised platform of wide planks front-to-back (also gray), around which, at the front and sides of the stage-proper, sere leaves were parsimoniously strewn. Blue and white cloud forms streaked diagonally across the walls at times to add (with the leaves) a touch of credibility to the outdoor scenes, and flats were lowered to suggest the various locales; a wall at the rear with classical doorway flanked by glass-doomed bookcases for Professor Leeds' study; a more rustic downstage wall with door, their paint peeling, for the front of the Evans' home; a wall with tied-back bead curtains in its central portal for Sam and Nina's Long Island sitting room; and a low railing across the rear, with a deck and flag pole behind it, for the last-act terrace which, in this production, served as the eighth-act setting as well. And each locale featured a spare but adequate assortment of furniture and bric-a-brac that, like the costumes by Deidre Clancy, made up in authenticity for their lack of contemporary appeal.

The incidental music by Benedict Mason, that bridged the interact pauses, complemented the settings in its spareness (piano, violin and a few woodwinds) and also matched the play's own blend of neat surface realism and chaos beneath: its melange of melodic fragments redolent of Americana—march, dance, and hymn tunes (probably original, though "Bringing in the Sheaves" seems to surface occasionally)—frequently veered contrapuntally into dissonance in the manner of Charles Ives at his least transcendental.

But it was the actors—above all, the central British quartet—who make the long evening memorable, even glorious. Glenda Jackson adopted a persistent tic—a three or four-step upward jerking of her head—that seemed real enough for one to hope it *was* adopted, but that failed to gauge any change in Nina's nature, since it was present from beginning to end. (One would expect it to diminish, at least, once she had achieved her goal to "pass beyond desire" and "rot away in peace" with her "nice Charlie doggy"—but it didn't. The rotting was not *all* peace, and the gratuitous tic offered less nuance than nuisance.) But it was her voice that made her ideal for the part: her ability, even at midsentence, to switch from mellifluous purr to venomous rasp, so appropriate for Nina, who runs the gamut of feline emotions. (Something in its timbre made one wish that Katharine Hepburn had essayed the role in earlier days.) Every nuance of Nina's lines was lovingly revealed, subtext vied with text in the delivery, and the periodic apostrophes to "Mother God" had the warm ring of long-standing conviction. I still resist the view of Nina as archetypal Everywoman, but Jackson managed to create a believable human being out of O'Neill's anthology of female stereotypes.

Nina's "three men"—semi-satirical portraits of the artist, the businessman and the scientist—are harder to humanize, but Jackson's co-stars did very well indeed. Edward Petherbridge almost stole the show as Charles Marsden, conveying all the repressions of the prissy penman (legs crossed, arms crossed, hands held together when one wasn't picking at the immaculate fingernails of the other) and mining every vitriolic vein in the lines with which he needles others and responds with bitchy wit to every real or supposed affront. Even the more fluid, overwritten passages seemed fully believable: this was how such a writer *would* speak. His drunk scene in the eighth act, when he reelingly cast off all his usual inhibitions, was the evening's comic highlight. But this Marsden was not clown. He showed real pain when forced to consider that his mother may have cancer; and the tender triumph of his closing line—"God bless dear old Charlie...who, passed beyond desire, has all the luck at last!"—brought a final glow to the evening's twenty-five years of turmoil.

James Hazeldine (Sam Evans) aged convincingly from brash, likable clod to vested, paunchy, red-faced business success, and his eighth act stroke was ghastly in its lifelikeness. Brian Cox (Ned Darrell) captured all the forces that turn a promising scientist into a self-rebuking derelict for whom we feel as much pity as scorn, even though he is burdened with the wildest of the evening's assorted "thoughts." (Cox's "Got to go!...can't go!...got to go!..," when trying to flee from Nina in Act Five, earned ubiquitous titters—only partly because of its rapid-fire delivery—that could hardly have surprised the author.) The American players in the smaller roles were serviceable at best, except for Tom Aldredge, who caught a touching quality in Professor Leeds, torn between loneliness and stoical self-reliance, that I'd never found in the text.

There is little point in niggling about the accents of the British quartet....They all captured the complex essences of their respective roles and achieved a level of ensemble performance seldom equalled these days in the commercial theatre.

Many a flashy production dissolves on recollection. This one had abundant surface fireworks *and* continued to deepen and expand in the memory afterwards. It may not have won any of the Tony awards for which it was nominated, but it was a performance to cherish.

Eugene O'Neill Newsletter, 9 (Spring 1985): 46-49.

Lazarus Laughed Produced on Coast

George C. Warren

Eugene O'Neill's mystic drama, *Lazarus Laughed*, had its first performance on any stage tonight at the Pasadena Community Playhouse before an audience that filled the house to its utmost capacity, and was received with tremendous enthusiasm.

The play is simpler in content than anything O'Neill has written since he entered the realm of psychology with *The Great God Brown*, of which it might be called a continuation in a way, for it is based on the dying Dion's last speech. In the new drama O'Neill makes concession of faith in a guiding Omnipotence, affirms his belief in life beyond the grave and makes a plea for men to love life and laughter and to forget sorrow and death.

The production of the play presents almost insuperable difficulties and an outlay of money that is prohibitive to the commercial producer. It was because the Pasadena Players are a community body with several thousand workers that it was possible to make the production here. When it is stated that there are used in its presentation 400 costumes, 300 masks, which include the double size masks of Greek tragedy, the half face of the commedia del arte and the ordinary full faced mask, and as many wigs, it will be seen the expense of production is extraordinary. The play is in four acts and eight scenes, but by the use of a geometric, architectural setting, which permitted the rearrangement of platforms, sets of stairs and huge columns, this expense while considerable, was lessened.

The production was a triumph for Gilmor Brown, the director, of the Playhouse—the crowning of fifteen years of work in Pasadena with the first performance anywhere of an important drama by America's most distinguished dramatist.

It is as a pageant, perhaps more than a play, interesting as the text is, that *Lazarus Laughed* succeeded tonight. The play is a mass play, and Brown had a body of 125 supernumeraries and choristers trained to the minute, to give effect to the mobs that are a continual procession before the audience.

In this respect nothing greater in mass acting has been seen in California with the exception of Reinhardt's *The Miracle*, which had greater space for manoeuvres and numbers. The capacity of the playhouse stage was taxed, but the crowds never became mere mobs.

The use of chorus and crowds that speak take the play to the period of Greek tragedy, but O'Neill has superimposed on the base a structure of melodrama, effective, tense, terrible.

Brown's problem was to harmonize these various elements, and to do this he stylized his action, unified the movements of his crowds and produced richly colored tableaux. The most effective moments were those of the second and the final scenes, where the action of the crowds made superb pictures. In the first of these episodes two levels were used, with Lazarus and his followers above, while below the warring factions among the Jews, the followers of Jesus and the Orthodox Hebrews fought and killed, while the Lazarites danced and laughed. In the final scene the crowd, on a high platform, watched the martyrdom of Lazarus at the stake, the flames lighting the faces of the Roman mob which, when Lazarus began to speak swarmed down four flights of stairs and into the arena, bringing the play to an end on a magnificent piece of stage direction.

Lazarus Laughed begins just after the miracle of his resurrection and the departure of Jesus, who is not seen. The joy of parents and people at his return to life is soon overshadowed by their bigotry and that of the people, and presently they battle over him, while the Roman legions come to take him to Rome, for Tiberius Caesar had heard the story of his return from the grave and hopes that the Jew may bring him renewed youth. Failing to win a way of new life from Lazarus, he has him burned at the stake.

"There is no death," the cry of Lazarus, is made the theme for many of the choruses, the music for the play having been written by Arthur Alexander, formerly head of the Eastman Orchestra at Rochester, N.Y. His score has dignity, much of beauty and a great deal of dramatic intensity.

More than twenty of the characters in the play speak, but there are only five that stand out. Lazarus was played superbly by Irving Pichel, whose technical equipment is tremendous. The laughter, which at one time runs without cessation for four minutes, calls for absolute repose and poise, and Pichel's splendid and resonant voice carried him to a triumph.

Gilmore Brown chose one of three human roles in the play, that of Tiberius, and scored by a fine impersonation. Victor Jory scored as Caligula, making him half animal, with dangling arms and bended knees, and giving him snarling speech. Dore Wilson, cast for Pompeia, played the cruel wanton with distinction and power and Lenore Shanewise made much of the gentle Miriam, wife of Lazarus.

New York Times, April 10, 1928.

Seen on Stage: *Dynamo*

David Carb

Eugene O'Neill describes *Dynamo*, his latest drama, as "the first of a trilogy that will dig at the roots of the sickness of to-day as I feel it—the death of an old God and the failure of science and materialism to give him any satisfying new one for the surviving primitive religious instincts to find a meaning for life in, and to comfort its fears of death with. It seems to me that any one trying to do big work nowadays must have this big subject behind all the little subjects—or he is simply scribbling around on the surface of things and has no more real status than a parlour entertainer—"

Unfortunately, the "big work" O'Neill appears to think he has been working at comes nearer to the intemperate outpourings of an adolescent than to bigness from any angle; it tells us what we already know—that organized religion has neglected to adapt itself to the conditions of life and to the ways of thinking of this time, that all about us we may observe are groping for a new conception, or at least a readjustment—it tells us that and leaves us there. It offers no solution, no theory, not even a dream or a hope; it reveals a triangle—the old fashioned hell-and-damnation preacher, the brash atheist, and the preacher's son who rejects his father's God, deifies electricity in the form of a huge, solid, completely material dynamo, and loses his reason, his love, and his life in the process. O'Neill states the problem, but in terms as artificial and so extreme that it remains an objective thing framed in a proscenium—inconclusive, boringly repetitious, flatulent, not infrequently maudlin, and often smudged with the baroque.

Moreover, *Dynamo*—to use the author's own words—is not only not "parlour entertainment;" it is no other kind of entertainment. Occasionally, its wild raving is relieved by a pulsating dramatic scene in the author's fine early manner, but those occasions come so seldom that they fail to do more, either as illumination or as fire, than the sparks of a lighter that has no fuel.

O'Neill calls *Dynamo* "a symbolical and factual biography of what is happening in a large section of the American soul right now." That did not come across the footlights of the Martin Beck Theatre to at least two members of the audience—it may have reached the others. The unrest is stated, but no more. And the statement has been made in such an awkward manner and in terms so lugubrious, when not downright silly,that the impression comes early and persists throughout the evening that one is listening to the loud ululations of a schoolboy.

The hero rebels against formalized religion, but his rebellion is entirely negative; it has no aspiration in it. And rebellion without aspiration has no place in art. There can be no tragedy without frustration, and frustration must be preceded by aspiration. Reuben Light fixes on a dynamo made of metal and stone for his god because it happens to be handy when his father's narrow creed restricts his life too much; if a Ford car had been near—. The hurt that comes from something fine, noble, a reaching-out defeated, is not in him. Also, in making him insane when he embraces his new god, O'Neill dilutes the "message," if he indeed does not altogether negate it; whatever tragedy there is becomes the tragedy of a mind awry. *Strange Interlude*—still playing to large congregations at the John Golden Theatre—asserts endlessly that "God is a mother." O'Neill seems to have changed his mind in the few months since he wrote that "experimental" drama. This dynamo-God, it is true, is feminine, but, otherwise, a careful search fails to reveal anything about her that could possibly be considered maternal or convertible into the maternal. However, spiritual awakenings come suddenly, and, perhaps, the dramatist rejoices that the two plays are running simultaneously, desiring the same people to see both in order that they may realize his growth, or his change of mind—however he chooses to regard the revelation that has come to him.

As drama, *Dynamo* suffers from the same causes as its immediate predecessor. It utilizes the aside and the soliloquy, and with as little reason. Most of the things they uncover are already known, or the action could easily reveal them; in many places, they are substituted for the expository dialogue, one of the fundamentals of playwriting, upon which the expert dramatist expends his skill because it gives his work the illusion of naturalism. The first two acts show the houses of the preacher and of the atheist skeletonized so that the living rooms and the up-stairs bedrooms are open to the audience's view. When Helen Westley as Amelia Light thinks aloud about the preacher's glamorous courtship of her, he and his neighbours must sit deaf and dumb; when the Reverend Light castigates himself for having given in to the "sins of the flesh," the others must let their power of speech and hearing fall into abeyance; and so on. A crude—and, in these two plays, unnecessary—device that O'Neill attempts to dignify and fix on the drama of his time by dubbing "Interludism." (He seems to think he invented it.) It serves merely as a lazy way out of technical problems, and it slows the action and gives it an unusual artificiality.

Little of the poetic feeling that bestowed such beauty and power on the early O'Neill work animates *Dynamo*, and the play as a whole reinforces the conviction some of us have held for a long while that O'Neill's talent is not versatile, that it consists solely of depiction the conflict of raw emotions, and that when he ventures away from that, especially into the field of ideas, he shows himself a mere tyro.

He has never been strong on characterization; most of the people in his theatre have been types. But until lately, they have been types closely observed and with individualizing mannerisms. The figures of *Dynamo* are drawn in conventional, general strokes. The New England preacher, for example, comes out of innumerable books and plays; he might even derive from Frank Simon's phrase describing some one else: "The trouble with John Jones is that he's a New Englander, so he's never happy unless he's crucified every night before he goes to bed." May Fife is drawn as no more and no less than "a silly ass woman," or in our current argot, "a regular dumbbell." And so down the whole list of dramatis personae.

The man who wrote *The Emperor Jones*—the best of American plays—parts of *The Hairy Ape*, a scene or two of *The Straw*, the short dramas of the sea and that nearly perfect first act of *Anna Christie*, does not belong in the intellectual drama. Whenever he ventures there, he exhibits shallowness, immaturity, becomes muddled, and resorts to technical trickery to cover those limitations. His three latest plays have been thus marked. The way he employed the mask in *The Great God Brown* was as clumsy and of as little use as it well could be; the soliloquies and asides of *Strange Interlude* tell nothing that the action could not make clear without effort—the scenes in which he falls back on straight, direct drama are the moving ones—,and, in *Dynamo,* the same devices throw the stress on themselves in a futile, though very likely unconscious, attempt to conceal the thinness of the idea, to justify the wild, florid raving.

Lee Simonson's two sets are dramatic and harmonious. They evoke emotion. The one showing the house of the minister and that of the atheistic superintendent of the local electric plant separated by a picket fence expresses the temperaments of the people who live in them exactly, is excellent for the purpose, and pictorially effective. And the Light and Power Company's hydroelectric plant, with its several glass platforms, its operating boards, its switches, its enormous round dynamo, is both accurate and imaginative—which happens not to be the paradox it seems.

George Gaul's interpretation of the Reverend Light has as much verisimilitude as the author permits. Helen Westley plays the brief role of his wife with intensity and conviction. Fife, the atheist, becomes both a credible and a likable person in the hands of Dudley Digges. And Claudette Colbert brings her tingling, invigorating femininity to bear on Ada Fife. As for Glenn Anders, who is cast for Reuben Light, the lad who finds a new god in the dynamo, he shows again a bearing, a resource, a passion, a command of means rare among the young men of our stage.

Because *Dynamo* proves it a second time, I must repeat here what I said of

Dynamo 125

O'Neill in reviewing *Strange Interlude*, more than a year ago. Looking along the whole line of his plays, from *Beyond the Horizon* to this latest, one is impressed by the fact that, while all of them have frequent passages illuminated with that happy kind of phraseology we call poetic, none of them possesses that poetry of conception known as imagination. They all—until the four most recent—come from definite, well remembered experiences. But, you say, imagination itself comes from experiences. True, but not from remembered ones. The bar of a song, a breath of perfume in a crowd, the line of a profile may start the fancy soaring; may bring forth from some hazy depths a contact, an emotion a sentiment long forgotten; it feels familiar, but cannot be placed—its origins are lost in mists, an unbridgeable hiatus separates the present sensation from the event responsible for it. And identification has become impossible.

Until he began writing synthetic plays, all of O'Neill's works came from actual, vivid experience—even *The Emperor Jones*, his nearest approach to "imaginative drama." When he wrote that, he was extremely poor, and his friends found a defence for their poverty, an alibi, in considering those who had comfort and security bourgeois; they pretended to think it little short of disgraceful to go above Fourteenth Street or even Washington Square....That was the spirit of the young Greenwich Village artists in those days. And behind it lay a strong feeling of persecution, of being hounded by the rich who were in the nature of things smug—the Emperor Jones was but themselves in black face.

Then O'Neill achieved success. The admirers who gathered about him insisted he was an intellectual, a psychologist, a psychiatrist, and the like; it looks as though he had made himself agree and were now trying to convince himself and them. He is too vital, too fervent a playwright to be those things. His forte, I insist, is the conflict of raw emotions. The dramas he has fabricated under the new influences have emphasized technical tricks at the expense of pulsating emotion. He now announces *Without Ending of Days*, and *It Can Not Be Had* as sequels to *Dynamo*, and a *Big Grand Opus*, neither a play nor a novel, but "there will be many plays in it, and it will have greater scope than any novel I know of....Beside it *Strange Interlude* will seem like a shallow episode." So it looks as though he were definitely committed to writing out of the top of his head.

Vogue, March 30, 1929.

The Theatre: The American Dramatist

George Jean Nathan

Let this chapter be devoted to a consideration of American dramatists and to an effort to ascertain what place if any, they presently occupy in the theatrical sun.

That O'Neill is the outstanding figure in the catalogue under discussion is now denied only by such critics as employ the denial, against their honest and better judgment, to lend their writings that share of fillip which always attaches to a marching out of step. Their insincerity is easily penetrable, for while they eloquently argue that O'Neill is not the outstanding force, they do not tell us who is. With the production last season of *Dynamo*, a very poor piece of work, the hostility toward its author and the skepticism over his hitherto loudly proclaimed talents took on full sail, and we were entertained by an over-night shifting of the critical course. Because he had written a bad play, O'Neill, his antecedent work forgotten, was denounced as an overestimated and even ridiculous dramatist, and it was argued that, since this one play was so bad, doubtless his previous good plays were not really so good as they had previously been thought to be. In this we engaged no novelty, for the tactic is a commonplace one in American criticism, whether literary or dramatic, and familiar to everyone who follows the critical art as it is manoeuvred in God's country.

If O'Neill is not the leader among American playwrights, *Dynamo* or no *Dynamo*, it is pretty difficult to make out who the leader is. While it is perfectly true that in one or two of his other plays as well as in *Dynamo* he has exposed at times a juvenile indignation, a specious profundity and a method of exaggeration that has verged perilously on travesty, he has nevertheless written a number of plays of very definite quality, a number of plays that outdistance any others thus far written by Americans and, whether in better work or poorer, shown an attitude and an integrity—to say nothing of a body of technical resource—far beyond those of any of his American rivals. The truth about O'Neill is that he is the only American playwright who has what may be called "size." There is something relatively distinguished about even his failures; they sink not trivially but with a certain air of majesty, like a great ship, its flags flying, full of holes. He has no cheapness, even in his worst plays. *The First Man, Welded* and *Dynamo*, for example, are mediocre affairs as drama goes, but in them just the same there is that peculiar thing that marks off even the dismal efforts of a first-rate man from those of a second-rate.

The American Mercury, August 1929.

Tragedy Becomes O'Neill

J. Brooks Atkinson

Although most of us have been brought up to bow and genuflect before the majesty of Greek tragedy, it has remained for Mr. O'Neill to show us why. His modern psychological play, *Mourning Becomes Electra*, brings the cold splendors of Greek tragedy off the sky-blue limbo of Olympus down to the gusty forum of contemporary life. For the divine omniscience of the gods he substitutes the discovery of modern science, since knowledge is what this civilization pits against the solemn councils of the gods. We have lost a great deal, I suspect. To believe is to hope in a wild and vaulting fashion; to know is to be resigned, although

Socrates would not say so. But the essential mystery of life still fills us with terror and wonder and fills *Mourning Becomes Electra* with the same baleful alarms. There are many remarkable things about Mr. O'Neill's single clear-cut masterpiece. But nothing is so remarkable as the discovery that in modern speech and modern environment the impersonality of a great tragic story still lives in terms of mute foreboding. However much you understand the doomed inhabitants of this fourteen-act play and the causes of their calamities, you recognize their helplessness in the face of powers they cannot control. For Mr. O'Neill has lifted his tragedy out of the miasma of petty emotions to the impersonal plane of inevitable things.

In its dramatic patter *Mourning Becomes Electra* is a modern rendering of the Electra-Orestes legend, successively employed by Aeschylus, Sophocles and Euripides. The New England house of Mannon is the house of Atreus; Ezra Mannon is Agamemnon; Christine Mannon, his wife, is Clytemnestra; Lavinia, his daughter, is Electra; Orin, his son, is Orestes; Captain Brant is Aegisthus. The hired man and his rude companions of the town are the chanting, apprehensive chorus. The Civil War from which Ezra Mannon is returning is the Trojan War from which Agamemnon came wearily home. The cool pillars of Robert Edmond Jones's New England house are the portals of the Greek temples before which the tragedies were acted. Although Mr. O'Neill has deliberately gone to these sources for his modern drama, even writing it in three-play trilogy form like the Orestes trilogy by Aeschylus, he has not played the sedulous ape to his Hellenic forebears, and he has even introduced the Oedipus story in Greek tragedy, arriving at modern conclusions. Especially in the third play, which in Aeschylean tragedy was the moral and religious finale, Mr. O'Neill has pursued his own course as a modern playwright. What he has attempted to accomplish in that final play is best told in one of his own footnotes to the play:

> The Electra figure in the Greek legend and plays fades out into a vague and undramatic future. She stops, as if after the revenge on her mother all was well. The Furies take after Orestes, but she is left alone. I never could swallow that. It seemed to me that by having her disappear in nice conventionally content future (married to Pylades, according to one version of the legend) the Greeks were dodging the implication their own belief in the chain of fate. In our modern psychological chain of fate certainly we cannot let her make her exit like that. She is so inevitably worthy of a better tragic fate! I have tried to give my Yankee Electra an end tragically worthy of herself. The end, to me, is the most inevitable thing in the trilogy. She is broken and not broken. By her way of yielding to the Mannon fate she overcomes it.

During several years of strain and bluster most of us have been on Mr. O'Neill's side as a dramatist, though not without misgivings. Although he has been straining after large themes, his reach has often fallen short and his mind has been truculent and rebellious. What makes *Mourning Becomes Electra* his only masterpiece, to my mind, is the cool deliberation with which he has dominated it. The fret and fever of his early work, the truncated thinking, the turgid writing, the elaborate symbolism of masks, the subterfuge of asides, the inarticulation and the collapse into grandiose generalities—have disappeared. Even now he is prolix.

Eager to explain all that he has been exhibiting, he permits his characters repeated self-analyses that should be implicit in dramatic thinking but that are superfluous and egregious as passages of dialogue. Mr. O'Neill still wants reticence. But he grows more ambitious year by year. While his contemporaries are pottering around with the trifling platitudes of shop worn playmaking, he insists upon regarding the drama as one of the major arts. Originally, *Mourning Becomes Electra* was designed for three separate evenings in the theatre. Even now, cut and compressed, it takes six hours, excluding the dinner intermission after the first play. But huge though it is in size, Mr. O'Neill has kept it simple and lucid as a narrative, and the contour of the story rises and falls like the long, mighty heave of the waves in midocean.

Mr. O'Neill is not the only master-craftsman in this enterprise. The Theatre Guild, which has been floundering, has risen to the occasion with a magnificent production, and Philip Moeller, who put *Strange Interlude* on the stage, has assimilated *Mourning Becomes Electra* completely. For pace and coherence, for the prescience of doom in the acting and the spectacle, for climaxes and flow, the performance he has directed is superb. Having written a play that is preeminently actable, Mr. O'Neill makes it possible for his players to appear to their best advantage. And I must confess to having been quite unprepared for the studious, malevolent stateliness of Alice Brady's unearthly Lavinia, and the preternatural grace of Mme. Alla Nazimova's Christine, which is one of the loveliest and most sinister character studies I ever saw. Both of these portraits take on a visual majesty from the ominous costumes the actors wear. Earle Larimore, as the brother, has likewise developed into full maturity as an actor; there is a substantial fullness to his acting; it has solidity and diversity. No one familiar with Robert Edmond Jones's artistry could be the least bit surprised by the incandescent vitality of his scenic designs. Of all the scene designers his is the one whose inspired idealism is great enough to comprehend the play. His interiors and exteriors of a New England mansion have not only beauty and humility but the vibrancy of the theme, and, like the play they belong exclusively to the theatre.

Amid the babble of excitement occasioned by this splendid achievement it is possible to discuss a big question. Is this a great play? It falls short of true greatness, I believe. To be great a tragedy needs some traces of genuine nobility in the characters. For the Greeks that was easy. They had royalty to represent a standard of nobility that need not be fulfilled in the individual characters. Royalty was, by common consent, heroic, and all the passions royalty developed were thus heroic also. In transcribing the Electra legend in modern psychological terms Mr. O'Neill has no royalty to fall back on; and when the house of Atreus becomes the house of Mannon you recognize the true ignobility of their personal characters. Nor can modern characters speak verse. They speak, in Mr. O'Neill's trilogy, the simplest, most unobtrusive style of prose, which, on Mr. O'Neill's part, is as honestly deliberate as all the workmanship he has squandered on the play. But prose is an earthly instrument unless the thoughts expressed are sublime and highminded. Although the Mannons are strong and resolute, animated by unconquerable wills, they are an ignoble lot. I can admire their fortitude without being stunned by their disasters. For great tragedy you must have, if not heroes, then characters as superior as the chief figure in *The Father*, who has something besides his life to lose. *Mourning Becomes Electra* is Mr. O'Neill's masterpiece and also one of the supreme achievements of the modern theatre. It rises out of our moribund drama like a lily from the black slime of the swamp. Although Mr. O'Neill for the first time sees life steadily, he does not, in my opinion see it whole. In this world of debased values none of us dies. That is our eternal misfortune. Nor shall we have true greatness in government, business or art until someone has the courage and capacity to look on life with his "welkin eye."

New York Times, November 1, 1931.

The Theatre: Top

Robert Benchley

In the midst of the acclaim with which Eugene O'Neill is being so justly hailed for his latest and most gigantic *tour de force, Mourning Becomes Electra*, and in the confusion of cross-references to the Greek dramatists from whom he derived his grim and overpowering story, are we not forgetting one very important source of his inspiration, without which he might perhaps have been just a builder of word mountains? Was there not standing in the wings of the Guild Theatre, on that momentous opening night, the ghost of an old actor in a white wig, with drawn sword, who looked on proudly as the titanic drama unfolded itself, scene by scene, and who murmured, with perhaps just the suggestion of a chuckle: "That's good, son! Give 'em the old Theatre!"? The actor I refer to needs no introduction to the older boys and girls here tonight—Mr. James O'Neill, "The Count of Monte Cristo" and the father of our present hero.

Let us stop all this scowling talk about "the inevitability of the Greek tragedy" and "O'Neill's masterly grasp of the eternal verities" and let us admit that the reason why we sat for six hours straining to hear each line through the ten-watt acoustics of the Guild Theatre was because *Mourning Becomes Electra* is filled with good, old-fashioned, spine-curling melodrama. It is his precious inheritance from his trouper-father, his father who counted "One," "Two," Three" as he destroyed his respective victims, one at the curtain of each act; it is his supreme sense of the Theatre in its most elementary appeal, which allows Eugene O'Neill to stand us on our heads (perhaps our heads would have been more comfortable) and keep us there from five in the afternoon until almost midnight. In this tremendous play he gives us not one thing that is new, and he gives us nothing to think about (unless we are just beginning to think), but he does thrill the bejeezus out of us, just as his father used to, and that is what we go to the theatre for.

Just run over in your mind the big scenes in *Mourning Becomes Electra*. A daughter upbraiding her mother for adultery, the mother plotting with her lover the murder of her husband, the poisoning of the husband and the discovery of the tablets in the fainting mother's hand, the placing of the tablets on the breast of the corpse to frighten the mother into a confession (and what a scene *that* was!), the brother and sister peering down the hatch of a sailing ship to spy on the mother and later to murder her lover, and the tense moments of waiting for the offstage shots which would tell of the successive suicides of the mother and the brother. Greek tragedy my eye! The idea may have been the Greeks', but the hand is the hand of Monte Cristo. If the Greek idea of revenge, murder, incest, and suicide is so thrilling, why isn't Margaret Anglin busier than she is? *Mourning Becomes Electra* is just the old Greek story put into not particularly convincing New England talk, but it is a hundred times better show than *Electra* because O'Neill has a God-given inheritance of melodramatic sense. So let's stop kidding ourselves about the Verities and Unities and take a grand, stupendous thriller when we find it and let it go at that.

In the face of such an overwhelming victory over Time, Space and the Daily Press as that which Mr. O'Neill has won, it is perhaps puny in a single commentator to admit such a personal reaction as fatigue during the last of the three sections of the drama (for they are *not* three plays, as advertised, but one play in fourteen successive acts). But, willing as the spirit may be to take punishment, the human frame is not equipped for such a session as that which is imposed upon it in the Guild Theatre (at any rate, mine isn't, and I have a pretty good equipment), and, starting with a pretty bad scene (go ahead, strike me dead, Jove!) of comic relief at the beginning of the section called *The Haunted*, I began to be cushion-conscious. This uneasiness was heightened as I saw approaching that margin of Diminishing Returns in Tragedy which I alone seem to be conscious of in O'Neill's dramas, when one more fell swoop of Fate, one more killing, one more father in love with one more daughter, or one more sister in love with one more brother, and the whole thing becomes just a bit ridiculous. It was when I saw those magnificent scenes of the middle section becoming confused with a grand finale of bad comedy, incest, and extra suicide that Miss Brady's agonized cry, "I couldn't bear another death!," struck home, and I began to realize that, for me personally, *Mourning Becomes Electra* was getting to be just about one hour too long. I know that this is a purely individual and unworthy reaction, quite out of place in a serious review of a great masterpiece, but, as this page is nothing if not personal, I am setting it down. And the final scene of all, in which Electra, or Lavinia, closes herself up in the great New England Greek temple for the rest of her unhappy life, content that mourning is her *métier*, made up for everything.

And now we come to Miss Alice Brady and to Alla Nazimova and to all the rest of the splendid cast which the Theatre Guild has assembled to do homage to Mr. O'Neill's *magnum opus*. Without them, and without Robert Edmond Jones's superb settings, I am not so sure just how effective this drama would be. I can imagine its being pretty bad, as a matter of fact, if only moderately well done. We thrill to the scenes between the mother and daughter on the steps of the cold New England mansion, but how much credit do we give to Mr. Jones and to Mr. Philip Moeller, who gave us this picture of two women in black on the white steps of a Greek temple? (It may have been so nominated in the script, but without Mr. Jones to give it being, it might have remained just a stage-direction.) Alice Brady has at last come into her own, in voice and bearing the perfect Electra, and Nazimova, in spite of her Russian accent, which rings so strangely in Suffolk County, made so much of the sinning Clytemnestra that the drama lost much when she withdrew into the shades of the House of Mannon never to return. Earle Larimore, too, as Orin-Orestes, gave the role a human quality which could hardly have been expected in the writing, and Thomas Chalmers, with an opera trained speaking voice, not only overcame the trick sound-currents of the theatre but gave a healthy robustness to the rather murky proceeding which was reassuring, as long as it lasted. Lee Baker, the first of a long string of entries to die, may have seemed a little stiff, but I suspect that it was a rather stiff part. In short, Philip Moeller in his direction, and the cast in their interpretation, and especially Mr. Jones in his settings, all did more than their share to raise Mr. O'Neill to the undisputed, and probably for a long time uncontested, eminence of the First Dramatist of Our Time....But while we are on our feet, let us drink once again to the Count of Monte Cristo.

New Yorker, November 7, 1931.

Our Electra

Joseph Wood Krutch

Except for a dinner intermission Eugene O'Neill's new trilogy, *Mourning Becomes Electra* (Guild Theater), runs from five o'clock in the afternoon until about eleven-fifteen in the evening. Seldom if ever has any play received a reception so unreservedly enthusiastic as this one was accorded by the New York newspapers and, to begin with, I can only say that I share the enthusiasm to the full. Here, in the first place, are those virtues—intelligence, insight, and rapid, absorbing action—which one expects in the best contemporary dramatic writing. But here also are a largeness of conception and a more than local or temporary significance which put to rest those doubts which usually arise when one is tempted to attribute a lasting greatness to any play of our generation. O'Neill, though thoroughly "modern," is not dealing with the accidents of contemporary life. He has managed to give his—I am almost tempted to say "our"—version of a tale which implies something concerning the most permanent aspects of human nature, and it is hard to imagine how the play could lose its interest merely because of those superficial changes which take place from generation to generation. For this reason it may turn out to be the only permanent contribution yet made by the twentieth century to dramatic literature.

As the title suggests, O'Neill's fable follows, almost incident for incident, the main outlines of the Greek story. Though he has set the action in New England just after the Civil War, his Clytemnestra murders Agamemnon and his Electra persuades Orestes to bring about the death of their common mother. Nor do such changes as are necessarily made in the motivation of the characters so much modify the effect of the story as merely restore that effect by translating the story into terms which we can fully comprehend. It is true that Electra loves her father and that Orestes loves his mother in a fashion which the Greeks either did not understand or, at least, did not fully specify. It is true also that the play implies that the psychological quirks responsible for the tragedy are the result of a conflict between puritanism and healthy love. But this is merely the way in which we understand such situations, and the fact remains that these things are *merely* implied, that the implications exist for the sake of the play, not the play for the sake of the implications. It is, moreover, this fact more than any other which indicates something very important in the nature of O'Neill's achievement.

Hitherto most of our best plays have been—of necessity perhaps—concerned primarily with the exposition and defense of their intellectual or moral or psychological backgrounds. They have been written to demonstrate that it was legitimate to understand or judge men in the new ways characteristic of our time. But O'Neill has succeeded in writing a great play in which a reversal of this emphasis has taken place at last. Because its thesis is taken for granted, it has no thesis. It is no more an exposition or defense of the tenets of the Greek religion, even though it does accept the one as Aeschylus accepts the other. It is on the other hand—and like all supremely great pieces of literature—primarily about the passions and primarily addressed to our interest in them. Once more we have a great play which does not "mean" anything in the sense that the plays of Ibsen or Shaw or Galsworthy usually mean something, but one which does, on the contrary, mean the same thing that "Oedipus" and "Hamlet" and "Macbeth" mean—namely, that human beings are great and terrible creatures when they are in the grip of great passions, and that the spectacle of them is not only absorbing but also and at once horrible and cleansing. Nineteenth century critics of Shakespeare said that his plays were like the facts of nature, and though this statement has no intellectual content it does imply something concerning that attitude which we adopt toward *Mourning Becomes Electra* as well as toward Shakespeare. Our arguments and our analyses are unimportant as long as we attempt to discover in them the secret of our interest. What we do is merely to accept these fables as though they were facts and sit amazed by the height and the depth of human deeds. Perhaps no one knows exactly what it means to be "purged by pity and terror," but for that very reason, perhaps, one returns to the phrase.

To find in the play any lack at all one must compare it with the very greatest works of dramatic literature, but when one does compare it with *Hamlet* or *Macbeth* one realizes that it does lack just one thing and that that thing is language—words as thrilling as the action which accompanies them. Take, for example, the scene in which Orin (Orestes) stands beside the bier of his father and apostrophizes the body laid there. No one can deny that the speech is a good one, but what one desires with an almost agonizing desire is something not merely good but something incredibly magnificent, something like "Tomorrow and tomorrow and tomorrow..." or "I could a tale unfold whose lightest word...." If by some miracle such words could come, the situation would not be unworthy of them. Here is a scenario to which the most soaring eloquence and the most profound poetry are appropriate, and if it were granted us we should be swept aloft as no Anglo-Saxon audience since Shakespeare's time has had an opportunity to be. But no modern is capable of language really worthy of O'Neill's play, and the lack of that one thing is the penalty we must pay for living in an age which is not equal to more than prose. Nor is it to be supposed that I make this reservation merely for the purpose of saying that Mr. O'Neill's play is not so good as the best of Shakespeare; I make it, on the contrary, in order to indicate where one must go in order to find a worthy comparison.

Space is lacking to pay fitting tribute to the production and acting of the play. It must suffice to say that both they and the setting do it justice. Both Nazimova as Christine (Clytemnestra) and Alice Brady as Lavinia (Electra) contribute performances hardly less notable in their own way than the play, and, indeed, everyone concerned in the production may be said to share somewhat in the achievement. *Mourning Becomes Electra* reads well; when it comes to life on the stage of the Guild Theater it is no less than tremendous.

Nation, November 18, 1931

The Circle Moves Up

Jack Kroll

In an oddly quiet way, the opening of the new Circle in the Square marks the end of an era—the era of the original off-Broadway movement which the Circle, founded in 1951 by Theodore Mann, helped to initiate. The Circle's new uptown house, officially called the Joseph E. Levine Theatre for the movie magnate and longtime circle supporter, is the second of the "Lindsay plan" theaters built into new Broadway-area office buildings to open....There is always some danger in the legitimization of theatrical energy that occurs in moves such as these. In the case of Circle in the Square, however, such legitimization took place long ago; under men like Mann and José Quintero, more square than circle crept into the sensibility that purported to inherit the anti-commercial, experimental attitude of the old Provincetown Playhouse which nurtured Eugene O'Neill. Appropriately the new Circle opens with a revival of O'Neill's massive *Mourning Becomes Electra*, and if middlebrows can produce such a thing as strong middle vibes, this occasion certainly has them.

When the original production of *Mourning Becomes Electra*, opened in 1931, Robert Benchley in *The New Yorker* imagined the spirit of James O'Neill, the playwright's matinee-idol father, calling from the shades: "That's good, son! Give 'em the old Theatre!" Benchley was being an effete Algonquin snob, but there was something to his barb. The play, modeled on the Orestia trilogy of Aeschylus, is on one level a titanic soap opera. But on another level it is one of the biggest triumphs of O'Neill's astonishing emotional authenticity over his naïveté and clumsiness.

Whatever one says about O'Neill's night-school Freudianism, his boardinghouse reach across cultural history to appropriate the epic resonance of Greek tragedy, this play not only has a cumulative power but a clear draftsmanship that builds the tensions and agonies, the homicidal loves and suicidal hatreds of the Mannon family into a dramatic structure as alive as an anthill and as secure as a geodesic dome.

The middleness comes from Mann's production. He has cut the work so that it runs less than four hours rather than the original five. This gains speed but loses time—the O'Neill Standard Time that builds a mountain of heartbeats making you feel the crescendo of your own life to some inescapable accounting of flesh and spirit. As a director Mann blocks the play but doesn't tackle it; the production does not escape a piety that colors it sober black rather than letting it bleed its own black blood.

This middling quality, this stone-stepping rather than water-walking, is shared by most of the performances, including that of Pamela Payton-Wright as Lavinia, the New England Electra who drives her brother to kill the mother who has killed their father. As Christine, the mother, Colleen Dewhurst, whose career has been so bound up with Circle, comes close but not all the way to being larger than life. I liked Stephen McHattie, who played Orrin-Orestes as a young man trapped in an inescapable hysteria as the immense gravitational pull of his doomed family pulls him away from his own development to their destiny.

Newsweek, November 27, 1972

Masking Becomes Electra: O'Neill, Freud, and the Feminine

S. Georgia Nugent

O'Neill's detailed stage set for *Mourning Becomes Electra* describes the Mannon mansion with its Greek "temple portico like an incongruous white mask fixed on the house to hide its somber gray ugliness." We might characterize the trilogy itself with a reversal of this image: O'Neill's work affixes a projecting façade of Freudian concepts to an underlying structure derived from Greek tragedy. Freudian theory would seem to offer the playwright a means of illumining the psyche of the Electra figure. Instead, O'Neill uses Freud not to reveal but to mask a darkness, specifically "the dark continent" of feminine sexuality. Overtly, *Mourning Becomes Electra* seems to be about unresolved Oedipal attachments. These, however, are *so* overt as to lack Freudian resistance and repression altogether. Something else, however, *is* systematically repressed in the trilogy—namely, non-Oedipal sexual relations and particularly feminine desire and sexual activity.

I shall argue here that O'Neill, in the process of writing and re-writing the play, consistently cut passages revealing feminine desire or sexual activity and replaced them with passages which displace and conceal that activity. Moreover, that *suppressed* sexuality (we discover) is displaced onto the author's own writing. An analysis of the trilogy clearly demonstrates O'Neill's fear of confronting or portraying desire, but the playwright's own commentary on the trilogy reveals a consistent system of sexual metaphor involving both male adequacy of performance and female parturition. The eroticism displaced from the play's narrative is transferred to the act of writing like a Freudian "return of the repressed." Within the work itself, O'Neill's eroticization of writing is translated into epistolary terms with the result that in *Mourning Becomes Electra* a refusal to write signals an aggressive and dangerous entry into sexuality.

From Fate to Freud. Most obviously by his naming of the trilogy (and by the use of the trilogic structure itself) O'Neill designates that his work is to be understood in the context of Greek tragic theater and, most especially, as a modernization of Aeschylus' *Oresteia*, the only complete Greek trilogy extant. Each major narrative element of the Greek drama finds its counterpart here. The war hero (Agamemnon/Ezra Mannon), returning home, is treacherously murdered by his unfaithful wife (Clytemnestra/Christine) with the aid of her lover, also a dispossessed heir of the household (Aegisthus/Adam Brant). Subsequently, the children (Electra/Lavinia, Orestes/Orin) take their vengeance upon both lover and mother and, in the final play, must come to terms with their own part in the family's history of crime and punishment. In other details as well, from providing a narrative background of lust and betrayal in the previous generation to experimenting with the formal use of a "chorus" of townspeople to introduce the plays, O'Neill attempts to transfer Greek tragedy to the American stage.

In addition to specific narrative and formal elements of the *Oresteia*, what O'Neill has carried over into his modern version is the powerful force of a family curse working its way through generations. While others have seen economic determination as the modern equivalent for the ancient concept of tragic fate, O'Neill sees in its place psychological complexes.[1] He insists that "fate from within the family is the modern psychological approximation of the Greek conception of fate from without, from the supernatural."[2]

While O'Neill's debt to classical tragedy is undisputed, the extent of his familiarity with and exposure to psychoanalytic theory remains a topic of some debate.[3] The playwright himself demurs when the question of his psychologizing in *Mourning Becomes Electra* is raised.[4] Yet his working notes for the trilogy clearly indicate from the beginning his desire to experiment with the possibility of introducing psychological compulsion in the place of Greek tragedy's motivating Fate.

If one of O'Neill's major motives in writing the trilogy was to explore the psychological translation of the Greek notion of fate, another was his desire to explore the Electra figure herself. We know from his working notebooks that as early as 1926 he had read versions of the Electra story and conceived the idea of transferring the Greek tragic plot to a modern setting.[5] O'Neill speaks of Electra as "the most interesting of all women in drama."[6] Electra is indeed the only figure for whom we have a full, extant treatment by each of the great Greek tragedians (Aeschylus' *Choephoroi*, Sophocles' and Euripides' respective *Electra*'s). Despite this considerable attention in ancient drama, however, O'Neill is quite right in identifying a curious gap in the treatment of her tale. "Why," he asks, "did the chain of fated crime and retribution ignore her mother's murderess?—a weakness in what remains to us of Greek tragedy that there is no play about Electra's life after murder of Clytemnestra" ("Notes," p. 530). The modern dramatist seeks to redress the balance by focusing on this female protagonist rather than on the Orestes figure as had the Greek tragedians.

In theory, O'Neill's decision to wed psychoanalytic theory to the Greek mythic material seems well-motivated. Of course, Freud himself frequently appealed to Greek mythic material and especially to the Oedipal tragedy in naming what he calls "the central phenomenon of the sexual period in early childhood."[7] In practice, however, O'Neill's choice of classical Freudian theory to explore the female psyche via Greek tragedy makes strange bedfellows indeed. The Greek tragic stage was capable of creating female figures of remarkable power and complexity and of exploring feminine interiority with extraordinary insight.[8] Freudian theorizing of the feminine, on the other hand, has been an area of psychoanalytic theory repeatedly challenged and contested (first in the 1930's and recently by a new generation of feminists) as inadequate or misconceived.[9] The weaknesses of the Freudian imagination in this regard work directly counter to O'Neill's desire to trace and illumine the character of Electra. However, Freudian theory may have served O'Neill very well as a way to mask his own fears and inadequacies in the portrayal of the feminine psyche.

One key to understanding O'Neill's superimposition of Vienna on Greece is his fascination with the mask, which as we shall see provides a bridge for him between Greek dramatic convention and psychoanalytic theory. In the stage directions of *Mourning Becomes Electra*, the mask is a constantly recurring feature. *All* of the Mannons are said to possess mask-like faces, and one of O'Neill's "choral" figures makes this explicit for the audience early on. While O'Neill had already experienced with the use of masks (notably in *The Great God Brown*, produced in 1926), he eventually chose not to use actual masks in this production. Yet, his concept of the mask *is* central to his particular fusion of the classical and the psychoanalytical.

An essay by O'Neill which is contemporary with the trilogy expresses his endorsement of masking as a theatrical convention: "the mask is dramatic in itself...."[10] But, more importantly, the essay documents for us how theater and psychology met for O'Neill in the concept of the mask. Consider the following passages:

> The use of masks will be discovered eventually to be the freest solution of the modern dramatists's problem as to how...he can express those profound hidden conflict's of the mind which the probings of psychology continue to disclose to us.
>
> Dogma for the new masked drama: One's outer life passes in a solitude *haunted* by the masks of others; one's inner life passes in a solitude *hounded* by the masks of oneself [italics mine; cf. the titles of the trilogy's plays, *The Hunted* and *The Haunted*, as well as Orin's comment on Lavinia: "You'll have to haunt and hound her for a lifetime!"]
>
> For what, at bottom, is the new psychological insight into human cause and effect but a study in masks, an exercise in unmasking?

In terms of the theater, then, O'Neill sees the mask as a way of directing the audience's attention inward, to the characters' interior states rather than dissipating it on the superficial (for example, as he notes, on a "star" performance). In terms of psychoanalysis, however, O'Neill sees the journey to the interior as an *unmasking*. And yet the psyche itself, it seems, is constituted of masks. In other words, while O'Neill speaks of analysis as an unmasking, that process itself can only yield the discovery of more masks. On this view, O'Neill seems to constitute the self as structured like an onion. Mask after mask might be removed, but underneath would lie only other masks and, ultimately: nothing, *horror vacui*.

If masks are so deeply implicated in O'Neill's conceptions both of the theater and of the self, the first thing that might strike us about *Mourning Becomes Electra* is the *absence* of masks. On the most obvious level, O'Neill decided to eschew the use of actual masks in favor of stage directions repetitively characterizing the Mannons as having mask-like faces. Those faces, however, reveal much more than they conceal. In O'Neill's explicit directions, virtually every flicker of emotion is registered melodramatically on the faces of his protagonists. More significantly than these aspects of the staging, however, is the fact that the psyche itself in this trilogy requires no un-masking, no psychoanalysis. "An exercise in unmasking" is *not* what O'Neill's trilogy provides. Oddly enough, the truth seems always there, right before the audience and (more curious still) evident to the protagonists as well. With the single exception of Vinnie's strong attraction to Brant (to which we shall return), O'Neill's characters are remarkably *un*deceived about their passions, fantasies, and motives. Indeed a number of lines are almost embarrassingly direct in voicing these:

> Vinnie (to her father): "You're the only man I'll ever love."
>
> Ezra (to his daughter): "I want you to remain my little girl."
>
> Orin (to his mother): "You're my only girl."
>
> Christine (to her son): "We had a secret little world of our own in the old days, didn't we?"

These family members might have stepped out of a textbook of Freudian neuroses immediately onto the stage.

The problem seems to be that O'Neill has allowed an over-dose of Freudian theory to rob his characters of life and credibility.[11] Doris Alexander, however, has pointed out that this is a misdiagnosis. In fact, O'Neill's representations of the Oedipal complex are *so* explicit that they cease to be Freudian at all. She specifies the non-orthodox nature of O'Neill's "Freudian" ideas; the dramatist's "peculiarly non-Freudian version of the Oedipus complex," she writes, "lacks the most important elements of Freud's, ambivalence and unconsciousness."[12] More than simply diagnosing the heterodoxy of O'Neill's apparent Freudianism, however, Alexander's important article offers a convincingly documented explanation for its origin.

She shows that O'Neill's non-orthodox version of Freudian theory was highly influenced by a book published in 1929 by his friend and correspondent,

Kenneth Macgowan.[13] The book, entitled *What is Wrong with Marriage?* Was in turn a popularization of an academic psychoanalytic study, *A Research in Marriage*, completed by Dr. G. V. Hamilton, based on his analysis of two hundred married men and women. Among the research subjects was O'Neill himself, who participated in the study in exchange for Hamilton's services in treating his drinking problem. O'Neill's peculiar form of the Oedipal complex—in which intricate, subtle, and unconscious affinities (as Freud theorized them) are replaced by straightforwarded attractions, voiced without hesitation and based on obvious physical resemblance—can be seen to have a clear parallel in Macgowan's book. Both literalize and reify concepts which in Freud may exist on a level of *relations* rather than objects and be *metaphorical* rather than literal.

What Alexander carefully and convincingly documents in a scholarly analysis has been expressed in a satiric vein but nonetheless accurately by Eric Bentley:

> O'Neill has boasted his ignorance of Freud but such ignorance is not enough. He should be ignorant also of the watered-down Freudianism of Sardi's and the Algonquin, the Freudianism of all those who are ignorant of Freud, the Freudianism of the subintelligentsia. Now what is it that your subintellectual knows about Freud? That he "put everything down to sex." Precisely; and that is what O'Neill does with the [Electra] myth....*Mourning Becomes Electra* is all sex talk. Sex talk—not sex lived and embodied but sex talked of and lingered....O'Neill is an acute case of what Lawrence called "sex in the head." Sex is almost the only idea he has—has insistently—and it is for him *only* an idea.[14]

My contention here will be that Eric Bently is fundamentally correct. However arch his criticism may sound, he has hit upon the basic problem of *Mourning Becomes Electra*. And that problem does not have to do with the pathologically intense Oedipal relations so insistently displayed before us on the stage. They are merely a screen. Indeed, the very reason they are so openly presented and voiced is that they are *not* what is psychologically at stake in the trilogy. In fact, all is *not* openly voiced and displayed. The plays still circle about a center of darkness and the unknown. It is the origin of all subsequent action, and it remains almost entirely obscure. What is really at issue is confrontation of the female as a sexual being. This "sex talk"—via a popularized version of Freud—serves as a way for the playwright to mask "sex lived and embodied" and to displace it from his treatment of the Electra tragedy.

Repression. Despite O'Neill's explicit *claim* to investigate the Electra figure, in practice he has rigorously and systematically repressed feminine sexuality, initiation, and satisfaction. For this purpose, the vagaries of Freudian theory on the feminine are perfectly well-suited. "O'Neill always had a problem depicting women," notes one scholar.[15] Surely, that is an understatement. In O'Neill's canon, women seem capable of occupying only two positions; child-like or domineering, they remain in either case secretive, manipulative, dangerous, and incomprehensible.[16] Freudian psychology does not illumine these characters, it merely provides new masks.

In *Mourning Becomes Electra*, several crucial moments which motivate the action and yet are never directly confronted can be identified: all concern feminine sexuality, its awakening, and its threatening quality. This is true through three generations. For not only Christine's wedding night, but also Marie Brantôme's attraction for the Mannon brothers and Vinnie's attraction to Brant (as well as, subsequently, to the native Avahanni) remain (as Freud says of feminine sexuality) "shadowy and incomplete." The female's sexual desire or activity is consistently and systematically repressed in the play, yet is actually the motive of the action. In terms of plot, the apparently pathological relations within the family are of second-order importance. The first order, the prime sources of narrative are two non-Oedipal, non-aberrant sexual moments—the sexual relations of David Mannon with Marie Brantôme and of Ezra Mannon with his wife Christine.[17]

Given the seething passions supposedly lurking at the heart of the action, the trilogy itself is remarkably reticent in touching upon those passions. In the first generation, the original attraction between the governess Marie Brantome and one (both?) of the Mannon brothers is almost as completely suppressed in the drama as it is in the family history. Despite multiple allusions to the tale (by the chorus, Seth, and Brant), the narrative remains rather obscure, both because of its compressed complexity and because of the very different points of view of the narrators. Since its informant's views are diametrically opposed and equally highly prejudiced, the audience acquires an unclear and fragmented knowledge of the affair.

In the subsequent generation, the wedding night between Ezra and Christine, for all its centrality to the play, is more radically suppressed. Concerning this nuptial moment, O'Neill never reveals more than that the experience was "disgusting." This adjective recurs several times in the trilogy, all but once in the context of feminine sexuality and initiation:

> CHRISTINE....I loved him once—before I married him...He was silent and mysterious and romantic! But marriage soon turned his romance into—disgust! (*Homecoming*, Act 2)
>
> LAVINIA. So I was born of your disgust! (*Homecoming*, Act 2)
>
> CHRISTINE....I loved you when I married you! I wanted to give myself! But you made me so I couldn't give! You filled me with disgust! (*Homecoming*, Act 4)
>
> ORIN....the naked women [of the Islands] disgusted me...(*Haunted*, Act 1, Scene 2)
>
> LAVINIA. Orin! Don't be disgusting! [At the suggestion that she fell in love with the Islanders.] (*Haunted*, Act I, Scene 2)
>
> LAVINIA. How can you make up such disgusting fibs? [In the same context as the preceding reference] (*Haunted*, Act I, Scene 2)

The playwright's refusal to confront the nuptial scene directly—which makes of this moment the unfathomable origin of what transpires on stage may be a counterpart to Freudian notions of "the primal scene," the coupling of parents which the child barely glimpses (or merely imagines) and yet realizes is fraught with meaning.[18] In Freudian theory, the "primal scene" plays a crucial role in the generation of subsequent neurosis, as Christine's "disgusting" wedding night generates the subsequent aberrance in the family. Only in his notes does O'Neill comment on the source of the problem in the Mannon marriage: "reason for Clytemnestra's hatred for Agamemnon sexual frustration by his Puritan sense of guilt turning love to lust..." ("Notes," p. 531). This explanation bears comparison with O'Neill's earlier outline of the play's characters. Of "Clementina" (who will later become "Christine"), he remarks: "her passionate, full-blooded femaleness had never found sex-satisfaction in his repressed morally-constrained, disapproving sex-frigidity" (Cited in Floyd, *Work*, p. 188). It is worth remarking the reversal of typical gender stereotypes here, with the female seeking "satisfaction," the male afflicted by "frigidity."

If Christine's initiation into marital "duty" is hidden under the designation "disgusting," her second initiation, into fulfilling sexuality with Brant, is also displaced by O'Neill as far as possible: removed, mediated, and downplayed. The illicit couple's rendezvous are of course remote from the Mannon home, staged in distant New York. Our knowledge of them comes, via hearsay, from Vinnie's detective mission to the city. She reports the results of her spying, which significantly culminates in what she has *heard* outside of Brant's room. And what she has heard is "kissing". O'Neill's choice to represent the lover's affair in this way departs substantially from his initial scenario. Originally, the lover's passion was verified by the written evidence of love letters exchanged between the two—letters which spoke explicitly, for example, of Christine's white body in her paramour's arms. In addition, the couple were to embrace passionately onstage and verbally recall moments of their affair (Floyd, *Work*, pp. 193-94, 200). Though *The Hunted* does include a scene of embrace between the two, at the time their passion is unquestionably subordinated to fear. Thus the erotic relations between the lovers have been suppressed in the final text.

Not only Christine's erotic nature but also Vinnie's figures in the trilogy. But it is a figure well hidden. Perhaps the only truly repressed and unspoken Oedipal desire in the drama is that of Lavinia for Adam Brant. Before Lavinia's final "Freudian slip" (when, in a passionate embrace with Peter, she cries out, "Want me! Take me, Adam!"), only unreliable intimations indicate the extent to which a thwarted passion for her mother's lover motivates her single-minded vengeance. Although Christine and Orin both charge Vinnie with a jealous passion for Brant, the jealousy of the accusers themselves leads us substantially to discount their accusations. O'Neill's documentation of his writing shows, however, that the recognition of Lavinia's love for Brant had been quite explicit in the early scenario and in fact was excised from the final text at the last moment. In the original scenario, the "Vinnie" character (called "Elena" at this point) feels "a strange conflict is going on within her, she cannot help being fascinated by the idea of being his [i.e., Brant's] wife, in bed with him" (Floyd, *Work*, p. 195). Later, Elena, having discovered the correspondence between the lovers is "repulsed—but attracted by the love letters she has read. She would make him forget her mother in her arms!" (Floyd, *Work*, p.196). In fact, Lavinia, until the last of the play's six revisions, explicitly acknowledged her love for Brant in the dialogue. A small journal, kept while travelling in the Canary Islands and dedicated to his wife Carlotta, indicates that not until 8 March 1931 (i.e., three weeks before deciding he had truly completed the five-year writing process) did O'Neill cut the "one passage" which "reveals what is only implied in the published text—that Lavinia loves her mother's lover" (Floyd, *Work*, p. 208).

As with Christine's second sexual initiation, so Lavinia's second erotic attraction is remarkably displaced in the text. This concerns, of course, her mysterious relation to the "native," Avahanni. Again, the association, whatever we are to make of it, is distanced geographically, this time not merely from New England to New York, but much further to "the Islands," which function as a mythologized landscape throughout the plays. Again, all that we know initially of the relation we learn through hearsay, this time through Orin rather than Lavinia. Whereas Lavinia had, however, at least heard *something* (however slight, however mediated), Orin's evidence of Lavinia's alleged sexual attraction is even more attenuated. He accuses Lavinia of an unspecified incident at which he was not present either to see or to hear. Rather, he infers her guilt from looking at her face—and projects it into the future as well with his claim that "If we'd stayed another month, I know I'd have found her some moonlight night dancing under the palm trees—as naked as the rest!" To this Vinnie twice objects that Orin is being "disgusting." She herself, however, will later complicate the picture by the now familiar strategy of concealing/revealing. Her thoroughly romantic and sensual evocation of the Islands to Peter seems to confirm Orin's thinly-attested accusation. Subsequently, she will twice claim sexual intimacy with the native Avahanni—and each time, immediately withdraw and repudiate that claim. In this case, then, not only is the representation of the woman's sexual satisfaction or initiation displaced and suppressed; in fact, it is completely unclear whether there has even been such a scene of initiation.

What *is* represented on the stage is the relation between Vinnie and Peter, her would-be fiancé. Here, it is clear that the woman has been transformed by her voyage to "the Islands." In this case, O'Neill registers ambivalent messages about the female's assumption and open expression of sexual desire in the stage directions rather than directly in the dialogue. Thus we learn that, when Lavinia impulsively embraces and kisses Peter passionately, "*He returns it, aroused and at the same time a little shocked by her boldness.*" Later, he will be "*shocked and repelled by her display of passion.*" Finally, when he believes that Lavinia had "lusted" with Avahanni, Peter "*stares at her with a stricken look of horrified repulsion.*" Of course, Peter has no inkling of Vinnie's role as accessory in the deaths of Brant, Christine, and Orin. But, for him, her entry into sexual relations takes on the dimensions of criminal offense. In horror at the thought that Vinnie has been initiated into sexuality, he cries, "you are bad at heart—no wonder Orin killed himself—God, I—I hope you'll be punished...." He then runs offstage. Thus O'Neill effects an important transposition, which manages to equate or replace criminal activity with sexual activity. The punishment which might indeed be meted out to the woman on the grounds of her implication in multiple deaths is here seen as merited on the grounds of her participation in sexual relations.

Each of the trilogy's encounters with female desire remains "shadowy and incomplete." Each, however, is a source of anxiety to be displaced, mediated, and replaced by various textual strategies. O'Neill has exfoliated a series of complexities, like a series of masks, around a central problem—confronting female desire, initiation, and satisfaction. *This* is what is systematically repressed throughout the plays. Even more striking is the fact that this repression, which takes the particular form of revealing too much of the inessential (Oedipal neurosis) in order to hide and deflect attention from the essential (feminine desire), is replicated in O'Neill's writing of the trilogy itself. If O'Neill has effectively resisted the representation of female desire by displacing it from the final text of the trilogy, yet sexuality does surface elsewhere—namely, in O'Neill's own relation to the drama and its writing. His documentation of that process reveals the return of the repressed.

The Return of the Repressed—in Writing. It is at this point that we must psychoanalyze the plays themselves, as it were. Of course, the autobiographical elements which pervade O'Neill's work are well known. In a very real sense, the plays *are* the man, and more than one critic has remarked that O'Neill's theater is in fact an unmediated presentation of self, that the dramatist's audience is often less engaged with the *characters* of O'Neill than with the man himself.[19] It is all too tempting, therefore, to launch into a reading of O'Neill's psychosexual history as it is (irrepressibly) represented in his drama. What I shall attempt here is *not* a psychobiography, but rather to *psychoanalyze* (if that is not too grand a term) the trilogy itself and O'Neill's *writing* of the trilogy as displaying a coherent set of symptoms and strategies. When we examine the playwright's notes—and other documentation relevant to the writing of the trilogy—we find a pattern of metaphor emphasizing exposure/concealment and a strikingly sexual relation to the writing.

O'Neill's production of the Electra trilogy entails a peculiar pattern of hiding and exposing. (We might compare Ezra's confession to Christine: "Something queer in me keeps me mum about the things I'd like most to say—keeps me hiding the things I'd like to show.") On the one hand, O'Neill was uncharacteristically secretive about the work.[20] In contrast to his usual practice, he did not reveal his material to friends; in a letter to Benjamin de Casseres of 20 April 1930 he noted only that the work is a "psychological drama of lust," but that this description is sent "*in strictest confidence.*"[21] Oddly enough, however, while he was anomalously tight-lipped to others concerning the project, he was also anomalously complete in his private record of the work (Floyd, *Work*, p. 186). Then uniquely, O'Neill agreed to introduce these private notes into the public sector by publishing them not once, but twice![22] Curiously, however, the notes themselves insist by their over-determined title ("Working Notes and Extracts from a Fragmentary Work Diary") upon their incompleteness, as if something were still hidden and inaccessible. The publication manages, therefore, both to reveal and conceal at the same time.[23] Something of the same may be said of O'Neill's drama itself. Having completed his first draft, he exclaims that "reading this first draft I get the feeling that more of my idea was left out of the play than there is in it!" ("Notes," p. 532). In an article on *Mourning Becomes Electra*, Barrett Clark makes a strikingly similar observation: "What appeals to me most strongly in those of...[O'Neill's] plays I most respect and like is this uneasy undertone that hints at something not completely expressed."[24] Indeed, something very similar is what I claim—that the completed text *symptomatically* "leaves out" or represses disturbing sexual material, and that this project leaves its traces in the process of the writing itself.

At the same time that female sexuality is being edited out of the work, O'Neill's set of metaphors for the creation of the play consistently refers to adequacy/inadequacy of male sexual performance. Very early in his "Working Notes," O'Neill states his objective: to give Electra a tragic ending worthy of her, since in Greek versions she merely "peters out into undramatic married banality" ("Notes," p. 520). After his first attempt, O'Neill alludes to his "scrawny first draft." Having completed his second draft, however, he "feel[s] drained out." Rereading this draft a week later, he is heartened, but finds that his technique "causes[s] action to halt and limp" ("Notes," pp. 533-34).

Particularly intriguing is his "solution" to the problem of writing—an insistent, monotonous rhythm, a breakthrough so appealing he insists on describing it three times. It should not escape us that this is the prose model selected to represent a tragedy significantly motivated by the sexual inadequacies of Ezra Mannon as a cold, unimaginative, and unsatisfying lover. (Relevant here as well is Orin's discussion of his father's nickname in the Army, "Old Stick": "Father was no good on an offensive but...[he'd] stick in the mud and hold a position until hell froze over!") The day after expressing the fear that his drama is "limp," O'Neill exhorts himself to "try for prose with simple forceful repeating accent and rhythm which will express driving insistent compulsion of passions" ("Notes," p. 534). So pleased is he with his "new conception" that he describes it yet again the next day: "think I have hit on right rhythm of prose—monotonous, simple words driving insistence" ("Notes," p. 534). Upon reading his third draft two months later, he is still obsessed with rhythm—which now expresses itself more openly in sexual terms, in his instructions to himself: "get all this in naturally in straight dialogue—as simple and direct and dynamic as possible...stop doing things to these characters—let them reveal themselves—inspite of (or because of!) their long locked-up passions, I feel them burning to do just this!" ("Notes," p. 535).

Through three more re-writings, however, the drama continues to be recalcitrant. George Jean Nathan recalls that the writing of this work was uniquely difficult for O'Neill, who wrote him at one point: "I'm beginning to hate it and curse the day I ever conceived such an idea."[25] Later, however, when the work was finally completed, he wrote again to Nathan: "I have a feeling of there being real size in it, quite apart from its length."

Despite O'Neill's difficulties in writing the trilogy, as documented in his letters and notes, upon completion of the drama he was enthusiastic about the work accomplished. To Nathan he wrote: "It has been one hell of a job! Let's hope the result in some measure justifies the labor I've put in." The most striking document, however, is the inscription with which he dedicated the script to his newly married third wife, Carlotta Monterey. As Croswell Bowen records,

> Mrs. O'Neill sent fifty copies of the inscription to friends with the following printed note:

Fifty copies of Eugene O'Neill's inscription to the final longhand manuscript of *Mourning Becomes Electra* have been reproduced in facsimile. This copy is No.___.[26]

In stark contrast to this public dissemination of the inscription text is the intimacy of the terms in which O'Neill describes therein the production of the trilogy. He begins with "the impenetrable days of pain in which you privately suffered in silence that this trilogy might be born." Oddly, although he alludes to the work as "this trilogy of the damned!" he immediately continues: "These scripts are like us and my presenting them is a gift which, already, is half yours." He speaks of "the travail we have gone through for its sake" and concludes with the remarkable closing: "Oh, mother and wife and mistress and friend!—And collaborator! I love you."

That the dedicatee chose to commercialize this document by circulating it to fifty of her closet friends is a topic which we shall not broach here. What *is* relevant to our inquiry, however, is the curious birthing process of the trilogy which O'Neill's metaphors describe. Consistently, the language associated with the completion of the work is that of midwifery. But the mother in question vacillates between being O'Neill's wife and himself.

Michael Manheim has called attention to a kind of gender-free identification in O'Neill's plays—that is, that "a character's sex has little to do with the figure he or she represents in O'Neill's mind."[27] Such bi-sexuality seems to inform O'Neill's view of his relation to the Electra trilogy. On the one hand, the "Working Notes" employ a metaphorics of male performance and adequacy. On the other hand, the author's dedication of the work casts him as its mother, with the writing presented, as a child to the spouse (Carlotta). Of course, we could view this in Freudian terms (as the negative Oedipal complex of the male child, who wishes to present a baby to the father).

Re-Inscription. Rather than turning to theory external to the trilogy, however, let us consider O'Neill's relation to his own writing by examining his characterization of writing *within the plays*. As I have noted above, in O'Neill's original scenario an exchange of letters between Christine Mannon and her lover, Adam Brant, played an important, revelatory role. In the re-working of the trilogy, this correspondence has disappeared altogether. Yet the act of writing has by no means disappeared from the published drama. On the contrary, the epistolary genre recurs intermittently, retaining erotic associations throughout, and other acts of writing as well prove crucial in the narrative.

The association of writing and eros is established very early in the trilogy when Peter confides to Vinnie: "Hazel feels bad about Orin not writing. Do you think he really—loves her?" From this point on, the *absence* rather than the presence of epistolary exchange often is significant. The next unanswered letter of which we learn is that of Adam's mother to Ezra Mannon—a letter containing Adam's charge that because "he never answered her," Ezra is "as guilty of murder as anyone he ever sent to the rope when he was a judge!" From Seth's exposition of the Mannon past, we know that Ezra too, like his father and uncle, was attracted to Marie Brantôme: "He was only a boy then, but he was crazy about her." Confronted with the knowledge of her sexual relations, however, he rejects his earlier feelings: "he hated her worse than anyone when it got found out she was his Uncle David's fancy woman." This repudiation of erotic attraction is thus reenacted by his refusal to respond to her writing. In *The Hunted*, Orin rebukes his mother bitterly for her failure to write (which, as we know—and he senses—signals her transfer of erotic involvement from her son to Adam). Orin rebuts her claim of loneliness with the exclamation: "So lonely, you've written me exactly two letters in the last six months!" And later complains: "Your letters got farther and farther between—and they seemed cold! It drove me crazy!"

If correspondence broken off (like coitus interruptus) is a source of frustration, yet to engage in writing itself in the trilogy is consistently threatening and/or dangerous. The act of writing is in both of these ways distinctly eroticized in O'Neill's work. To refrain from writing is to refuse erotic involvement; but to write is to enter into an economy of life-and-death, as is entry into the sexual cycle. Thus, acts of writing in the plays are consistently bound up with death—for oneself or another. Marie Brantôme's desperate letter to Ezra Mannon will be the prelude to her death. Ezra's own letter home from the front, describing his heart condition, will supply a pretext for his own murder. That murder will be set in motion by Christine's writing out for Adam the prescription for poison. At the same time, she recognizes that this act of writing binds Adam irrevocably to her. Having passed the note to him, she observes triumphantly, "You'll never dare leave me now, Adam."

The use of writing as a threat (more specifically, as a means of coercion on the sphere of one's own erotic fantasies) seems one of the many characteristics inherited from Christine by her children. For both Vinnie and Orin engage in similar practices of coercive writing. Vinnie, by writing to her father and Orin "Only enough so they'd be suspicious," inserts herself between her father and mother, forces Christine into her power and, through the threat of writing again (more completely), keeps her there. The most significant scribal act of the trilogy, however, is surely Orin's writing in the final play. Orin at first has difficulty carrying out his intention to wire the family's history, for he is resistant to the realization that relations between himself and Vinnie replicate the relation between their parents ("That's the evil destiny out of the past I haven't dared predict. I'm the Mannon you're chained to!"). Having completed the document, he presents it first to the would-be wife, Hazel. Soon, however, he withdraws his text from her and represents it to the mother/sister, Lavinia using his writing as a means to coerce her consent to incest. In this way, the act of writing is virtually festishized, for in Orin's fantasy the completion of the text yields power to fulfill the Oedipal desires. That desire is not fulfilled, however; in the end, the completion of the text "stands in" for engagement in the sexual cycle.

Throughout the trilogy, writing maintains a consistent status, one which associates it closely with erotic activity. The refusal of epistolary intercourse is a sign of a concomitant refusal of sexual intercourse. We can see this in the cases of Orin and Hazel, Ezra and Christine (for he has evidently written to Vinnie concerning his homecoming, but not to his wife), Ezra and Marie Brantôme, Christine and Orin. But daring to write bestows an almost magical potency, rendering one capable of binding others, often in the realm of sexual desires (whether explicit or implicit). Thus, Vinnie writes to her father and Orin—and threatens to write more—Christine writes a formula which will bind Adam to her, and Orin writes a text intended both to bind Lavinia irrevocably and illicitly to himself as well as to sever her from Peter.

That text, the history of the Mannon family, must bear a great resemblance to the text of the trilogy itself. Orin's history, therefore, and O'Neill's trilogy invite comparison. I suggest that, with Orin's writing of the family history and his bestowal of it, O'Neill has re-inscribed within the text his own textual production of the trilogy—and his presentation of it to the mother/wife, Carlotta. In this way, O'Neill has employed a strategy of displacing sexuality to textuality in such a way that the mastery of authorship becomes a means of confronting feminine desire. Underlying the surface of mere "subintelligentsia Freud," this displacement of erotic empowerment, from sexual to textual relations, is the mask behind the mask in *Mourning Becomes Electra*, the truly psychoanalytic basis of the trilogy.[28]

NOTES

1. Cf. Doris V. Falk, *Eugene O'Neill and the Tragic Tension: An Interpretive Study of the Plays* (New Brunswick, N.J.: Rutgers Univ. Press, 1958), p. 26.

2. Eugene O'Neill, "Working Notes and Extracts from a Fragmentary Work Diary," in *European Theories of the Drama with a Supplement on the American Drama*, ed. Barrett H. Clark, rev. ed. (New York: Crown, 1947), p. 534; hereinafter cited in my text as "Notes."

3. See Arthur H. Nethercot, "The Psychoanalyzing of Eugene O'Neill," *Modern Drama*, 3 (1960-61), 357-72, and "The Psychoanalyzing of Eugene O'Neill: A Postscript," *Modern Drama*, 8 (1965-66), 150-55. The first of these largely recapitulates views expressed by other critics, notably Edwin A. Engel, *The Haunted Heroes of Eugene O'Neill* (Cambridge: Harvard Univ. Press, 1953), and Falk, *Eugene O'Neill and the Tragic Tension*. The second draws upon the biography of Arthur and Barbara Gelb, *O'Neill* (New York, 1962), to document further O'Neill's actual knowledge of what he called merely "the new psychology." For the relevant view of a practicing psychoanalyst, see Philip Weissman, "Conscious and Unconscious Autobiographical Dramas of Eugene O'Neill," *Journal of the American Psychoanalytic Association*, 5 (1957), 432-60.

4. See his personal letter to Barrett H. Clark, cited in Clark's article," Aeschylus and O'Neill," *English Journal*, 21 (1932), 710: "critics...read too damn much Freud into stuff that could very well have been written exactly as is before psychoanalysis was ever heard of....And I am no deep student of psychoanalysis. As far as I can remember, of all the books written by Freud, Jung, etc., I have read only four [Nethercot, p. 153, identifies three of these as *Totem and Taboo*, *Beyond the Pleasure Principle*, and Jung's *Psychology of the Unconscious*] and Jung is the only one of the lot who interests me." For the Jungian aspects of O'Neill's work—and, indeed, his anticipation of several "neo-Freudians," notably Karen Horney—see Falk, *Tension, passim*.

5. Virginia Floyd, *Eugene O'Neill at Work: Newly Released Ideas for Plays* (New York: Frederick Ungar, 1981); hereinafter cited in my text as Floyd, *Work*, p. 185: "While the first idea for *Mourning Becomes Electra* appears in the notebook in 1928, O'Neill's statements indicate his decision to write the "Greek tragedy" dates to spring 1926 after he had read Arthur Symon's translation of Hugo von Hofmannstahl's *Electra*." During 21-27 June 1929, O'Neill read Greek plays in translation (Floyd, *Work*, p. 196). The trilogy was begun in 1929 and, after six revisions, completed in 1931.

6. Letter to Robert Sisk, 28 August 1930, as quoted in Floyd, *Work*, p. 185.

7. Sigmund Freud, "The Passing of the Oedipus Complex" (1924). Freud himself rejected the use of the Jungian term *Electra complex*; he preferred instead to speak of the female Oedipus complex ("Female Sexuality," 1931).

8. On the apparent discrepancy between women's inferior social position in classical Athens and their powerful portrayal on the Athenian stage, see M. Shaw, "The Female Intruder: Women in Fifth-Century Drama," *Classical Philology*, 70 (1975), 255-60; Helene Foley, " 'The Female Intruder' Reconsidered: Women in Aristophanes' *Lysistrata* and *Ecclesiazusae*," *Classical Philology*, 77 (1982), 1-21; F. I. Zeitlin, "The Dynamics of Misogyny: Myth and Myth-Making in the *Oresteia*," *Arethusa*, 2 (1978), 149-84; and H. Foley, "The Conception of Women in Athenian Drama," in *Reflections of Women in Antiquity*, ed. H. Foley (London, 1982), pp. 127-68.

9. Juliet Mitchell presents a clear summary of so-called Jones-Freud controversy over feminine sexuality in "Freud, the Freudians, and the Psychology of Women," *Psychoanalysis and the Feminism* (New York: Pantheon, 1974), pp. 121-31. Critiques of the Freudian view of the feminine which remain within the psychoanalytic discourse may be found in Mitchell's book as well as in Janine Chasseguet-Smirgel, *Sexuality and Mind: The Role of the Father and Mother in the Psyche* (New York Univ. Press, 1986), pp. 9-28. Another such voice, which acknowledges the authority of Freud while at the same time significantly re-interpreting the understanding of the feminine, is of course that of Lacan. See Jacques Lacan and the école freudienne, *Feminine Sexuality*, ed. Juliet Mitchell and Jacqueline Rose (New York: Pantheon, 1985).

10. "Memoranda on Masks," *The American Spectator* (November 1932) p. 3.

11. For such a view, see Ahuja Chaman, *Tragedy, Modern Temper, and O'Neill* (Atlantic Highlands, N.J.: Humanities Press, 1984), p. 96: "But O'Neill *did* read Freud before writing *Strange Interlude*....His mind seething with case-histories, he merely gave dramatic shape to such material as might have been useful for the mental clinics but was patently questionable for the theatre." Certainly the explicitness with which the interlocking Oedipal attractions of this family are voiced violates our sense of verisimilitude. But O'Neill indicates that, rather than reality, he was striving to achieve an "unreal realism" ("Notes," p. 534). CF. Leonard Chabrowe, *Ritual and Pathos: The Theatre of O'Neill* (Lewisburg: Bucknell Univ. Press, 1976), p. 161.

12. Doris M. Alexander, "*Psychological Fate in Mourning Becomes Electra*," PMLA, 68 (1953), 923-34.

13. A letter to Macgowan, dated 14 June 1929, playfully alludes to "you psychosharks!" (cited in Floyd, *Work*, p. 150). By this term O'Neill means those who would read autobiography into his *Days Without End*.

14. Eric Bently, "Trying to Like O'Neill," in *In Search of Theatre* (New York: Alfred A. Knopf, 1952), p. 246.

15. Virginia Floyd, *The Plays of Eugene O'Neill: A New Assessment* (New York: Ungar, 1987), p. 405.

16. Is it mere coincidence that O'Neill who was no stranger to Spanish-speaking regions, should give the name of "Nina"—in Spanish, "little girl"—to the protagonist of what he called his "women's play," *Strange Interlude*.

17. Cf. Chabrowe, who locates the first "visible link in the chain" of Mannon tragedies as the

marriage relationship of Ezra and Christine (p. 149), but also notes that the events of the trilogy are all to be traced to Abe Mannon's act of jealousy" and that this origin seems both overdetermined and "too arbitrary a beginning" (p. 162).

18. Freud's most elaborate exposition of the primal scene occurs in the Wolf Man case history *From the History of an Infantile Neurosis*, pt. 4 (1918). For a discussion of whether the parental coitus is actually viewed or merely imagined (i.e., "recollected" or "constructed"), see pt. 5. Recently, the concept of the primal scene has been subjected to new scrutiny, as has the narrative of the Wolf Man itself. See A. Esman, "The Primal Scene: A Review and Reconsideration," *The Psychoanalytic Study of the Child*, 28 (1973), 49-81; H. Blum, "On the Concept and Consequences of the Primal Scene," *Psychoanalytical Quarterly*, 48 (1979), 27-47; H. Blum, "The Pathogenic Influence of the Primal Scene: A Re-Evaluation," in *Freud and His Patients*, ed. M. Kanzer and J. Glenn (New York, 1980); and Patrick J. Mahony, *Cries of the Wolf Man*, History of Psychoanalysis, 1 (New York: International Universities Press, 1984).

19. Francis Fergusson, "Eugene O'Neill," *The Hound and Horn*, 3 (1930), 145-60; rpt. in *Literary Opinion in America*, ed. Morton D. Zabel, 3rd ed. (New York: Harper, 1958), III, 518-19. See also Harold Clurman, "Long Day's Journey Into Night," *The Nation*, 3 March 1956, and Falk, *Tension*, pp. 12, 119.

20. Travis Bogard, *A Contour in Time: The Plays of Eugene O'Neill* (New York: Oxford Univ. Press, 1972), p. 334.

21. Bogard, *Contour*, p. 335.

22. First in the *New York Herald Tribune* of 3 Nov. 1931. Then, in response to a request from Barrett Clark, O'Neill suggests their re-publication in Clark's *European Theories of the Drama* volume.

23. Cf. Clark's speculation on O'Neill's "own private notes" on *Morning Becomes Electra*: "are these notes complete?" (Aeschylus and O'Neill," *English Journal*, 21 [1932], 699). Obviously, Floyd's subsequent publication of O'Neill's notebooks (itself only partial) shows that they were not (Floyd, *Work*, pp. 185-209).

24. Clark, "Aeschylus," p. 701; cf. Falk, *Tension*, p. 139.

25. George Jean Nathan, "Portrait of O'Neill," *The Intimate Notebooks of George Jean Nathan* (New York: Alfred Knopf, 1931-32).

26. Croswell Bowen, *P.M.*, 3 November 1946.

27. Michael Manheim, *Eugene O'Neill's New Language of Kinship* (Syracuse: Syracuse Univ. Press, 1982), p. 78.

28. For his always patient and perceptive readings, I thank my toughest editor, First Lieutenant Thomas J. Scherer of the U. S. Army I would also like to thank my colleagues David Konstan and Coppelia Kahn as well as my anonymous referee for helpful suggestions and encouragement.

Comparative Drama, 22 (Spring 1988): 37-55.

Ah, Wilderness!

A Great American Comedy

Euphemia Van Rensselaer Wyatt

E. A. Robinson once said to me some twenty years ago that the best man on our stage was George M. Cohan. Just before she died Mrs. Fiske said the same to Mr. Cohan's daughter. After such opinions it seems to make very little difference if I announce I agree with them. For the first time in his whole life, Mr. Cohan is acting in a play not written by himself. That the authors of *The Hairy Ape* and *Little Johnny Jones* should come together in their prime is one of those happy events that appear anomalous and are perfectly logical. Genius makes for kinship. But the Theater Guild never did a better deed for the American Theater than when they invited George M. Cohan to grace Eugene O'Neill's first comedy. *Ah, Wilderness*, is a play everyone must see who wants to have something to boast about to his grandchildren, for Cohan's Nat Miller will rank with Jefferson's Rip Van Winkle.

It is all very sudden and a tremendous help to the theater for although Mr. O'Neill has been expected to write the great American tragedy, hometown comedy lay unsuspected in his inkwell. He admits now that it was a surprise to himself and that he dashed it off in six weeks, in between the second and third acts of his next tragedy. We are not so surprised as we might be, as we have never been unduly alarmed over Mr. O'Neill's morbid tendencies. Mr. O'Neill has never confused right with wrong no matter how much sinners figured in his dramas, and in this day when sin is barely recognized, that is a very important stand point. O'Neill is really a Catholic at heart. *Marco Millions* carried a finer spirituality and a fiercer warning against materialism than most of its audiences seemed to appreciate. *Ah, Wilderness* is the perfect sequel to the Holy Father's Encyclical on Marriage. No more tender plea could be made for the family.

Because it is confessedly reminiscent, O'Neill has framed his tale in the fashions of 1906, which is a very wise proceeding for a comedy that will probably be a heritage for future generations, as the greatest frailty of the Comic Muse is her tendency to highly topical humor that fast becomes dated. The humor of *Ah, Wilderness* is so purely and richly human that staleness will not molder it. Uncle Sid's entrance after the Fourth of July picnic will be just as good ten years from now. So will his remarks at dinner.

In 1906, young Richard Miller was enjoying his first pains of love. He was reading Ibsen and Khayyam—hence the title—and life was all Wilderness and very far from Paradise for instead of singing beside him, she had been forbidden to see him again. The Book of Verses was but poor consolation on the Fourth of July and young Richard, at the invitation of a gay Yale friend of his brother's, goes forth to forget his sorrows in a barroom. The Jug of Wine was all very well but when it came to its concomitant in petticoats, Richard buys deliverance with $5.00 and staggers home where only Uncle Sid quite understands the immediate emergency. Nat Miller talks to his son; its beauty lies in what is left unsaid. A great actor gives us the thoughts that hide behind the spoken word and a great playwright so builds up his scenes that those thoughts are natural and clear. Mr. Cohan's pauses are as eloquent as speech. All the inarticulate affection that holds us together is shown in that interview between the father and the son.

"You're all right, Son," says Nat Miller, and then Richard, before he goes out to think of Muriel in the moonlight, kisses his Father goodnight. "He hasn't done that for years. That meant something," says Nat to his wife.

Mr. O'Neill never makes fun of his Miller family. The Millers do that for themselves. Besides the four children there is Uncle Sid, the incorrigible Uncle Sid, who has proposed and been refused for his weak ways by Aunt Lily Miller for the last twenty years. But of course everyone in the family knows that she really loves him just the same. To enter into the Miller family made me think of a home as the equivalent of a high voltage wire where all the active energy is bound together by a single thread. The mystery of it all is clearer when we leave Nat Miller and his wife together at the end. There had been no short current in their love.

If there seems to be a large dash of sentiment in what we have just said let us hasten to assure the more modern minded that they need have no fear. O'Neill's writing is always straight. There is nothing mawkish in the Miller family ties and the scene in the barroom is quite frank. It is difficult to imagine how the Theater Guild could have improved upon the production. Mrs. Don Marjorie Marquis is Mrs. Miller and she enjoys the humor of her family as much as anyone. As Uncle Sid, Gene Lockhart scores a triumph and Elisha Cook, Jr., as Richard opens a new vista for his career. After all the tough boys he has been invited to play he shows his understanding of the finer grain. It might have been Richard's play had Mr. Cohan been young enough to be Richard. As it is he steps as much into the background as the space permits but whenever the action presses him forward he simply can't help taking the play. His acting isn't acting but a fuller life.—*At the Guild Theater.*

Catholic World, November, 1933.

Ah, Wilderness **Revived by Guild**

John Anderson

Since it seems impossible to get O'Neill's numerous new plays out of his desk and on to a stage crying for them, it is good to have the old ones around, and doubly gratifying to have one of them used by the Theatre Guild in starting off its season of popular-priced revivals last night in the Mother House.

Ah, Wilderness, to be sure, doesn't seem to be a very old play, for it was only eight years ago to the very night that the Guild put the curtain up on the opening performance. It was then that a somewhat astonished but delighted audience discovered that our Master of Tragedy had turned his mind back to his own youth to write a comedy of deep tenderness and wise humor about the growing pains of a sensitive lad back in Connecticut in 1906.

Within his slowing reminiscence, O'Neill caught a perfect picture of an average American family and set it true, and funny, and sad, and altogether endearing. The mood of affectionate retrospect never softens to sentimental reverie, or mere cloying sweetness. It is as strong, spiritually, as O'Neill's more serious work, but warmly human and gently heart-breaking—a play to be seen, and seen again, and cherished among the happiest of playgoing memories.

Here, in the powerful strokes of the First Dramatist, are simply folks, the salt, as they say, of the earth, concerned with the universal problems of youth and age, of growing up and growing old. Young Dick Miller, in the throes of adolescence, threatens to kick over the traces, goes on a binge over what he thinks, poetically, is a broken heart, gets plastered and then pulls himself together, with the guidance of a wise father, a patient mother and a loving sweetheart.

All of the characters of a big family group are superbly drawn, and since he is a realist O'Neill knows the whole picture can't be pretty and happy. Uncle Sid is a worthless, but engaging sot wasting his life away, and Aunt Lily, who loves him, prefers to be a jittery old maid rather than marry the rascal. Young Dick's effort to forget his youthful sorrows in sin includes a bawdy scene with a prostitute in the back room of a saloon and suggests both the tragedy and comedy of the situation; and the final scene of father and son, in mutual understanding and respect, is profoundly touching, without slushy emphasis or cheap effect.

In the original production, George M. Cohan seemed practically perfect as Nat Miller. He suggested vividly the genial humor and inner strength of the character, his goodness and abiding integrity, and in addition he gave the whole play the impact and vitality of a high tension performance.

To say that Harry Carey is not George M. Cohan is one thing, but to say he is not Nat Miller is quite another. He is not as good a Nat Miller, not as benignant, nor as shrewd, nor as sensitive; but he is a Nat Miller of compassionate nature, a little too solemn, plain, fatherly, and not very interesting. His performance, as kindly as it is, lacks the propulsion of full-bodied playing, and he misses the sly subtleties by which the one and only George M. Cohan gave his own sharp comments on family and other life.

Under Miss LeGallienne's direction, the others vary considerably. Tom Tully is immensely amusing as the drunken uncle, and in the hangover scene of repentance, genuinely touching. Enid Markey emphasizes the humor more than the heartbreak of Sid's disappointed sweetheart, and the younger members of the family are attractively played, notably by William Prince as young Dick in a performance of poignant and vivid effect. Dennie Moore plays the back-room wench with much gusto; and while Miss LeGallienne's direction serves the broader intentions of the script, it is not a complete or vigorous illumination.

It seems a pity that O'Neill hasn't worked a little over the scene on the beach and cut it down, especially the opening soliloquy, which is awkward and unnecessary.

But defects and all, it is a fine comedy of true values and enduring interest, and as I was saying eight years ago, when we were interrupted, I recommend it heartily.

New York Journal American, October 3, 1941.

Singing in the Wilderness: The Dark Vision in Eugene O'Neill's Only Mature Comedy

Thomas F. Van Laan

The consensus about Eugene O'Neill's *Ah, Wilderness!* characterizes the play as nostalgic, light-hearted, sunny, wholly approving of the life and people it depicts, and—in the words of Joseph Wood Krutch—"quite unlike anything else O'Neill ever wrote."[1] O'Neill himself described the play, shortly after he wrote it, as "out of my previous line";[2] and he probably encouraged the usual view by calling it "a comedy of recollection" and "a dream walking,"[3] by offering a remarkably non-committal note for the Wilderness Edition of his plays in which he *seems* to praise "the spirit of the American large small-town at the turn of the century,"[4] and by claiming that the play was not autobiographical but "a sort of wishing out loud. That's the way I would have *liked* my boyhood to have been."[5] Since the appearance of *Long Day's Journey Into Night*, the consensus has included a realization that *Ah, Wilderness!* dramatizes some of the same material from which O'Neill would eventually create profound tragedy; this realization has generally altered not the response to *Ah, Wilderness!* but merely the terminology in which this response is phrased, for it is now customary to describe the play as the other side of the coin,[6] the "bright counterpart to the dramatist's final self-assessment."[7]

There have, of course, been some departures from this consensus. A few readers—Sheaffer in part, Raleigh in part, John T. Shawcross, and most notably Adler and Carpenter—attribute dark undertones to the play, including a genuine awareness of evil and a suggestion of spiritual despair. However, none of these readers has discussed these undertones in much detail or sufficiently indicated their sources within the play.[8] Two critics, finally, recoil from *Ah, Wilderness!* with something approaching, and in one case definitely crossing into loathing. Engel dismisses the play as a falsification of experience, which, among other distortions, bestows upon its heroes, father and son, a set of rewards that "exist only in the sentimental pipe dream."[9] For Ruby Cohn, "*Ah, Wilderness!* conceals smug acceptance of a double standard, hypocrisy of American family life, and unfocused boredom of July 4th, America's national holiday." "Were O'Neill not the author of *Ah, Wilderness!*," Cohn concludes, "it would have faded into the oblivion it deserves."[10]

In one sense, the play *has* virtually faded into oblivion. Many have written about it, but almost no one has attempted to discuss it in detail, to discern exactly what is happening in it and what O'Neill is doing with his supposedly sunny and sentimental material. It is not oblivion that *Ah, Wilderness!* deserves but serious consideration which views it as worthy of the kind of careful, detailed analysis to which O'Neill's other major plays have been subjected and on which all good drama thrives. Analysis of this sort reveals that *Ah, Wilderness!* is far more complex than has yet been realized, that the consensus about the play contains much more sentimentality than the play itself, that the critics who discern dark undertones have apparently merely scratched the surface, and that the sentimentality and smugness of which Engel and Cohn complain stem less from the dramatist than from his characters.[11]

The title of the play, as is well known, constitutes O'Neill's slight modification (changing "Oh" to "Ah") of the first two words in the last line of the most famous quatrain from FitzGerald's translation of *The Rubaiyat of Omar Khayyam*. This quatrain posits a distinction between an existing reality, the wilderness, which is barren, desolate, and lifeless, and the hypothetical transformation of it, "paradise enow," which *could* take place given certain desiderata—the loaf of bread, the jug of wine, and "thou" singing "beside me." Although most commentators on O'Neill's play treat it as if it dramatized—or sought to—the implicit "paradise enow" evoked by its title, this title in fact emphasizes the wilderness. Perhaps these commentators are in part misled by the "Ah," but as *Webster's New Collegiate Dictionary* explains, "Ah" is an interjection "used to express delight, relief, regret, or contempt," and it would be quite arbitrary to single out any of these usages before seeing which of them the play itself endorses. My reading of the play convinces me that the "ah" of delight belongs chiefly to the characters, who unconsciously or otherwise misperceive the nature of their reality, while their creator, in addition to sharing his characters' misperception to a small degree, is primarily torn between regret and contempt. Far from depicting a paradise—pure or flawed, fool's or otherwise—the play actually depicts a wilderness. The surface light-heartedness, sunniness, and sense of satisfaction are for the most part merely examples of singing in the wilderness—which is a rough equivalent to whistling past a cemetery—by characters who are no more able to face the desolate reality confronting them than are the denizens of Harry Hope's saloon or the four haunted Tyrones.

The fundamental strategy of the play involves something comparable to altering the "ah" of delight to one more suggestive of contempt. *Ah, Wilderness!* emphasizes three familiar American clichés, compares them to the actuality they distort, and concludes that as truths they are sham but as sustaining pipe dreams they are serviceable and necessary. These three clichés, which I list in the order I plan to discuss them, are: first, the gallery of sentimental stereotypes in the mode of Norman Rockwell; second, the Fourth-of-July myth of independence and equality; and third, the notion of family life as the ideal form of existence.

Many readers of *Ah, Wilderness!* have noticed, some of them complainingly, the characters' resemblance to key sentimental stereotypes readily found in the wish-fulfillment fantasies of the American middle class. Indeed, the opening sequence of the play looks as if O'Neill aimed at nothing other than providing us with whatever satisfactions this resemblance may afford. This sequence methodically introduces the various members of the family, each of whom is assigned the appropriate appearance, manner, language, preoccupations, and activities of a familiar stereotype. Eleven-year-old Tommy is a cute little dickens, an oh-that-boy! with "a rim of milk visible about his lips" (p. 6).[12] Fifteen-year-old Mildred is the boy-crazy, awkward adolescent girl, largely caught up in teasing her older brothers, especially nineteen-year-old Arthur, who, "solemnly collegiate" (p. 7) and self-consciously watchful against assaults upon his dignity, strives manfully but without entire success to appear mature and sophisticated. Mrs. Miller (her name is "Essie," but speech headings and stage directions invariably refer to her as "Mrs. Miller") possesses "a bustling mother-of-a-family manner" (p. 8); she is "the Mother's Day Mother," as Engel calls her,[13] pointedly deferential to her husband, constantly hovering over her brood to correct and protect. Aunt Lily, shy and kindly, "conforms outwardly to the conventional type of old-maid school teacher, even to wearing glasses" (p. 8). Mrs. Miller's brother, Sid Davis, "with the puckish face of a Peck's Bad Boy who has never grown up" (p. 9), is the carefree, jovial, fun-loving uncle. Nat Miller is the "understanding and ever-smiling father,"[14] who, as befits the head of the household, governs his various charges with a fine balance of severity and indulgence.

What has not been clearly realized about these stereotypes is that O'Neill by no means intends that we perceive them as the actual identities of his characters; on the contrary, he soon defines them—for the adult members of the family, at least—as roles that his characters have adopted or have had imposed on them. The idea of behavior as role-playing is familiar enough in O'Neill's plays and it is explicitly established in *Ah, Wilderness!* by the clownish antics of Sid and the tortured posing of Richard Miller, who is a prototype for Con Melody of *A Touch of the Poet*. Richard, moreover, is called a "child actor" (p. 71), and both he and Sid, we hear at separate times, "ought to be on the stage" (pp. 40, 47). But even before Richard enters and Sid fully warms up, the idea of role-playing has already been implicitly introduced through the difficulty Lily and Sid have in trying to maintain the stereotypes associated with them. Sid would genuinely like to be the jovial uncle, but his drinking and Lily's attitude toward it fill him with self-loathing and self-pity, and so he is driven to melodramatic overacting in his vain efforts to turn his situation into a joke. Lily pretends to find contentment in her husbandless and childless lot, but she cannot-or will not—conceal her underlying anguish and particularly the pain that Sid's weakness constantly causes her.[15] The discrepancy between Lily's mask and her reality is most fully revealed in Act Two (pp. 37-38), and it is at this same time that Mrs. Miller, with the men gone, drops her normal pose as the deferential, reverent wife. "Men are weak," she assures Lily (p. 36), and a few minutes later, as she talks about tricking Nat into eating bluefish, she reveals how she actually feels about his opinions, and since she believes that she not only can but ought to deceive him, she also reveals her convictions of her own superiority.

The ubiquitous discrepancy between pose and actuality is perhaps most interesting and most important in the case of Nat Miller, however, because readers of the play almost uniformly see him as the embodiment of an ideal type. O'Neill may use greater subtlety with Nat than with the others, but he nonetheless manages, and in several ways, to indicate that for Nat, too, the surface is a mask that cannot quite conceal the reality lurking behind it. I shall here point to only one instance. During his confrontation with McComber, Nat loses his temper, thereby momentarily forfeiting his role as all-wise controller of every situation. But this fact is of less significance, than what it occasions after McComber leaves, for here Nat must assure Sid (and evidently himself) that his loss of control is not characteristic of him, and he must elicit from Sid reassurances that he really is what everyone who knows him regards him to be. It is clear from this episode that while Nat is not always able to be what he wants to be—or thinks he has to be—he is also determined that no one, including himself, will be permitted fully to discern his failure.[16]

It is Richard who alerts us to the second cliché examined in *Ah, Wilderness!*, the Fourth-of-July myth of independence and equality, when shortly after his initial entrance, he bursts out in vehement denunciation: "I don't believe in this silly celebrating the Fourth of July—all this lying talk about liberty—when there is no liberty...! The land of the free and the home of the brave! Home of the slave is what they ought to call it—the wage slave ground under the heel of the capitalist class, starving, crying for bread for his children, and all he gets is a stone! The Fourth of July is a stupid farce!" (p. 15). Richard's denunciations remind us that the era in which the Millers lived also knew social injustice and human suffering of a sort that none of the Millers or their friends had ever experienced and that all of them, Richard included, are ignorant of or indifferent to. But Richard's excessive, adolescent rhetoric and the responses of his father (a twinkle in the eye, a scarcely concealed grin) define the speaker of these denunciations as a buffoon, and this definition allows us either to dismiss the denunciations as irrelevant, or worse yet, to laugh off or laugh at the abuses and suffering they invoke. On the other hand, O'Neill undoubtedly expected some members of his audience to experience a more complicated relation to this material, and to be troubled not only by the callowness of Richard's version of these issues and Nat's complacent indifference to them but also by the ease with which they themselves have been provoked to laughter about matters deserving a response of a much different kind.

More important than the immediate impact of Richard's denunciations—whatever it may be—is the fact that the contrast he introduces here pertains even to the narrow world that the play directly depicts. The immediate milieu of *Ah, Wilderness!* is innocent of sweatshops and starving children, but even the Millers and their associates exist within an oppressive social reality that diverges sharply from the independence and equality promised by the myth. This social reality is what causes the characters of the play to engage in their role-playing, the reason for which is twofold. On the one hand, they are trying to conform to an established network of roles which they assume to be valid. On the other, this network is so oppressive for most if not all of them that they try to lose themselves in its individual units in the same way that other O'Neill characters turn to sustaining pipe dreams. They try to convince themselves that they *are* what they have to be in order to ward off the pain and anguish caused by their having to be exactly that.

What makes this network of roles oppressive is the fact that it has been cast in the form of a rigid hierarchy that relegates most of its members to outcast or second-class status. The clearest example of an outcast, and hence a representative of the bottom of the hierarchy, is Belle, the prostitute, everybody's victim, whom we last see, appropriately, being brutalized by the Bartender. The Bartender himself is not much better off; he is, after all, striking out at her because of his own vulnerability, expressed in his fear that Nat Miller will have him "run... out of town" for serving drinks to his son (p. 75). The second-class citizens abound, for they include all children, all women, and all males who for some reason fall short;

as Arthur does, in part because he is not yet quite a man and in part simply because his father dislikes him; as McComber does, because he lacks a sense of proper proportions; and as Sid does, because he is totally without self-discipline. Perched on top of this hierarchy—albeit, as we have seen, a bit precariously—is Nat Miller, who holds this position because he is a respectable, professionally successful, adult male with more common sense, wisdom, and self-discipline than the other adult males of the play.[17]

In relation to Nat, according to the language of the play, the other characters lack full adult status. McComber has sufficient age, but he is an "old fool" (p. 21) and an "old idiot" (p. 29). Arthur, though nineteen, is at one point ordered by his father to "skedaddle" with the rest of the "kids" (p. 93). Belle and her kind, according to Sid, are "babies" (p. 96), while Sid himself, according to Richard on one occasion, is "a bigger kid than Tommy is" (pp. 28-29). Interestingly enough—since O'Neill is not only demonstrating the existence of the hierarchy but also implicitly criticizing it—as Nat Miller heads for bed at the end of the play, he asks his wife's permission to skip his prayers; "You're worse than Tommy!" she exclaims fondly, but then with a note of motherly indulgence she grants his request (p. 131).

O'Neill dramatizes this hierarchy throughout the play and by a variety of means, including the entire scene in the bar, Nat's belittling generalizations about women, the joke which assumes that women and children are unfit to know the specific "wickedness" committed by Oscar Wilde, and Nat's refusal to take Richard's rebellious protests more seriously than as signs of a stage he is passing through. To my mind, however, the episode that most strikingly evokes the hierarchy and its implications is the one in which Nat sends his wife out of the room in order to have a man-to-man talk with Richard. Readers of the play who mention this scene praise it for its humor and for the fine impression of Nat and of the father-son relationship that it conveys.[18] The scene has funny moments certainly, but as often in *Ah, Wilderness!*, the humor is subtly blended with nasty undertones that threaten to turn humor into satire. For what Nat accomplishes, in effect, is to enlighten Richard with regard to one of the ways in which "human society [is] organized"; the fact that "a certain class of women" has been set aside for the purpose of satisfying the sexual needs of the male members of society. Nat concedes that it is probably best to avoid "girls like that" entirely, but, after all, human nature is human nature, and the only real wrong, from his point of view, would be "to ever get mixed up with them seriously"; "You just have what you want and pay 'em and forget it" (p. 128).

If the third cliché examined in *Ah, Wilderness!*, the idealization of family life, were true, then most of its characters would remain unaffected by the oppressive social reality encompassing them, because they participate in family life and thus have constant access to the loving nurturance it supposedly provides. In some ways the play seems to be an endorsement of the notion that middle-class family life is the ideal form of existence, especially when Richard and Muriel vow to marry someday, and when, at the end of the play, Nat and Mrs. Miller affirm that being together lends beauty to the autumn and even to the winter—that, in other words, it is an effective means for converting wilderness to paradise. One must not, however, emphasize these final notes at the expense of countless earlier notes insisting that, far from compensating for the wilderness of existence, family life in fact constitutes one of its most oppressive elements. These notes, located throughout the play, occur in special abundance in two of its scenes, Act Three, scene two, in which the other members of the family await Richard's late-night return, and the dinner scene that takes up the second half of Act Two.

The latter episode is among the best scenes O'Neill wrote. It is extremely funny and yet, at the same time, it makes us painfully aware of how harrowing domestic existence can be. According to this scene, the function of the family is not to nurture and sustain but to curb and inhibit, and alternatively, to provide captive victims for relieving one's hurt and frustration. If one member of the family expresses exuberance, as Nat does when he "slaps [his wife] jovially on her fat buttocks" (p. 46), this necessarily causes distress or worse to another, and the victim must immediately find relief by turning to attack some member of the family who is in an even more vulnerable position. If one member of the family tries to assert his individuality by indulging some idiosyncrasy—as Nat does in imagining bluefish poisons him or in endlessly retelling the same stories about himself—he cannot simply be ignored or tolerated; he must instead be made a laughing-stock so that he will learn to conform—though it is far more likely that he will instead precipitate an attack on one of the others, most probably the one who was least involved in the attack on him. There is by no means any vast gulf between the family dynamics of this episode and the far more obviously destructive interaction uniting the Tyrones of *Long Day's Journey Into Night*. Interestingly enough, moreover, both plays include a servant girl who suggests a better way. In Act Three of *Long Day's Journey*, as Mary Tyrone complains to Cathleen about her husband's many failings, thereby assigning blame for her torment and suffering, she is unable to shake the servant girl's dogged conviction that Tyrone—and, it is implied, all people—is to be accepted, no matter what his faults. And Cathleen is merely echoing the Millers' Norah, who cheerfully excuses Sid's outrageous behavior at dinner with "Ah, Miss Lily, don't mind him. He's only under the influence. Sure, there's no harm in him at all" (p. 51).

It might be objected to this reading of *Ah, Wilderness!* that O'Neill does, after all, end his play with the emphatic notes of affirmation already referred to. In response, four points can be made. First, and this is a possibility offered without much insistence, no dramatist wants to alienate totally the potential audience upon whom the commercial success of his work depends. Second, although the vision of the Millers' world which O'Neill presents is a dark one, *in form* he never entirely breaks with the genre of nostalgic family comedy, and this ending is appropriate to the genre. Third, it should be noted that these final scenes of affirmation are drenched in moonshine, and this is perhaps O'Neill's way of suggesting that his characters are here behaving pretty much as they do in Act Three, scene two, when Arthur sings his sentimental songs and the other Millers instantly surrender to the maudlin lure. Additional suspicious qualities of the very last episode include Nat's acting like a big kid (in trying to get out of his prayers), the suggestions that the characters are striking poses rather than behaving spontaneously (Nat's "Let her go, Gallagher" and his perceiving Richard as "like a statue of Love's Young Dream," pp. 131-132), and the final stage direction, which has Nat and Mrs. Miller moving "back into the darkness of the front parlor" (p. 132).

The fourth point, which seems to me to afford the interpretation most responsive to the play, can perhaps best be approached through considering O'Neill's presentation of his central character, Richard Miller. Richard is caught between two locations of the hierarchy, the child who he has been and to whom he frequently returns, and the man who he is supposed to become. His rebellious outbursts and actions are the result of his efforts to play the man in the only way he can conceive of, since he is as yet unable to fulfill the requirements for doing so in the approved manner, that of his father. By the end of the play, however, it is clear that he is well on his way toward fulfilling these requirements, and his father can affirm with relief, "I don't think we'll ever have to worry about his being safe—from himself—again" (p. 131). Richard's reading, as is well known, reflects that of his creator; so also does the content of his outbursts; and Richard is the only character in the play who is at all in touch with the critical attitude O'Neill has toward the smug complacency of the Millers' narrow world. Yet O'Neill, as well as Nat, sees Richard in his rebellious attitudinizing as a figure more of mirth than of truth, and he presents Richard's development in the later scenes not as the tragic loss of a possibility for full emancipation but, in Bogard's terms, as a reclamation, as a return to the proper path.[19]

To some extent this presentation of Richard can be accounted for as a response to genre—comedy often views any deviation from the social norm as preposterous, and nostalgic family comedy demands an harmonious conclusion. But there is also present here, it seems to me, a genuine ambivalence on O'Neill's part which is typical of his entire relationship to the material of *Ah, Wilderness!*. Despite his critical attitude, O'Neill never wholly succeeds in detaching himself—or us—from the values in which the Millers try to believe. In the same way that he is able to laugh at Richard, and make us laugh at him, even while no doubt privately agreeing with what Richard has to say, he also, I think, genuinely tries to find something worth celebrating in the Millers' existence and to celebrate it. However, he is too knowledgeable about the human capacity for self-deception, and too honest in reporting accurately what he sees, to submit with any deep conviction to the sentimental pipe dream most of the characters have accepted. As a result, *Ah, Wilderness!* is a much richer and more interesting play than it is generally taken to be.

NOTES

1. *Literary History of the United States*, Fourth Edition, ed. Robert E. Spiller, et al. (New York, 1974), p. 1244.

2. Quoted by Arthur and Barbara Gelb, *O'Neill* (New York, 1962), p. 769.

3. Quoted by Barrett H. Clark, *Eugene O'Neill: The Man and His Plays* (New York, 1947), p. 137.

Ah, Wilderness! 159

4. Quoted by Clark, p. 138. The full statement is as follows: "My purpose was to write a play true to the spirit of the American large small-town at the turn of the century. Its quality depended upon atmosphere, sentiment, an exact evocation of the mood of a dead past. To me, the America which was (and is) the real America found its unique expression in such middle-class families as the Millers, among whom so many of my own generation passed from adolescence into manhood."

5. Quoted by Louis Sheaffer, *O'Neill: Son and Playwright* (Boston, 1968), p. 232.

6. Gelbs, p. 81.

7. Travis Bogard, "Introduction" to *The Later Plays of Eugene O'Neill* (New York, 1967), p. xxiii.

8. Sheaffer, *O'Neill: Son and Artist* (Boston, 1973), pp. 405-406; John Henry Raleigh, *The Plays of Eugene O'Neill* (Carbondale, Ill., 1965), pp. 80, 139; John T. Shawcross, "The Road to Ruin: The Beginning of O'Neill's Long Day's Journey," *Modern Drama*, 3 (1960), 295-296; Jacob H. Adler, "The Worth of *Ah, Wilderness!*", *Modern Drama*, 3 (1960), 280-288; Frederic I. Carpenter, *Eugene O'Neill* (New York 1964), pp. 136-138, 145-147.

9. Edwin A. Engel. *The Haunted Heroes of Eugene O'Neill* (Cambridge, Mass., 1953), p. 277.

10. Ruby Cohn, *Dialogue in American Drama* (Bloomington, Ind., 1971), pp. 40, 41.

11. The difficulty of perceiving the complexity of *Ah, Wilderness!* is compounded by inadequate, unresponsive productions that also fail to take the play seriously. The most prominent production of recent years, which originated at The Long Wharf Theatre, moved to New York City's Circle in the Square during the 1975-1976 season, and eventually reached a very wide audience through inclusion in the Theater in America series on P.B.S., conformed to the consensus by presenting a heavily edited text. We need more productions like that directed by Irene Lewis for the Milwaukee Repertory Theater during the 1977-1978 season, where *Ah, Wilderness!* was presented in repertory with *Long Day's Journey* (also directed by Ms. Lewis), utilizing the same set and the same principal actors. This enjoyable production, presenting the play substantially as O'Neill wrote it, captured most of the qualities of *Ah, Wilderness!* that are the concern of this essay.

12. All quotations from *Ah, Wilderness!* are from *The Later Plays of Eugene O'Neill* (see note 7).

13. Engel, p. 273.

14. John Gassner, *Eugene O'Neill*, Pamphlets on American Writers No. 45 (Minneapolis, 1965), p. 34.

15. Some would argue that the actual "identities" Sid and Lily try to conceal behind their appropriate stereotypes are themselves familiar theatrical stereotypes. This claim is to a large extent true, but on the other hand, these revealed stereotypes are characteristic of melodrama rather than nostalgic family comedy.

16. Engel is probably in part responding to this aspect of Nat's character when he calls him, "Mrs. Miller's little boy" (p. 273). Adler (p. 283) rightly objects to this remark as excessive. More to the point and more interesting is Engel's perception that Harry Hope is in many respects a reincarnation of Nat Miller (pp. 291-292).

17. The overall pattern of this hierarchy is recapitulated in its various subdivisions: among the women, so that Lily as a non-wife and non-mother must take a back seat to Mrs. Miller (literally, in the play, she "goes diffidently to the straight-backed chair...leaving the comfortable chairs to

the others," p. 8); and among the children, whose differentiation goes according to age, except that Richard, for a variety of reasons, is preferred to Arthur.

18. For example, Richard Dana Skinner, *Eugene O'Neill: A Poet's Quest* (New York, 1935), pp. 231-232; Arthur Hobson Quinn, *A History of American Drama from the Civil War to the Present*, Revised Edition (New York, 1936), Vol. Two, p. 259.

19. Bogard, p. xxv.

Modern Drama, 22 (March 1979): 9-18.

Great Day for the Irish

John Simon

Disappointing is the word for **The O'Neill Plays**, as the mini-repertory of *Ah, Wilderness!* and *Long Day's Journey Into Night* is billed. *Ah, Wilderness!* is Eugene O'Neill's only shot at comedy, and there is a certain wistful charm about this imaginary, idealized family and adolescence he invented for himself. Yet just as the facts are falsified (for the truth we must go to *Long Day's Journey*), so there is something spurious and synthetic about the comedy: It is as if Strindberg were trying to be Booth Tarkington. The situations and laughs are stock; the poignancies, supremely stock. No wonder the play is a stock company staple.

Even so, there is enough craft in the play, overlong as it is for what it has to offer, to make it palatable in the right production. A dozen years ago, Arvin Brown, the present director, brought such a production to the Circle in the Square; this time round, he is less nimble, the cast is less felicitous, and the last scenes drag to the point of making *Long Day's Journey Into Night*, by comparison, an afternoon's jaunt. Colleen Dewhurst comes off best, as Essie, the mother; her performance holds no surprises, but neither does it miss a trick: Everything is in its place, with the proper timing and emphasis. Good, too, in the threadbare part of the hooker, Belle, is Annie Golden, as is Jamey Sheridan in the small and easy role of the bartender. Extremely weak, however, are Kyra Sedgwick, Steven Skybell, Jane Macfie, and Nicholas Tamarkin, while a couple of others pass muster. The big trouble, though is the other principals. Jason Robards relies exclusively on his old charm and tricks, which with the years, have become less charming and much too tricky. Although he has given some memorable performances, they have been variations on the poetic weakling, the mired illusionist; Nat Miller, the father, is no such thing. Robards's Nat is cute—no less and, sadly, no more.

A similar problem afflicts George Hearn's Uncle Sid, the talented but self-destructive drunkard hopelessly in love with the prim spinster, Aunt Lily. A gifted performer, Hearn fails to be moving here: He gets across the comedy of Sid, though even that is rather labored, but he flubs the pathos. And Elizabeth Wilson, aside from being too old for Hearn's Sid, is relying on her stock-in-trade, the hemmed-in older woman who represses even flutters, although they ooze out of odd corners of her being. It's a neat piece of craft, but Miss wilson has done it so many times that even she seems to have lost interest in it, never mind *us*. Finally, and crucially, Raphael Sbarge is not up to Richard, O'Neill's pipe dream of himself as a boy lurching toward young manhood. Sbarge is puppyish in love (fine), coltish in joy (okay, but overdone), and doltish in suffering (bad).

New York Magazine, July 11, 1988.

The Theatre: L'amour et—Mon Dieu

George Jean Nathan

  Those critical spirits in our midst who contend that not Eugene O'Neill but everyone else from Mr. Robert Sherwood to the Hattons is the first dramatist of the American theatre will find great comfort in O'Neill's most recent play. *Days Without End*, which is not only, along with *Welded* and *Dynamo*, one of the poorest things he has written but which, in addition, is one of the dullest that has come to the more ambitious stage in some time. Further comfort, if it be needed, will be afforded them in the undeniable fact that it is one of the most unbroiled plays that has been composed upon its general theme. And to make matters worse for those of us who believe in O'Neill's very considerable talent and better for those who don't, the fellow actually considers it the best play he has ever written!
  From beginning to end, save for two brief flashes, this *Days Without End* is a tournament in collegiate theorizing artlessly bamboozled into a superficial aspect of grave experimental drama by a recourse to masks and to the technical device—favorite of Viennese and Hungarian playwrghts like Schnitzler and Molnar in the years before the War—of coordinating the narration of a hypothetical fiction story with the actual lives of the immediate characters.
  It comes to the old tale: when O'Neill goes in for pure emotion, he is a sound and enormously effective dramatist; but when he ventures into theorizing and philosophizing, he is—to be very gallant about it—far from palatable. In the present play, he had a play of pure emotion, exalted emotion even. But every time it pops up its head he gives it a mortal clout with a pseudo-ratiocinative bladder. The result is chaos—and tedium.
  Days Without End, a reconstruction of the Faust idea (with Faust and Mephistopheles imagined as one) and seeking its resolution under the Cross of the Catholic Christ, cries piteously for a poetry that is nowhere in it. Its lines are not only banal and humdrum, but—worse—at certain moments when only the high and thrilling beauty of the written English word might bring it a second's exaltation, the author descends to such gross argot as "Forgive me for butting in" and the like. The net final impression is of a crude religious tract liberally sprinkled with a lot of dated Henry Arthur Jones sex in an effort to give it a feel of theatrical life. O'Neill subtitles his play, "a modern miracle play." It is not modern, as he himself should realize, since he originally wrote it with the scene set back something like

fifty years. And, if he knows the miracle plays, which he most assuredly does, he certainly realizes that this forced, tortured and hocus-pocused slice of greasepaint drama is anything but a miracle play in the sense of such a play's cool simplicity, and innocence, and moving dignity.

In this work of his, O'Neill—as in other of his unsuccessful theorizing matches—again suggests a bulldog ferociously battling a Haldeman-Julius Little Blue Book. It shows nothing of the cold, hard, calm critical gift which, paradoxically enough, he exercises upon his unadulterated emotional plays. In place of that cold self-criticism, which has provided our American stage with some of its finest plays, we find here an intoxication with what may be called logicalized emotionalism, which turns out to be neither logic nor emotion but only a bogus Siamese twin. The passion that should have gone into the play's emotional and spiritual fabric is spent upon what the author evidently cherishes as a sacrosanct amorous ethic, an ethic that seems more and more dubious as his passion continues indignantly to inflame and apotheosize it. Aiming at a climactic exaltation of the spirit, he succeeds infinitely less in accomplishing his purpose than whoever the play-carpenter was who years ago made the honky-tonk version of *Faust* for Lewis Morrison....

The Theatre Guild gave the play, in most particulars, a careful production, especial credit being due to Mr. Lee Simonson for some imaginative settings and some excellent lighting. Earle Larimore acquitted himself nicely in the central role, and Stanley Ridges, as his masked *alter ego*, did all one supposes any actor could do, his director permitting. Robert Loraine managed the small priest role well enough. But whoever cast the flint-hard and resolute Miss Selena Royle for the delicate, highly sensitive wife owes an explanation to a large portion of the head-scratching audiences.

Vanity Fair, March 1934.

O'Neill Discovers the Cross

Fred Eastman

A few months ago I wrote an article in *The Christian Century*, "Eugene O'Neill and Religion." In it I held that O'Neill had not yet achieved the stature of a great artist and that he would not do so until he developed certain insights and attitudes which religion at its best cultivates. I said:

> No other playwright of modern times has developed a greater intensity of power in the crises he has contrived for his characters. No other has revealed more souls naked and stripped of all pretense. But it is equally true that he has seldom found beauty in the characters he has revealed. As he has stood on the brink and looked down into the crater of a human soul he has found only selfishness and torment. Seldom nobility, never divinity....He has found *great struggles*—but *little men* engaged in them. Wherever, in the souls he has opened, he has found God and the Devil struggling against each other, he has

nearly always found the Devil winning out. He does not rejoice that the Devil wins, but that's what he sees and so he records it.

This is not to say that the struggles he portrays issue in immorality. Nothing could be farther from the truth. He is sternest of moralists. The censor boards which have excluded his plays from certain cities have been exceedingly shortsighted. Jonathan Edwards never preached hell-fire with more passion than Eugene O'Neill. Over and over again the doctrine that "the wages of sin is death" is illustrated in the lives of his characters. But never, I think, has he discovered the other half of that doctrine—that "the gift of God is eternal life." He believes—if one may judge by his works—in the Calvinistic doctrine of predestination. Most of his characters are foreordained to be damned. But he has apparently not heard of the doctrine of grace. Or of forgiveness.

When a man has had such (a deeply religious) experience...his eyes are opened, his ears unstopped. He sees now the sacredness of her life as well as its insanity. He see the injustice still, but he does not seek to escape it, but to fight it, and to fight with hope. His understanding is deepened, his sympathy broadened. Religion sends him back to struggle and wrestle with the difficulties of life, but with a happy heart, and a feeling of fellowship with the good and the great who have gone before him.

Some day Mr. O'Neill may discover this sort of religion....We need have no fear that it will make him a sentimentalist or a propagandist. Rather, it may make him immortal.

Tonight I have just finished reading O'Neill's new play, *Days Without End*, and I want to be the first to leap into these columns, waving the book aloft and crying, "He's done it!" For no mere craftsman in the art of play-making could have achieved this great drama. Only a man who had, in his own insight, penetrated to the heart of the Christian religion could have wrought it. No detached observer could have broken open the character of John Loving and seen within it the redeeming work of the cross. Such an observer might have found Freudian complexes and tremendous struggles of the will. But only a man whose own soul had something of what the old theologians called grace could possibly have found the strait and narrow way to salvation and guided John Loving so surely, though painfully, along it. But all this will seem incoherent ranting to the reader who does not know at least the outline of the story. Here it is:

As a boy, John Loving, the central character, had been brought up a devout Catholic. His parents' piety had a genuine, gentle and mystic quality. They were in no sense ignorant or bigoted. Their God "was one of infinite love, not a stern self-righteous being who condemned sinners to torment, but a very human, lovable God who became man for love of men and gave his life that they might be saved from themselves." In this God the boy trusted implicitly until one day his parents met with a terrible accident. He prostrated himself at the foot of the cross and prayed for a miracle, believing that they could yet be spared him—but no miracle happened. They died, and something snapped in him. On his knees then, when people thought he was praying, he cursed God and forsook him forever.

Thereafter he followed other gods and preached them. First it was atheism; then atheism wedded to socialism; next it was anarchy, followed by communism. An excursion into oriental philosophy brought him successively to Lao-Tze and Buddha, but these had to make way in his allegiance to Pythagoras and the Greek philosophers, and then to mechanistic materialism. But at this point he met Elsa and in her he found the fulfillment of all the yearnings of his hungering heart.

Two specters now rise to haunt him in his happiness. One is an act of adultery which he has committed and which he fears Elsa will some day discover. He has cursed himself for a fool for this act to which he had been seduced by Lucy, an old friend whose husband had been unfaithful and against whom she had plotted revenge. Knowing Lucy as he does, he has grounds for fear that when she is drunk she will some day tell their secret, and it will reach out and stab Elsa. Elsa does discover the fact, and it gives her a mortal wound. John's house of happiness comes crashing about his head. In the last act of the play we find him a distraught soul, hovering over Elsa begging forgiveness as she tosses between life and death in a fever.

The second specter is his own cynical self which he has nourished and fed since the death of his parents and the loss of his faith. This cynical self O'Neill treats as an alter ego. He uses two actors constantly to represent John Loving. One of them plays John, the hopeful, eager, faithful searcher after truth and love; the other plays Loving, with a mask "whose features reproduce John's face—the death mask of a John who has died with a sneer of scornful mockery on his lips and this mocking scorn is repeated in the expression of the eyes which stare bleakly from behind the mask." Throughout this device O'Neill visualizes the inner conflict which now comes to a climax as Elsa lies dying.

John's uncle, Father Baird, a lovable priest, who has maintained an affectionate interest in his nephew through all his spiritual wanderings in a far country, stands by him in this hour of trial. He urges him to pray, but John cannot pray until he staggers back to the foot of the cross where he had forsaken God in his youth. There he casts himself down, and out of his broken heart rises this tragic cry:

> O Son of Man, I am Thou and Thou art I! Why hast Thou forsaken me? O Brother Who lived and loved and suffered and died with us, Who knoweth the tortured hearts of men, canst Thou not forgive—now—when I surrender all to Thee—when I have forgiven Thee—the love that Thou once took from me!

The cynical figure of Loving has followed him and desperately tried to prevent the prayer. With a cry of hatred Loving defies God and curses him again, but John's prayer has been answered, and in a voice trembling with awakening hope and joy, he speaks:

> Ah! Thou hast heard me at last! Thou hast not forsaken me! Thou hast always loved me! I am forgiven! I can forgive myself—through Thee! I can believe!

There at the foot of the cross John, the believer, and the other side of his personality, Loving the cynic, wage their battle for John's soul. John wins, and his cynical self surrenders and dies, with this address to the cross upon his lips:

> Thou hast conquered, Lord. Thou art—the End. Forgive—the damned soul—of John Loving!

Elsa, too, has been fighting for her soul and for the power to forgive John, and now as Father Baird brings to John word that she has won her battle, John meets him with exultation in his voice, crying, "I know! Love lives forever. Death is dead....Life laughs with God's love again."

All of this gives no hint of the interplay of character on character, of idea on idea, as the conflict within John and within Elsa rises to its climax. But I am not trying to give a dramatic criticism of the play. My interest here is in the man behind the play. For fifteen years I have read O'Neill's works and watched him grow. I have seem him rise through Freudianism and materialism and cynicism. In this play he lifts his head above all the petty philosophers of the passing hour. He is venturing here upon the plane of faith, where true artists have always found their ultimate home. A great craftsman has become a great artist.

For here is beauty. Here is nobility. Here are characters worth knowing and remembering. Here is a mirror held up to the struggles of our own souls. Here is a playwright who has climbed the hill of Calvary and knelt in understanding humility before the eternal figure of forgiving love. O'Neill days of greatness have begun. May they be *Days Without End.*

Christian Century, February 7, 1934.

Eugene O'Neill

Lionel Trilling

Whatever is unclear about Eugene O'Neill, one thing is certainly clear—his genius. We do not like the word nowadays, feeling that it is one of the blurb words of criticism. We demand that literature be a guide to life, and when we do that we put genius into a second place, for genius assures us of nothing but itself. Yet when we stress the actionable conclusions of an artist's work, we are too likely to forget the power of genius itself, quite apart from its conclusions. The spectacle of the human mind in action is vivifying; the explorer need discover nothing so long as he has adventured. Energy, scope, courage—these may be admirable in themselves. And in the end these are often what endure best. The ideas expressed by works of the imagination may be built into the social fabric and taken for granted; or they may be rejected; or they may be outgrown. But the force of their utterance comes to us over millennia. We do not read Sophocles or Aeschylus for the right answer; we read them for the force with which they represent life and attack its moral complexity. In O'Neill, despite the many failures of his art and thought, this force is inescapable.

But a writer's contemporary audience is inevitably more interested in the truth of content than in the force of its expression; and O'Neill himself has always been ready to declare his own ideological preoccupation. His early admirers—and their lack of seriousness is a reproach to American criticism—were inclined to insist that O'Neill's content was unimportant as compared to his purely literary interest and that he injured his art when he tried to think. But the appearance of *Days Without End* has made perfectly clear the existence of an organic and progressive unity of thought in all O'Neill's work and has brought it into the critical range of the two groups whose own thought is most sharply formulated, the Catholic and the Communist. Both discovered what O'Neill had frequently announced, the religious nature of all his effort.

Not only has O'Neill tried to encompass more of life than most American writers of his time but, almost alone among them, he has persistently tried to *solve* it. When we understand this we understand that his stage devices are no fortuitous technique; his masks and abstraction, his double personalities, his drum beats and engine rhythms are the integral and necessary expression of his temper of mind and the task it set itself. Realism is uncongenial to that mind and that task and it is not realistic plays like *Anna Christie* and *The Straw* but rather in such plays as *The Hairy Ape, Lazarus Laughed* and *The Great God Brown*, where he is explaining the world in parable, symbol and myth, that O'Neill is most creative. Not the minutiae of life, not its feel and color and smell, not its nuance and humor, but its "great inscrutable forces" are his interest. He is always moving toward the finality which philosophy sometimes, and religion always, promises. Life and death, good and evil, spirit and flesh, male and female, the all and the one, Anthony and Dionysus—O'Neill's is a world of these antithetical absolutes such as religion rather than philosophy conceives, a world of pluses and minuses; and literary effort is an algebraic attempt to solve the equations.

In one of O'Neill's earliest one-act plays, the now unprocurable *Fog*, a Poet, a Business Man and a Woman with a Dead Child, shipwrecked and adrift in an open boat, have made fast to an iceberg. When they hear the whistle of a steamer, the Business Man's impulse is to call for help, but the Poet prevents him lest the steamer be wrecked on the fog-hidden berg. But a searching party picks up the castaways and the rescuers explain that they had been guided to the spot by a child's cries; the Child, however, has been dead a whole day. This little play is a crude sketch of the moral world that O'Neill is to exploit. He is to give an ever increasing importance to the mystical implications of the Dead Child, but his earliest concern is with the struggle between the Poet and the Business Man.

It is, of course, a struggle as old as morality, especially interesting to Europe all through its industrial nineteenth century, and it was now engaging America in the second decade of its twentieth. A conscious artistic movement had raised its head to declare irreconcilable strife between the creative and the possessive ideal. O'Neill was an integral part—indeed, he became the very symbol—of that Provincetown group which represented the growing rebellion of the American intellectual against a business civilization. In 1914 his revolt was simple and socialistic; in a poem in *The Call* he urged the workers of the world not to fight, asking them if they wished to "bleed and groan—for Guggenheim" and" give your lives—for Standard Oil." By 1917 his feeling against business had become symbolized and personal....

Although we now see the often gross sentimentality of the *S.S. Glencairn* plays and remember with O'Neill's own misgiving the vaudeville success of *In the Zone*, we cannot forget that, at the time, the showing of a forecastle on the

Eugene O'Neill   167

American stage was indeed something of a torpedo. Not, it is true, into the sides of Guggenheim and Standard Oil, but of the little people who wallowed complacently in their wake.

But O'Neill, not content with staggering middle class complacency by a representation of how the other half lives, undertook to scrutinize the moral life of the middle class and dramatized the actual struggle between Poet and Business Man. In his first long play, *Beyond the Horizon*, the dreamer destroys his life by sacrificing his dream to domesticity; and the practical creator, the farmer, destroys his by turning from wheat-raising to wheat gambling. It is a conflict O'Neill is to exploit again and again. Sometimes, as in *Ile* or *Gold*, the lust for gain transcends itself and becomes almost a creative idea, but always its sordid origins makes it destructive. To O'Neill the acquisitive man, kindly and insensitive, practical and immature, became a danger to life and one that he never left off attacking.

But it developed, strangely, that the American middle class had not strong objection to being attacked and torpedoed; it seemed willing to be sunk for the insurance that was paid in a new strange coin. The middle class found that it consisted of two halves, bourgeoisie and booboisie. The booboisie might remain on the ship but bourgeoisie could, if it would, take refuge on the submarine. Mencken and Nathan, who sponsored the O'Neill torpedoes, never attacked the middle class but only its boobyhood. Boobish and sophisticated: these were the two categories of art; spiritual freedom could be brought at the price of finding *Jurgen* profound. And so, while the booboisie prosecuted *Desire Under the Elms*, the bourgeoisie swelled the subscriptions of the Provincetown Playhouse and helped the Washington Square Players to grow into the Theatre Guild. An increasingly respectable audience awarded O'Neill no less than three Pulitzer Prizes, the medal of the American Academy of Arts and Sciences and a Yale Doctorate of Letters.

O'Neill did not win his worldly success by the slightest compromise of sincerity. Indeed, his charm consisted in his very integrity and hieratic earnestness. His position changed, not absolutely, but relatively to his audience, which was now the literate middle class caught up with the intellectual middle class. O'Neill was no longer a submarine; he had become a physician of souls. Beneath his iconoclasm his audience sensed reassurance.

The middle class is now in such literary disrepute that a writer's ability to please it is taken as the visible mark of an internal rottenness. But the middle class is people; prick them and they bleed, and whoever speaks sincerely to and for flesh and blood deserves respect. O'Neill's force derives in large part from the force of the moral and psychical upheaval of the middle class; it wanted certain of its taboos broken and O'Neill broke them. He was the Dion Anthony to its William Brown; Brown loved Dion: his love was a way of repenting for his own spiritual clumsiness.

Whoever writes sincerely about the middle class must consider the nature and the danger of the morality of "ideals," those phosphorescent remnants of dead religion with which the middle class meets the world. This had been Ibsen's great theme, and now O'Neill dramatized its simpler aspect in *Diff'rent* to show the effects of the repression of life. Let the ideal of chastity repress the vital forces, he was saying, and from the fine girl you will get a filthy harridan. The modern life of false ideals crushes the affirmative and creative nature of man; Pan, forbidden the light and warmth of the sun, grows "sensitive and self-conscious and proud and revengeful"—becomes the sneering Mephisthophelean mask of Dion.

The important word is *self-conscious,* for "ideals" are part of the "cheating gestures which constitute the vanity of personality." "Life is all fright if you let it alone," says Cybel, the Earth Mother of *The Great God Brown.* But the poet of *Welded* cannot let it alone; he and his wife, the stage directions tell us, move in circles of light that represent "auras of egotism" and the high ideals of their marriage are but ways each ego uses to get possession of the other. O'Neill had his answer to this problem of the possessive, discrete personality. Egotism and idealism, he tells us, are twin evils growing from man's suspicion of his life and the remedy is the laughter of Lazarus—"a triumphant, blood-stirring call to that ultimate attainment in which all prepossession with self is lost in an ecstatic affirmation of Life." The ecstatic affirmation of Life, pure and simple, is salvation. In the face of death and pain, man must reply with the answer of Kublai Kaan in *Marco Millions*: "Be proud of life! Know in your heart that the living of life can be noble! Be exalted by life! Be inspired by death! Be humbly proud! Be proudly grateful!"

It may be that the individual life is not noble and that it is full of pain and defeat; it would seem that Eileen Carmody in *The Straw* and Anna Christie are betrayed by life. But no. The "straw" is the knowledge that life is a "hopeless hope"—but still a hope. And nothing matters if you can conceive the whole of life. "Fog, fog, fog all bloody time," is the chord of resolution of *Anna Christie.* "You can't see vhere you vas going, no. Only dat ole davil, sea—she knows." The individual does not know, but life—the sea—knows.

To affirm that life exists and is somehow good—this, then, became O'Neill's quasi-religious poetic function, nor is it difficult to see why the middle class welcomed it. "Brown will still need me," says Dion, "to reassure him he's alive." What to do with life O'Neill cannot say, but there it is. For Ponce de Leon it is the Fountain of Eternity, "the Eternal Becoming which is Beauty." There it is, somehow, glorious, somehow meaningless. In the face of despair one remembers that "Always spring comes again bearing life! Always forever again. Life again!" To this cycle, even to the personal annihilation in it, the individual must say "Yes." Man inhabits a naturalistic universe and his glory lies in his recognition of its nature and assenting to it; man's soul, no less than the stars and the dust, is part of the Whole and is willing to be absorbed by it. In short, O'Neill solves the problem of evil making explicit what men have always found to be the essence of tragedy—the courageous affirmation of life in the face of individual defeat.

But neither a naturalistic view of the universe nor a rapt assent to life constitutes a complete philosophic answer. Naturalism is the noble and realistic attitude that prepares the way for an answer; the tragic affirmation is the emotional crown of a philosophy. Spinoza—with whom O'Neill at this stage of his thought has an obvious affinity—placed between the two an ethic that arranged human values and made the world possible to live in. But O'Neill, faced with a tragic universe, unable to go beyond the febrilely passionate declaration, "Life is," finds the world impossible to live in. The naturalistic universe becomes too heavy a burden for him; its spirituality vanishes; it becomes a universe of cruelly blind matter. "Teach me to be resigned to be an atom," cries Darrell, the frustrated scientist of *Strange Interlude*, and for Nina life is but "a strange dark interlude in the electrical display of God the father"—who is a God deaf, dumb and blind. O'Neill, unable to support it with man's whole strength—his intellect and emotion—prepares to support it with man's weakness: his blind faith.

For the non-Catholic reader O'Neill's explicitly religious solution is likely to be not only insupportable but incomprehensible. Neither St. Francis nor St. Thomas can tell us much about it; it is neither a mystical ecstasy nor the reasoned proof of assumptions. But Pascal can tell us a great deal, for O'Neill's faith, like Pascal's is a poetic utilitarianism: he needs it and *will* have it. O'Neill rejects naturalism and materialism as Pascal had rejected Descartes and all science. He too is frightened by "the eternal silence of the infinite spaces." Like Pascal, to whom the details of life and the variety and flux of the human mind were repugnant, O'Neill feels that life is empty—having emptied it—and can fill it only by faith in a loving God. The existence of such a God, Pascal knew, cannot be proved save by the heart's need, but this seemed sufficient and he stood ready to stupefy his reason to maintain his faith. O'Neill will do no less. It is perhaps the inevitable way of modern Catholicism in a hostile world.

O'Neill's rejection of materialism involved the familiar pulpit confusion of philosophical materialism with "crass" materialism, that is, with the preference of physical to moral well-being. It is therefore natural that *Dynamo*, the play in which he makes explicit his anti-materialism, should present characters who are mean and little—that, though it contains an Earth Mother, she is not the wise and tragic Cybel but the fat and silly Mrs. Fife, the bovine wife of the atheist dynamo-tender. She, like the other characters in the play, allies herself with the Dynamo-God, embodiment both of the materialistic universe and of modern man's sense of his own power. But this new god can only frustrate the forces of life, however much it at first seems life's ally against the Protestant denials, and those who worship it become contemptible and murderous.

And the contempt for humanity which pervades *Dynamo* continues in *Mourning Becomes Electra*, creating, in a sense, the utter hopelessness of that tragedy. Aeschylus had ended his Atreus trilogy on a note of social reconciliation—after the bloody deeds and the awful pursuit of the Furies, society confers its forgiveness, the Furies are tamed to deities of hearth and field: "This day there is a new Order born"; but O'Neill's version has no touch of this resolution. There is no forgiveness in *Mourning Becomes Electra* because, there is as yet no forgiving God in O'Neill's cosmos, there is no society either, only a vague chorus of contemptible townspeople. "There's no one left to punish me," says Lavinia. "I've got to punish myself."

It is the ultimate of individual arrogance, the final statement of a universe in which society has no part. For O'Neill, since as far back as *The Hairy Ape*, there has been only the individual and the universe. The social organism has meant nothing. His Mannons, unlike Atreides, are not monarchs with a relation to the humanity about them, a humanity that can forgive because it can condemn. They act their crimes on the stage of the infinite....

Forgiveness comes in *Ah, Wilderness!* the satyr-play that follows the tragedy, and it is significant that O'Neill should have interrupted the composition of *Days Without End* to write it. With the religious answer of the more serious play firm in his mind, with its establishment of the divine law, O'Neill can, for the first time, render the sense and feel of common life, can actually be humorous. Now the family is no longer destructively possessive as he has always represented it, but creatively sympathetic. The revolt of the young son—his devotion to rebels and hedonists, to Shaw, to Ibsen and Swinburne—is but the mark of adolescence and in the warm round of forgiving life he will become wisely acquiescent to a world that is not in the least terrible.

But the idyllic life of *Ah, Wilderness!* for all its warmth, is essentially ironical, almost cynical. For it is only when all magnitude has been removed from humanity by the religious answer and placed in the Church and its God that life can be seen as simple and good the pluses and minuses of man must be made to cancel out as nearly as possible, the equation must be found. The hero of *Days Without End* has lived for years in a torturing struggle with the rationalistic, questioning "half" of himself which has led him away from piety to atheism, thence to socialism, next to unchastity and finally to the oblique attempt to murder his beloved wife. It is not until he makes an act of submissive faith at the foot of the Cross and thus annihilates the doubting mind, the root of all evil, that he can find peace.

But the annihilation of the questioning mind also annihilates the multitudinous world. *Days Without End*, perhaps O'Neill's weakest play, is cold and bleak; life is banished from it by the vision of the Life Eternal. Its religious content is expressed not so much by the hero's priestly uncle, wise, tolerant, humorous in the familiar literary convention of modern Catholicism, as by the hero's wife, a humorless, puritanical woman who lives on the pietistic-romantic love she bears her husband and on her sordid ideal of his absolute chastity. She is the very embodiment of all the warping, bullying idealism that O'Neill had once attacked. Now, however, he gives credence to this plaster saintliness, for it represents for him the spiritual life of absolutes. Now for the first time he is explicit in his rejection of all merely human bulwarks against the pain and confusion of life—finds in the attack upon capitalism almost an attack upon God, scorns socialism and is disgusted with the weakness of those who are disgusted with social individualism. The peace of the absolute can be bought only at the cost of blindness to the actual.

The philosophic position would seem to be a final one: O'Neill has crept into the dark womb of Mother Church and pulled the universe in with him. Perhaps the very violence of the gesture with which he has taken the position of passivity should remind us of his force and of what such force may yet do even in that static and simple dark. Yet it is scarcely a likely place for O'Neill to remember Dion Anthony's warning: "It isn't enough to be [life's] creature. You've got to create her or she requests you to destroy yourself."

New Republic, September 23, 1936.

3
The Late Plays

Eugene O'Neill's New Play Is Powerful and Moving

Richard Watts, Jr.

Eugene O'Neill's first play in twelve years is, among other things, certain to be the most controversial dramatic event of the season, with sides taken violently and the admiration and damnation rising to great heights. Since the battle lines are no doubt being drawn at the moment, I shall get into the fray at once by expressing my dogmatic conviction that *The Iceman Cometh* is a superb drama of splendid and imposing stature, which is at once powerful, moving, eloquent and compassionate.

Being a playwright of monumental proportions, Mr. O'Neill gives us works in which both the virtues and flaws are on an impressive scale, and there is no denying that *The Iceman Cometh* has its share of the latter. There is a wild, cascading power in O'Neill dramas, which, if tamed, would destroy the freedom and scope of his fierce and brooding imagination, and the excessive length, the sometimes unnecessary verbiage and the deceptively leisured interludes of an O'Neill play are a small price to pay for keeping his essential quality intact. Editing might make *The Iceman* seem more efficient, but it would endanger the magnitude of its spirit.

Superficially, it would be possible to describe *The Iceman Cometh* by comparing it to an alliance between Saroyan and Gorky, the Saroyan of *The Time of Your Life* and the Gorky of *The Lower Depths*. The William Saroyan aspect would lie in the warm, almost tender attitude toward the boozy philosophizing of alcoholics. The Maxim Gorky contribution, which is less superficial, would have to do with the setting, which is a refuge for derelicts, and the central character, who is a rather mysterious visitor with ideas of bringing peace and comfort to lost souls. Such comparisons, while they come almost inescapably to mind, are certainly not to be pushed far, since O'Neill uses his material for very different purposes.

One charge certain to be brought against the play is that it is immoral. The indictment will not deal with such minor matters as the frequent frankness of the dialogue or the presence of prostitutes in the cast of characters. It will be based on the no doubt shameless fact that *The Iceman* seems to be an eloquent and persuasive defense of getting drunk. There is no getting around it: the poor derelicts of the drama have a very satisfactory time with their dreams when they are filled with poisonous five-cent whisky, and they are terribly miserable when they are approximately sober.

It happens, however, that drink, while important to both the play and the characters, is not the vital thing in what O'Neill has to say. He is merely proclaiming the humanitarian doctrine that mankind, being lost and lonely in a hard and bitter world, is entitled to some sort of illusion to comfort it in exile, even if that illusion can be supplied only by alcohol, and that the best intentioned meddler interferes with this right at his own peril.

Whenever there is a new O'Neill play there is a lot of talk, some of it rhapsodic but most of it contemptuous, about symbolism and messages and cryptic profundities. In part O'Neill, himself, is to blame for such talk, since his scorn for the conventional in his drama and his often ponderous brooding on the universe do a great deal to encourage it. In truth, though, most of his works are essentially simple, just as in the case of *The Iceman Cometh*. The new play, whatever any one may say of it, is not heavily symbolic. It has a lot to say about miserable humanity, but says it in story, not symbols.

What seems to me important about the drama is that its barroom characters, who had once been soldiers, anarchists, newspapermen, gamblers, lawyers, policemen and circusmen, are richly, humorously, compassionately and knowingly drawn, and that their talk, their history and their entanglement in the tragedies of a hardware salesman, who would play providence to them, and a boy, who comes to an old anarchist for help, are movingly, if often too languorously, dramatized.

Of course, *The Iceman Cometh* is far more than that, too. "Compassion" is a word that can hardly be avoided in the consideration of an O'Neill play, and it is present in its most eloquent form here. The seeking of inner-meaning in such a work has at least the justification that the brooding spirit, the melancholy contemplation of man and his fate, the frank contemplation of human defeat and despair and the manner in which such despair is even given a certain nobility, which are all present in *The Iceman Cometh*, give the simple story of men reduced to simplicity its stature and strange beauty.

This remarkable drama, which on the first night ran from 4:30 to 10 p.m.—with an hour and a quarter dinner intermission—presents great problems of production and casting. On the whole, they have been handsomely surmounted. Robert Edmund Jones' barroom sets are brilliant, the cast is mostly splendid and Eddie Dowling's direction is characteristically sympathetic and understanding. There are a number of extremely fine performances and at least one is superb. The veteran Dudley Digges is nothing short of magnificent as the sentimental old proprietor of the derelict's saloon.

The most difficult role in the drama, that of the hardware salesman, is played by James Barton, whose acting problems include a moving and dramatic speech which lasts some fifteen minutes. Mr. Barton is an excellent and experienced player, and, on the whole, he is quite brilliant. It is no doubt unfair to him, but somehow I could not help thinking that Mr. Dowling, himself, would have been far more touching and impressive in the role.

There are some fine portrayals in the lesser roles. In fact, all of the barroom denizens, male and female, are admirably presented and it is fairly arbitrary to pick out a few of the names for special mention. But I recall particularly Paul Crabtree's understanding impersonation of the doomed son of a celebrated anarchist heroine; E. G. Marshall's Harvard Law School alumnus, John Marriot's Negro ex-gambler, Russell Collins' one time Boer War correspondent, Tom Pedi's bartender and Nicholas Joy's broken down British officer.

Then, too, there should be special mention of Carl Benton Reid, who plays the important role of a despairing ex-anarchist, and gives it a fine air of broken down intellectual integrity.

The Iceman Cometh goes about its story-telling too slowly and at too great length and it has its share of other faults, too. But it is a drama that gives the entire American theatre dignity and importance.

New York Post, October 10, 1946

O'Neill—at Long Last

Howard Barnes

Eugene O'Neill's erratic genius flames uncertainly in *The Iceman Cometh*. Breaking a silence of a dozen years, he has peopled the stage of the Martin Beck with fascinating characters, has involved them in a magnificent riddle of life and death, and then has left them and an audience singularly untouched. It is a long play, starting in late afternoon and pausing for the dinner hour. During four acts the celebrated dramatist stirs the bitter dregs of human experience in a waterfront saloon of 1912. With a reverent Theater Guild production and generally inspired acting, the play has a savage undertow and moments of bleak and tragic majesty. That it remains essentially earthbound and monotonous is a flaw inherent in the work.

The more vivid and individual the gallery of bums becomes in *The Iceman Cometh*, the greater is the compulsion for some dynamic resolution of their various whip-sawings by destiny. Most of the figures are content in their palace of pipe dreams, drinking the proprietor's 15-cent rotgut and kidding each other malevolently. O'Neill has drawn them masterfully, from Harry Hope, the irascible host, to the ex-wobbly, Larry, who likes to think he has taken a philosopher's grandstand seat at this pageant of the lower depths. What he has failed to do, as Dostoievsky did, is to shape their personal tragedies to an upheaval which might illuminate their existence.

The dramatic catharsis in *The Iceman Cometh* is mystical and mystifying. It occurs when a hardware drummer whose arrival has been eagerly awaited by the derelicts, turns a brawling birthday party for Harry into a wake. Hickey, as he is known, should have been the life of the festivities, joshing the old anarchist, the broken-down British officer, the tarts and the touchy Negro and telling his old gag about his wife and the iceman. Instead, he announces that he has found peace by denying his particular pipe dream and lures each pitiful human wreck into attempting the same experiment. It is a striking and even sensational plot twist, but it is coiled tight and then allowed to unravel in a disappointing climax.

One may select a variety of interpretations for this major theme. In terms of overt stage exposition, it finds the bums in Harry's dump taking on the horrible guises of death itself until Hickey confesses that he has killed his loving and beloved wife and takes sanction in insanity by damning her. There are profundities aplenty in the last two acts of *The Iceman Cometh*, particularly since there is a subplot in which the son of Larry's former mistress in the I.W.W. confesses he has turned her in for a life stretch and tries to atone for his sin by committing suicide. The stuff of a great and moving tragedy gleams through scene after scene of the drama, but it has not been properly refined.

The performances do not fail whatever it is that O'Neill has sought to communicate in stage terms. Dudley Digges is superbly crotchety as the sinner among sinners, who cherishes the bums he shelters and grieves sentimentally for a nagging wife. His Harry is a full-dimensioned and understandable Irishman no matter how murky the action becomes. James Barton has the difficult assignment of making Hickey a recognizable and vaguely appealing figure. For much of the time he is excellent, but he plays the final stanzas with less knowledge than rather bewildered intensity. Carl Benton Reid is fine as the philosopher who likes to think he has forsaken his cause and Nicholas Joy is seedily jaunty as the Boer War veteran.

Several of the lesser parts, being remote from O'Neill's restless probing into the human spirit, stand out with astonishing clarity. Morton L. Stevens is slyly amusing as a circus grifter, Leo Chalzel is excellent as a sodden old Anarchist; Dan Parritt makes the visiting boy peculiarly obnoxious and Marcella Markham, Jeanne Cagney and Ruth Gilbert are immense as tarts who insist on being called just that. Then there are Russell Collins, as an ex-foreign correspondent who really likes to drink, and Tom Pedi, who is excellent as a bartender. Eddie Dowling has kept all the characters alive and vibrant in his staging against Robert Edmund Jones's realistic setting. Neither of them can keep *The Iceman Cometh* from conversational monotony and final dramatic confusion.

New York Herald Tribune, October 10, 1946.

Iceman Returns

J. Brooks Atkinson

When O'Neill's *Mourning Becomes Electra* was produced in 1931, Robert Benchley made an acute observation. He said he suspected that the ghost of O'Neill's father—James O'Neill—was in the wings of the theatre and applauding.

For James O'Neill was famous as the swashbuckling Count in the romantic melodrama *The Count of Monte Cristo*, in which, as a matter of fact, Eugene once played a small part when he had no settled employment. Benchley's allusion to the romantic sweep of an O'Neill tragedy has never been forgotten. Despite the gloom and the pessimism of his plays, O'Neill did have a romantic streak in his nature.

He enjoyed the spectacle of tragedy, as he enjoyed the spectacle of men struggling against the indifference of the universe. Romantic things appealed to him—the sea, ships and foreign ports, gold prospecting in Honduras, the raffish part of city life, the bums, the seedy intellectuals, the hospitality of saloons.

He had romantic tastes in literature. He liked Omar Khayyam, Dowson, Swinburne and Kipling. In his youth he had a romantic interest in revolutionary writers like Nietzsche, Shopenhauer and Marx. In *Long Day's Journey Into Night*, the ailing lad who represents O'Neill's youth had a dreamy, romantic view of himself and remarks that he ought to have been created as a sea gull or a fish. He romantically thinks of himself as a character in literature.

If O'Neill did not have a romantic streak in his nature he might not have been able to sustain his long career as a dramatist in the face of his sense of futility and doom. What drove him on to write the greatest body of tragedy of any American? It was not hatred. It was more likely a romantic dream of beauty and peace that are unattainable.

Although he had no hope he was in love with the spectacle of man in conflict with fate. There was a romantic tinge to his brooding. It was his style of poetry—never angry, but wistful and reconciled. He was not crying with rage and scorn, like Strindberg. He was not trying to reform society, like Ibsen. He was not a revolutionary like Gorki. He was a poet who was full of gloom but essentially sweet-natured. He did not set himself apart from the world he was writing about.

Thanks to José Quintero, the artistic genius of Circle in the Square, one of O'Neill's Promethean plays, *The Iceman Cometh*, has just been beautifully restaged. When it was first produced, in 1946, it was generally admired, but it was not an overwhelming success with the public. It ought to have a long run this time. For the intimate environment of Circle in the Square provides the ideal setting for this saloon saga. And Mr. Quintero's direction is extraordinarily perceptive. It expresses not only the boozy bickering of the saloon but the philosophy of the play.

The performance lasts nearly five hours. Although a playgoer may be exhausted when it is over, he will not be exhausted from boredom, but from the relentless reiteration with which O'Neill and the actors drive the theme home. *The Iceman Cometh* shows a collection of representative vagrants sustained from one periodical drunk to another by illusions about themselves. They are romantics. They are heroes to themselves. Each of them has some fondly cherished alibi that keeps him from acknowledging the sordid truth about himself.

The dreams are disturbed by the arrival of a fanatical reformed drunk who tries to help the saloon inmates by making them face the truth. The results are not only distressing but disastrous. The truth does not set these men free. It makes their life unbearable. Illusions—or "pipe dreams," in the O'Neill vernacular of 1912—are essential to sustain the will to live.

Although *The Iceman Cometh* was written in 1939, the characters and the environment were already familiar. These are the men and women that O'Neill wrote about in the S. S. Glencairn plays and *Anna Christie*, and these are the counterparts of the riffraff he associated with in Jimmy Priest's grog-shop on the waterfront in 1910 or thereabouts—tarnished soldiers of fortune, anarchists, radicals, con-men, gamblers, black sheep, bartenders and prostitutes. If they did not shape his thinking, they at least confirmed what he was already thinking a year or two previous to the part of his life described in *Long Day's Journey Into Night*.

When O'Neill was writing about such characters thirty-five or forty years ago, they seemed to be realistic. His attitude toward them seems romantic now. But in *The Iceman Cometh* they are portrayed candidly as romantics, and his attitude toward them seems to be brutally realistic in terms of his tragic philosophy. They are so far gone in dreams of past heroism or future regeneration that reality is like death to them—something they haven't the strength to face. After disturbing them with truth, O'Neill lets them fall back into drunken stupor in the last act—reunited in the shabby fellowship of the damned.

Ten years ago nearly everyone regarded *The Iceman Cometh*, despite its virtues, as long, lumbering and repetitious. Very likely the same criticisms will be urged against it now. But this department, without being sure, is inclined to regard the length of *The Iceman Cometh* as an essential part of its power. It lets the characters destroy themselves in their own fashion—languid, garrulous, confused, acrimonious, frightened, sullen and resigned. The length and the torpid pace are parts of O'Neill's basic statement that the universe is not hostile but indifferent.

In a sense, *The Iceman Cometh* is an affectionate play. O'Neill was fond of these delegates to oblivion. For the most part, they are not vicious men, but men who have always taken the easy way out. They are weak men in a strong world. On the whole, they like each other. Certainly, they are good company in the theatre. In any rational view of life, they emerge as comic characters who speak a sardonically amusing jargon.

Although O'Neill knew the bitter truth about them in 1939, he still had a romantic attachment for them. At a time of his life when his mind was settled and his craftsmanship perfected, he portrayed them pungently and vividly in a titanic drama....

New York Times, May 20, 1956

The Iceman and the Bridegroom: Some Observations on the Death of O'Neill's Salesman

Cyrus Day

> While the bridegroom tarried, they all slumbered and slept. And at midnight there was a cry made, Behold, the bridegroom cometh. (Matthew 25:5-6)

The Iceman Cometh is a play about the death of a salesman; its central theme is the relationship between men's illusions and their will to live. The salesman, Theodore Hickman, or Hickey, as he is called, is a more complex character than Arthur Miller's Willie Loman, and O'Neill's diagnosis of the spiritual *malaise* of the twentieth century is more profound than Miller's. Loman is depicted from the outside: he is the victim of a false and wholly external conception of what constitutes success. He wants, in a worldly sense, to solve the riddle of life, but the questions he asks are superficial and relatively easy for an audience or a reader to answer.

Hickey is depicted from the inside. He is more successful as a salesman than Loman, but he is the victim of a far more insidious disease. He is not versed at first hand (as O'Neill was) in philosophic nihilism, but he has somehow become aware, presumably through a sort of intellectual osmosis, that modern man no longer believes in objective reality and truth. Loman is adrift in contemporary American society; Hickey is adrift in the universe. The difference is a measure of the difference between O'Neill's aims and the aims of almost all other modern dramatists.

A few days before *The Iceman Cometh* opened on Broadway in 1946, O'Neill told a reporter that he had tried to express its "deeper" meaning in its title, and in an interview with S.J. Woolf he said that the verb form "cometh" was a "deliberate reference to biblical language." The play itself, he gave Woolf to understand, had religious significance. It is difficult to see what he can have meant by these hints, for *The Iceman Cometh* has few readily discernible connections either with religion or with the Bible. However, since O'Neill was not in the habit of talking at random about his own work, we would do well, if we want to come to terms with the "deeper" meaning of *The Iceman Cometh*, to assume that he had something specific and important in mind, and to try to discover what it was.

O'Neill looked upon himself, we must remember, as a spiritual physician, and he thought that his mission as a dramatist was to "dig at the roots of the sickness today," which he defined as the death of the old God (echoing Nietzsche) and the failure of science and materialism to provide a new one satisfactory to the remnants of man's primitive religious instincts. Most dramatists write about the relationship between man and man, but he was more interested, he said, in the relationship between man and God. His plays, accordingly, often have a metaphysical basis, but since he had lost his faith in God at an early period in his life, and since he thought that it would take a million years of evolution for man "to grow up and obtain a soul," they are seldom religious in any generally accepted sense of the word.

Days Without End, which preceded *The Iceman Cometh*, is an exception. Written in 1934, during a brief period of personal happiness, it is a Christian play. The protagonist, a young man very much like O'Neill himself, is torn by religious doubts, but in the final act he enters a Catholic church, prostrates himself before an image of the crucified Jesus, and becomes at last an integrated personality, at peace with himself and with God. O'Neill, in 1934, appeared to have come to the end of his spiritual pilgrimage.

Actually, *Days Without End* was a "mere interlude," as he admitted later, and did not reflect his personal religious convictions. For the moment he may have supposed that he could return to the Christian fold, but by 1939, when he wrote *The Iceman Cometh*, his mood had changed from tentative hope to unqualified despair. World War II was beginning, and the human race was obviously "too damned stupid" (this was O'Neill's phrase) to realize that its salvation depended on one "simple sentence": What shall it profit a man if he gain the whole world and lose his own soul? Perhaps, O'Neill told a reporter, mankind ought to be dumped down the nearest drain and the world given over to the ants.

These are hardly Christian sentiments, despite the quotation from the New Testament, and *The Iceman Cometh* cannot, therefore, have the same sort of religious significance as *Days Without End*: it cannot be a Christian play. Can it be a recantation of the point of view of *Days Without End*? Can it be, in any sense, a repudiation of Christianity?

Since O'Neill himself has given us the hint, let us begin our inquiry with the title. On the surface, the iceman is a reference to Hickey's ribald jest that he knows his wife is safe because he has left her with the iceman in the hay. On a "deeper" level, the iceman represents death, as O'Neill pointed out in 1946, and as Larry Slade points out in the play when he learns that Hickey's wife is dead. "It fits," Slade says, "for Death was the Iceman Hickey called to his home."

It is not enough, however, merely to identify the iceman with death. We must realize also that the iceman is the foil of the bridegroom of Scripture, and that he stands for the opposite of everything the bridegroom stands for. In the symbolism of theology, the bridegroom is always Christ, giver of life eternal. Waiting for the bridegroom symbolizes man's hope of redemption. Union with the bridegroom, conceived as a marriage, is the "final end and realized meaning"[1] of the life of every Christian, the "fulfillment of promise and [the] consummation of hope." Union with the bridegroom signifies victory over death and salvation in the world to come.

Union with the iceman, conceived as adultery, must, then, be a parody of union with the bridegroom, and signify surrender to death and acquiescence in personal annihilation. Evelyn Hickman, after her husband kills her, finds the peace of oblivion in the arms of the symbolical iceman. The other characters in the play will eventually find the same kind of peace when they abandon their illusory hope of happiness, whether here and now on earth, or in a hypothetical Christian hereafter.

Construed in this way, *The Iceman Cometh* (on one of its many levels of meaning) is seen to be a parable of the destiny of man. All men are waiting for the iceman, but only those who have shed their ultimate illusions are aware that the "final end and realized meaning" of their lives is death. "I'm the only real convert to death Hickey made here," says Slade, who speaks for O'Neill in the play. "From the bottom of my coward's heart I mean that now."

"I want to go to the chair," says Hickey, when he realizes that his love for his wife was an illusion, and that he killed her because he hated her. "Do you suppose I give a damn about life now?" he asks the detective who has arrested him. "Why, you bonehead, I haven't got a single damned lying hope or pipe dream left." The other derelicts in Hope's saloon (the world of illusions) lack Slade's philosophic detachment and Hickey's psychopathic insight, and are afraid to face the truth: that waiting for the iceman constitutes the chief employment of their futile lives.

The paradox of fulfillment through annihilation is a concept that O'Neill could have derived either from Schopenhauer or from Freud, who reached the conclusion previously reached by Schopenhauer, though by a different route, that the goal of life is death. The immediate stimulus to his imagination, however, may have been Waldo Frank's novel *The Bridegroom Cometh*, in which the heroine gives herself to a succession of bridegrooms, both spiritual (Christ, Freud, Marx) and material (a husband and several lovers). Only Marx satisfies her need for love, and in the end she finds fulfillment through identification with the masses. O'Neill, unlike Frank, never supposed that a political or sociological nostrum could cure the diseases of the soul.

A second key to O'Neill's attitude toward Christianity in *The Iceman Cometh* is the role of the hardware salesman Hickey. When the curtain rises on Act I, the derelicts in Hope's hotel, slumbering and sleeping in their chairs, are waiting for Hickey to visit them on one of his periodical benders. "Would that Hickey or death would come," says Willie Oban. But Hickey has tarried: a prostitute has seen him standing at the next corner, and to her surprise he is sober....

Hickey, when he arrives, is greeted by a very different cry from "Behold, the bridegroom cometh." "Here's the old son of a bitch," says Rocky; and "Bejees, Hickey, you old bastard, it's good to see you!" says Hope.

But Hickey is no longer the irresponsible drunkard the derelicts once knew and loved. He is on the wagon, and he proposes a stern remedy for what ails them. What he has to sell, in other words, is symbolic hardware, and he himself represents all self-appointed messiahs and saviors who meddle in other people's affairs and tell them how to live. Hence he can be fruitfully compared to Gregers Werle in Ibsen's *Wild Duck*, to Luka in Maxim Gorki's *Lower Depths*, and to the mysterious strangers in Jerome's *Passing of the Third Floor Back* and Kennedy's *Servant in the House*.

He also has something in common with Sigmund Freud, and his program of salvation is similar, in a general way, to psychoanalysis. He invites the derelicts to re-examine their pipe dreams (wish fulfillments) and to get rid of them by coming to terms with reality (the reality principle). This, he imagines, will make them happy. It doesn't, of course; and after their abortive attempts to resume their former occupations, they stagger back, demoralized and defeated, to the security of Hope's saloon. They cannot endure life unsupported by illusions, and instead of making them happy, Hickey deprives them of the will to live. Hickey has the last speech in each of the first three acts, and his last word in each is an ironical "happy." The notion that men can be happy in this worst of all possible worlds is an illusion.

Another illusion, or so Freud tells us, is religion. Man does not need consolations, he says in *The Future of an Illusion*, nor can he remain a child forever. Rather he must venture out into the hostile world and be educated to reality. "Man can endure the cruelty of reality. What, you fear he will not stand the test? But it is at least something to know that one has been thrown on one's own resources."

This is very much like Hickey's program for the individual derelicts in *The Iceman Cometh*. Over and above their private illusions, however, stands Christianity, the collective illusion of what O'Neill thought of as our bankrupt Western civilization. Religion is an illusion, O'Neill evidently agreed; but unlike Freud, he did not think that the "swine called men" could live without it. Thus, by an extraordinary reconciliation of opposites, he equates the drunken Hickey with the secular savior Freud and the Christian Savior Christ, and at the same time rejects the gospels preached by both. Says Slade:

> Honor or dishonor, faith or treachery, are nothing but the opposites of the same stupidity which is ruler and king of life, and in the end they rot in the same grave. All things are the same meaningless joke to me, for they grin at me from the one skull of death.

That O'Neill had this anti-Christian undertone in mind when he compiled his medley of illusions in *The Iceman Cometh* is further substantiated by several tantalizing resemblances[2] between the play and the New Testament. Hickey as savior has twelve disciples. They drink wine at Hope's supper party, and their grouping on the stage, according to O'Neill's directions, is reminiscent of Leonardo da Vinci's painting of the Last Supper. Hickey leaves the party, as Christ does, aware that he is about to be executed. The three whores correspond in number to the three Marys, and sympathize with Hickey as the three Marys sympathize with Christ. (The implications of this resemblance are not without precedent: Christopher Marlowe, it will be recalled, was accused of saying that the women of Samaria were whores.)

One of the derelicts, Parritt, resembles Judas Iscariot in several ways. He is the twelfth in the list of *dramatis personae*; Judas is twelfth in the New Testament lists of the Disciples. He has betrayed his anarchist mother for a paltry $200; Judas betrayed Christ for thirty pieces of silver. He is from the far-away Pacific Coast; Judas was from far-away Judaea. Hickey reads his mind and motives; Christ read Judas's. Parritt compares himself to Iscariot when he says that his mother would regard anyone who quit the "Movement" as a Judas who ought to be boiled in oil. He commits suicide by jumping off a fire escape; Judas fell from a high place (Acts 1:18) or "hanged himself" (Matthew 27:5).

In the light of O'Neill's remarks concerning the Biblical and religious significance of his play, these resemblances can hardly be coincidental. They are no more than an undertone, to be sure—one of many undertones or subordinate layers of meaning—but they are consistent with the main theme of the play, and they account for some of its otherwise unaccountable features: for example, the emphasis on midnight (see Matthew 25:5-6) as the hour appointed for Hope's party, and the unnecessarily large number of derelicts in Hope's saloon. If O'Neill's only purpose had been to show that everyone, no matter how degraded, has one last pipe dream to sustain him, four or five derelicts, instead of twelve, would have sufficed, and the play would have been less redundant than, in fact, it is.

O'Neill was fond of hidden symbols and multiple layers of meaning. The nine acts of *Strange Interlude* and the name of the heroine, Nina, symbolize the nine months of a woman's pregnancy. Christine Mannon in *Mourning Becomes Electra* is called Christine (to correspond with Clytemnestra in Aeschylus's trilogy) instead of some other name beginning with "C" because O'Neill wanted to suggest that she is a sort of female anti-Christ or pagan martyr, crucified by a repressive Puritanism for her faith in sexuality. Lavinia Mannon is called Lavinia instead of a name beginning with "E" (to correspond with Electra) because "levin" means lightning or electricity. The name Mannon, from the last part of Agamemnon, suggests Mammon, the figurative divinity of all genuine Mannons. Examples of this sort of ingenuity, culled from other plays by O'Neill, could be multiplied indefinitely.

In addition to Hickey and Christine Mannon, O'Neill likens several other characters to Christ. In *The Fountain*, Bishop Menendez advises Juan to surrender the Indian Nano to the mob.

> Juan (*with wild scorn*). Ah, High Priest! Deliver him up, eh?
> Menendez. Juan! You are impious! (*Angrily*) It is sacrilege—to compare this Indian dog—you mock our Blessed Savior! You are cursed—I wash my hands—His will be done!

Nina, in *Strange Interlude*, cherishes the illusion that her dead lover Gordon Shaw is the real father of her son. "Immaculate conception," Marsden mutters in an unpublished manuscript version of the play.[3] "The Sons of the Father have all been failures!" Nina says, referring both to her son and to Christ. "Failing, they died for us...they could not stay with us, they could not give us happiness."

Allusions such as these abound in O'Neill's plays. *Where the Cross Is Made*, to cite a final example, contains what I surmise is a double reference to the sustaining power of illusions (the central theme, as we have seen, of *The Iceman Cometh*). As the curtain falls on the last scene, Nat Bartlett cries out with insane frenzy: "The treasure is buried where the cross is made." On the surface, this means that Nat, like his father, is obsessed by the belief that the trinkets on the island represent a fortune in gold. But the words also suggest that Christianity, symbolized by the Cross, is as much of an illusion as the gold. In view of the way he worked and thought, O'Neill cannot have been unaware of this implication in his title.

These considerations bring to mind an ironic scene in *The Great God Brown*. Dion Anthony, one of O'Neill's favorite characters and a recognizable self-portrait, designs a cathedral which, he boasts, is "one vivid blasphemy from the sidewalk to the tips of the spires!—but so concealed the fools will never know! They'll kneel and worship the ironic Silenus who tells them the best good is never to be born!"

When Brown inherits Dion's soul, he too introduces secret motifs into his work. Of a new state capitol that he designs, he says:

> Here's a wondrous fair Capitol! The design would do just as well for a Home for Criminal Imbeciles! Yet to them, such is my art, it will appear to possess a pure common sense, a fat-bellied finality, as dignified as the suspenders of an assemblyman. Only to me will that pompous facade reveal itself as the wearily ironic grin of Pan as he half listens to the laws passed by his fleas to enslave him.

Did O'Neill, in writing *The Iceman Cometh*—the question inevitably presents itself—did O'Neill do what Dion and Brown do in *The Great God Brown*? Did he, that is to say, introduce concealed blasphemies into his play, just as Dion and Brown introduce concealed blasphemies into their architectural designs? And did he laugh in secret at the critics who supposed that he had written a compassionate play in *The Iceman Cometh*, just as Dion and Brown laugh at the fools who do not see through their mockery?

André Malraux once asked if man in the twentieth century could survive after God had died in the nineteenth. O'Neill's answer in *The Iceman Cometh* is no. The derelicts in Hope's saloon, all of them childless, symbolize a humanity that is engaged in the laudable act of committing suicide. As the play ends, Larry Slade stares straight ahead (O'Neill's habitual way of depicting disillusionment) and waits for release from the intolerable burden of life. O'Neill's prolonged search for faith has led him, not to faith, but to despair.

Could there have been in 1939, a more prophetic anticipation of the self-destructive compulsions of the Age of Nuclear Fission? Is there in dramatic literature a more nihilistic play than *The Iceman Cometh*?

NOTES

1. See L. A. Zander's discussion of the problem of the bridegroom in his *Dostoevsky*, 1948, pp. 97-137.

2. First called to my attention by Mr. Philip Taylor.

3. Yale M.S. 52, not at present available to scholars, but discussed by Miss Doris Alexander in her brilliant doctoral thesis entitled *Freud and O'Neill: An Analysis of Strange Interlude* (New York University, 1952).

Modern Drama, 1 (May 1958): 3-9.

Stage: *Iceman Cometh* to Broadway

Clive Barnes

Pace was always a prime concern with America's greatest dramatist, Eugene O'Neill. He dared time. He wrote long plays, but never carelessly. His plays were long because the best of them are essentially plays of theme rather than exposition. They are markers to a drowned life, autobiographical, intense and acquiring their dramatic flavor from an atmosphere that seduces its audience into the very past of a time experienced. This obsession with the practically direct communication of experience, as opposed to story-telling, reaches its peak in the three great plays—the plays where after so many fumbling stumbles to the summit O'Neill finally achieves unquestionable mastery of his material.

Of the last great trilogy, *A Moon for the Misbegotten*, *Long Days Journey Into Night*, and *The Iceman Cometh*, it is the last that is the most difficult, and even the least immediate. It was given last night at the Circle in the Square Joseph E. Levine Theatre. See it—it is the kind of theater that jumps between life and drama. But it never forgets that it is really drama, and, indeed, at times it can be overly theatrical. But this is a small price to pay for poetic insight.

You expect a great playwright to be a great writer. Oddly enough, O'Neill is a very changeable writer, even in his last climatic period. He uses words uncertainly—there is too often a trace of ease, a slip of cliché—but such falters give the humanity to his genius. The theme of *The Iceman Cometh* is simple. Illusion is better as a reality than reality is as an illusion. We live with pipe dreams, and support those dreams the best we may. For some, the people O'Neill understood, tomorrow is more of a drug than a promise, and its withdrawal pressures may be so severe that the heroism it demands is impossible. In this play O'Neill gives us three life heroes—one who is led away to the electric chair on a charge of murder, one who jumps from a fire escape and one who is left, all conscience and bleeding. O'Neill never suggested life was easy.

This deeply moving play—this excursion into another life—might be compared to Maxim Gorki's *The Lower Depths*. They are both great plays of this century that show existence through the microscope of degradation. O'Neill did it with more humor and, in my opinion, more understanding.

The scene is a downtown West Side hotel in Manhattan. It is the summer of 1912. A hotel bar—more a bar than a hotel—is owned by Harry Hope. Don't forget the symbolism—this is a hope not quite abandoned. We begin slowly with drunks. They slouch somnolently around liquor-splashed tables. As they awake, we are awaiting a friend—a man who will rush into their bleak world carrying illusions and dispensing drink. The awaited visitor is a salesman called Hickey.

At last Hickey comes. But he is "the iceman of death." He has forfeited his illusions. Slowly he attacks—with his old bonhomie and salesman's gusto—all of the bar's inhabitants. He shows them the life of illusions that they are leading. He shows them that life, and destroys it. Bullied by the conscience-prickings of his eloquence, they try reality, try neglecting the soft pillows of their failures, and fail once more. Hickey's realities seem to work no better than the bar's illusions.

Yet O'Neill is going deeper than this. The profound act of the play—the final card, the last issue—is a man embracing death from a fire escape. O'Neill always thought that life was a debt that had to be paid by death, with a certain interest on the side represented by suffering. The setting for the play is perfect. The scenery by Clarke Dunham, the lighting by Jules Fisher and costumes by Carrie F. Robbins evoke time and place like a loving lithograph. Theodore Mann's direction is careful, reverent but lacks something in immediacy. These strange aquarium characters should walk out into life nervously dripping with actuality. The acting was fine, but there were certain nuances untouched.

James Earl Jones as Hickey was all right but all wrong. He is a thoughtful actor rather than an impassioned one. He teases climaxes rather than rides them, and it is difficult to see him as the good-natured, ill-determined Hickey. He looks and sounds as if he is selling insurance rather than dreams.

Many of the individual performances did seem to strike at the heart of the play. I was especially impressed, for example, with the ashen fire suggested by Michael Higgins as Larry, the one-time anarchist and now self-styled grandstand observer of life. Mr. Higgins brought just the right air of urgent bewilderment to the play and was very moving. Among the others—a good group—I liked the tattered gentility of Jack Gwillim as the Captain and Tom Aldredge as the seedily decayed newspaperman. This is a wonderful play that takes you into its own world. We are lucky to have it on Broadway—it is one of the most absorbing plays of our century. It leaves its mark on you.

New York Times, December 14, 1973.

Absence As Presence: The Second Sex in *The Iceman Cometh*

Bette Mandl

The principal women of O'Neill's *The Iceman Cometh* remain offstage. They never appear to the audience in full complexity as characters to engage us in various ways, to elicit a range of response. This design has special virtues for a consideration of some aspects of O'Neill's treatment of women in his work. The invisibility of the significant female figures, Evelyn and Rosa, brings their purpose in the play into relief, uncomplicated by their presence. O'Neill makes palpable here the contribution of women to the symbol pattern of *The Iceman Cometh*, to the ways in which it makes meaning.

Three women do, of course, figure in lively exchanges at Harry Hope's. But O'Neill's stage directions describe Margie and Pearl, who are somewhat younger versions of Cora, as "sentimental, featherbrained, giggly, lazy, good-natured and reasonably content with life."[1] The description alerts us to their marginality in a setting where alcohol and a protective male camaraderie are the substance of life. The "tarts" are external enough to the central movement of the play, and innocuous enough in this context, for Travis Bogard to call Hope's saloon "a world without women."[2] There are no women present who will impinge on the experience of the men.

The habitués of the backroom have managed to sustain a long-term, uneasy harmony—an equilibrium that is disturbed by the unexpected entrance of the tormented Parritt, and the eagerly awaited arrival of Hickey for Harry Hope's birthday. The force of the two men's impact on the backroom is directly related to the experiences they have just had with women. Parritt has betrayed his mother, Rosa, by giving the police the information that led to her arrest; and Hickey has murdered his wife, Evelyn. The stasis of life in the saloon has been contingent on keeping at bay the influence of women outside this haven. The center no longer holds once the proximity of such influence increases.

Simone de Beauvoir says of woman in her book, *The Second Sex*, "she is defined and differentiated with reference to man....He is the subject....She is the other."[3] The "otherness" of Rosa and Evelyn is intensified for us by their invisibility. They emerge exclusively in relation to the male characters. Rosa Parritt is a "new woman," dedicated to the Movement, to anarchy and free love. She seems a foil for Evelyn, a traditionally submissive wife. "Sweet and good" (p. 233), Evelyn maintained an unshakable faith in Hickey, forgiving his drinking and his sexual escapades, even when he infected her with venereal disease.

The audience quickly understands the frustration and hostility such women might have provoked. O'Neill need use little more than a kind of shorthand of familiar feminine images to suggest the fiercely, though ambivalently, independent woman, as well as the long-suffering wife, something of a martyr. John Henry Raleigh says of Rosa and Evelyn, "so fully drawn are they, the strong and domineering woman and the sweet self-effacing one...that they hover over the play like ghosts.[4] We help to fill in the sketch O'Neill provides with detail from a reservoir of notions about types of women.

Jean Rhys in her novel, *Wide Sargasso Sea*, imagines a life for Bertha Rochester, the madwoman in the attic of *Jane Eyre*. We might—with some wistfulness—be tempted to conceive of Rosa as a modern female hero living a life of commitment and risk. Or we might consider what the experience of Evelyn might have been, the isolation and thwarted possibilities of her life. What these women as protagonists in their own dramas might have been like, we can't know from *The Iceman Cometh*, because in this work, as in so many others, the women tend to be merely representative of that which men struggle with and against in enacting their destinies.

Throughout there are clues to the nature of the process that distances woman as "other." The pipe dreams themselves that give "life to the whole misbegotten mad lot of us, drunk or sober" (p. 10) turn out to be, for the most part, dreams about women which barely conceal the underlying nightmares. The extent to which a woman is inextricably linked with these illusions is a measure of the degree to which she has been removed from the realm of experience and located in an individual symbol system. When Rocky gives expression to his pipe dream early in the play, he sets out features of fantasy that will recur. He claims that he is not a pimp for Margie and Pearl, but just a bartender who is "pals" with them, and who takes their money because, "Dey'd on'y trow it away" (p. 12). His illusion is a comic, parodic prelude to the other pipe dreams to be articulated. Rocky's fantasy about himself distorts his actual relationship to the women he depends on. The major characters have corresponding dreams of self that deny the truths of their attachments.

When Hickey arrives and sees Parritt, he recognizes something about him. "We're members of the same lodge—in some way" (p. 84), he says, sensing that they have in common some essential guilt. He also intuits accurately that at the heart of Parritt's trouble is an anguished experience with a woman. "Hasn't he been mixed up with some woman? I don't mean trollops. I mean the old real love stuff that crucifies you" (p. 118). Of course, Hickey has no suspicion that the "woman" involved is Parritt's mother; but his good guess suggests that if a man is going through some profound turmoil, a woman is likely to be implicated.

Still, it is not a woman herself who is necessarily the problem. Arthur and Barbara Gelb report, "The truth of the play, as O'Neill explained to (Dudley) Nichols and to two or three other close friends, was that Hickey had long ago begun to harbor a murderous hatred for his wife; she represented his own, punishing conscience."[5] O'Neill, then, was highly aware of the symbolic function of Evelyn for Hickey. He also had great insight into the risk of violence inherent in a too-seamless fusion of person and symbol.

The revelations about women that emerge in the play are revelations of hatred. Parritt's early outcry, "I hate every bitch that ever lived!" (p. 71), foreshadows the confessions to be made. When pipe dreams are temporarily dispelled, Harry Hope, who had clung to a sentimental vision of his marriage and a claim that Bessie's death is the reason for his inactivity, makes a telling remark to Hickey; "Bejees you're a worse gabber than that nagging bitch, Bessie, was" (p. 202). And Ed Mosher talks of his delight in cheating Bessie, who was his sister: for him, "Dear Bessie wasn't a bitch. She was a God-damned bitch!" (p. 132). Similarly, Jimmy Tomorrow acknowledges that he had been a drunkard long before his wife committed adultery, though he's always offered her infidelity as his perennial excuse for his drinking. In fact, he felt no love for her.

Helen Muchnic points out:

> The poor harmless souls at Harry Hope's—good natured, easy going, and rather appealing with their vague beliefs in love and honor so long as they remain in their drunken stupor—exhibit, as soon as they are forced to consciousness, unsuspected deep-seated murderous hatreds.[6]

And, with great consistency, the hostility is directed toward a woman. Winifred Frazer compares *The Iceman Cometh* with *No Exit*, suggesting that in both, "'Hell is other people,' especially people of the female variety."[7]

Hickey, adopting an evangelical stance, offers to bring his somnolent friends release and serenity. He believes that he killed his wife, whom he says he'd always loved, because murder was "the one possible way to free poor Evelyn and give her the peace she'd always dreamed about" (p. 226). The truth, however, is wrenched out of him, as he describes his torment. "There's a limit to the guilt you can feel and the forgiveness and the pity you can take. You have to begin blaming someone else too" (p. 239). A woman comes to share in the blame in this case as in the others. Finally, he shocks himself by recalling what he said to Evelyn at the last: "Well, you know what you can do with your pipe dream now, you damned bitch!" (p. 241)

Parritt, who at first concealed that it was he who betrayed Rosa, gradually admits to more hostility toward his mother while Hickey makes his extended confession. As Travis Bogard says, "There are not many moments in theatre comparable to the canonical weaving of the narratives of betrayal, Hickey's and Parritt's, toward the end of the play.[8] As an intermediate step, Parritt says that he betrayed Rosa for money, a motive that seems less reprehensible to him than his own. And finally, at the moment when Hickey is about to utter his ultimate secret, Parritt, limp with "exhausted relief," says, "I may as well confess, Larry. There's no use lying any more. You know, anyway. I didn't give a damn about the money. It was because I hated her" (p. 241).

The outbursts of hostility are as similar as the cacophonous, joyful songs at the conclusion of the play are disparate. The power with which they are invested no doubt derives, in part, from O'Neill's own troubled personal experience, as Louis Scheaffer suggests:

> In the interlocked stories of Hickey and Parritt, he at last gave full vent to his fury against Ella Quinlan O'Neill, drug addict, the chief source of the bad conscience and the feeling of self-hatred that would fester in the playwright till the end of his days.[9]

But O'Neill manages to convey more here than a parable of misogyny. He recognizes, and gives eloquent expression to his understanding, that women are often interposed between men and the realities of life and death they have to face. Simone de Beauvoir says, "In all civilizations and still in our day woman inspires man with horror: it is the horror of his own carnal contingence, which he projects on her.[10] In *The Iceman Cometh*, the hatred of woman that emerges is itself something of a screen. After the betrayals are enacted and the confessions are made, vital tasks still remain to be done. Hickey has to face judgment, and Parritt must go to his suicide. As the former said to Harry Hope when prodding him to take his walk, "You've got to keep a date with yourself alone" (p. 194).

The responses to the confessions of Hickey and Parritt emphasize further woman's place in this cosmos. Harry Hope, feigning aggrieved indifference, wishes Hickey would interrupt his compelling story: "Give us a rest, for the love of Christ! Who the hell cares? We want to pass out in peace!" (p. 240). And all but Parritt and Larry loudly second him. Of course they don't want to hear, as Larry says, "things that will make us help send you to the chair" (p. 227). More significantly, however, in the backroom—where fantasies mask feelings that approximate violence toward women—evidence that such violence can be acted out is threatening and unwelcome. Even Hickey himself had come to see Parritt as a dangerous intruder. While he recognized their kinship at the outset, Hickey later says, "I wish you'd get rid of that bastard, Larry. I can't have him pretending there's something in common between him and me" (p. 227). Parritt later concurs. "You know what I did is a much worse murder," he says to Larry. "Because she is dead and yet she has to live" (p. 247).

It is not only because Rosa is consigned to a living death that Parritt's was "a much worse murder." He has come close to committing matricide, an act that evokes a feeling of primal horror. And matricide in this context is also the ultimate embodiment of the varying degrees of hostility toward women that find expression throughout the play. Raleigh refers to Parritt as a "moral leper."[11] No doubt he inspires such repulsion because, by his own example, Parritt locates in the mother-child bond the genesis of the tormented relationships the men have experienced and mythologized. Hickey might get a light sentence if judged insane. Parritt, on the other hand, seems a scapegoat, whose death is necessary for the restoration of order and life-sustaining illusion.

The iceman, prominent symbol of the play, is almost invariably linked with women. Rocky, for example, associates the iceman with Hickey's wife: "Remember how he woiks up dat gag about his wife, when he's cockeyed, cryin' over her picture and den springin' it on yuh all of a sudden dat he left her in de hay wid de iceman?" (p. 13) And Chuck later says of women that they can't be trusted: "De minute your back is toined, dey're cheatin' wid de iceman or someone" (p. 214).

O'Neill had discussed the iceman's role with Dudley Nichols, whose report of the playwright's comments is recorded by the Gelbs:

> The iceman of the title is, of course, death....I don't think O'Neill ever explained, publicly, what he meant by the use of the archaic word, "cometh," but he told me at the time he was writing the play that he meant a combination of the poetic and biblical "Death cometh"—that is, cometh to all living—and the old bawdy story...of the man who calls upstairs, "Has the iceman come yet?" and his wife calls back, "No, but he's breathin' hard."[12]

Cyrus Day extends the analysis by tracing parallels between the iceman and Christ as bridegroom: "Waiting for the bridegroom symbolizes man's hope of redemption."[13]

Women are expected to betray men with the iceman. They are, indeed, his proper consort here. Like him they bear the signs of death, sexuality, and salvation. Not simply creatures of the imagination as the iceman is, however, they suffer for having been transmuted into symbol by the men in their lives. Although the feminine is cast into protean forms—Evelyn and Rosa are strikingly contrasting figures—woman here is always the second sex.

Chuck's pipe dream of a happy marriage to Cora functions as relatively gentle mockery of all such aspiration. His picture of Cora, the whore as bride, settled with him on a farm out in the country, seems an absurd reminder of the failed unions of the play. When pimp and prostitute irritably evade marriage in spite of Hickey's prodding, the couple seem spared the ancient enmities of male and female that arise when the real vies with the illusory.

The theme of woman's otherness is, perhaps, made most clearly manifest in the transformation that Larry Slade undergoes during the course of the play. While much of our attention is riveted on Hickey and his struggle to promote and achieve a catharsis, it is Larry whose pipe dream is the first to be revealed and the only one to be absolutely dispelled. Still more engaged in life than he can acknowledge,

Larry imagines that his illusions are behind him and that he is waiting dispassionately for death. He no longer sees himself as an anarchist:

> I saw men didn't want to be saved from themselves, for that would mean they'd have to give up greed, and they'll never pay that price for liberty....(p. 11).

He claims, that is, that his motives are philosophical, political, impersonal. Not only is he in error about the degree to which he is aloof from experience; he is also deceiving himself about the "purity" of his reasons for detachment.

The events of the play are cumulatively a catalyst for change in Larry. In some important way, what happens in *The Iceman Cometh* happens to Larry Slade. Though he tries to remain an observer, he is forced to move beyond the inertia he cultivates. The drama he would be content to be audience for, turns out to be a participatory one for him. Parritt, desperate in his need for Larry to play, if not to be, his father, knows intuitively that he must get Larry to face the truths of his own experience before he will respond to him. So he goads him about his relationship with Rosa, trying to show him that she is responsible for the wreckage of Larry's life as well as his own.

Early in their exchange, Parritt asks, "What made you leave the Movement, Larry? Was it on account of Mother?" And Larry retorts, "Don't be a damned fool! What the hell put that in your head?" (p. 29) But Parritt is on the right track. He remembers an important quarrel Larry and Rosa had had before Larry's departure, and reacts "with a strange smile" to Larry's reply that their quarrel was about Larry's disenchantment with the Movement. When Parritt talks insistently about Rosa's behavior as a sexually "free woman" (p. 32), Larry's defensiveness is revealing. Then, when Hickey shows up, with his perspicacity about the pipe dreams of others, he hurts Larry by suggesting that he hasn't retired from life and offering to "make an honest man" (p. 83) of him, to Parritt's satisfaction. Later Hickey says to Larry, "Hell, if you really wanted to die, you'd just take a hop off your fire escape, wouldn't you?" (p. 116)

By this point Larry is ready for a confrontation with self. The direct assault on his pipe dream by Parritt and Hickey, and the climate of Harry Hope's, in which de-illusionment reigns for this short while, prepare him for the steps he must take. Parritt advances now, pursuing further the subject of Rosa's infidelity and its effect on Larry:

> That's why you finally walked out on her, isn't it?...I remember her putting on her high-and-mighty free-woman stuff....I remember that you got mad and you told her, "I don't like living with a whore, if that's what you mean!" (p. 125)

When Larry says it's a lie, Parritt softens the blow by talking of Rosa's respect for Larry for rejecting her: "I think that's why she still respects you, because it was you who left her....She just had to keep on having lovers to prove how free she was." (p. 125)

Unable to evade these intense exchanges, Larry is finally moved. He gives Parritt sanction for his suicide, which, it had become apparent, was what he had hoped for from Larry. Ultimately, Larry simultaneously admits and denies, "I sit here, with my pride drowned on the bottom of a bottle, keeping drunk so I won't see myself shaking in my britches from fright, or hear myself whining and praying: Beloved Christ, let me live a little longer at any price!" (p. 197) The truth is out.

Implicit in Larry's transformation is an addition to the indictments of woman as mother, wife, sister, mistress and prostitute that abound here. Having been vouchsafed a critical insight—that his motives for leaving the Movement were alloyed with his disgust at Rosa's promiscuity—Larry no longer has a pipe dream: "Be God, I'm the only real convert to death Hickey made here. From the bottom of my coward's heart I mean that now!" (p. 258)

At the conclusion, Harry Hope's is newly peaceful. Illusion has been restored for all but Larry, whose final bleak vision, though it lacks generativity, seems a kind of triumph. Larry can now face his own reality directly. Woman as other has been exorcised.

NOTES

1. Eugene O'Neill, *The Iceman Cometh* (New York: Random House, 1946), p. 62. Subsequent page references to the text will appear in parentheses following the quotations.

2. Travis Bogard, *Contour in Time: The Plays of Eugene O'Neill* (New York: Oxford University Press, 1972), p. 416.

3. Simone de Beavoir, *The Second Sex*, (New York: Bantam Books, 1961), p. xvi.

4. See John Henry Raleigh's introduction to his edition of *Twentieth Century Interpretations* of *"The Iceman Cometh"* (Englewood Cliffs, NJ: Prentice-Hall, 1968), p. 11.

5. Arthur and Barbara Gelb, *O'Neill* (New York: Harper and Row, 1973, p. 832.

6. Helen Muchnic, "The Irrelevancy of Belief: *The Iceman Cometh* and *The Lower Depths*," *O'Neill and His Plays: Four Decades of Criticism*, ed. Oscar Cargill, N. Brillion Fagin and William J. Fisher (New York: New York University Press, 1961), p. 440.

7. Winifred Frazer, *Love as Death in "The Iceman Cometh"* (Gainesville: University of Florida Press, 1967), p. 21.

8. Bogard, p. 409.

9. Louis Sheaffer, *O'Neill: Son and Artist* (Boston: Little, Brown and Co., 1973), p. 495.

10. de Beauvoir, p. 138.

11. John Henry Raleigh, *The Plays of Eugene O'Neill* (Carbondale: Southern Illinois University Press, 1965), p. 163.

12. Gelb, p. 832.

13. Sheaffer, p. 495.

Eugene O'Neill Newsletter, 6 (Summer/Fall 1982): 10-15.

Robert Brustein on Theatre: Souls on Ice

Robert Brustein

When *The Iceman Cometh* was first produced by the Theatre Guild in the mid-1940's, hostile intellectual critics invidiously compared it with Ibsen's *The Wild Duck* and Gorki's *The Lower Depths*. After it was successfully revived ten years later by Circle in the Square, commentators began to recognize that, for all its clumsy, repetitiveness, and schematic plotting, the play was a great work that surpassed even those distinguished influences in depth and power. Today, almost 40 years after its initial appearance with James Barton and Dudley Digges, *The Iceman Cometh* has been restaged at the Lunt-Fontanne Theatre by the original director of the Circle in the Square revival (José Quintero) with the same Hickey (Jason Robards) and, despite arthritic moments in the production, emerges not only richer than ever but as the inspiration for much that has been written for the stage since.

The play resonates. It is at the same time familiar and strange. One is caught in its potent grip as by a gnarled and crippled hand. Jason Robards, with his past history of alcoholism and air of personal suffering, has always been the American actor who shows the greatest personal affinity with O'Neill's spiritual pain, and this blood kinship, coupled with a valiant heart, carries him through the handicaps of playing Hickey in his late 60's. Hair darkened, face rouged, mouth dentured, energy flagging, Robards would now appear to be too old for the part, and there are times when he seems less to be living his role than remembering it. Still, if the performance is a bit of an overpainting, Robards has belonged to Hickey for many years, and when this remarkable actor makes his first entrance in a boater and off-the-rack pin-striped suit, throwing his bankroll at Rocky the bartender and exhorting the inmates of Harry Hope's saloon in his slurred whiskey bass, there is a thrill of simultaneous immediacy and recognition.

Age has given Robards an extraordinary translucency—pallid skin, transparent eyes. His Hickey continually promises his drunken friends the reward of spiritual peace (each act but the last ends on the word "happy"), but for all his drummer's energy, finger snapping, vaudeville physicality, and carny shill delivery, he is a ghost from the moment he walks on stage. Robards is continually undermining his character's professed optimism, as when he gets "sleepy all of a sudden," trips over a chair, and falls into a faint; Robards's face goes slack as though he's had a minor stroke. For while Hickey has the remorseless cheeriness of an American evangelist (he was no doubt inspired by Billy Sunday or by Bruce Barton's characterization of Jesus as the world's greatest salesman), only Larry Slade looks as deeply into the abyss of life without hope or redemption.

Robards is surrounded by a fine cast, the one weakness being Paul McCrane's rather flaccid Parritt. Barnard Hughes is a roistering Harry Hope, John Christopher Jones an intellectually degenerate Willie Oban, James Greene a gaunt Jimmy Tomorrow, and Donald Moffat a dignified Larry Slade, while most of the smaller roles are played with strength. Still, Robards's realism, even when unfulfilled, is of such intensity that it sometimes makes the others seem a little "classical." Take Barnard Hughes, so ingratiating and roguish when holding court in his saloon but not quite anguished enough when his "pipe dream" is exposed, or Donald Moffat, quietly eloquent and detached throughout the play, yet resorting to languorous legato cadences in his time of agonizing self-recognition.

And I wish that Quintero had been a little bolder in his approach. Ben Edwards's bar setting is selectively seedy, and Jane Greenwood's costumes really look like secondhand clothes that have been rotting on the bodies of the characters. But apart from the opening scene, with the stubble-bearded living-dead derelicts sleeping open-mouthed under Thomas R. Skelton's pasty light, there has been little effort to suggest that this is a world at the bottom of the sea or that *The Iceman Cometh* has a reverberant symbolic interior as well as a naturalist facade. Quintero acknowledges O'Neill's hints (in his archaic title and elsewhere) that Hickey and his 12 companions bear a strong resemblance to Christ and his disciples—Parritt being Judas and Larry being Peter, the rock on which he builds his church—and that Harry Hope's birthday party is based on the Last Supper (his actors fall into poses inspired by Leonardo da Vinci's painting, Hickey hovering over them with his palms outstretched).

But otherwise the production is a retread of the one staged in 1956, as if nothing had happened to the theater in 30 years. Even the exits and entrances seem designed for Broadway applause. I don't mean this version is old-fashioned—it has too much life for that—and I admit that a more imaginative interpretation might very well have obscured the play's intentions. Still, O'Neill was a very reluctant convert to Ibsenite realism ("holding the family Kodak up to ill-nature, as he called it) and never truly abandoned his devotion to symbolic substructures. A play as thickly faceted (and familiar) as this one deserves more audacious treatment.

Even conventionally staged, however, *The Iceman Cometh* has lost none of its consuming power. The play is long—it lasts almost five hours—and sometimes painfully repetitious, since each character is identified by a single obsession that he continually restates. Thus, each act offers a single variation on the theme of illusion. The action never bursts into spontaneous life; and the characters rarely escape O'Neill's rigid control as, say, Falstaff escapes Shakespeare's or Mother Courage escapes Brecht's. Still, one must recognize that the work consists not of one but of 13 plays, each with its own story; O'Neill has multiplied his antagonists in order to illuminate every possible aspect of his theme, and every rationalization, whether religious, racial, political, sexual, psychological, or philosophical, with which humankind labors to escape the truths of raw existence. And in some crazy inexplicable way, the very length of the play contributes to its impact, as if we had to be exposed to virtually every aspect of universal suffering in order to feel its full force.

This exhaustiveness of design probably accounts for the influence of *The Iceman Cometh* on so much subsequent work; seeing the play today is like reading the family tree of modern drama. Surely, *Death of a Salesman*...owes a strong debt to *The Iceman Cometh*, with its O'Neillian theme of an illusory tomorrow embodied in another philandering drummer cheating on another saintly wife in out-of-town hotels. (The name Willy Loman even unconsciously echoes O'Neill's character Willie Oban.) Hickey's long-delayed entrance ("Would that Hickey or

Death would come") may have inspired a similar long-awaited figure, Beckett's Godot, who, like Hickey, stands in an almost supernatural punitive relationship to hapless derelicts. And there is no question that Jack Gelber's dazed junkies in *The Connection* owe a great deal to O'Neill's drunks in Harry Hope's "End of the Line Cafe," just as it is likely that if the play were written today, the characters would have been drug addicts.

I cite this partial list of influences not to swell the secondary reading list of the dramatic lit syllabus but to suggest how a great play over time becomes a seedbed of riches. And *The Iceman Cometh* is as great as the modern theatre has produced. The current production brings no new insights. It is occasionally badly paced and laborious, especially in the overly schematic third act; and the actors, gifted as they are, sometimes draw back from the precipice. But by the conclusion of this long evening, this masterwork has managed to cut to the bone, and that makes the production a single event in any Broadway season.

New Republic, October 28, 1985.

Theatre: *Long Day's Journey Into Night*

Walter Kerr

In *Long Day's Journey Into Night* Florence Eldridge plays a shattered mother—her white hair drifting mistily about the damaged prettiness of her face—who has convinced herself, with the help of morphine, that her arthritic hands are the true cause of all her pain. She stretches them out before her in the blurred light of a foggy seaside afternoon and exults, "They can't touch me now—I see them, but they're far away! The pain is gone."

This, I think, is what Eugene O'Neill was doing when he put to paper the searing and sorry record of the wreck of his family. He has held up his mother, his father, and his brother at the arm's length of the stage, looked at everything that was ugly and misshapen and destroyed in them, and now the pain is gone.

It is gone, too. Though the four-hour, endlessly savage examination of conscience on the stage of the Helen Hayes is deliberately, masochistically harrowing in the ferocity of its revelation, the agony that O'Neill felt whenever he contemplated his own beginnings is not passed onto his audience. It is in some curious and even exalting manner exorcised, washed away, leaving in its place an undefined dignity, an agreed-upon peace, a powerful sense of exhilarated completion.

Long Day's Journey Into Night is not a play. It is a lacerating round-robin of recrimination, self-dramatization, lies that deceive no one, confessions that never expiate the crime. Around the whiskey bottles and the tattered leather chairs and the dangling light-cords that infest the decaying summer home of the Tyrones (read O'Neill's), a family of ghosts sit in a perpetual game of four-handed solitaire, stir to their feet in a danse macabre that outlines the geography of Hell, place themselves finally on an operating table that allows for no anesthetic. When the light fails, they are still—but are not saved.

How has O'Neill kept self-pity and vulgarity and cheap bravado out of this prolonged, unasked for, improbable inferno? Partly by the grim determination that made him a major dramatist: the insistence that the roaring fire he could build by grinding his own two hands together was the fire of truth. You can disbelieve, but you cannot deny him his heat, his absolute passion.

And partly by a talent he must have picked up from that greedy and grandiose father of his: a talent that puts words together so that actors can chew them, spit them, tear at one another's skins with them. Director José Quintero has seen to it that every one of his present players knows how to handle that whip.

Fredric March cracks down on the skinflint monarch that O'Neill remembered as his father with majestic authority from the outset. Laughing a bit too much and a bit too hollowly, working off his nerves with a restless cigar, snapping at every insult like a guilty bulldog, he foreshadows the whole sodden fantasia of the midnight to come. When he reaches that last grim debacle, and is forced to stumble to his feet in slavering but heart-breaking tribute to his lost glory, he is in every way superb.

Hot on his heels is Jason Robards, Jr. as the dissolute elder brother who may have led the consumptive Edmund (read Eugene) into every sort of vice to help square away his own failings. Mr. Robards lurches into the final scene with his hands, his mouth, and his mind wildly out of control, cracks himself in two as he pours out every tasteless truth that is in him, and subsides at last into the boozy sleep of the damned. The passage is magnificent.

Florence Eldridge makes the downward course of an incapable mother utterly intelligible. She does not have the deep, resonant notes that will sustain her woman through the blinding, tragic memories of the center of the play; she cannot quite fight fury with fury. Yet there is a hidden delicacy that is often touching in the shallow gayeties and transparent pretenses of a convent girl who could not survive in the world.

Bradford Dillman handles the exceedingly difficult and soul-searching soliloquies of his poet who "didn't have the makings just the habit" with swift, sensitive skill, and Katherine Ross is excellent in the brief role of a "second girl" who is permitted to tipple while her mistress mourns. The David Hays setting is a perfect echo—curving and empty—of the universe these characters wander.

For any one who cares about the American theatre, *Long Day's Journey* is, of course, an obligation. But it is more than that. It is a stunning theatrical experience.

New York Herald Tribune, November 8, 1948.

Theatre: Tragic Journey

J. Brooks Atkinson

With the production of *Long Day's Journey Into Night* at the Helen Hayes last evening, the American theatre acquires size and stature.

The size does not refer to the lengths of Eugene O'Neill's autobiographical drama, although a play three and three-quarter hours long is worth remarking. The size refers to his conception of theatre as a form of epic literature. *Long Day's Journey Into Night* is like a Dostoevsky novel in which Strindberg had written the dialogue. For this saga of the damned is horrifying and devastating in a classical tradition, and the performance under José Quintero's direction is inspired.

Twelve years before he died in 1953, O'Neill epitomized the life of his family in a drama that records the events of one day at their summer home in New London, Conn., in 1912. Factually it is a sordid story about a pathologically parsimonious father, a mother addicted to dope, a dissipated brother and a younger brother (representing O'Neill) who has TB and is about to be shipped off to a sanitarium.

Roughly, those are the facts. But the author has told them on the plane of an O'Neill tragedy in which the point of view transcends the material. The characters are laid bare with pitiless candor. The scenes are big. The dialogue is blunt. Scene by scene the tragedy moves along with a remorseless beat that becomes hypnotic as though this were life lived on the brink of oblivion.

Long Day's Journey Into Night could be pruned of some of this excesses and repetitions and static looks back to the past. But the faults come, not from tragic posturing, but from the abundance of a great theatre writer who had a spacious point of view. This summing-up of his emotional and artistic life ranks with *Mourning Becomes Electra* and *Desire Under the Elms* which this department regards as his masterpieces.

Like those dramas, it comes alive in the theatre. Although the text is interesting to read between covers, it does not begin to flame until the actors take hold of it. Mr. Quintero, who staged the memorable *The Iceman Cometh* in the Village, has directed *Long Day's Journey Into Night* with insight and skill. He has caught the sense of a stricken family in which the members are at once fascinated and repelled by one another. Always in control of the turbulence of the material, he has also picked out and set forth the meaning that underlines it.

The performance is stunning. As the aging actor who stands at the head of the family, Fredric March gives a masterly performance that will stand as a milestone in the acting of an O'Neill play. Petty, mean, bullying, impulsive and sharp-tongued, he also has magnificence—a man of strong passions, deep loyalties and basic humility. This is a character portrait of grandeur.

Florence Eldridge analyzes the pathetic character of the mother with tenderness and compassion. As the brother, Jason Robards Jr., who played Hickey in *The Iceman Cometh*, gives another remarkable performance that has tremendous force and truth in the last act. Bradford Dillman is excellent as the younger brother—winning, honest, and both callow and perceptive in his relationship with the family. Katherine Ross plays the part of the household maid with freshness and taste.

All the action takes place inside David Hays' excellent setting of a cheerless living room with dingy furniture and hideous little touches of unimaginative decor. The shabby, shapeless costumes by Motley and the sepulchral lighting by Tharon Musser perfectly capture the lugubrious mood of the play.

Long Day's Journey Into Night has been worth waiting for. It restores the drama to literature and the theatre to art.

New York Times, November 8, 1956.

Off Broadway: Return Journey

Edith Oliver

Arvin Brown, the artistic director of the admirable Long Wharf Theatre, in New Haven, has directed a first-rate revival at the Promenade of Eugene O'Neill's *Long Day's Journey Into Night*, and it seems to me better than the original production. (I liked the play better, if that is a test.) Never have three and a half hours—the approximate running time of the show—gone more quickly for me. The first three acts, which fifteen years ago seemed an endless prologue to the tremendous fourth, are now completely absorbing. There is no star performance of the calibre of Fredric March's or Jason Robards', but the company, under Mr. Brown's, deft direction, is very good. Along with greatness in performance, much of the portentousness has gone; the steam has evaporated and the characters emerge life-size and human.

The day's journey, as I probably needn't tell you, is O'Neill's own into the night of his tortured spirit and memory. The action takes place (presumably to observe the dramatic unities of classical tragedy) in the summer cottage of his family, here called the Tyrones, on the single day and evening in August, 1912, when O'Neill (Edmond Tyrone) learned that he had tuberculosis, and when his mother was finally defeated by the morphine addiction that had trapped her and—as woeful spectators and victims—her husband and two sons. The father, James Tyrone, Sr.—a great popular actor and pathological miser—has denied his wife proper medical treatment, and about to deny it to young Edmund, intending to send him instead to a state-run sanatorium in the belief that he will probably die anyway. The older son, Jamie Tyrone, an unsuccessful actor, is a profligate alcoholic whose hatred of his father is so fierce it is almost palpable. In the fourth act, his drunken, agonized confession to his younger brother and lifetime crony, and his warning that there is as much hatred as love for Edmund in what is left of his heart, makes the most striking passage in the play. All the characters are plagued and tortured by the past, except for young Edmund—it is the future that haunts him—and when the evening is over there is nothing that they do not know about one another, or about what they have done to one another, and there is more to the calm at the end than just exhaustion.

In performance, every moment is believable, which takes some doing with O'Neill. In spite of the underlying tension throughout, there are light, light even casual, scenes, and those high-flown lines that Wolcott Gibbs rightly objected to in his review of the original production for this magazine have had much of the stuffing taken out of them by the sense and sensibility of the actors speaking them. I don't know whether the play has been cut or not, but I was not nearly as aware of repetitiousness as I was the first time. As James Tyrone, Robert Ryan, his face pinched with worry but his eyes bright with intelligence and humor, is better than I have ever seen him, Tyrone is as quick to tenderness as he is to resentment, and Ryan's guilt-ridden speech, in which he acknowledges his stinginess and its consequences and then traces it back to the ghastly poverty of his childhood as an Irish immigrant, is very moving indeed. As his wife, Geraldine Fitzgerald is considerably more than just touching and pathetic as her nerves tighten and then as she slips further and further out of focus, babbling, babbling, babbling. We also realize that she has inflicted as much damage as she has received, and not only because of the morphine; the loneliness for which she reproaches her husband without letup is partly the result of her priggish refusal to make friends with his theatrical troupe and of her outsize devotion to her father. As Jamie, jaunty in his straw boater, cynical, self-hating, and in utter despair, Stacy Keach, is, as always, a fascinating actor to watch, and James Naughton, making his New York debut as the younger brother and dramatist's surrogate, is so strong—so attentive and vulnerable—that he almost shifts the balance of the two roles. Mr. Naughton is quite a discovery. Mr. Arvin Brown has also had the good sense to cast delightful Paddy Croft in the part of the family's Irish maid. The character is a stereotype, but Miss Croft makes her a person. The setting, by Elmon Webb and Virginia Dancy, is appropriately shabby, and Ronald Wallace, the lighting designer, has conjured up summer sunshine and summer fog.

New Yorker, May 1, 1971.

Theater: The Haunted Tyrones

Jack Kroll

Long Day's Journey Into Night is not just the greatest American play, it is the only really great American play, the only one to reach the magnitude of Chekhov, Strindberg or Ibsen. In order to touch that pinnacle Eugene O'Neill had to reach not only a certain point as an artist but a certain point as a human being. As Eric Bentley put it, he had to learn sincerity. In his early 50's O'Neill finally could see his tormented family whole, including himself. Now he was able, as he put it in the dedication of the play to his third wife Carlotta, "to face my dead at last and write this play—write it with deep pity and understanding and forgiveness for all the four haunted Tyrones."

No one ever worked harder than O'Neill to become an artist. His plays are full of the sound of American carpentry, the artist banging his forms together out of anything at hand. All those gimmicks—the masks, the soliloquies, the home-fried expressionism—have disappeared in *Long Day's Journey*. Now there are only four people—the father, the mother and their two sons, living and talking through a long day in 1912 at their summer house in New England. The result is overwhelming, reminding us that the greatest mode of Western art is what might be called transcendent realism. In play after play O'Neill manipulated his life and his family's lives into different patterns. You could call this the activity of a prodigiously gifted child. In *Long Day's Journey*, the childishness, the both touching and exasperating American innocence, has vanished. O'Neill's sheer relentlessness has earned him grace, the artist's grace of transcendent perception.

"When he started *Long Day's Journey*," said Carlotta O'Neill, "it was a most strange experience to watch that man being tortured every day by his own writing. He would come out of his study at the end of a day gaunt and sometimes weeping. His eyes would be all red and he looked ten years older than when he went in in the morning." O'Neill undoubtedly wept back in 1912 when he was a young would-be poet and erstwhile sailor, tubercular, married but psychologically still bound by love-hate to his overbearing father, a famous actor whose fear of poverty had turned him into a pathological miser, to his drug-addict mother and his older brother, Jamie, who wallowed away his despair in booze and whores. O'Neill's tears then were those of a trapped animal. The tears his third wife saw were those of an artist free to see those four people with piercing clarity, as predators and victims caught in a circle of carnivorous love.

The result is the one American play that has true tragic power and size. The notorious O'Neill clumsiness, the "stammering" that Edmund (as O'Neill calls himself in this play) refers to as his "native eloquence," has been replaced by a powerful sense of form and language. The play does not depress, it lifts you with the strength of truth and the buoyancy of art. It's even funny; O'Neill makes you laugh at the stratagems human beings devise to inflict misery on one another.

In the production Jason Robards has staged for the Kennedy Center, which is now at the Brooklyn Academy of Music, Robards (who played Jamie in the play's 1956 premiere) also plays the father, James Tyrone. He has not been able to create a true ensemble with his four first-rate actors—himself, Zoe Caldwell as Mary Tyrone and Michael Moriarity and Kevin Conway as the sons, Edmund and Jamie. Moriarity is the obvious odd man out: he has become increasingly mannered in concept, behavior and voice. As the whoremongering Jamie, Conway gives another of his strong, intelligent performances. Jason Robards opts for absolute reality, depriving himself of some of James's darker colors, but rightly emphasizing the humanity that has turned monstrous. Zoe Caldwell is special, woundingly lovely as she slowly vanishes from sanity. The last shattering act—a collision among three men drenched in alcohol and a woman dissolved in drugs—is surely the greatest passage ever written by an American playwright. That act is O'Neill's ticket to sit in the shades with Sophocles.

Newsweek, February 9, 1976

Long Day's Worth the Journey

Clive Barnes

Possibly some of my lily-livered colleagues will find objection to be made to Eugene O'Neill's *Long Day's Journey Into Night* being given by a black cast. It opened officially last night at the Common, the theater at St. Peter's Church in the Citicorp Building.

However, the color of Tyrone's family that fateful Connecticut day in August, 1912, is no more the issue of the play than were the unashamed English accents of two of the mostly celebrated interpreters of Tyrone—Ralph Richardson and Laurence Olivier.

In front of quality we gladly suspend our disbelief. This performance is a signal demonstration of the rights, even the duty, of certain black actors to assume the birthright of their mother tongue on the classic stage.

Why is *Long Day's Journey* such a great play? The writing scarcely sparkles; even given the special circumstances of a theatrical family, the language is at times unduly fustian; and the play tales an inordinately length of time to get going, and once moving seems all too ready to make the odd backtrack of repetition.

Yet it sears its way into the heart. It grabs you and changes you. It is probably the dramatic concept of a soul's journey. We are in the house of a famous, but disillusioned old actor James Tyrone, who has sacrificed his once considerable artistry for the lure of easy cash. For years he has played virtually only one role, the Count of Monte Cristo.

His elder son, also an actor of sorts, is an alcoholic Broadway bum, his younger son (in reality O'Neill himself, for it was his own story he was telling) is sensitive and possibly has TB, while his wife, put on morphia by a quack to ease the pain after her second pregnancy, has become an addict, "a dope fiend."

On this sunny August day, as we work our way from soon after noon to just after midnight, the whole family history is brought up, examined and resolved. Nothing, nothing at all, will ever be the same for the Tyrones. They have passed through the watershed, and the curtain falls on clear if drunken eyes.

That is O'Neill's secret. This family interests us in a way few stage families will ever interest us—we hang on their words as if we are eavesdropping on history. This cast is not only good in itself, it plays around one another with the wariness of familial tigers in a dangerously small cage. The superlative director, Geraldine Fitzgerald, was herself a notable Mary Tyrone, playing opposite Robert

Ryan's James, and perhaps Ryan's ruggedly splendid, underplayed portrayal served as a skeleton model for the play's key.

The James here is Earle Hyman, much more cultivated than Ryan, but with the same confused gentleness, now and again bursting into histrionic fury, and the same nervous parsimony of a man who has known hard times.

Gloria Foster as Mary is the most glamorous Mary I have ever seen—not for her the wan, wraithlike figure created by Florence Eldridge and matched by almost everyone else. Miss Foster is almost flamboyant in her tragedy, which gives the role a new feeling, particularly as she collapses into the drug-spent night.

The brothers flash at one another like sabers at midnight. Al Freeman Jr. plays the complex and dissolute Jamie with his nerve-ends exposed and a violent vulnerability, with explosive and impotent at the same time.

Almost equally as good is Peter Francis-James as a brooding yet spirited Edmund struggling through to the acceptance and poetic realization of his family. As Cathleen, the always pert servant girl, Samantha McKoy gets deliciously tipsy and shows the right contrasting reality to the high-flying Tyrones.

New York Post, March 4, 1981.

Reviews of O'Neill's Plays in Performance: *Long Day's Journey Into Night*

Steven F. Bloom

This *is* a short *Long Day's Journey Into Night*, a feature apparently meant to make the drama more appealing, or at least less intimidating, to the theatregoing public. A *short Long Day's Journey*, however, is a contradiction in terms: you can no more make O'Neill's *Journey* a short one than spend a cold day in Hell—an apt metaphor, since it suggests the second, and related, problem with the current revival. Not only is this a *short Long Day's Journey*; it is also a very cold *Long Day's Journey*.

Director Jonathan Miller has cut the play's running time from the usual four hours or so to about two hours and forty minutes, not by making extensive cuts in the text (although there are some unfortunate ones), but primarily by using overlapping dialogue. When the Tyrones speak, nobody listens; everybody talks at once. Now, Miller is quite right that, realistically, in the heat of family arguments, one person rarely has the courtesy to wait for another to complete a well-crafted speech; and this an acceptable notion with reference to the Tyrones. Furthermore, it is certainly true that much of what the Tyrones say to each other is repetitious, often ritualistic; so that the characters barely do attend to each other's words since they have heard them so many times before.

So it is true, then, as Miller contends, that we do not miss any especially important lines of dialogue because of this approach. To say, however, that if we do not miss any dialogue, then we do not miss any of O'Neill is to fail to recognize that the essence of O'Neill's drama does not lie in the words themselves.

Long Day's Journey Into Night

To say that, since it is all so repetitious anyway, we do not have to hear all of the repetitions, is to deny what is now so well-known about O'Neill's dramaturgy: he wrote for the theatre, not for the easy chair, and he certainly meant for an audience to experience the repetition, which is a central reality of the lives of his characters....To understand the Tyrones, you must spend time with them, *their* time, at *their* pace. You have to understand the "horrible burden of Time weighing on your shoulders and crushing you to the earth," as Edmund puts it quoting Baudelaire. The Tyrones cannot escape this burden, try as they may; and by allowing the audience to escape an hour and twenty minutes early, Miller denies us the full experience of the play.

The pace-setter in this production, especially for the first three acts, is Bethel Leslie in the role of Mary Tyrone. Apparently the idea here was that rapid speech might be symptomatic of her morphine intoxication, and I would not argue with Dr. Miller about the accuracy of that diagnosis. In performance, however, there are at least two problems with this notion. First, Ms. Leslie speaks very rapidly from the opening curtain, when Mary has just begun to take the morphine again, and the pace only increases from then on. There are not enough variations to indicate how much morphine she has taken, or to indicate the onset of withdrawal symptoms, and she never seems to attain that peaceful sense of calmness which, presumably, is what she is after by taking the drug in the first place. She remains nervous and high-strung at virtually all times. Second, her rapid-fire delivery becomes rather monotonous, making her a distant and cold Mary Tyrone. Now, while these are certainly *aspects* of the character, in Ms. Leslie's portrayal they *define* the character....

Because Mary seems so detached and cold, we have little sympathy for her, and therefore we have too much for James. Granted, O'Neill does seem to be more severe toward his mother than his father in the text, and he does give the father his confessional moment and the subsequent implied forgiveness from his son. Still, this production oversimplifies the situation. As Mary says, everyone is to blame, and no one is to blame; yet in this production it is too easy to blame Mary.

Aside from Ms. Leslie's portrayal of Mary, another factor that contributes to this effect is Jack Lemmon in the role of James Tyrone. Mr. Lemmon is a very fine actor, and he has some wonderful moments in this play. One of the most memorable comes towards the end of Act Two, Scene One, when James returns from working outside, after Jamie and Edmund have had clear evidence of Mary's return to morphine. After Mary's first speech with James in the room, the stage directions state that "Tyrone knows now. He suddenly looks a tired, bitterly sad old man," and this is exactly what happens. When Mr. Lemmon turns to the audience here, after observing the now obvious signs of his wife's condition, he is indeed a man transformed, shot through by a reality that visibly shakes him to his very soul. He is suddenly deflated, all the life taken out of him by this one glimpse of his wife and the recognition of her return to the "cursed poison." From this point on, Mr. Lemmon noticeably deteriorates, looking more and more like a lost, broken old man....

The moment of deflation, in Act Two, Scene One, is moving but at the same time, indicative of the overall interpretation of the play. Tyrone is the wounded victim, portrayed from the outset as a basically good man who occasionally becomes defensive and obstinate....If he is a victim, his own stubbornness is at least partially responsible. Indeed, it can easily be argued that James has a stake in maintaining Mary's dependence on morphine, and that he has done little to really help her; she, after all, gives him a good reason to get drunk. Long Day's Journey requires a delicate balance between James and Mary, so that one recognizes the complexities of both characters and their relationship....

This distance is also a serious problem in Mary's relationship with her sons, especially with Edmund, who believes that Mary takes the morphine to get "beyond our reach, to be rid of us, to forget we're alive." He is, of course, correct; Mary does build a "blank wall" around herself. This is a process, though; the audience should see her build the wall, and therefore, she must begin *within* the family's reach in order to move *beyond* it. In the text, she is especially attentive to Edmund's health, even if her concern is ambivalent; and she does vacillate between mothering him and denying that there is anything wrong with him. It may not be necessary to go to the extreme of excessive physical contact, as in the 1962 film with Katharine Hepburn; yet without a sense of any warmth or affection between mother and son, with virtually no physical contact, it is difficult to feel Edmund's pain when Mary "departs" at the end of the play.

Mary's coldness, conveyed mostly by avoiding eye contact while speaking rapidly and unfeelingly, also has ramifications for Jamie. The home should feel like a home to him and his father; Mary should seem to be a mother to her sons. Since Ms. Leslie misses the nurturing, maternal quality of Mary's character from the beginning, Jamie's cynicism tends to seem entirely justified. It is difficult to imagine why he would be anything but cynical with such a cold, distant mother. But this oversimplifies matters: Jamie's cynicism should be part of the family's problems, not an easily understandable and acceptable solution for him.

Among the cuts that Miller has made in the text is Jamie's recitation of "A Leave-taking" in the last scene of the play. It would not make sense, though, for this Jamie to attempt to reach out for his mother at the end, so he is virtually eliminated from the final scene. His last memorable line in this production is "The Mad Scene. Enter Ophelia," which is played mostly for laughs, so that Jamie seems too unaffected by his mother's condition; he is too much the devil-may-care cynic. While Kevin Spacey gives an excellent performance as Jamie, and even captures flashes of the self-hatred that lies beneath the cynical bitterness (especially in the climactic confessional scene with Edmund), yet he is denied his proper "leave taking," and thus remains the sneering cynic, rather than the bitter, broken, lost young man he should be at the play's end.

It is, indeed, in these final moments of the production that Mr. Miller has most egregiously cut and altered the text, doing a great disservice to its potential impact. First, Jamie announces his mother's entrance, wobbling drunkenly on the sofa as she descends the staircase. Granted, "The Mad Scene. Enter Ophelia" is meant to provide momentary relief from the wrenching confessions of Act Four, but the line should also suggest the anticipated horror of what is yet to come. Here Mary descends *wearing* her wedding gown, rather than dragging it behind her; she looks disheveled, confused, and rather old, not "youthful" at all. Since she wears the dress over her clothing, she looks rather ridiculous, not innocent and "girlish," thus adding inappropriately to the humorous impact of Jamie's line....

Furthermore, during this final scene, only Edmund tries to reach Mary, whereas in the text he is the last of the three men to try, and he almost breaks through. These final attempts to reach her serve to isolate each character in succession, punctuated by Jamie's resigned refrain, "It's no good." In the text, they also attempt to have a final drink together, which is then cut off by Mary's final speech. In this production, the drink is not suggested. With the audience's attention thus focused on Mary, the men do not seem as affected by her "departure" as they should be....

Generally, the depiction of the younger Tyrones is much more satisfying than that of the elders (although the fault lies not in the stars but in the director, I suspect). In addition to Mr. Spacey's fine performance as Jamie, Peter Gallagher sensitively plays an appropriately understated Edmund. His illness never distracts from the ritualistic patterns within the family, yet is always subtly in evidence, reminding the characters and audience of the fragility of this young man, and thus of the romantic dreams that he espouses....

The costumes by Willa Kim are fine, the use of white providing an effectively stark contrast to the bleakness of the lives portrayed. The lighting by Richard Nelson is very effective at dimly illuminating these scenes of darkening hopes. The only problem is the apparent lack of fog which is a design problem that involves the scenery by Tony Straiges...

If more people sit through this faster version of *Long Day's Journey* than would sit through a more than four-hour version, however, then perhaps this production may serve an important function. Such a reinterpretation of a great play breeds debate and controversy, and therefore publicity and curiosity; it raises interesting and important questions about the text, about the nature and structure of the drama itself. Perhaps some of the people in the audience, who may never have considered it otherwise, will now wonder what the "original" is really like. In many ways, Mr. Miller's production betrays O'Neill's text, but perhaps it will prompt another director to assemble another fine cast soon for another major production, to prove Jonathan Miller wrong—about the audience and about the play—perhaps another director who trusts O'Neill and will serve the text.

Eugene O'Neill Newsletter, 10 (Summer/Fall 1986): 33-39.

Communal, Familial, and Personal Memories in O'Neill's *Long Day's Journey Into Night*

John Henry Raleigh

The human memory, on one of its many levels, manifests itself in three overlapping categories: the historical and communal; the familial and social; the autobiographical and personal. At one end of the scale is the constellation of collective memories, given by one's socio-economic class, ethnic background, education, religion, the historical period of one's life, nationality, and so on. At the other end of the spectrum, in a purely private shrine in one's own unique ego, there are those individual memories that no one else, past, present or future, will ever share or know. Social-familial memories tend to connect to both categories, the public and the private. At the extremes of the spectrum there appears to be on the communal side, an assertion: "We are what we are," and at the private end a question: "Who am I?"

The most compact—compact because it is a drama, albeit a lengthy one—dramatization of this triadic aspect of memory in our literature is O'Neill's *Long Day's Journey Into Night*; it is also one of the most powerful such dramatizations, powerful because the communal-familial memories are so distinct and intense, and because the private memories, the "Who am I?" constituent, are so moving, poignant and problematical.

To take the historical-communal aspect first, the Tyrones are an Irish-American family in whose collective consciousness the "Irish" side is probably more important than the "American" side. There were few other emigrant groups in America who so insistently proclaimed their native identity as did the American Irish Catholics, from the middle of the nineteenth century on down into the twentieth (the phenomenon has lessened but has by no means yet disappeared in the 1980's). Indeed the scope, longevity, and intensity of the Irish-American fixation on its own, unique past has by now engendered a very large historical-scholarly literature on the subject of the Irish emigration to the United States, larger, I believe, than is the case for any other group of emigrants.

The latest, and in my opinion the best, book in this area is Kerby Miller's massive *Emigrants and Exiles* (1985), which is not only a description and analysis of the Irish in America but also a comprehensive history of Ireland itself, Miller's point being that one cannot properly understand the emigrants if one does not fully understand the culture from which they came. Miller's principal thesis is threefold: that the Irish regarded emigration as involuntary exile (Irish wakes were held in Ireland for those about to depart, as if they were already dead; they were called both "American Wakes" and "Living Wakes"); that this outlook was a deeply-rooted and long-standing constituent of Irish culture, the product of a world-view long preceding the English conquest; and that this exilic outlook had much to do with their American experience, often not in happy ways. As Miller narrates his lengthy, complex and rich story, at almost every juncture a member of the O'Neill clan comes to mind. The Irish, says Miller, agreeing with other students of the subject, were the "the most homesick of all immigrants."[1] Letters written home to Ireland, memoirs (Miller had access to some five thousand of these), songs, and ballads all have this pervasive note of sadness. Many Irish emigrants shared a nostalgia rooted in the idyll of childhood memories, which even success in America could not eradicate. Miller quotes from the autobiography of the fabulously successful financier Thomas Mellon, who himself wondered at the poignancy of his recollections of Ulster after sixty years in Americas: "It must not be only true that we learn more in the first five years of life than in any ten years afterward, but also that we retain whatever we learn in those five years incomparably better than anything we learn at a later date" (p. 131). Any student of O'Neill is immediately reminded of James O'Neill's seemingly maudlin statement: "It was in Kilkenny, where I was born one opal-tinted day in October, 1847 [actually it was 1846]."[2] And maudlin it may have been, but it is also realistically expressive of a deeply-cherished collective memory of the Irish emigrants, the bulk of whom had no such success as Mellon. Much more typical would be the story of the hardships of James Tyrone's childhood, as related in Act IV of *Long Day's Journey*, all of which would have made the slow-paced, simple, communal life of Ireland, with its green land and temperate climate, appear to be almost paradisal (provided there is no famine); in any event a sense of being out of place was endemic with many of the Irish emigrants: "With the ideas of old movements, still clinging to us like the memories of childhood, we can scarcely keep pace with it [i.e. the speed of life in America]" (p. 326). "We are a primitive people wandering wildly in a strange land, the Nineteenth Century" (p. 326). Indeed some ten percent of the post-famine emigrants did return, a fact that immediately brings to mind the O'Neills once more, and the strangest and most problematic fact in the welter of multifarious strange and problematical facts concerning this modern house of Atreus: the desertion by the original emigrant Edmund O'Neill of his wife and eight children to return to Ireland to die, which he shortly afterwards did (with a suspicion of suicide).

By the early 1870's enough Irishmen had succeeded in making financial successes, in occupations above brute labor, so that the phenomenon of the "lace curtain" Irish emerged, and, once more, one thinks of an O'Neill—Ella Quinlan O'Neill—and one of the most potent and divisive of the memories of Mary Tyrone; the discrepancy between her background and that of her husband, and the difference, harped on incessantly in *Long Day's Journey*, between her "lace-curtain" early life and her married life to an Irish peasant who is a hard-drinking and peripatetic actor. Again it was the post-famine Irish emigrants who created American-Irish nationalism, calling to mind James O'Neill-Tyrone whose real religion, as has been said, was not Catholicism but Irish nationalism. Even in the twentieth century and even with success many Irish Americans never overcame deep-seated feelings of inferiority and insecurity, and preserved the old wounds, ever fresh. Miller quotes James Michael Curley, who never forgot that he had been despised by the Yanks in his Roxbury boyhood (he was Gaelic-speaking then). At that point in his argument Miller brings in O'Neill and *Long Day's Journey*, although the O'Neill scholar will already have thought of the essential isolation of the Tyrone family in New London, despite the father's professional and financial success, and of James Tyrone bowing elaborately to the Chatfields as they drive by Monte Cristo cottage in their Mercedes. As Miller expresses the problems of many of the financially successful Irish:

> Generally, such conflicts were internalized, mitigated through religious devotion or later expressed in autobiographic fiction such as O'Neill's *Long Day's Journey Into Night.* (pp. 498-499)

However, Miller goes on, the conflicts often assumed self-destructive dimensions which although they rarely eventuated in actual suicides often issued in chronic drinking. There were, says Miller, quoting the historian John Duffy Ibsen, "tensions sewn into the lace curtain" (p. 499). Several times in his book Miller quotes another quite expressive phrase, taken from the Irish historian David N. Doyle, that the Irish-American experience had engendered in Irish groups and families, even successful ones, "a self-indulgent communal morbidity" (p. 7). These two phrases pretty well describe the ambiance of the Tyrone family in *Long Day's Journey*. At its most elemental level such morbidity issued in a felling of simply not belonging, a kind of cosmic loneliness:

> As it is, I will always be a stranger who never feels at home, who does not really want and is not really wanted, who can never belong, who must always be a little in love with death.
>
> ***
> You're glad they're gone.
> *She gives a little despairing laugh.*
> Then Mother of God, why do I feel so lonely?[3]

Accompanying the sense of isolation was the sense, so deep-set in all peasant societies, of fatalism. The real religion of the Russian peasant, said many observers, was not the Greek Orthodox religion but fatality—so too with the post-famine Irish peasants and many of their descendants:

> None of us can help the things life has done to us. They're done before you realize it...everything comes between you and what you'd like to be, and you've lost your true self forever. (p. 61)

Loneliness and fatalism, in turn, help to generate a fixation on the past (wherein, at sometime, you lost that true self), and this feeling is expressed most absolutely and powerfully by the Jamie Tyrone of *A Moon for the Misbegotten*:

> There is no present or future - only the past happening over and over again - now. You can't get away from it.[4]

So far I have been talking of what might be called a collective or communal memory, several varieties of which appear in O'Neill's plays. In *The Emperor Jones* there is clearly a collective racial memory at work. In *The Iceman Cometh* a collective social memory operates for some of the characters, evoking the good old days—"dem old days"—in the 1890s when Tammany corruption was at its height and they were in on the take. In the Irish plays, like *Long Day's Journey, Moon,* and *A Touch of the Poet*, the history and culture of Ireland is ever-present for many of the characters. That collective or group memories do in fact exist has been documented by students of the workings of memory. Indeed the French sociologist, Maurice Halbwachs, argues that there is hardly such a thing as individual memory: "In reality, we are never alone."[5] We also know that familial memories are among the most powerfully "fixed" memories that we have, indelibly inscribed and never forgotten; thus when a powerful and distinctive communal memory coincides with a passionate and distinctive family memory as with the O'Neill-Tyrones, the twin effect is sometimes overpowering, so much the more so in such an intense, turned-in-on-itself, and long-standing family group as the Tyrones. The two sons, one thirty-three and the other twenty-three, are still living at home with their parents and having adolescent "allowances" doled out to them by their begrudging father, as the family relives, over and over again, year after year, its troubled Irish-American communal-familial memories.

But the human memory in its fullness is individual and unique: in the whole history of the human race no two human memories have been quite the same. In that massive disquisition on memory, *Remembrance of Things Past*, Proust makes the following claims for the uniqueness and the power of memory: it is our ultimate privacy (no two are ever alike); our ultimate fixity (the world is flux while memory is stable); our claim on immortality (through its agency we triumph over, by rising above, time); our sole access to reality—"reality takes shape in the memory alone"; and our only real continuity in time—"my past...projected before me that shadow of itself we call our future."[6] As many observers have said, we are what we remember. So in *Long Day's Journey* while the collective, communal Irish-American memory described above provides the generic outlines of the four memories for the Tyrone family, each individual memory is unique; that is to say, no two people, even man and wife or siblings, ever remember all the same things, and when they do remember in common, as they often do, they do not remember those same things in the same way. One of the many reasons for this is that memory is often self-serving: it operates, generally speaking, to enhance rather than to tear down one's ego and self-esteem. So even guilt-ridden Mary Tyrone must make her childhood and adolescence more idyllic than in fact they were.

For the workings of individual memories O'Neill was as acute as he was with his dramatization of the workings of the collective memory. In *Strange Interlude* O'Neill had Darrell in one of his interior musings speculate on some of the properties of human memory: "Memory is too full of echoes!...memory is lined with mirrors!" (Act VI). An echo chamber lined with mirrors: this is a quite perceptive metaphor for the workings of individual memories, and can take its place in that long succession of metaphors descriptive of memory generated by some of the seminal writers of Western culture, beginning with Plato and coming down through Augustine's *Confessions*, Rousseau and Wordsworth, among others, to culminate in Proust. Darrell sees that a certain kind of memory does not simply remember the past, but is self-perpetuating, and has a tendency to feed upon itself and to dilate and expand (as does Mary Tyrone's).

When one turns to the actual working of individual memories in *Long Day's Journey*, one is struck by the preponderance of the memory of Mary Tyrone; in fact one could say that for the first three acts this is what the play is about; not only is she the dominant figure in the play, the dominant thing about her is her ever-exfoliating memory. A rough tabulation shows that in Act I she memorializes some six times; in Act II, Scene One another six; in Act II, Scene Two fourteen; and in Act IV some eighteen. Although it is true that while she is off-stage in Act IV the detailed picture by James Tyrone of his past and the respective revelations of the sons considerably reduce the preponderance of the Mother's memory, still she comes on at the end of Act IV to dominate the conclusion of the play and to give a fairly full recapitulation of her key memory sequence: convent-nun-piano-wedding dress-happy wedding. Furthermore, O'Neill appears to have believed in the existence of a kind of physical or bodily memory, that is to say, the person you have once been many years before never absolutely goes out of existence and can suddenly reappear, and not as a ghost either. So near the beginning of Act I when James kisses Mary:

> *Suddenly and startlingly ones sees in her face the girl she had once been, not a ghost of the dead, but still a living part of her.* (p. 28)

So at the end, at "The Mad Scene. Enter Ophelia!":

> *The uncanny thing is that her face now appears so youthful. Experience seems ironed out of it. It is a marble mask of girlish innocence, the mouth caught in a shy smile.* (p. 170)

So, literally, the young Mary Tyrone encircles the whole play (how an actress in her fifties gets this across is quite another matter). In between lies her constantly active memory, ever getting more extended, and quite repetitious, and ever more immersed in her various conceptions of her past. On the other hand, the major memorials of the three males are mostly all packed into Act IV, and their evocations of the past appear, surprisingly, rather infrequently in Acts I, II, and III, although the long-standing hostilities between the father and the sons are always there and frequently find voice.

So in *Long Day's Journey Into Night* O'Neill has put at the center of his play an extended memory that runs through Acts I, II, III, disappears during the first seven-eights of Act IV, and then comes on once more to take over at the end of Act IV and conclude the play, just as, in Act I, it had begun the play—that is, the real play. This memory is extended, complex, on occasion contradictory, problematical, obsessive, regressive, a veritable "echo-chamber lined with mirrors."

Then as counterpoint to this central memory O'Neill introduces in Act IV three memories that give in straightforward, compact form either a narrative, as the father tells the story of his life, or recount a moment of cosmic insight, as Edmund describes his estatic experiences at sea, or make a revelation, as Jamie tells his brother of his own half-hatred and jealousy of him. Unlike the mother's memories those of the three males are straightforward, unambiguous, non-obsessive, and unlike some of hers, "true," i.e. they constitute a reasonably accurate reflection of the past.

So what is going on in the mother's memory? Many things, of course. Empirical studies of memory show that normally we tend to highlight happy memories and repress unhappy ones (one informed estimate says that fifty percent are pleasant, thirty percent are unpleasant, and twenty percent neutral).[7] In Mary Tyrone this balance is altered. A rough calculation shows that Mary's come out about fifty-six percent unhappy, forty-four percent happy, a rather higher percentage in this respect than one might have expected, and none neutral. The interesting thing is that she roughly reverses the normal percentages of a normal memory; so what we are seeing is the workings of a memory in an abnormal state, as we well know anyway. However, to put the opposite side of it, her memory is exhibiting the tortures of being unable to escape past guilt, a theme that we associate especially with O'Neill but which is in fact one of the important themes of serious twentieth-century literature, and can be found in Joyce, Proust, Strindberg, Eliot, Hemingway, and others. It appears to be one of the many facets of the malaise of twentieth-century culture. (It is certainly not such an obsessive theme in nineteenth-century culture.) At the same time she is using her unhappy memories not only to make herself suffer but to make every one else suffer as well; in other words, memories are weapons, yet another phenomenon of twentieth-century literature, as in Strindberg, or as in Harold Pinter's *Old Times*, which is a kind of contest as to which of the three central characters can conjure up the most devastating recollection of the others (in Pinter's world these "recollections" do not even have to be true). The single most horrific weapon of memory Mary Tyrone employs in the play is used against the male she loves the most (naturally), her beloved son Edmund, when she tells him in Act III—"*with a hard, accusing antagonism—almost a revengeful enmity*"—(p. 116) that is was his birth that began the rheumatism that now has crippled the once beautiful hands, about which we have heard so much.

Viewed in the large, Mary Tyrone's memories reveal an evolution over the play as a whole which embodies a dialectical movement: thesis, antithesis, and synthesis, or, put in psychological terms, it is a schizophrenic tug-of-war between the remote past and the past-to-present continuum of her post-martial existence, with finally one event of the remote past at last winning out. The thesis, the past-to-present continuum, is asserted repeatedly, insistently throughout Acts I and II—the cheap hotels, the trains, the doctors, the New London home, the Packard car, the dead baby, *et al. ad infinitum*. It is in Act III than an antithesis appears, and for two reasons: she is deeper into her morphine stupor and she is talking to Cathleen, a person who arouses no hateful personal memories. And thus issues forth the other Mary Tryone: the well-brought-up convent girl, her father's pet, the potential nun and pianist. But alongside these memories, somewhat embellished, as James Tyrone tells us in Act IV, there also arises the memory of the most important, and the happiest, event of her life, described in great detail to Cathleen, her falling in love with the actor James Tyrone: "I've loved him dearly for thirty-six years" (p. 101). So what is really going on in Mary's memory is an interaction between three components: the happy childhood (exaggerated); the unhappy marital existence (probably exaggerated once more in some respects—later Tyrone says that he did not drag her on the train trips—she wanted to be with him); and one unqualifiedly "true" and happy memory: meeting, falling in love with, and marrying James Tyrone. But, it should be added, that when this most prized event does not escape at least one corrosive touch: "What is so wonderful about the first meeting between a silly romantic schoolgirl and a matinee idol?" (p. 107).

The single most complex and interesting stretch of Mary Tryone's memory is in the second half of Act III when Tyrone and Edmund have returned, where she is alternately extremely hostile and even vengeful to the two males and to herself (she even mentions her own suicide attempt which earlier in the play she could not bear to think of) and tender to both of them, with Edmund, her "baby", and Tyrone, her life-long love. But her single longest reminiscence in this section is about that wedding gown; just as in the sequence with Cathleen the single longest reminiscence is about the meeting and falling in love with James Tyrone. What appears to be happening in her memory is that both the hapy childhood and the unhappy married life are getting pushed aside by her central remembrance of things past: her courtship and marriage whose tangible memento is that wedding gown. As Proust said, "the true paradises are the paradises that we have lost" (*Remembrance*, III, p. 903).

Interestingly enough, the shape of her memory is very much like that of Molly Bloom at the conclusion of *Ulysses*, who also divides her life between a romantic and expectant girlhood, and adolescence and a married life, which, after the early years, had become boring and routine, and who places at the center of her memory the two great romantic meetings of her life: her first kiss on Gibraltar in 1885, and being kissed and proposed to by Bloom atop the Hill of Howth, in May 1887. These events constitute her respective "lost paradises," and, like Mary, she concludes her reverie with a remembrance of them.

As the content of Mary Tyrone's memory gradually changes over the play as a whole—by the end we are in a totally different part or compartment of that memory than we were at the beginning—so its form changes as well. In the first two acts it consists of a series of verbal ejaculations, brief, insistent, hostile, obsessive, and atemporal. Her memory jumps about in time, now in the far past, now in the near past, now in the middle distance. By Act III it has begun to settle into the far past and to take on a leisurely, narrative reminiscent quality, as she tells the story of the great romance of her life to Cathleen. And, of course, in her final appearance it is a narrative of her life up to her marriage that she tells. She has succeeded, thanks to the powers of morphine and memory, in her chief aim: to transport herself back to the time before she knew her true self. In a wild, weird, crazy O'Neillian way, one could almost say that for her anyway the play has a "happy ending": she has recovered the "lost paradise."

The two most important memories in *Long Day's Journey* are those of Tyrone and his wife, seemingly as different as night and day in both content and form, as in most respects they are. Yet they have correspondences as well. Both, in good Irish-American fashion, have much of that "self-indulgent communal morbidity," redolent of the "tensions sewn into the lace curtain," and both are "exilic." Each character had seen the Promised Land—Mary by the end of the play has convinced herself that she once was in the Promised Land—but has since lost out: that malign fatality that they believe hovers over their lives has defeated them. Strictly speaking, Mary is more the fatalist while Tyrone believes more in self-responsibility, but also in another overriding power, the workings of chance; either way, fate or chance, our lives are not our own. The most touching and poignant resemblance between the two memories is that each thinks that somewhere in the fated Monte Christo cottage lies buried, among the tangible and concrete memorabilia that a family accumulates over the years, an object that constituted at one time a kind of passport into the Promised Land. For Mary it is, of course, the wedding gown, and although she finally finds it, when it first comes into her memory in Act III she is not quite sure where it is:

> Where is my wedding gown now, I wonder? I kept it wrapped up in tissue paper in my trunk...*Where is it now, I wonder?* [emphasis added] (p. 115)

The high point of James Tyrone's life was connected with his profession; in 1874 in Chicago he played a series of matching roles with the great Edwin Booth, Cassius to his Brutus one night, Brutus to his Cassius the next, and so on. The first night that he played Othello to Booth's Iago, Booth said to the manager of the theater—in the most important words that James Tyrone ever heard—"That young man is playing Othello better than I ever did" (p. 150). Tyrone had the manger write down Booth's exact words and he kept this sacred message in his wallet and used to reread it until, after years in the dungeon of Monte Cristo, his Shakespearean career gone aglimmering, he could no longer bear to look at it. But it still exists:

> *Where is it now, I wonder?* [emphasis added] Somewhere in this house. I remember I put it away carefully - (p. 152)

At which point Edmund says, ironically, that, maybe it's in the trunk with Mary's wedding dress. So both Tryones had carefully put away their respective passports to a promised but never realized human felicity. I do not know if "Where is it now, I wonder?" is *the* key line of the play, but it is certainly one of the key lines.

If one is looking for an apt and concrete metaphor for the workings of memory in *Long Day's Journey*, then the play itself provides it, but it occurs off stage and has to be imagined by James and Edmund Tyrone (and the audience). It will be remembered that periodically during Act IV the two men in the living room hear a movement on the floor above them and know that Mary is rummaging about in the attic looking for the wedding dress. We are to imagine the potent symbol of a person alone in the dark ransacking the concrete memorabilia of the past, accumulated willy-nilly in a completely haphazard way over a long period of time and yet containing somewhere, somehow, a completely meaningful constituent, reverberating with life-long consequences. Her quest represents each persons search for the meaning of one's life, of which only memory has the secret, which it sometimes reveals and sometimes does not, sometimes happily, sometimes unhappily. All these portentous matters are suggested by Mary Tyrone's search alone and in the dark for the fated wedding dress. So do we all alone in the dark rummage around in the attics of our memories looking for the secret of the meaning of our existence. And although, like the Tyrones, we thought we had put it away carefully, we still say, "Where is it now, I wonder?"

NOTES

1. Kerby A. Miller, *Emigrants and Exiles* (New York, 1985), p. 4. All further references to this book appear in the text.

2. Louis Sheaffer, *O'Neill Son and Playwright* (Boston, 1968), p. 27.

3. Eugene O'Neill, *Long Day's Journey Into Night* (New Haven, 1956), pp. 153-4, 95. All further references to this play appear in the text.

4. Eugene O'Neill, *A Moon for the Misbegotten*, in *Later Plays of Eugene O'Neill* (New York, 1967), p. 378.

5. Maurice Halbwachs, *The Collective Memory*, trans. Francis J. Ditter, Jr. and Vida Yazdi Ditter (New York, 1980), p. 23.

6. Marcel Proust, *Remembrance of Things Past*, trans. C.K. Scott Moncrieff and Terence Kilmartin (New York, 1981), I, pp. 201, 873. All further references to this book appear in the text.

7. I.M.L. Hunter, *Memory* (Harmondsworth, 1957), p. 272.

Modern Drama, 31 (March 1988): 63-72.

Great Day for the Irish

John Simon

Disappointing is the word for **The O'Neill Plays,** as the mini-repertory of *Ah, Wilderness!* and *Long Day's Journey Into Night* is billed....

In this *Long Days's Journey*—a great play if ever there was one—nothing quite works. José Quintero, an old hand at directing this and other O'Neill plays, has become a tired hand as well. but even the lackluster direction would suffice if the acting were what it must be here: flawless. Can you imagine a string quartet with even one inadequate player? At the play's premiere, Jason Robards was a superlative Jamie, Fredric March an incomparable James Tyrone. The others though good were not spellbinding. In the may productions I have seen since there has always been a weaker link or two; here nobody is quite right.

The worst offender is Robards, who performs as if from numbered filing cards, each listing one of his terrific effects: the falsely modest smile (No. 6), the exasperating foot-stamping (No. 17), the despairing wave of the arm (No. 22), and so on. He can plot his entire performance meticulously by the numbers: 19, 16, 3, 22, 10, etc. He gives us the effect, but cannot show the cause, the path whereby a thought or feeling wends its way toward expression. Colleen Dewhurst starts out well as Mary, hiding her guilt under an excess of sweetness and righteousness, and always innocently perplexed by her family's probings. But with the great final scene, where Mary, heavily drugged, reverts to childhood, she cannot cope. There is no vulnerability, no coming apart at the seams, no collapse—Geraldine Fitzgerald, Zoe Caldwell, Inga Tidblad (in the epochal Swedish production) all managed this much better. Miss Dewhurst merely turns her flame to low and thinks the rest will take care of itself.

Her real-life son Campbell Scott is an interesting actor with a haunting voice, and he handles much of Edmund splendidly. Yet when he comes to the really splendid passage—the poetic recollection of life at sea—he never catches the true lyric spark. As Jamie, Jamey Sheridan grins a bit too much at first, but then does very well until his last scene: His late, drunken homecoming and sudden, horrified sobering up lack the vehemence against which Mary's quasi-sleepwalking finish can fully deploy its ghostly pianissimo. And—something unseen till now—the seemingly foolproof part of the maid is mangled by Jane Macfie, whose attempts at a brogue are as pitiful as her stabs at acting.

Despite all this—despite even Ben Edwards's customarily unimaginative but oh, so inexpensive setting—the play somehow intermittently shines through. Even in this severely dented production, it is worth a dozen *Ah, Wilderness*es—at least it is never boring.

New York Magazine, July 11, 1988.

O'Neill Opus Long but Fiercely Great

John McClain

The power and the grandeur of Eugene O'Neill are again evident in *Moon for the Misbegotten*, his last play, which was presented last night at the Bijou Theatre. Like *Long Day's Journey Into Night*, to which this is at least a partial sequel, it has the same fierce qualities of introspection, the ruthless examination of forces and frustrations which pursued his tragic family to their separate graves.

Here he is concerned with the fate of his brother Jim, whose early problems with drink and dollies are intrinsic in the plot of *Journey*. Now, with his mother dead, Jim seeks security at the breast of his tenant farmer's king sized daughter; there is an evening of gentle magnificence, then they go their separate and inevitable ways.

With a gift superior to anybody writing our language today, O'Neill is able to bring poetry to this almost squalid consideration of Irish immigrants on a poor Connecticut farm. His scenes proceed endlessly—rising and falling, stopping short and starting all over again, sometimes trailing off into trivialities. But he never loses control or understanding of his characters, or of their importance.

It seemed to me that much of the three-hour drama might not have suffered by adroit deletion, but the general effect depends upon its very verbosity, the creation of a mood, and it would be difficult and dangerous to select the point of incision. Certainly there are moments in the first act that could be condensed, but from there onward the overpowering progression of the play, however long-winded, is justified.

Mr. O'Neill in describing his heroine, the farmer's daughter, had indicated that she be a female behemoth, weighing "around 180 pounds." Wendy Hiller, who plays the part, carries no such weight but by force of sheer animal vigor and some ingenious pads is able to create the desired effect. She gives one of the memorable performances of her career—tender, earthy and primitively proud.

Cyril Cusack, an Abbey Theatre alumnus making his Broadway bow, is superb in the role of the Irish father—the sad, scheming inebriate, whose last links with life are his farm and his daughter.

Franchot Tone, as James Tyrone Jr., turns in an assured and brilliant portrayal of the alcoholic brother who is lost in the torment of his weakness at the time of his mother's death. Reclining in Miss Hiller's arms, he has one of the longest expositional speeches in recent history, and he does it wonderfully well. Glenn Cannon has a brief moment, and a good one, as one of Mr. Cusack's fugitive children, William Woodson is a properly stuffy landowner. I thought Carmen Capalbo's direction was always forthright and never intrusive, and the stark premises of a Connecticut farm, as designed by William Pitkin, were excellent.

There will be those who will find *Moon* over-lengthy and under-clear. But not me. I am an O'Neill fan, and I think it's just great.

New York Journal American, May 3, 1957.

The Stage: The Image and the Search

Richard Hayes

It is the ironic virtue of *A Moon for the Misbegotten* to remind us of the claims not only of piety, but of art. Eugene O'Neill's last play arrived at a salutary moment: having done this season past, with that generosity which is ever an American grace, justice and homage to a most considerable figure in our literature, the tide of feeling runs high. It will not be swelled by this work; one hopes, indeed, some movement of control may set in. For *A Moon for the Misbegotten*, hoary, ruminant, immutable yet baggy with total recall, full of a sucking guilt and reddened with whiskey, as Miss Mary McCarthy observed, like a bloodshot eye, invites not so much response as endurance. It is built of private obsessions which, unlike those of *Long Day's Journey Into Night*, stubbornly refuse to take a public investiture, and inundated by its weary factuality, I reflected that Gertrude Stein must have had reference to something like this when she observed that anecdotes are not literature. Even the mesmeric midnight scene, which gathers one irresistibly into its moist claw of remorse, seems to me inadvertently, if at all, to enter the kingdom of art: it inhabits rather a climate of moral pathology, and I resign happily to the theologian the task of charting that weather.

The O'Neill Problem: one adds it to the James problem, the Dreiser problem, the Melville problem, and the problems of Poe, Fitzgerald, Hemingway and Mrs. Wharton: it would seem that only in the public thoroughfare of their diverse stresses do American writers meet and touch. The O'Neill problem *vis-à-vis* *A Moon for the Misbegotten* is centrally one of language and form. Insensibility to the first—to its luster or resistance, shimmer or weightiness—harassed O'Neill all his days: the durable images of his work are either visual, or the achievement of some intolerable personal pressure; his attempts to realize them in language are muddy and clotted. Even *Long Day's Journey,* which forges out of domestic speech a kind of tragic poetry of remembrance and loss—even here some excess might be rinsed away, the whole moulded to a richer expressiveness and finality.

In *A Moon for the Misbegotten,* this insensibility expands into the larger indifference to anything like selection. One's mouth, ears, nostrils are crammed, not with the intense, the difficult or abstract, but rather with an aimless and literal redundancy. The sense persists that to the later O'Neill, the reality of language and form deteriorated; he saw them only as part of the tedious machinery of making the spirit manifest. Indeed, the Manichean burden of *A Moon for the Misbegotten,* is embodied in its form, for we have here not so much a play, as a piece of drama, dominated but by an aesthetic tone or a vision of reality (however meager), but by an *image*: that of the withered husk of a sensualist, and the randy, yearning virago uniting to deny the reality of physical love and the flesh, finally of matter itself.

This scene, rising like a gutted moon over what has gone before, is of uncommon power and quality: raddled with private tension, it is able to exact what Mr. Lionel Trilling, in a subtle discrimination, has called acquiescence without assent. However decisively one rejects its lamentable psychology and perverse values, the want of intelligence it flaunts—its lordly indifference to the testimony of common experience—the thing has nonetheless romantic authority and a terrible truth. For it brings to light the fantasy world of a kind of Irish-American Catholicism by which we have all been fingered. Such a scene, I might add, could be written only by a lapsed Irish-American Catholic, and whatever its dubious worth as art, as a document of contemporary experience it could not be more relevant.

Its critical significance is to dramatize inescapably O'Neill's failure to acquit what Mr. T. S. Eliot has called the central task of the poetic dramatist—the devising of a form to arrest the flow of spirit. My designation of O'Neill as poetic dramatist may surprise, but it is obvious that these later plays may be said only peripherally to fall within the tradition of realism; their real animation is metaphysical horror, and their real passion the attempt to register that in all its shock. Yet the Manichean heresy is intolerable to literature as it is to theology; within the terms of art, spirit cannot exist without embodiment. It seeks ever the conditions of form, and the impatience of O'Neill's later plays with this necessary search—their solipsistic obsession with the undifferentiated image—may mark the limits of his art. One is indeed curious to know what later generations may make of these works, when all their paraphernalia of contemporary reference is sloughed off, and they stand only by the inarticulate, shuddering authority of their pain.

Mr. Carmen Capalbo's production of *A Moon for the Misbegotten* is the sketch of a work in progress, the tribute of a devoted amateur, in which one may question not the homage but the want of finish and aesthetic awareness. The theatre of O'Neill is so patchy and eclectic and void of anything like a dominant style, that it can be made to "work" only by the organization of personal obsession: varieties of realism, however individually effective, can bring it only to chaos. Nothing like this unity binds Mr. Carmen Capalbo's production into coherence: Mr Cyril Cusack plays with a garrulous, Abbey Theatre amiability which is doubtless authentic, but which dwindles into the unintelligible, and Mr. Franchot Tone with a wry, soiled elegance, always admirably taut. Mr. Tone "projects," as one says, with unfailing authority, yet the role runs cross-grained to his sensibility, and I could not feel him happy in it. Miss Wendy Hiller is the somewhat tarnished Demeter of O'Neill's vulnerable conception, and her performance, into which has gone much personal resource, baffles nonetheless by its shifts in style. Miss Hiller is at first the raffish tartar we have known on so many Tobacco Roads; she later dilates this quality, with a lovely jet of feeling, into the vital tenderness and obliteration of the midnight scene. Her closing moments strain, a trifle visibly, after the enclosed peace and acquiescence of a conventional tragic poise. This fluctuation would seem to be Miss Hiller's response to the impossible components of the role, and it may be said of her approach that she sometimes makes them possible; often, too, she sounds a note of resonant pathos. One regrets only that the part permits no scope to the quality of luminous, energetic intelligence which is such a feature of Miss Hiller's distinction.

Two highly pertinent commentaries on the published version of *A Moon for the Misbegotten* have been written by Miss Mary McCarthy (in *Sight and Spectacles)* and Mr. Eric Bentley (in *The Dramatic Event*).

Commonweal, August 30, 1957.

Theatre: *A Moon for the Misbegotten* "and yet..."

Anthony West

There is something about the work of Eugene O'Neill that always brings to mind the old definition of "rude plenty" as "plenty that gives rise to rude remarks." The talent behind *A Moon for the Misbegotten* is real enough, the play itself is stiff with theatrical virtues, and the superb production that it has been given by the Mann-Libin-Walker team at the Circle in the Square does manage to make it look awfully like an authentic classic of the American theatre—and yet, and yet....

The trouble is, in part, that the bad fairy that came last of all to O'Neill's cradleside to nullify the gifts bestowed upon him by all the others knew exactly what she was about when she picked a humourless innocence as her contribution. This is not to say that O'Neill couldn't be funny when he wanted to, but it is to insist his ideas about the nature of the inner life of his characters were astoundingly naive, and that his efforts to contrive hammer-blow-of-fate-type disasters for his characters would lead him into the realms of Rabelaisian farce just about as often as not.

This is unhappily the case with the present play. O'Neill is insistent that what is going on has the weight and tension of Greek tragedy, and the people at the Circle in the Square are rightly loyal to him in treating him with the total seriousness he demands. But the crux or hinge of the whole thing, the event that is to establish the play's hero as a tragic and doomed figure, is one that can only anchor him in our minds as a grotesque or a caricature. This dire off-stage happening is a four-day transcontinental train trip made by James Tyrone, junior, after his mother's death. He was bringing her body home to Connecticut and while she lay there stiff and stark in her long box in the baggage car, he was taking in a tankful of guilt by entertaining himself with a prostitute in his drawing room back along the train.

It took great naïveté and great unawareness of the drift of things to write Tyrone junior's confession to this piece of compulsive self-abasement in terms of a confession to unforgivable sin twenty full years after Joyce had written his account of Bloomsday and while Yossarian was, literally, in the air. But O'Neill had what it took, and to spare. So that as one watches Salome Jens, Mitchell Ryan, and W.B. Brydon doing marvelous things in the way of convincing their audiences and themselves that the characters are real people, really involved with each other, one is slowly overwhelmed by a feeling that one of the three, it wouldn't matter which, should be Zero Mostel or Milo O'Shea, arching eyebrows to question the basis of the whole thing. It doesn't seem possible that O'Neill, being more or less a contemporary, could have held such a dazzlingly and utterly non-contemporary view of the proceedings.

And, alas, it isn't only the sense that O'Neill was behind his own time that is troublesome; there is, too, the lack of measure. The huge theatrical engine he wheels up is dealing with the refusal of two young persons to respond to the world or to each other on the adult level. When all has been said and done it just doesn't seem that important that Josie Hogan should have arranged to spend the rest of her life playing with her father the game that Dr. Berne (of *Games People Play*) calls Uproar, or that young Tyrone should have wriggled out of having his manhood tested yet again. O'Neill may have wanted to give us another Hamlet, but what we get is a lush Peter Pan.

Vogue, September 15, 1968.

Theatre

Harold Clurman

To say that *A Moon for the Misbegotten* is the best production of the best play of the season is to say very little. One might ask why it has taken so long for the reviewers and the public to recognize its unique distinction in O'Neill's work. For the play, written in 1943, failed dismally at its try-out tour under the Theatre Guild's auspices in 1947 and was still held weak when it was done on Broadway in the spring of 1957 with Wendy Hiller, Franchot Tone and Cyril Cusack. It achieved acceptance in its revival at the (old) Circle in the Square in 1968, but only now at the Morosco Theatre has it become an unqualified success.

The play's initial failure was to some degree the fault of its author and producers. They insisted that the girl in the play, Josie Hogan, be acted by someone of Irish blood who is "almost a freak—five foot eleven in her stockings and weighs around one hundred eighty." These physical attributes were considered so important that the actress who played the role—tall, but not heavy enough—was asked to sign a contract which read "the artist agrees to gain the necessary weight required for the role." This stupid and horrible clause may very well have led to the actress' death shortly after the play's production. None of the actresses who played it subsequently answered to the playwright's description of the character's size nor were they, as far as I know or as anyone could tell, Irish.

Both Wendy Hiller and Salome Jens are good actresses, but the productions in which they were cast were either not successful or only partially so. I am rather pleased to relate that Colleen Dewhurst, now in the role, was asked to play it for me while she was still a beginner, in one of my private classes, before I had ever seen the play. She played it in Spoleto (Italy) during one of its summer festivals which, for all her suitability to the part, was not enough to render that production impressive. In such a play the entire cast, its direction and the spirit of the whole must be coherent, unified. A play on the stage is not a good play simply because it may be one in its text. Theatre is something different from literature...it may be more or less, but it is not the same.

The historian Henry Steele Commager, writing about O'Neill, complained that he was obsessed by sex—and he was not the only one to do so. (As a joke, I once said that since there are only three or four things a person can be obsessed by, sex obsession might be considered as good as any of them.) But the truth is that O'Neill was ambivalent in the matter—it could be maintained with sufficient evidence that he had a certain horror of it. *A Moon for the Misbegotten* is a love story—almost the only one O'Neill ever wrote. Because it is that, *sex* occupies a peculiarly oblique role in it.

The love story in this play is a thwarted one. Yet that, in a certain sense, (O'Neill's sense) is one of the reasons why the love is realized. For the two people involved are "misbegotten." Josie Hogan believes herself unattractive because she is physically lumpy and perhaps even more because she is the daughter of a widowed and indigent farmer, working unyielding soil in a vicinity where the neighboring males are louts. She is ashamed of her condition and tries to mask it by pretending to a promiscuity which her natural fineness and pride shun. She is in fact a virgin. Old man Hogan understands Josie's plight and goes along with her game, while he sorrows over it. With all his being, he wishes that she may find a good man whom she might love and who would love her.

James Tyrone, Jr. is such a man. But he too is "misbegotten." He is an actor's son, morbidly attached to his now dead mother; his father's profession and person both alienate him to the degree that he has become an alcoholic who finds little gratification in life except through the frequenting of "Broadway tarts." His experience with these creatures makes him regard sex as dirty. In Josie, he finds purity, the maternal tenderness, the loving sensibility which reaches out to comfort him in his hurt.

Their love is a "moon"—a romance, an ideal, a dream, the opposite of a reality by which they might love. Thus, they cannot consummate a union of the flesh. The perfection of love to which they both aspire is impossible for them: he is too far gone in self-abasement, in his death-in-life; she perceives that the last remnant of his manhood resides in his enraptured regard for her and that she must forgo any expectation of redemption for him. Yet in their momentary contact they fulfill something of their dream by knowing they have experienced love in their one ecstatic and fleeting moment of mutual recognition. She knows that in a special way she has been truly loved; he knows that selfless love is possible, and what he desires even more, forgiveness, which he had never believed would be vouchsafed him.

What makes the play so absorbing and affecting is that O'Neill, without preachment or turgid poetizing, has poured into it all the ache of his confusion, all his drive toward perfection. He longed for the "absolute" in everything, strove toward it wildly, felt his inadequacies for achieving it and understood that only in his impassioned reaching for it did he attain the stature he hoped for.

O'Neill said his plays dealt with man's relation to God; what he meant was that he was concerned with purity, a life without taint or compromise. His weakness in confrontation with the circumstances of his own existence made him feel disgraced in his own eyes, so that all that remained to him was to pray for forgiveness as he himself, after his long day's journey into night, managed to forgive those who he imagined, despite himself, were responsible for his failings and wounds.

There is an affinity in Jason Robards with O'Neill's spirit. That is why he has reached the apogee of his career here in the role of James Tyrone, Jr. He was a perfect Hickey in *The Iceman Cometh*, admirable as the same but younger James Tyrone, Jr. in *Long Day's Journey Into Night*; but Hickey is limited compared to Tyrone in *A Moon*, and the junior Tyrone of O'Neill's masterpiece is caught within the complexities of that play's other personages. In *A Moon* James, Jr. is both subjectively and objectively essentialized. Objectively, he is O'Neill's brother; subjectively, he is O'Neill himself. (One wonders if O'Neill realized this.) And Robards is able, through inner motives and analogy, to convey the cracked vessel that is Tyrone, Jr. Robards' voice, with its buried sob and its suppressed laughter, its drunken despair so close to cynicism, its Broadway randyness and its shamefaced apology, the "hamminess" of it all, together with its humanity, go to the heart of O'Neill's creation. Robards and James Tyrone, Jr. are one.

Colleen Dewhurst brings a powerful womanliness to the part of Josie. She is of the earth, warm and hearty. She looks and sounds a person who can do her own and her father's hard work; one, moreover, who possesses the vast sexuality she boasts of, as well as a woman chaste through the very force of that sexuality.

The play begins as comedy—very old-fashioned comedy at that—and it is an aspect which could mislead an audience into expecting something other than what follows and which therefore doesn't often come across as part of the play's deeply affectionate quality. In Edward Flanders' performance, dryly understated yet sharply indicative of stout fiber, bereftness, sorry slyness and fatherly devotion, Hogan becomes, for the first time, wholly alive and integral to the play's texture and scheme.

José Quintero's direction is his best. The play flows in easy and precise rhythm. There is no impediment, waste movement or ponderousness in it. Without being "stylized," it is free of petty realism and without rhetorical inflation, rises to its own inherent grandeur. The direction is well aided by Ben Edwards' setting and lighting, which combine poetic theatricality with the specificity of the play's environment.

A Moon for the Misbegotten has at last become a wonderful evening in the theatre.

Nation, January 19, 1974.

A Moon for the Misbegotten

John Simon

A Moon for the Misbegotten was Eugene O'Neill's last finished play, a lament, conciliatory offering, and funerary monument for his older brother, Jamie, to whom he may have felt he did not do justice in *Long Day's Journey Into Night*. Here Jamie is shown away from his Broadway tarts on a farm owned by his family; he is being decent to the wily tenant farmer, Phil Hogan, and having a platonic one-night stand with Josie, Hogan's 28-year-old daughter, a sardonic, tough, sexually wild giantess with, like Jamie himself, a hidden craving for love.

Josie is Eugene's fictitious gift to his brother, though, clearly, also what the playwright himself yearned for. Five-foot-eleven and weighing 180 pounds, she is stronger than any man around, yet extremely feminine, with large breasts that are frequently extolled, but more as pillows than as objects of erotic play. She is that well-known fantasy figure Mother-Wife-Whore, with an emphasis on the first. Although the play contains some comic intrigue involving possession of the farm, its main concern is the moonlit *nuit blanche* during which Jamie and Josie find each other as fellow sufferers from the illness of living, and his longing, confession of guilt about his mother, and need to expiate are met with absolution, mothering, and the gift of peaceful sleep on the wished-for breasts. But Jamie is too far gone for sexual consummation, let alone marriage; he can only be eased toward a merciful death by Josie, to live on as a bright and aching memory in her equally stunted life.

For the play to work, it must be flawlessly cast. The present production was engineered by Kate Nelligan, who coveted the fat part of Josie. But Josie, like Jamie, must be "misbegotten": a huge thing who, because of her size and energy and appetite—and perhaps also her superior intelligence and emancipatedness—will never satisfy or be satisfied by the men in her purview. The actress who plays her must have the uberousness of the Triple Goddess, mother, mistress, and spouse. Miss Nelligan, though highly accomplished, lacks Josie's opulence of stature, her large-eyed warmth and expansive smile, her unforced, all-enveloping sexuality. The actress conveys much better high-strung, urban edge-teeterers; her anxieties and acerbities ring truer than her mellowness. How much finer a Josie was Colleen Dewhurst the last time round; still Miss Nelligan has authority (though not as O'Neill specifies, of the unmannish sort), exemplary elocution, and a stock of strong emotions that seem, however, commandeered into action rather than spontaneously exuded. Bluntly put, her appearance (down to an unfortunate wig) and personality are not warm and winning, and her bosom seems more suited for uneasy catnaps than sleep that brings oblivion. Moreover, her strong Irish accent, thicker than her father's seems less suited to Josie from Connecticut than to Pegeen Mike from County Synge.

Even so, she is vastly preferable to Ian Bannen, an interesting actor wildly miscast as Jamie. Bannen is too pinched, too ominous, too old for the mercurial, romantic Jamie, and has great problems with his American accent. With a face and voice more apposite to scheming villainy, he comes across even colder than his co-star. His line readings are often extremely idiosyncratic, but not, to my mind, tenable. And he must fumble in the footsteps of Jason Robards, whose Jamie was definitive. As Hogan, Jerome Kilty gives a performance that is bold and fascinating, but a bit too excogitated, sonorous, histrionic. He invests the pig farmer Hogan with the self-dramatizing poetry of a Falstaff or Richard II....

Brian Vahey's set is elegantly stylized and sculptural, but more suited to Sam Shepard than to O'Neill; above all, it lacks the spaciousness from which Jamie and Josie must wrest their bit of moon encircled intimacy. But Marc B. Weiss's lighting is faultless, and David Levaux has directed sparely and purposively, giving the actors their head, though I wish he had called less attention to the facade of the Hogan house folding itself open (and, later, shut) in accordion pleats. It is not really his fault if, in this version, the play's mother fixation emerges with more pathology than pathos.

New York Magazine, May 14, 1984.

The Metatheatrics of *A Moon for the Misbegotten*

James A. Robinson

In *Forging a Language*, Jean Chothia mentions an intriguing aspect of Eugene O'Neill's late plays. "Within the conventional performing of the play itself," she notes, "his characters perform for each other," as illustrated by Con Melody's posing in *A Touch of the Poet*, Don Parritt's histrionic curtain line in *The Iceman Cometh*, and the self-conscious recitations by the Tyrone men *In Long Day's Journey Into Night*. Chothia does not contend that these performances break the illusionistic plane of the plays, for they are always integral to plot and in character. "And yet," she continues, "they also bring consciousness of performance and playing into the audience's minds, in much the same way as does the reiterated play metaphor in Shakespeare's drama."[1]

This consciousness of playing is what today's criticism has come to term "metatheatre." As used by most critics,[2] metatheatre (or metadrama) designates a self-reflexive theatrical style which not only reminds a play's viewers that they are watching a performance, but explicitly explores the conflicts between role and self, art and life. While a modern coinage, metatheatre is not an exclusively modern phenomenon. Thus, *Hamlet*, with its ubiquitous role-playing and crucial inner play, provides the primary model for such modern metadramas as *Rosencrantz and Guildenstern Are Dead*. Still, the father of modern metatheatre is commonly acknowledged to be Luigi Pirandello, whose *Henry IV, Six Characters in Search of an Author* and other theatre plays examine the discrepancies between personality and role, life and theatre. Similar metatheatrical motifs are also apparent in Eugene O'Neill's final play, *A Moon for the Misbegotten*. On its primary levels of plot and theme, the play remains firmly within the American naturalistic mainstream, displaying the interests in psychological motivation and family conflict that were characteristic of O'Neill throughout his long theatrical career. However, the play also subtly develops more self-conscious themes via theatrical references—references possibly motivated by O'Neill's heightened awareness of his artistic medium as he reluctantly prepared to leave it.

In marked contrast to O'Neill's other late plays, the structure of *A Moon for the Misbegotten* is strikingly artificial, with so much plotting in its first two acts that (as Frederic Carpenter has observed) it "seems like a maze of false clues and blind alleys."[3] The maze quietly parodies the contrivances of theatrical art. Moreover, the play's three major characters are all figuratively masked actors who perform before one another. Accordingly, the opening acts present several short inner plays, as well as anecdotes about previous performances. Finally, the play's protagonist (modelled on O'Neill's brother Jamie, who was an actor) yearns to abandon role playing but finds himself trapped in his parts, thereby offering a mildly metatheatrical variation on O'Neill's obsessive themes of death, fate and the past. To be sure, that is only one aspect to this character's complex, divided personality; and the play's self-conscious touches in both structure and characterization are subordinate to its central, dramatically "realistic" explorations of the emotional relationships between a guiltridden man and his virgin lover. But the metatheatrical subtext I have identified nonetheless invests this final play with a self-reflexive dimension which may make it more contemporary than scholars have previously realized.

The agonizing circumstances of the play's composition may partially explain its self-consciousness. The scenario and manuscript versions were composed between October 1941 and May 1943, a period when, for a variety of reasons, O'Neill (in the words of his biographer Louis Sheaffer) "sank, both mentally and physically, to a nadir."[4] Several factors contributed to his depression—among them the highly publicized behaviour of his socialite daughter Oona, and the outbreak of World War II—but the major cause was the intensification of a long-standing tremor in his hands. In February 1942, shortly after O'Neill finished the first draft of *A Moon for the Misbegotten*, a doctor diagnosed the illness as Parkinson's disease. The incurable condition grew steadily worse, the medication failed to alleviate the painful tremor. Writing to George Jean Nathan in October of the same year, he confided that "there are days when it is physically impossible to write at all."[5] In December, he repeated this ailment in a letter to Theresa Helburn. "Some days I can't write—I mean physically can't write longhand—and couldn't type even if the old dog could change tricks and compose on a typewriter."[6] He purchased a Soundscribe (an early version of the tape recorder) and, Sheaffer reports, "tried to dictate the ideas developed in his mind and pressing to be born, but his creative process balked at the new approach."[7] Sadly, that creative process experienced repeated frustration as outlets for its expression closed up. By 1943, O'Neill was beginning no new projects, and had to content himself with revising unproduced plays.

Arthur and Barbara Gelb speculate that during this time, O'Neill started "suspecting that his writing days were nearly at an end";[8] and *A Moon for the Misbegotten*, composed intermittently during this trying time and completed in manuscript in the middle of 1943, was the last play he would ever complete. Beset by a progressive, incurable disease, O'Neill may have reluctantly concluded during *Moon's* composition that his active career as a writer was over. Whatever his conscious realizations or intentions, the product of this poignant period was a play which has reminded at least one scholar of Shakespeare's *The Tempest* another final play which comments upon the theatrical arts which its creator is about to abandon.[9] If the play is indeed O'Neill's valedictory to the theatre, its subtle exploration of role-playing, plays within plays, and the conflict between self and role is hardly surprising.

Several lines in the play's early scenes hint at O'Neill's metatheatrical subtext. The action takes place in 1923 outside the rural Connecticut shanty of Phil Hogan, a cunning Irish-American tenant farmer who is worried that his landlord Jim Tyrone might, in a drunken moment, sell their farm to a neighbouring Standard Oil magnate. Scheming to prevent this, Hogan muses to his oversized daughter Josie about the possibility of tricking Tyrone into a marriage with her. Her response is revealing: "I never can tell to this day, when you put that dead mug on you, whether you're joking or not."[10] Able to bewilder his own daughter, Hogan is a master of the deadpan style and a manipulator of masks, which he puts on and discards at will until the final act. Thus, when he persists in promoting his scheme in act one, Josie—who sees herself as "an ugly, overgrown lump of a woman" who could not possibly seduce Tyrone—warns Hogan not to "play the jackass with me" (28). Shortly afterwards, her comments point up a brief inner play between Hogan and Tyrone, when she first asks her father to "play the old game about a drink" with the landlord, then delightedly recognizes them "playing that old game" when they do so (36,46). Hogan and Josie subsequently play before their Yankee millionaire neighbor the roles of the outraged peasant and his scandalized daughter, driving the plutocrat from the premises. By the end of the first act, Hogan has emerged as a comic gamester, the trickster figure common to folklore and the plots of Old Comedy. And intriguingly, he also resembles the comic playwright, weaving comic plots for purposes of entertainment and fooling his audiences along the way—like a vulgar, farcical, Celtic variation on Shakespeare's Prospero.[11]

Those plots become complicated in the second act, which explicitly identifies the daughter as co-performer. Labelled by her father as "a great proud slut who's played games with half the men around here," Josie is later accused by him of "playing the virgin" when she turns scrupulous about seducing Tyrone—forcing the daughter to vow to "play whore" to get revenge on the landlord whom she mistakenly thinks is about to dispossess them (80, 94, 95). But Josie's role-playing is attended by multiple ironies. Josie has in fact "played games" with the men in town, but not the wanton one she advertises: she remains a virgin, having teased numerous men into desiring her only to reject them. Her father, while overtly accepting her promiscuous mask, knows this. But in the scene described above he successfully plays a game on *her*, misleading her into thinking Tyrone has sold the farm so that her anger will prompt her to trick Tyrone into bed and marriage. The subsequent scheme fails. Tyrone arrives and, after eventually confessing to sexual episodes with a prostitute on the train bearing his mother's dead body home from California, falls asleep on Josie's comforting breast. For Tyrone also sees through Josie's promiscuous mask, which helps explain his attraction to her. Her actual chastity and her large, maternal figure make her an ideal mother-substitute, and he has sought her out to play a role in his fantasy scenario of reunion with, and confession to, his dead mother.

Beneath the various masks and schemes of the characters lie two more levels of plot and response, the first sentimental and the second tragic. Tyrone and (especially) Josie do feel genuine love for one another, and Hogan devises his scheme as "the only one left to bring the two of you to stop your damned pretending, and face the truth that you loved each other. I wanted you to find happiness" (175). This act-four confession adds an unexpected dimension to Hogan, who had shortly before been berated by Josie after her discovery of the "scheme behind [his] scheme" (159): to fool her into seducing Tyrone as revenge before she realized no betrayal had occurred. Hogan's deeper, loving motive again points up a resemblance to comic playwrights, but this time the practitioners of New Comedy, who devise sentimental schemes to unite young lovers. Sadly, the scheme must fail. O'Neill, the tragedian, abandons his comic mask in the last acts.[12] The grieving, guilt-ridden Tyrone loves death more than Josie; and the audience's romantic expectations are denied as Tyrone exits, grateful for Josie's comfort but beyond her love's redemptive powers. On the deepest level of the play thus resides O'Neill's obsession: the tragic fact of death, the ultimate reality which renders futile all schemes of men and playwrights.

"Everything in this play has double bottoms," the late O'Neill scholar Timo Tiusanen once wrote, echoing Carpenter's remark about the play's maze-like quality.[13] As the above summary suggests, the plot's twists and turns repeatedly expose the artificiality of theatrical constructions. In his final creation, the playwright unexpectedly toys with the complicated, arbitrary plot devices of comedy, embodying this comic impulse in the figure of Phil Hogan. By so doing, he calls into question the very notion of dramatic plotting by first exaggerating it, then exposing its futility.[14] Josie's rueful, ironic curtain line at the end of the third act hints at this. As she realizes that neither her plots nor her love can save the life of the man whose sleep-stilled face has *"the drained, exhausted peace of death,"* she stares at the sky and proclaims, "God forgive me, it's a fine end to all my scheming, to sit here with the dead hugged to my breast, and the silly mug of the moon grinning down, enjoying the joke." (153). While the line is perfectly in character for Josie, it could also be O'Neill describing the play itself. Despite all its "scheming" (the ingenious plots of the Hogans), it leaves the playwright once again hugging death to his breast, in its shift from the Hogans to Tyrone, from comedy to tragedy. And the moon's laughter at the scheme's futility suggests a religious theme: the contempt for man's plans of the distant, ironic life force, a theme which obsessed O'Neill throughout his career. Indeed, Josie's remark may even represent the playwright's retrospective overview of that career. For the scheming also represents all the plots the playwright has ever invented—plots on which the final curtain is about to fall, as his career draws to an end—to the wry amusement of the moon, the cosmic force which knows the destiny of death that awaits those plots and their creator.

A more overt self-consciousness manifests itself in the three small plays within the play, which likewise expose the artificiality of dramatic structures. The first, which commences upon Tyrone's entrance in act one, has already been mentioned. Tyrone and Hogan stage a witty, good-natured comic scene of landlord and tenant, *"like players at an old familiar game where each knows the other's moves, but which still amuses them"* (37). They appreciate one another's jokes about a college prank and the farm's sterility until the playlet's plot reaches the climax indicated in advance by Josie: as a "game about a drink," its final movement consists of apparently idle talk about the heat that leads to Tyrone's broad requests for some whiskey, which Hogan at first resists but ultimately fulfills. Like the first two acts of *Moon*, the miniature play—complete with protagonist (Tyrone), antagonist (Hogan) and audience (Josie)—hints at the contrived, plotted nature of dramatic construction, with each line written with a preconceived end in mind.

Moreover, this playlet also anticipates O'Neill's larger strategy of questioning theatrical contrivance by contrasting it with life. Interrupting this comic set piece are nineteen lines of dialogue between Tyrone and Josie which offer a glimpse into their genuine emotional needs and sexual desires. Josie dons her mask of wanton woman as she teases Tyrone about his Broadway "tarts." Tyrone twice admonishes her to "cut out that kind of talk," finally stopping her with his declaration that "I like them tall and strong and voluptuous now, with beautiful big breasts"—a description of Josie herself (43). Tyrone had earlier dropped *his* comic mask briefly when he confessed to having had "one of those heebie-jeebie nights when booze keeps you awake instead of—," then *"catches [Josie] giving him a pitying look"* and concludes *"irritably,"* "But what of it!" (41). Tyrone's understanding of Josie's true nature, his Oedipal desire for her, and her compassion for him all receive expression in this subtle scene within the playlet. The scene thus foreshadows the sentimental love plot which will emerge later from beneath the intrigues, and the deeper death obsession of Tyrone (notice his desire for the whiskey to obliterate his consciousness) that will frustrate *that* plot as well. Finally, the structural contrast between the skilful game-playing of Tyrone and Hogan (which surrounds this inner scene) and the aborted game between Tyrone and Josie also suggests a Pirandellian contrast between art and life. The witty perfection of the former presents a striking contrast to the earnest imperfection of the latter, where unexpected emotions destroy the artificial role-playing of Josie and Tyrone before one another.

The second inner play follows hard upon the first, when T. Stedman Harder is spotted approaching the house on horseback. Tyrone has warned Hogan that their wealthy neighbor will call upon them to complain about the tenant's pigs breaking down a fence to wallow in Harder's ice pond. Hogan and Josie respond like veteran performers looking forward to the challenge of active roles in a strong central conflict: exploited peasants vs. arrogant aristocrat. The ensuing scene combines brilliant comic improvisation with a scenario indicated in advance by O'Neill's stage directions. *"The experienced strategy of the Hogans in verbal battle is to take the offensive at once and never let an opponent get to hit back. Also, they use a beautifully co-ordinated, change of pace, switching suddenly from jarring shouts to low, confidential vituperation. And they exaggerate their Irish brogues to confuse an enemy still further"* (56). Hogan repeatedly twists his neighbour's words around, interrupts him, accuses him of bad manners, and finally berates him for breaking down his fence "to entice my poor pigs to take their death in your ice pond" (62), thereby decimating the herd. Hogan's quick mind, gifted tongue and ability to seize on his opponent's own words (as when Harder's interrupted "I didn't come here—" is turned by Hogan into a suspicion of Harder's sanity) renders the *agon*'s resolution apparent from the start: Harder is quickly routed.

More than the preceding playlet, this one highlights theatrical role playing, as Hogan and Josie consciously assume exaggerated roles. Hogan, for example, offers to "play politeness" with Harder by formally introducing Josie as "Miss Josephine Hogan" (57-8); after interrupting Harder's "I didn't come here—," Hogan *"takes off his hat and scratches his head in comic bewilderment"* (59). The scene reaches its hilarious climax when Hogan simulates the fury and fierceness of the outraged victim of a "pig-murdering tyrant" and throws Harder out, while Josie *"leers at him idiotically"* and seeks a lovers' rendezvous "tonight as usual, down by the pigpen" (63-4). The performing couple is also conscious of its effect, as father and daughter guffaw together *"while they watch the disconcerting effect of this theatrical mirth"* on their victim (58). And, as in the first inner play, the performers are also aware of their audience—this time, the hidden one of Tyrone, who witnesses the scene from within the shanty. His appreciation goads them on while (predictably) it has the opposite effect on Harder. When Harder hears a *"burst of laughter"* from the shanty, *"revelation of an unseen audience"* startles him. *He begins to look extremely unsure of himself"* (58). Harder is thereby exposed as an inferior performer, lacking presence, unable to improvise, incapable even of remembering his script—thereby pointing up the Hogan's dramatic talents in those very areas.

The final inner play occurs at the end of the second act. Josie has just been duped by her father into believing Tyrone has betrayed them, when the landlord is spotted coming down the road. Josie tells Hogan to allay Tyrone's possible suspicions about their conversation by pretending to be so drunk "you don't remember what he's done, so he can't suspect you told me" (89), while Josie pretends to be so outraged at her father's inebriation that she is driving him off the farm for the night. The miniature scene is over after ten lines, accomplishing its

A Moon for the Misbegotten

purpose of fooling Tyrone and clearing the stage for the intended seduction. The tone, however, quickly changes following Hogan's departure. The two lovers joke with one another, each having a plot in mind: Tyrone that of achieving forgiveness from his mother through Josie, and Josie that of revenging herself (and also satisfying her deeper yearnings) through sex with Tyrone. But the departure of the master comic schemer, Phil Hogan, ultimately permits the true feelings of love, sexual attraction—and the tragic futility of both—to emerge. Thus, this tiny inner play shifts the play from comedy to tragedy, and as the final scene in the three-scene sequence of inner plays, it also dramatizes another shift, this one in Jim Tyrone. In the first, he had been performer, trading witty lines with Hogan in a "game about a drink"; in the second, he served as expectant, knowledgeable audience, both amused by (and contributing to) the plot to rout Harder; in the last, he is ignorant audience, unaware that he is witnessing a contrived scene. Almost imperceptibly, O'Neill has removed the character from the centre of the comic inner dramas to their periphery. The playwright thereby suggests both the death wish of Tyrone, who wants to remove himself from the drama of life, and his corresponding desire to abandon role-playing altogether as a form of insincerity which masks the deeper reality of death.

The same shift from comedy to tragedy and from role to reality occurs in another set of events, these ones narrated by the three characters. Three anecdotes about performances by the Hogans and Tyrone are structured to move from distant to recent past, and from a comic con game which fools nobody to a histrionic display of grief which takes in everyone but the performer himself. The first reminiscence is shared by Josie and Hogan, and concerns their periodic visits from Jim Tyrone's father following their repeated failures to pay the rent when Josie was a girl. Hogan's script each time was to dress Josie up, make her "skip down the path to meet him, and make him a courtesy, and hold on to his hand, and bat [her] eyes at him and lead him in the house, and offer him a drink of the good whiskey [Hogan] didn't keep for company, and gape at him and tell him he was the handsomest man in the world" (25-6). Enter Hogan, threatening to "vacate the premises unless he lowered the rent and painted the house"; exit the elder Tyrone's intentions, for he would always succumb to the transparent performances and "by the time he left we were too busy cursing England to worry over the rent" (25-6).

However, this is not simply a tale of knave and fool. Josie recalls that Tyrone "always saw through [Hogan's] tricks," including his costuming and direction of Josie; and Hogan knew this, for "all I wanted was to give him the fun of seeing through them so he couldn't be hard-hearted" (26). The recounted episode serves to comment indirectly on the game performed by comedy as a genre, and by the play itself. Like his son, Tyrone *père* enjoys playing the game with Hogan, "telling stories and singing songs" while remaining aware that it is an artful contrivance designed to make him forget his purpose. He is simultaneously involved and detached, resembling the audience at a comedy like *As You Like It* or *The Importance of Being Earnest*—or the first two acts of *A Moon for the Misbegotten*—which enjoys the plot contrivances despite their violation of probability. And undeniably, it is difficult to be hard-hearted toward any of the characters of *A Moon for the Misbegotten* as a result. Later, however, O'Neill challenges the audience's comic detachment as he moves toward tragedy. That move exposes the artificiality of the previous comic contrivances, contrivances epitomized by this short narrative of a father and small daughter half-conning their elderly landlord; for the plotting is contrasted with the sobering, unredeemable reality of death, symbolized by Jim Tyrone, which resists all of man's attempts at seduction.

As the first anecdote foreshadows the later attempted seduction, so does the second. This description of a past performance involves the undergraduate Jim Tyrone and a prostitute. Introducing "Dutch Maisie" as his sister, he costumes her in black, gives her "a pound of Sen-Sen to kill the gin on her breath," and shows her around the campus with one of the priests; but the scheme explodes when she delivers her exit line, "Christ, Father, it's nice and quiet here away from the damned Six Avenue El. I wish to hell I could stay here!" (39). The slippage of the virginal role she had assumed is amusing (though it cost Jim his Bachelor's degree), but it also foreshadows Josie's surrender of her non-virginal role in the next act. Indeed, all three characters drop their masks in the play's later acts—as does the play itself, in its movement from comedy to tragedy. And the ambiguity as to whether or not her unmasking was "mischievous" or innocent becomes a more serious question when applied to the subsequent behaviour of Tyrone, who has difficulty differentiating between role-playing and sincere self-preservation.

Tyrone's problems with role-playing are the subject of the final performance anecdote. Describing his behavior at the viewing of his mother's corpse, Tyrone recalls how "I found I couldn't feel anything....But there were several people standing around and I knew they expected me to show something. Once a ham, always a ham! So I put on an act. I flopped on my knees and hid my face in my hands and faked some sobs and cried, 'Mama! Mama! My dear mother!' But all the time I kept saying to myself, 'You lousy ham! You God-damned lousy ham!'" (148). Unable to accept the form his grief has taken, the insecure Tyrone capitulates to (possibly imagined) audience demands for an overt sideplay of sorrow, and inwardly curses himself for the performance. Nor is this awareness of insincerity limited to a particular event, for he not only regrets his former "career as a third rate ham" (128), but also repeatedly admonishes Josie to discount his words in the present.

In this instance, Tyrone is clearly too hard on himself. However contrived the performance, the grief over his mother's death is genuine: hence, his pursuit of Josie as a mother-substitute, and his desire to join his mother in death. More pertinent to my concern is O'Neill's decision to explore this behavior in a character with a theatrical background. Admittedly, this aspect of Tyrone's character corresponds to his real-life model, Jamie O'Neill, who appeared in various minor roles in New York and on tour. But within the play, Tyrone's professional background gives his awareness of role-playing a certain authority, serving to emphasize the theatrical frame in which the play recurrently poses its psychological and existential questions. Via Jamie, O'Neill explores the Pirandellian theme of the differences between self and role; and his exploration illuminates the deeper themes of death and the determinism of the past which lie at the centre of the play.

Since Tyrone is a man of roles, he enters theatrically, performing a vaudeville routine with Hogan. So, we might recall, did Hickey perform upon entrance in *The Iceman Cometh*;[15] and like Hickey, Tyrone secretly yearns to confess the painful past experience his charming mask is designed to conceal. As noted above, Tyrone has also played the role of grieving son at the viewing of his mother's body—a role he repudiates as a histrionic counterfeit of sorrow. Another part he plays is that of a reciter of poetry, who quotes Keats, Rossetti, Shakespeare, and Dowson. This too is discounted, for on each occasion he either recites mockingly or afterwards chides himself for resorting to "the old poetic bull, eh? Crap!" (135). But even that cynicism is a pose, one which (unexpectedly) connects him to another late O'Neill protagonist, Con Melody of *A Touch of the Poet*. As Richard Hornby has recently observed, Melody is one of numerous examples of involuntary, compulsive role-playing found in modern drama;[16] and just as complex psychological factors drive Melody to masquerade as a English gentleman, guilt determines Tyrone's role of cynic, complete with *"habitually cynical expression"* (37).

Tyrone's cynicism masks the self-loathing exposed at the end of act two when, *"with intense hatred,"* he accuses himself of being a "rotten bastard" (107). Later, he thanks Josie for "not believing I'm rotten louse. Everyone else believes it—including myself—for a damned good reason" (133). The reason, of course, is his betrayal of his mother, which generates the desire for reunion with her in death. Paradoxically, the guilty yearning for self-annihilation constitutes the core to the self that lies beneath Tyrone's roles. For the protagonist, then, the battle between self and role expresses the existential conflict between death and life. "Look at him when he thinks no one is watching, with his eyes on the ground," remarks the sensitive Josie prior to Tyrone's entrance: "Like a dead man walking slow behind his own coffin" (25). In Josie's company, Tyrone is neurotically aware of the parts he plays, and is repeatedly driven by his self-contempt to repudiate them; when unaware of audience, Tyrone nakedly seeks that oblivion which would free him from all roles.

The result is occasional confusion between self and role, as in a crucial scene in Act Three which relates that confusion to Tyrone's struggle between fate and free will. Josie, having learned that Tyrone never betrayed them, finally yields to his sincere entreaties to abandon her "brazen-trollop act" (136), and (ironically) invites him into her bedroom. During her speech, *"a strange change has come over [Tyrone's] face,"* and *"he looks her over now with a sneering cynical lust"* and addresses her like a whore. When the horrified Josie resists, Tyrone first blames the drink, then mutters to himself, "Must have drawn a blank for a while. Nuts! Cut out the faking. I knew what I was doing. But it's funny. I *was* seeing things. That's the truth, Josie. For a moment I thought you were the blond pig" (137-8). The behaviour of Tyrone here reiterates his brotherhood with other compulsive characters like Hickey, Con Melody, and Mary Tyrone in *Long Day's Journey Into Night*, for whom a past role overwhelms the present ones. But Tyrone, the self-professed "third-rate ham actor," possesses more self-consciousness about role-playing than these characters; and this allows O'Neill to explore the character's inner struggle between will and fate in more theatrical terms.

"Cut out the faking": this line is central to Tyrone's character and attitudes.

Repeatedly, he entreats Josie to abandon her mask of trollop, and debunks or parodies his own performances. He desires for this one night to penetrate behind roles in order to expose his genuine guilt and suffering. But when he confuses Josie's loving sexual offer with the purchased favours of the blonde whore, he instinctively responds by slipping on the cynical mask again. Confronted by Josie's response, he quickly recovers, first denying responsibility ("must have drawn a blank"), but then assuming it: "I knew what I was doing." Characteristically, he strives to interpret his "sneering cynical lust" as willed behaviour typical of his "rotten" self. But clearly, the act is a spontaneous one in which a past role defeats (momentarily, at least) Tyrone's intention to be vulnerable before Josie.

From this angle, the scene distantly recalls the climactic moment in Pirandello's *Henry IV*, in which the protagonist suddenly stabs his enemy Belcredi, and thus condemns himself to continue in the role of madman which he longs to escape. Does Henry's violent act contradict his insane role, or confirm it? Is the murder attempt conscious and deliberate, or determined—fated—by unconscious drives? As in Pirandello, the line between self and role blurs here: is the "real" Tyrone the lusting cynic (as he believes), or the "dead man walking slow behind his own coffin" that Josie identifies? His past role on the train so haunts him that, unsummoned, it momentarily overtakes him in the present: it can scarcely be distinguished from the self. Thus (as is usual in the play), the mildly self-conscious exploration of a theatrical theme—the conflict between self and role—is here subsumed into a more dominant theme, the tyranny of the past. The past is Tyrone's fate, as he recognizes when he claims "there is no present or future. Only the past happening over and over again—now. You can't get away from it." (128). Tyrone's deepest self, beneath all roles, is fated by the past to destroy itself, as Josie reluctantly acknowledges following his confession. "Oh, Jim, Jim, maybe my love could still save you, if you could want it enough! *(She shakes her head)* No. That can never be" (153). The past as fatalistic determinant permeates Tyrone's behaviour, creating both the roles he yearns to abandon, and the longing for death which will furnish his vehicle of escape.

Tyrone's subsequent confession about the whore on his mother's funeral train again reveals the fated nature of his behaviour, this time in more explicitly theatrical language. Revealing his hope that the blonde hooker would help him forget his mother's death, he reconsiders: "No, it couldn't have been that. Because I didn't seem to want to forget. It was like some plot I had to carry out. The blonde—she didn't seem to matter. She was only something that belonged in the plot. It was as if I wanted revenge" (149-150). The speech puns on "plot" as a scheme (in a play full of them) and plot as a way of designing a dramatic action. In the latter sense, Tyrone once again feels himself trapped in a role in a "plot I had to carry out": here, a revenge scenario directed against his mother. But his realization that "it was as if I wanted revenge" reveals Tyrone's suspicion that he is author of this subconscious drama. Again, the role he plays actually seems fated, determined by unconscious drives that trap him in such plots until death. Like a Pirandello or Stoppard character, Tyrone here, and in the previous encounter with Josie, resembles an actor yearning to be free of his prescribed roles inside his play. But the only freedom for him lies in death, outside life altogether. For both the comedy of the opening acts and the tragedy of the closing ones demonstrate that role-playing is man's fate. Hogan, the play's comic spirit, responds to this by playing his roles with full awareness, and inventing plots which manipulate others. But Tyrone, the tragic spirit of the final acts, plays his roles with a disabling self-consciousness, and repeatedly finds himself in scripts over which he has no control.

As the creative artist still brimming with ideas for new plots as he began writing *A Moon for the Misbegotten*, O'Neill probably found it easy to project himself into Hogan; as the ailing semi-invalid who finished the script two years later, aware that he was fated to begin no more, O'Neill may have empathized more with Tyrone. But the past and present performances of both characters, as well as Josie, make it clear that self-conscious role-playing is a condition of existence in the play's dramatic world, and (by implication) in the "real" world as well. This, of course, is not the first time O'Neill has dramatized this idea. *The Great God Brown, Lazarus Laughed, Mourning Becomes Electra* and *Days Without End* all exhibit visual masquerading: the thought asides of *Strange Interlude* and *Dynamo* offer aural variations on the same theme. But however experimental those earlier works, none makes such extensive metaphorical use of the theatre as does *A Moon for the Misbegotten*. Its inner plays, as well as its anecdotes, continually remind us in subtle ways that we—like Josie and Tyrone in the opening act—are witnesses of a contrived performance. And the final acts make clear, in the anguished condition of the former actor Jim Tyrone, that to eschew performing is to deny life itself. Late in the fourth act, O'Neill finally announces his metatheatrical theme. Tyrone has awakened after falling asleep on the comforting Josie's breast after his confession, and is faced with a new feeling, whose origin he can't identify: "Sort of at peace with myself and this lousy life—as if all my sins had been forgiven" (171). Moments later, he faces the east and witnesses *"an exceptionally beautiful sunrise,"* and is *"profoundly moved but immediately becomes self-conscious and tries to sneer it off,"* proclaiming "God seems to be putting on quite a display. I like Belasco better. Rise of curtain, Act-Four stuff" (172). On the realistic plane, the behaviour is perfectly in character, as the insecure Tyrone claps on the cynical mask to hide his feelings; but it also comments on the play, aware of itself as theatrical artifact.

Characteristically, the play reverts quickly to its realistic core, as Tyrone's deeper emotions replace his self-conscious posing. "God damn it! Why do I have to pull that lousy stuff?" he mutters, and *"with genuine deep feeling"* admits "God, its beautiful, Josie! I-I'll never forget it—here with you" (172). The similar subtle self-reflexiveness displayed by O'Neill in crafting the characters and themes of this drama is not "lousy stuff," however, but his final, veiled commentary on his chosen medium; and as such, it provides insight into not only *A Moon for the Misbegotten*, but suggests a largely overlooked dimension of O'Neill's final plays.

NOTES

1. *Forging a Language: A Study of the Plays of Eugene O'Neill* (London: Cambridge University Press, 1979), 188-189.

2. Of the numerous studies of metatheatre, the most pertinent to my approach are those which deal (exclusively or in part) with modern theatre: Lionel Abel, *Metatheatre* (New York: Hill and Wang, 1963); Robert J. Nelson, *Play within a Play* (New Haven: Yale University Press, 1958); June Schlueter, *Metafictional Characters in Modern Drama* (New York: Columbia University Press, 1979); and Richard Hornby, *Drama, Metadrama and Perception* (Lewisburg, Pa.: Bucknell University Press, 1986).

3. *Eugene O'Neill*, 2nd edition (Boston: Twayne, 1979), 161.

4. *O'Neill: Son and Artist* (Boston: Little, Brown, 1973), 533.

5. Quoted in Arthur and Barbara Gelb, *O'Neill*, enlarged edition (New York: Harper and Row, 1973), 845.

6. Quoted in Gelb, 846.

7. Sheaffer, 541.

8. Gelb, 847.

9. See Michael Hinden, "Desire and Forgiveness: O'Neill's Diptych" (*Comparative Drama*, 14,3 [Fall1980], 240-250, which argues that Tyrone's reference to "Act Four stuff" in the play's Act Four "seems almost a farewell" which calls to mind Prospero's Epilogue in *The Tempest* (249). Also see Norman Berlin, *Eugene O'Neill* (New York: Grove, 1982), which briefly notes more general similarities between the plays of O'Neill's final phase and those of Shakespeare (129).

10. *A Moon for the Misbegotten* (New York: Random House, 1952), 23. All subsequent references will be documented in the next.

11. Michael Manheim, In *Eugene O'Neill's New Language of Kinship* (New York: Random House, 1982), also notices the resemblance between O'Neill and Hogan. Manheim describes "a Phil Hogan streak in [O'Neill's] own nature," from which he manufactures a mood for his audience suitable to Phil's comic intrigues," and "then pulls the rug out from under that audience" (194).

12. The movement from comedy to tragedy is typical of O'Neill's late plays. For recent analyses, see Carpenter, 148, 160; Berlin, 137-38, 142, 150, ; and my "Convergence and Divergences: Father and Son in *A Touch of the Poet* and *The Iceman Cometh*," *American Literature*, 59, 3 October 1987), [page numbers not yet available].

13. *O'Neill's Scenic Images* (Princeton: Princeton University Press, 1968), 312.

14. See Manheim: "It is then as a commentary upon the theatrical heritage he is rejecting...that O'Neill in the play knowingly tricks the audience" (*Kinship*, 194). That "heritage," asserts Professor Manheim, is specifically that of the well-made play. In a separate article, Professor Manheim claims that the play mocks, then transcends, the conventions of melodrama as well ("O'Neill's Transcendence of Melodrama in *A Touch of the Poet* and *A Moon for the Misbegotten*," *Comparative Drama*, 16,3 [Fall 1982], 238-50). I would go further than Professor Manheim and broaden the theatrical heritage to include all dramatic constructions—well-made, melodramatic, or otherwise—which are here exposed, but not necessarily rejected.

15. The stage directions for Hickey's initial appearance read, *"He immediately puts on an entrance act, places a hand affectedly on his chest, throws back his head, and sings in a falsetto*

tenor" (*The Plays of Eugene O'Neill*, III [New York: Random House, 1953], 619).

16. *Drama, Metadrama and Perception*, 82.

Perspectives on O'Neill: New Essays. Ed. Shyamal Bagchee. Victoria, British Columbia: University of Victoria, 1988, 61-75.

Portman, Hayes and Stanley Magnificent in *Touch of Poet*

John Chapman

What power Eugene O'Neill has! I know perfectly well that he died in 1953, and that the last play he ever completed was called *A Touch of the Poet*. But as I sat watching the first New York performance of this drama last evening at the Helen Hayes Theatre there slowly grew upon me a strange feeling that it was a living O'Neill, and not director Harold Clurman, who was driving Eric Portman toward and into the shattering, bloodchilling climax.

O'Neill was there—and up to now this season playwrights have been absent from their own plays. This is not great O'Neill, on the scale of *The Iceman Cometh*, *Long Day's Journey Into Night* or some of the earlier works, but it makes much of our contemporary theatre look pallid.

Never one to compromise with commercial formalities of the theatre, O'Neill began *A Touch of the Poet* very slowly, with a great deal of talk about off-stage characters and events—and without offering much in the way of event on the stage. Perhaps he knew—wrongly, as it turned out—that he had plenty of time and that this was merely the beginning of a long series of chronological dramas concerning one family.

But the dramatist moved implacably toward his objective, which was to show the birth of the first American in a dynasty of Americans. And this birth takes place in a middle-aged man—Portman. The agonies of this birth—the parturition of a man from himself—make the throbbing climax of the drama.

The time of the play is 1828 and the setting is a tavern in a village near Boston. The tavern is owned by a tempestuous Irishman, Con Melody, who is as proud as he is ill-tempered. He had been born with wealth in a castle. He had been a major with the Duke of Wellington at the Battle of Talavera. And now he is determined to show his pride and importance to the Yankee townsmen.

He makes a great show of it, cantering about on a blooded mare, quoting poetry at his majestic image in a mirror, donning his splendid British uniform and celebrating each anniversary of Talavera. But the show deludes only himself. He is an Irishman of humble origin in a strange and unfriendly civilization. He is totally in debt. His wife keeps the tavern going; unaccountably, this long-suffering woman adores him. His spirited daughter, whom he treats like a servant and berates as a slut, hates him. But his arrogance continues until at last he is beaten by the Yankee enemy—literally beaten into a coma.

So now he kills himself with a dueling pistol. Not by shooting himself, but by shooting his beloved mare, his one great show piece. This deed means the death of the past, the death of his pretensions, and the birth of a new Con Melody. This is a magnificent scene, and it is magnificently played by Portman.

Magnificent, too, are Kim Stanley as the daughter of Helen Hayes as the wife. Miss Hayes is simply wonderful as a tired, sloppy, bewildered Irishwoman who only knows what love is and that she loves her man. It is she who speaks at the end the obituary of the Con Melody she had loved so long: "He had to live all his life alone in the hell of pride." Once more, Eugene O'Neill gives stature to the theatre.

New York Daily News, October 3, 1958.

Theatre

Gore Vidal

Seven or perhaps eleven plays to encompass all things American from the Revolution to The Way We Live Now; after a number of false starts, the solemn burning of aborted fragments in a hotel room in Boston with only one completed play surviving, *A Touch of the Poet*, set in 1828. What could sound more unpromising? Especially in the wake of that stunning, mawkish bore *Long Day's Journey Into Night*, whose production and reception on Broadway resembled nothing so much as a state funeral, with black plumes waving and sonorous eulogies of the dead master from those who gave so little aid and comfort to the living master for his *The Iceman Cometh* in 1946.

I went to the theatre expecting the worst. Even before the curtain went up, irritable phrases formed in my mind (how often, I wonder, does this happen to professional reviewers?). "Rhetoric is the attempt of the will to do the work of the imagination": W.B. Yeats....I would definitely use that one, for if there was ever a rhetorician it was the late master. Then I recalled my old resentment against his misuse of the *Orestia* when, having crudely borrowed the relationship, the melodrama, the portentousness of Aeschylus, he blithely left out the whole idea of justice which was, to say the least, the point of that tragedy. And, finally the maddening urge of American primitives to include everything—to write cycles, tetralogies, epics, the whole hee-haw of the Thomas Wolfes as they list the rivers of America in alphabetical order, their minds innocent of civilization, their self-love filling the empty plains of a new continent which ought to have a tragedy, though just what it is no one has yet discovered.

The curtain rose. Two minor characters started talking. One's heart sank as they explained at length necessary secrets. By then I had worked through Henry James: "It takes a very great deal of history to make a very small bit of literature," when suddenly the stage was bathed in light: Helen Hayes and Stanley were on; the drama had begun and O'Neill blazed.

A Touch of the Poet is a beautiful play, beautifully presented. It has but one fault, to which I shall come last; its virtues more than compensate. The play is *rose* not *noire* and it has a deliberate artifice, which I prefer to the shapeless black melodramas O'Neill usually preferred. Then, too, 1828 is just right: Andrew Jackson; the rise of the democrats; the fall of J.Q. Adams and with him that oligarchical, gentlemanly society which began the nation. All this is symbolically right, and pleasing. It is time we used our bit of history; especially since the New York audience has practically no sense of the United States before the First War. Lincoln, of course, is recalled, glumly; it is known that there was some sort of Revolution at the beginning, and that's it—almost as if Van Wyck Brooks had never lived.

O'Neill reminds us of our past. He indicates the rise of the Yankee merchants, busy, practical contemptuous of the old aristocratic principle. With precision and—for him—economy, he sets the scene for his moral action which is the crushing of a man's false pride, his absorption into the main, his final realization that he has lived a bogus life, presuming a position both worldly and moral to which he has no right but the one—and this is significant—of wanting.

Cornelius Melody (Eric Portman) was born of Irish peasants, served bravely in the Peninsular campaign, became a British officer, got pregnant a peasant girl, married her, came to America, opened a tavern and failed. He torments his wife (Helen Hayes) and his daughter (Kim Stanley); he quotes Byron to himself in a mirror. He assumes the manner of a king in exile. He is laughed at by the Yankees, but adored by his wife who understands him perhaps more profoundly in O'Neill than she would in life: she sees how lonely he is in his vanity (very Meredithean, this) and she loves him. He is alternately mocked and served by his daughter, a finely realized character, part dreamer, part materialist, veering this way and that, ambivalent and strange.

The story is simple. The daughter loves a Yankee of the new merchant class. He has escaped his family to write poetry but eventually he will go into business—happily. The girl must marry him to escape the world of unpaid bills and false pride. She also loves him and wants to cheat neither of them. His family deplores the match. They try to buy her off. Melody, drunk, goes to a duel; he is beaten up by the police (dressed as a major of the British army); he returns, pride gone, and in a incredible *volteface* chooses reality to prideful illusion: he is only a Mick and a failure who loves his wife. The girl gets her Yankee, and all ends well.

What makes the play work thematically is the examination of Melody's dream world. It may well be that this is the most significant American theme, at least in the twentieth century. Reality does not please him; he chooses to invent his past; he tells lies; he believes the lies and for various reasons is abetted in them by those about him. O'Neill has often dealt with this theme (*The Iceman Cometh*, for example) and so have many of our best writers, most notably Tennessee Williams in *A Streetcar Named Desire*. Which brings us to an interesting question: What is it in modern American life (1828 is as good a date as any to start the "modern") which forces so many to prefer fantasy to reality? One observes them, at any cocktail party: charming people, boring people, intelligent, dull—people of all sorts, telling lies, which no one much minds. It is all a game. Who shall I be? Who am I? And the person who drops the brick of truth is the only villain.

It is to this that the audience of *A Touch of the Poet* most responds. There is an element of Melody in all of us and one watches with horrified fascination as he is brought at last to the truth about himself.

As for the production, it is splendid. Mr. Clurman has taken the three most mannered actresses in our theatre and imposed the play's manner on them with complete success. Miss Hayes is strong and direct and very moving; her cute pony-prancing severely curbed. Betty Field, whose old voice I always liked, has quite a new one which works admirably in her single scene. But the production's glory is Kim Stanley's performance. The old tricks are there but they glitter and she gets the character's ambivalence with such fairness that one is reminded of a character in Dostoevski: light and shadow mysteriously fluctuating; the "yes" and the simultaneous "no." It is fine work.

The play's flaw is the performance of Eric Portman. He is a fine technical actor whose attack here is unfortunately wrong. He belongs, at least when he plays bravuras, to what I think of as the "voice-music" school of English acting whose honorary president is Sir Ralph Richardson. The voice-musicians hear some strange melody in the wings to which in counterpoint they sing their lines. Their songs are often fascinating but almost always irrelevant to the play's meaning. Mr. Portman is far better in the small neat plays of Terence Rattigan, because in the naturalistic idiom one can gobble and honk and sigh and mumble and the meaning is always clear. Major Melody needs grandeur and thought, neither of which Mr. Portman provides. As I watched him strut about the stage on his spindly legs, his swollen body held tightly erect, like a pineapple on two sticks, I was haunted by *dèja vu;* not until the final scene did I recall who it was he reminded me of: a maleficent Mr. Micawber—and the moment one plays Melody like Micawber, O'Neill is brought down.

Happily, there are so many good things in this production—including the play—that the thing works, and one is pleased that Eugene O'Neill's last play should be at once so human and so gently wise.

Nation, October 25, 1958.

Theatre: Dream Addict

T.E. Kalem

O'Neill's magnificent obsession was that a life of illusions is unpardonable but that life without illusions is unbearable. This produces the fierce tension at the heart of his dramatic imagination.

In *A Touch of the Poet*, as elsewhere, O'Neill dramatizes, in the agitated course of a single day, the downward course of a lifetime. He tells of a man whose life would crumble except for his dreams and whose dreams themselves fall apart

A Touch of the Poet

at last. And as so often in O'Neill, *Poet* has centripetal force and centrifugal wastefulness, giant strength and giant sprawl, sure theatrical instincts and shaky dramatic structure. The present revival at Broadway's Helen Hayes Theater is like a tidal wave that seems to purge almost every defect of the play.

The setting is a tavern near Boston. The time in 1828. The hero is an O'Neill staple, the man of illusion-cum-sorrows, bottle-fed. With the aid of drink, Con Melody (Jason Robards) cultivates a highly colored remembrance of things past—the Gaelic gallant seducing the lovelies of Europe, the fearless cavalry major decorated on a Spanish field of honor by the great Wellington himself. In sorry reality, he is an impoverished tavern keeper too proud to tend bar as his father did in Ireland. Indeed, pride hagrides Con Melody, like the Greek Furies, except that he is driven more toward travesty than tragedy. In his scarlet dragoon's uniform, he preens before a mirror and loftily mouths stanzas from Byron. Playing the highborn gentleman, though fooling no one, Con charges over the countryside on a thoroughbred mare while reducing his daughter to a barroom slave. He sneers at the Yankees as vulgar traders while owing them money and enjoying none of their trade.

His fiery daughter Sara (Kathryn Walker) has a wealthy young Yankee in tow, and when it comes out that the boy's father wants no truck with the peat-bog Melodys, Con rides swaggeringly forth to avenge such an insult by issuing a dueling challenge. Terribly beaten by the police, Con stumbles home in a state of catatonic silence, all the posturing and pride crushed out of him. This time he goes forth only to kill the last emblem of his dream, his blooded mare, his Byronic self.

As confirmed a dream addict as any of the tosspots in *The Iceman Cometh*, Con Melody is unlike them in having a family around him—a low-born wife Nora (Geraldine Fitzgerald), who unfalteringly loves him, his mettlesome daughter Sara who is increasingly roused to hate. Yet each inspires in him only a more desolating sense of aloneness. In the costly family game of lies and consequences, Con bears more than a few resemblances to O'Casey's Paycock.

And a few, as well, to James Tyrone, the actor-patriarch of *Long Day's Journey Into Night*, whom O'Neill modeled on his own father. Con dwells on Wellington's praise of his combat heroics as Tyrone dwells on Edwin Booth's praise of his acting. Both men are united in a fear of the poverty of Ireland and a desire to conceal their peasant origins. Both loathe the modern currents of their times, Melody despises the Jacksonian rabble just as Tyrone reviles such (to him) modern playwrights as Strindberg and Ibsen.

An actor must be steeped in O'Neill to draw out the full resonances in the character of Con Melody. For over two decades, Jason Robards has displayed a symbiotic rapport with this great and haunted playwright. Director José Quintero's affinity is no less close. The pair seem attuned not only to O'Neill's text but also to his troubled soul. To the role of Con Melody, Robards brings the deepest brooding eyes of profound melancholy, the harsh self-lacerating laugh that masks inner pain, the actorish stance of assuming, while mocking, the grand manner, the human love that becomes inhuman cruelty under the distillation of alcohol. This is a performance that will go into the record books of acting.

The rest of the cast is undauntably fine. There is a quietly moving tenacity shining blade of courage. As the daughter Sara, Kathryn Walker beautifully balances an audacity of spirit with an awakening of sensual desire. She has a shatteringly powerful scene in which she goes up the stairs to claim by seduction the man she has lost in aborted courtship and later comes back down glowing in a bodily halo of fulfilled love. Like a gift of grace, all of the actors bring to this play what it sometimes lacks—the multipowered intensity of cumulative passion.

Time, January 9, 1978.

A Touch of the Poet: Memory and the Creative Imagination

Laurin Porter

A Touch of the Poet, the only surviving play of the cycle which O'Neill completed, encapsulates the themes that the historical cycle was to treat: the clash of cultures, the power of the past, the destructiveness of ambition. Set in 1828, *Poet*, which would have been the fifth of the eleven-play series, dramatizes the union of the Irish immigrant Melody clan with the aristocratic Yankee Harfords through the marriage of Sara Melody, the daughter of Con and Nora, and Simon, the son of Deborah and Henry Harford. As we reconstruct the stories of Simon's forebears from O'Neill's notes and work diaries, it becomes clear that each generation in the dynasty repeats in its own fashion the sins of its ancestors; the character traits and idiosyncracies of one generation reappear cyclically in the next. At the same time, we follow the linear progress of succeeding generations, representative of various stages in America's historical evolution. Deborah, Henry, and Simon Harford, for instance, represent three successive sociological generations of Yankees (a matter that is dealt with in *More Stately Mansions*...). Deborah is characterized by bizarre aristocratic fantasies that link her with the decadent European past from which the original Puritans fled; Henry is the rugged individual, the entrepreneur who builds the family empire; Simon, his son, rebelling against his father's materialism, places a Thoreauvian faith in nature and the goodness of the common man.

In Nora, Con, and Sara Melody, the principal characters of *A Touch of the Poet*, we see three corresponding generations of Irish immigrants. Con was born and raised on a country estate in Ireland purchased by his father, old Ned Melody, a "thievin' shebeen keeper who got rich by moneylendin' and squeezin' tenants and every manner of trick." According to Jamie Cregan, Con's cousin from Ireland who shows up the day before the play's action takes place, when Ned had saved enough money, "he married, and bought an estate with a pack of hounds and set up as one of the gentry" (*Poet* 11). Con's aristocratic past, of which he is fiercely proud, is somewhat qualified by its origins, as well as by the fact that he married Nora, the beautiful daughter of peasants on his estate. He achieved some status by going off to school in Dublin and later rising in the ranks of the British army, where he distinguished himself in battle. But after his promotion to major he was caught making love to the wife of a Spanish nobleman; a duel ensued, and when Con killed the Spaniard, he was forced to resign from the army in disgrace. He took his wife and infant daughter to America to try his fortune but fell on bad times. It is only through the hard work of Sara, now twenty, and the long-suffering Nora that Con is able to maintain his aristocratic pretensions.

In this configuration of characters, Nora, an untutored, hard-working woman who looks old beyond her years, clearly represents the first-generation immigrant. Her Celtic origins are evident in her thick brogue, Irish syntax, and peasant superstitions. Doctors bring bad luck, she says. Although she has abjured her faith to marry Con—she was pregnant at the time and thus married without the church's blessing—she still adheres to the simple belief that her "sin" with Con has brought bad luck upon the family that only a priest can vanquish. Her tolerant attitude towards Con's constant drinking illustrates the typical Irish acceptance of the ubiquitous bottle of whiskey. (Sara's priggishness about drinking represents the other side of this cultural coin.)

Nora's defining characteristic is her selfless devotion to Con, despite his insults and harsh treatment. Her love is the source of her pride and dignity; it is the very core of her existence and gives her life shape and meaning. When her daughter berates her for her slavish obedience to Con's unreasonable demands, she replies, "For the love of God, don't take the pride of my love from me, Sara, for without it what am I at all but an ugly, fat woman gettin' old and sick!" (*Poet* 26). She is an Irish matriarch through and through. As mediator between father and daughter, who are at odds much of the time, she stands at the center of the family unit.

It is this selfless love that wins the admiration of the inn's barkeeper, Mickey Maloy, another first-generation immigrant. Both he and Jamie Cregan prefer Nora to Sara, whom Mickey berates for her "grand lady's airs." What they sense is that Nora remains pure Irish; Sara, who has assimilated American values and mannerisms, has become a stranger in their midst.

Nora, then, along with Maloy and Cregan, represents the first-generation immigrant, still thoroughly Irish and loyal to the motherland. Con's free-loading drinking companions, Roche, O'Dowd, and Riley, also belong to this camp. As such, they retain a certain dignity, even though Con and Sara treat them like peasants. The fact is, they *are* peasants. Yet, though dressed in rags and tatters, they are not as helpless as they might seem. Irishmen all, they use their native wit to maintain a constant source of free whiskey, quite consciously playing peasant to Con's "master." When Con dons his officer's uniform in celebration of the anniversary of Talavera, O'Dowd calls Con "a lunatic, sittin' like a play-actor in his red coat." But when Roche curses him for wearing "the bloody red av England," O'Dowd replies, "Don't be wishin' him harm, for it's thirsty we'd be without him. Drink long life to him, and may he always be as big as fool as he is this night!" (*Poet* 100). Thus, while Con is using them to play supporting roles in his grand drama, they are also using him.

The second generation is represented by Con himself. Even though he, like Nora, is literally a first-generation immigrant, he acts out the aspirations of the second generation, combining mannerisms and attitudes of the old country with those of the new. For the bulk of the play, Con desperately insists upon his acculturation. He eschews the brogue and calls Sara a "peasant wench" when she uses it. He wants America to crush England in the next war (which he feels is "inevitable") only to revenge himself on England for disgracing him. Nora, typically, thinks solely in terms of the mother country. When England is driven from the face of the earth, "we'll free Ireland!" she says. Melody's contemptuous response is, "Ireland? What benefit would freedom be to her unless she could be freed from the Irish?" (*Poet* 40). To identify with America, he must sever ties with his Irish past.

Yet he still retains evidences of his Gaelic blood. It is peasant vitality that informs Con's view that the Yankees are "fish-blooded" when it comes to making love. "They lack savoir-faire," he says....And though he eschews the brogue in Sara and Nora, he himself slips into it unconsciously on occasion. When Riley sings "Modideroo," an old Irish hunting song, for instance, Melody's eyes light up and he "for[gets] himself, a strong lilt of brogue coming into his voice" as he recalls fondly the fox hunts on his father's estate (*Poet* 102).

The clearest proof of Con's Irishness, of course, is his response to Henry Harford's insulting bribe when he learns that his son intends to marry Sara. Prior to this point, although Con dismissed Harford as a "money-grubbing trader" and a "Yankee upstart," he was sufficiently impressed with the entrepreneur's wealth and power to regard Simon as a suitable son-in-law. But when he discovers through Henry's lawyer, Gadsby, that Harford is opposed to the match and willing to pay him $3000 to move,[1] Con reverts to his Irish ways. Harford becomes a "swindling trader" and Gadsby, "Yankee scum," and Con boots him down the street. He vows to duel Harford, even though Sara protests the inappropriateness of this response: "You're not in Ireland in the old days now. The days of duels are long past and dead, in this part of America anyway. Harford will never fight you" (*Poet* 125). But his blood is aroused, and his Irish pride must be vindicated. It is this episode that rallies all the Irish townsmen behind Con, though they've taken issue with his uppity ways heretofore; this incident would not be possible if he had totally assimilated American values.

It is significant that Melody's transformation at the play's end is to that of Irish *peasant*. The peasant-aristocrat polarity, like that of the Irish-Yankee one, becomes an axis around which the play's issues cluster. Con's history provides an illustration of the effort to rise through the social ranks, to advance from peasant to aristocrat. Old Ned Melody's efforts to establish himself as one of the gentry are doomed, of course, from the outset, since they occur outside the established social constructs. Ireland had no aristocracy of its own, so Melody tried to simulate the status of the British landowning class which then held sway. When none of the gentry would associate with him, he sent Con off to Dublin with "sloos of money to prove himself the equal of any gentleman's son. But Con found, while there was plenty to drink on him and borrow money, there was few didn't sneer behind his back at his pretensions" (*Poet* 12).

Con finally had to join the English to attain the status he sought. When he became an officer in the British army, he got the chance he wanted "in Portugal and Spain where a British officer was welcome in the gentry's houses. At home, the only women he'd known was whores" (*Poet* 13). Thus, in spite of his father's newly acquired wealth, Con must join forces with the British to achieve social status, and then, only when abroad. Even this does not last; he is ultimately forced to resign his commission in disgrace in spite of his valor in battle.

Because nineteenth-century Ireland did not allow for social mobility, Con left for America. In the land of opportunity and unlimited freedom, a country where "a rich gentleman's son" like Simon could spend a year "living like a tramp or a tinker" (which Nora, with her Irish soul, can never understand), social structures would seem to be nonexistent; a man of Con's wealth and education should rise readily through the ranks. This, however, does not come to pass—a fact which is at the root of Sara's scorn for her father. "He's the easiest fool ever came to America!" she says. "It's that I hold against him as much as anything, that when he came here the chance was before him to make himself all his lies pretended to be...." (*Poet* 26). Sara, as the third immigrant generation, articulates the American dream with passionate conviction. What she fails to understand is that it is Con's Irish mentality that prevents the dream's fulfillment. "The Yanks swindled him when he came here, getting him to buy this inn by telling him a new coach line was going to stop here," she recalls bitterly. Her anger, which is directed at Con, might be (and on some level, *is*) more appropriately focused upon the "Yanks" who took advantage of the immigrant's ignorance. A stranger in a strange land, Melody did not learn the new ways quickly enough (i.e., he did not become a Yankee) and so lived out the part of the traditional country bumpkin fleeced by the crafty locals.

Stripped of his fortune, Con is reduced once again to the level of peasant (or, more accurately, since an English-dominated Ireland did not allow for any other status, he is forced to acknowledge his true condition). But it is a role he refuses to accept. Desperately fighting to retain a sense of dignity which, for Con, only accrues to the upper class, he insists upon being regarded as a gentleman. He backs Quincy Adams over "that idol of the riffraff, Andrew Jackson" (*Poet* 37). He is not Melody, the innkeeper, but "*Major* Cornelius Melody."

Con has been cast aside—first, by a country that allowed no upward mobility, then by a society which held out a false promise of acceptance. The crux of his cultural dilemma, then, is not just the tension between his Irish and Yankee identities; it is his desire to be an aristocrat in the face of his peasant status. Neither Ireland nor America offers him viable cultural strategies and supports for ascending the social scale; neither system allows him dignity and self-respect. His alternatives are represented in Ned Melody, the "thievin' shebeen keeper," and Henry Harford, the cold-blooded, swindling Yankee trader. Thus it is significant that Con's regression at the play's end is not just to that of Irishman, but to Irish *peasant*. Similarly, Sara's plea that her father be "himself" again is in terms of his aristocratic pretensions: "Talavera—the Duke praising your bravery—an officer in his army—even the ladies in Spain" (*Poet* 178). In the character of Con Melody, O'Neill depicts the cultural dilemma of the Irish immigrant trying to become an American aristocrat. In the process, he dramatizes the complexities of both cultures, examining the dreams as well as the delusions each holds forth.

Sara Melody completes the cultural family portrait, manifesting both Yankee and Irish traits; predictably, she is even more Americanized than her father. Thus it is appropriate that she will bridge the cultural gap in marrying the Yankee, Simon Harford. Her appearance suggests another cultural polarity in the play. The stage directions indicate that Sara has a fine forehead, small ears, a slender neck, and a thin, straight nose, but her mouth is somewhat coarse and her jaw too heavy; she has large feet and broad, ugly hands with stubby fingers. This mixture of peasant and aristocratic features embodies the inner tension of Con Melody, suspended between the worlds of innkeeper and military hero. Indeed, Sara, perhaps the most complex character in the play, includes qualities of all three of the other major characters—Nora, Deborah, and Con.

In many ways, she is Nora's daughter and thus, instinctively Irish. She has inherited her mother's Irish beauty, with her black hair, fair skin, rosy cheeks, and beautiful, deep blue eyes....Although at first Sara is baffled by Nora's selfless devotion to Con, planning for herself only to "love where it'll gain me freedom and not put me in slavery for life" (Poet 25), by the play's end she, too, has surrendered completely to love. Her seduction of Simon, an act which will lead to a hasty marriage, also links Sara with her Irish mother.

At the same time, she is very much her father's daughter and has assimilated his ways. Like Con, she hates the Yankees, who remind her of her lowly immigrant status. For instance, although she can blarney Neilan, the shopkeeper, into holding their bill over for another month, she finds it humiliating to go "beggin' to a Yankee" (Poet 28). Yet she regards Riley, O'Dowd, and the others as "ignorant shanty scum" and eschews association with them or the old country. Sara has inherited her father's aristocratic pretensions (hence her desire for him to reassume his Major Melody identity at the play's end); she believes as he does that to advance in America she must sever ties with her Irish past. Her use of the brogue to taunt Con demonstrates this understanding; Melody's aristocratic pretensions, which extend to his dreams for Sara's future, are foiled when she slips into the brogue.[2] Likewise, when he wants to retaliate, he refers to Sara's "thick wrists" and "ugly peasant paws," thrusts which wound her to the quick. Con's aristocratic pretensions, like his ambivalent attitude toward his Irish heritage, are passed down to Sara.

But Sara responds to these pretensions in purely American terms. Significantly, she first appears on stage sitting at a desk checking figures in an account book (in anticipation of the desk she will occupy in Simon's office in More Stately Mansions). She is impatient with Nora's superstitious fears of doctors as well as her unwillingness to give her daughter full control of the finances. A pragmatist to the bone, she realizes the impracticality of feeding Con's mare with the money reserved for the family; Nora, with her Irish soul, sees only Con's need for the thoroughbred as a symbol of beauty and romance. Clearly, the manager in this family is Sara—shrewd, practical, with her eye on the main chance.

That chance, of course, is Simon, who will enable her to ascend the social and economic ladder. Unlike Con, who is not as concerned with rising above his station as he is in maintaining his aristocratic pretensions, Sara has completely assimilated the success ideology. She will attain more than just the appearance of wealth. And nothing will stand in her way—not even love. When she admits to her mother that she has fallen in love with Simon, she quickly adds, "But not too much. I'll not let love make me any man's slave...." (*Poet* 31). Thus, too, it is not Con's effort to increase his fortune in New England that Sara reviles, it is the manner in which he fails. Believing that money and education are sufficient to ensure success, she attributes his demise to his own stupidity. "If I was a man with the chance he had," she declares, "there wouldn't be a dream I'd not make come true!" (*Poet* 27). The audience tends to believe her; Sara's determination is matched by a shrewd Yankee pragmatism that has the smell of success about it.[3]

This trio of sociological generations, doubled by the allusions to the Yankee Harfords (all offstage except Deborah) underlies historical progression and the one-way, irreversible nature of chronological time.

This time dimension is reinforced by the fact that the action of the play encompasses a single day, a pattern O'Neill would later repeat in *Long Day's Journey*. As the devastating effects of that long day are reflected in Mary Tyrone's increasingly disheveled appearance and her regression further and further into her past, so the effects of time's passing in *A Touch of the Poet* can be measured by the changes that take place in Con as morning moves on to night. In *Long Day's Journey* O'Neill uses the structural device of family meals to mark off time and help us gauge the extent of change that occurs as the day unfolds, with the final gathering around the table in act 4 an ironic mockery of the shared after-breakfast laughter of the opening scene. In *A Touch of the Poet*, the markers are the four mirror scenes, which measure not only time but also Con's increasingly desperate and finally futile efforts to maintain his dignity by clinging to his Byronic pose.

In the first mirror episode it is morning, and Con's third drink has just begun to take effect. As he catches his reflection in the mirror, he "squares his shoulders defiantly" and stares into the glass, reciting from George Gordon Byron's "Childe Harold" as if it were "an incantation by which he summons pride to justify his life to himself." He completes the entire passage:

> "I have not loved the World, nor the World me;
> I have not flattered Its rank breath, nor bowed
> To its idolatries a patient knee,
> Nor coined my cheek to smiles,—nor cried aloud
> In worship of an echo: in the crowd
> They could not deem me one of such—I stood
> Among them, but not of them...." (*Poet* 43)

Just as he finishes, Sara walks in. He senses her presence and momentarily loses his composure, but he "immediately assumes an air of gentlemanly urbanity and bows to her," quickly gaining control of the situation (*Poet* 44).

The second incident occurs about half an hour and two drinks later. The stage directions inform us that this is "an exact repetition of his scene before the mirror in act I (*Poet* 67). Once again, he completes the chant, but this time he is so absorbed he does not notice when Deborah Harford enters the inn. When she addresses him, "Melody jumps and whirls around. For a moment his face has an absurdly startled, stupid look. He is shamed and humiliated and furious at being caught for the second time in one morning before the mirror" (*Poet* 68). Sara, who has witnessed this scene many times before, is merely contemptuous, a response

Melody deflects smoothly. Deborah stares incredulously, then "smiles with an amused and mocking relish" (*Poet* 67), a reaction that is considerably more devastating to Con's self-esteem.

By act 3, it is evening and Melody is drunk. He has endured humiliation at the hand of Deborah and exchanged bitter words with Sara, who embarrassed him in front of his cronies. The anniversary dinner, an annual ritual commemorating the Battle of Talavera, has failed to produce its usual effect, and Con's pride lies crumbled around him. Left alone at last, "his soldierly erectness sags and his face falls. He looks sad and hopeless and bitter and old" (*Poet* 116). But once again the mirror attracts him and he begins the familiar incantation. This time, however, he is only three lines along when a knock interrupts him. The intruder, Nicholas Gadsby, comes with the final blow to Melody's pride—a bribe from Harford to prevent Sara's marriage. This is the turning point for Con. He can no longer maintain his aristocratic pretense when a real aristocrat treats him like a peasant. From this point on, Con responds as an Irishman. True, he insists he will duel Harford, reverting to the tactics of Major Cornelius Melody over Sara's protestation that the days of duels are long past and gone. But his grandiose threat of revenge turns into a fiasco, and Melody and Cregan end up in jail together—an irony that does not escape Con.

Thus the fourth mirror scene becomes a mockery of the three which preceded it. Physically and psychologically defeated, Melody returns from the brawl after midnight, his scarlet uniform filthy and torn, his face and lips swollen and bloody. This time when his eyes fasten on the mirror, he leers into it and says, "By Jaysus, if it ain't the mirror the auld loon was always admirin' his mug in while he spouted Byron to pretend himself was a lord wid a touch av the poet—" (*Poet* 176). He "strikes a pose which is a vulgar burlesque of his old before-the-mirror-one," and, with Nora and Sara as his audience, recites the Byronic passage in a mocking brogue, guffawing contemptuously afterwards. Having put Major Cornelius Melody to rest, he prepares to join his Irish confreres in the bar: "Be God, *I'm* alive and in the crowd and they *can* deem one av such! I'll be among thim and av thim, too—" (*Poet* 177).

The Function of Memory

The repetition of this mirror scene serves several functions. While it allows O'Neill to shape the action around a central icon, Con's haughty, self-conscious pose in front of the mirror, it also allows the audience to observe the steady disintegration of his Major Melody identity, which depends upon the aloof superiority this ritual is designed to confer. As morning wears on into night and this stance is increasingly difficult to maintain, both Melody and the audience are prepared for Con's ultimate reversion to Irish peasant and his abandonment of his aristocratic aspirations. As such, this progression describes a linear movement. It can be measured, calibrated, divided into units, and its march into the future, like all experiences of historical time, is inexorable and irreversible.

At the same time, memory also plays a crucial role. As Con regards the shambles of his life, his fall from grace—whatever grace he has known—seems complete. Bad business decisions and mismanagement of funds have left him penniless, his dreams come to naught. To salvage what dignity he can, Melody must turn to his days as major of the Seventh Dragoons fighting against the French in Spain and Portugal. As Major Cornelius Melody, Con came into his own, and when that pose threatens to crumble, he performs his ritual incantation.[4] For, as he says to Nora during a poignant exchange in act 2, he has "no future but the past" (*Poet* 63).

The most concrete talisman of that past, of course, is his scarlet full-dress uniform, stored in a trunk of the attic (like Mary Tyrone's wedding gown) and retrieved for the anniversary of the Battle of Talavera, another highly ritualistic sequence at the center of the play which, like the mirror scenes, focuses the relationship between calendar and memory. From all his memories of past glory, Con has singled out one moment which represents value and dignity to him: "the most memorable day of my life," as he tells Deborah Harford. "It was on that glorious field I had the honor to be commended for my bravery by the great Duke of Wellington, himself" (*Poet* 71). This moment becomes an ideal for Con, an epiphany; he regards his life as a gradual but steady decline from that high point—a long slide into the boneyard. Chronological time is thus an enemy, removing Melody even further from his ideal and the possibility of wholeness.

Thus he turns to memory, which, if his imagination is strong enough, allows him to reenter the past and obliterate the interval between. His Byronic recitations are an effort in that direction, but, as we have seen, the present intrudes in the form of, first, Sara, then Deborah, and finally, Gadsby. Donning his scarlet uniform, however, perhaps because its very palpability performs the requisite magic, allows him to successfully turn back the clock. As he enters the room at the end of act 2 in full regalia,

> he looks extraordinarily handsome and distinguished—a startling, colorful, romantic figure, *possessing now a genuine quality he has not had before*, the quality of the formidably strong, disdainfully fearless cavalry officer he really had been. (*Poet* 88, emphasis mine)

Added to this is the arrival of Jamie Cregan, who was raised on the Melody estate and served as a corporal under Con in the Seventh Dragoons. With Jamie there to serve as chorus, Con reenacts the famous battle in which he so distinguished himself.

His efforts, we realize, are doomed to failure, as the stage action indicates. To re-create the scene, for instance, he rearranges the saltcellar and cutlery on the tablecloth to indicate the enemy lines. Sara, angry after a night of waitressing this drunken party, says in the mocking brogue she reserves for taunting her father, "I'll have your plate, av ye plaze, Major, before your gallant dragoons charge over it and break it" (*Poet* 97). But even more telling than Sara's interruptions are the intrusions of Patch Riley's Irish songs. Invited to fill out the numbers (though assigned to a separate table), Patch, Paddy, and Dan Roche, having a party of their own on Con's liquor, break into songs which distract Melody from his narrative as, despite himself, his eyes light up and his thoughts return to a still more distant past.

As Patch launches into his ballad, Melody "forgets himself," we are told (an interesting phrase), and with a "strong lilt of brogue coming into his voice,"exclaims,

> Ah, that brings it back clear as life! Melody Castle in the days that's gone!...Give me a orse to love and I'll cry quits to men! And then away, with the hounds in full cry, and after them! (*Poet* 102)

But Sara intrudes once again. The point is that Con's memories, whether of military glory or his life on the old estate, cannot escape both what he has been—his Irish roots (with the peasant retainers an ironic reminder of his origins)—and what he is now, the proprietor of a failing inn. Memory, however powerful, cannot obliterate the past, escape the present, or change the future.

The Failure of Ritual

In casting the mirror scenes and the Talavera celebration in a ritualistic mode, O'Neill consciously or not, raises the possibility of Con's entering the mythic dimension. But the incantations from "Childe Harold" and the anniversary celebration are more parodies than religious rites—rituals manqué, if you will. Both attempt to reenact the past, to make it present. The mirror scene, repeated four times in the drama, has, as Sara points out, a long history, as does the commemoration of Talavera, which, although it has no litany, has formulaic elements—the specially prepared dinner, for instance, the red coat and the invited guests, along with the narrative of the apotheotic experience.

The uniform suggests a sacramental feature, the outward sign of an inward conversion, and it does indeed produce a palpable transformation in Con, so much so that even Sara, who has witnessed this many times before, is momentarily overcome. The performance, too, has been repeated before; this is the nineteenth celebration of Con's glory, and it is rendered appreciably more meaningful by the presence of Jamie, the symbolic "community" of this event. While the three peasants contribute, however minimally, by simply being there to provide numbers (it is appropriate that they are all male, since the celebration commemorates an all-male experience), Jamie's chief contribution is that as witness and participant in the original event, he can testify to its validity and serve as acolyte. The incantations break down in this regard. Although they have a prop, the mirror, which produces and reflects the hoped-for transformation, the community of believers in this would-be ritual is reduced to one, Con, speaking only to his own image. And in both instances the outside world, the world of non-believers, intrudes.

The quasi-rituals, then, fail in the first instance because they are not truly communal in nature. (It is interesting in this regard that Patch and the others mock Con in the midst of his glory and that he mocks them, mocking him.) The ideal that they celebrate and strive to "make flesh" is individual only—Con's ideal conception of himself—with no communal component, no boon to the society at large, as the archetype dictates. Secondly, and perhaps even more significantly, the ideal moment that Con reenacts exists within, not outside, the boundary of time.

It occurred at a given moment in his own history; Con cannot become his own divine ancestor. The powers of memory are only momentary, because Con knows how his story turned out. At the height of his imaginative re-creation, for example, as he says to Jamie, "Brave days, those! By the Eternal, then one lived! Then one forgot!" he cannot forget. He stops at this point, and when he resumes he says bitterly, "Little did I dream then the disgrace that was to be my reward later on" (*Poet* 99). The epithet invoking the Eternal is ironic. Thus, neither the incantations nor the anniversary celebration, for all their ritualistic overtones, can work their magic for him. The only possible alternative is the abandonment of his aristocratic dreams and the resumption of his peasant status. He becomes, in the end, Ned Melody's son, not of Melody Castle, but of the shebeen.

Con's Return to Origins

In his return to his roots, it is significant that Con returns to a period prior to his own beginnings. He was born on the estate shortly after old Melody had established himself as one of the gentry. Thus, when he becomes a peasant at the play's end, he claims an identity he associates not with himself, but with his father. The fact is that without his imaginative reconstruction of reality, Con Melody is nothing more than a peasant—and when he arrives at Harford's mansion, he is treated as such. A butler informs Con and Cregan that "Mr. Harford don't allow drunken Micks to come here disturbing him" and that they actually should have come to the servant's entrance (*Poet* 155). Regarded as servants, they respond accordingly, forcing their way into Harford's home and brawling with his three lackeys until the police arrive and evict them. Con himself recognizes the discrepancy between the aristocratic pride that sent him on the mission and the ignominy of the actual event. "Bravely done, Major Melody!" he mutters to himself....When he is forced to relinquish his pretensions, what he sees is merely "the son of a thieving shebeen keeper." His shooting of the mare, a symbolic suicide, reflects this vision. Speaking of "the Major" in third person, Con explains to Nora and Sara, "He meant to kill her [the mare] first wid one pistol, then himself wid the other. But faix, he saw the shot that killed her had finished him, too" (*Poet* 169). From this point on, Con speaks and acts the part of an Irish peasant, a transformation which we are meant to understand as permanent.

This cyclic action, the return to Ireland and the shebeen, is not the mythic return of Eliade's archaic man or the Eternal Return of Nietzsche's Superman, but the paradigm of the classical historian who perceives history as a series of repetitive cycles. According to this view, because he is inherently limited, man will repeat the triumphs and the mistakes of those who have preceded him *ad infinitum*; it is an inescapable extension of the human condition.[5]

This view of history helps us understand why we experience Con's final transformation as a loss, which we are clearly intended to do. He lapses into a heavy brogue, and we are told that his face "loses all its remaining distinction and appears vulgar and common, with a loose, leering grin on his swollen lips" (*Poet* 167). He avows he will be "content to stay meself in the proper station I was born to" (*Poet* 179). As he moves into the bar to join the cronies he now accepts as equals, "his movements are shambling and clumsy, his big hairy hands dangling at this sides. In his torn, disheveled, dirt-stained uniform, he looks like a loutish, grinning clown" (*Poet* 175).

One might expect that since his illusions have been maintained at extreme cost—not only to Nora and Sara, but also to Con himself, who as Major Melody must remain aloof and alone, cut off from the warmth of relationships—the abandonment of these illusions would be regarded as a breakthrough, moving Con forward in the fullness of his humanity. In one sense this is true. Con is at last free to respond lovingly to Nora, who, as the play's moral touchstone, has had the audience's sympathy from the start. "Let you be aisy, darlint," he says to her, speaking of the Major in the third person: "He'll nivir again hurt you with his sneers, and his pretendin' he's a gintleman, blatherin' about pride and honor" (*Poet* 168). Shortly thereafter he kisses her tenderly and tells her thathe loves her, to Nora's astonished joy; "I've meant to tell you often, only the Major, damn him, had me under his proud thumb" (*Poet* 174).

But Sara (and the audience at large, I would argue) regards Con's relinquishmentof his illusions as a diminishment. Desperately, she pleads with him to reconsider. "I won't let you!" she exclaims. "It's my pride too!... So don't—I'll do anything you ask—I'll even tell Simon—that after his father's insult to you—I'm too proud to marry a Yankee coward's son!" (*Poet* 178). But Con can live in the past no longer. "For the love of God, stop—" he says to Sara. "Let me go!" As he closes the door to the bar behind him, greeted by the welcoming roar of drunken shouts, we are reminded of Deborah Harford's final entry into the summerhouse at the close of *More Stately Mansions*. Although Deborah finally chooses the world of imagination and madness while Con relinquishes imagination altogether, both represent a significant loss. They have exhausted all their other alternatives and close life's door behind them in their final, dramatic exit.[6]

Thus, in both the Con Melody plot and the Sara-Simon subplot, forward movement in time does not bring progress or growth; it merely removes Con further from his ideal moment. To combat the concomitant sense of loss, he travels backward in time to the pivotal Talavera experience, only to discover at last that his military glory cannot be recovered in the world of everyday experience. There is no mythic moment, no satisfactory ritual to transcend this stalemate; Con finally relinquishes his pretensions and accepts the identity of shebeen keeper.

Sara's case might seem to offer some hope. She has begun her climb up the American success ladder. Having seen the ultimate futility of Con's delusions of grandeur, she has set about transforming those dreams into reality in her own life by marrying Simon. She will indeed "wear fine silks and drive in a carriage wid a naygur coachman behind spankin' thoroughbreds, her nose in the air;..." as Con predicts (*Poet* 173). But her repetition of Nora's "sin" with Simon (a second cyclic action in the play)[7] calls into question the ultimate outcome of what promises to be a victory. In addition, the fact that Sara acts out of ambition as well as love, insisting that love itself is what matters, further casts a shadow over the impending marriage. As Con so accurately predicts at the end of the play, Sara will "have some trouble, rootin' out his [Simon's] dreams" (*Poet* 173), as *More Stately*

Mansions will reveal. Con himself will die within a few short years (see note 6).

Thus in this play about poetry and illusion, imagination and its powers, time remains the enemy. The future holds forth dubious promise, and memories of the past cannot redeem the present. It is a dilemma that will haunt O'Neill's characters throughout the historical-autobiographical cycle and will continue into the sequel, *More Stately Mansions*.

NOTES

1. Harford suggests they move to Ohio, a way-station for streams of Irish immigrants in the mid-nineteenth century—including the families of both Ella Quinlan and James O'Neill.

2. Like Jamie Tyrone in *Long Day's Journey*, another third generation immigrant, sociologically speaking, Sara uses her Irish heritage as a weapon against her father.

3. It is these Yankee traits that link Sara with the last major character of *Poet*, Deborah Harford, and which account for the otherwise inexplicable parallels between the two. We note, for instance, the interesting fact that Sara shares Deborah's admiration of Napoleon, in spite of the fact that Con fought on the British side. Like Deborah, Sara does not take seriously Simon's plan to transform the world with his idealistic dreams. Most importantly, her desire for freedom through power, which she locates in marrying Simon, parallels Deborah's fantasy of wielding control by winning the love of a Napoleon or a Louis XIV. Thus Sara can understand Deborah's motives when the innocent Nora cannot. When Nora protests that Deborah's coming against her husband's orders shows that she is on Simon's side, Sara answers, "Don't be so simple, Mother. Wouldn't she tell Simon that anyway, even if the truth was her husband sent her to do all she could to get him away from me?" (*Poet* 79). She is even capable of adopting Deborah's tactics in the battle for Simon's love: "I've got to be as big a liar as she was. I'll have to pretend I liked her and I'd respect whatever advice she gave him. I mustn't let him see—" (*Poet* 88). As O'Neill works back and forth in his mind from *More Stately Mansions* to *A Touch of the Poet*, he incorporates in the younger Sara those characteristics that would make her capable of the cultural reversal she undergoes in the later play.

4. O'Neill's allusion to this particular poem is apt in more ways than one. Byron, previously society's darling, writes "Childe Harold" from exile, a situation that bears striking parallels to Con's.

5. This is the position drawn upon by T.E. Hulme, for instance, in his famous essay "Classicism and Romanticism" (1924) in which he defines the classical perspective as one emerging from a view of human beings as inherently flawed, bound by limitations, as opposed to the romantic notion of infinite possibility.

6. That O'Neill regarded Con's choice as a diminishment—and permanent—is suggested by the opening scene of his uncut third draft of *More Stately Mansions*, which was included in the play's 1964 Broadway production. Jamie Cregan, mourning Con's premature death only a few short years after the Harford duel, says this at his funeral:

> He could have drunk a keg a day and lived for twenty years yet, if the pride and spirit wasn't killed inside him ever since the night that he tried to challenge that Yankee coward Harford to a duel and him and me got beat by the police and arrested" (Quoted in Michael Manheim: *Eugene O'Neill's New Language of Kinship* [Syracuse: Syracuse University Press, 1982] 116.

7. In Sara's seduction of Simon (which, as we learn in *More Stately Mansions*, results in a pregnancy), Nora's illicit affair with Con is repeated. Sara "becomes" Nora (hence, the similarity of their names and the unusual spelling of "Sara"). It may be an act which has a consecration all its own, to quote Hester Prynne; certainly Nora—and the audience—understand Sara's willingness to sacrifice everything for love. And it teaches Sara the wisdom of Nora's earlier statement that love was when "if all the fires of hell was between you, you'd walk in them gladly to be with him and sing with joy at your own burnin', if only his kiss was on your mouth!" (*Poet* 25). Sara even uses the same rhetoric when she describes her love for Simon. When Nora remonstrates that God will punish her for her sin, Sara replies, "Let Him! If He'd say to me, for every time you kiss Simon you'll have a thousand years in hell, I wouldn't care. I'd wear out my lips kissing him!" (*Poet* 149).

But there are also ominous overtones associated with the seduction. We have seen that Con throws their hasty marriage up to Nora and that she is convinced she will suffer in hell for it. This is a fact that bodes ill for Sara. Indeed, we will see in *Mansions* that the parallel holds true: Simon accuses Sara of using her body to force him to marry her—an issue which comes between them.

The Banished Prince: Time, Memory and Ritual in the Late Plays of Eugene O'Neill. Ann Arbor: UMI Research Press, 1988, 13-25; 114-115.

The Stage: Late O'Neill

Wilfrid Sheed

Anyone who wishes to extract the full juice from Eugene O'Neill's *Hughie* should first hie himself to Robert Brustein's chapter on O'Neill in *The Theatre of Revolt* (Atlantic, Little- Brown). This is by all means the best analysis of the pipe dream plays, to which *Hughie* forms an intriguing foot-note. Mr. Brustein contends that O'Neill had his own pipe-dream—that of being a "literary" playwright, full of arty tricks and classical razzle-dazzle—and that only when he had confronted this, played Hickey as it were to his own illusion, was he able to achieve real stature.

Hughie is an aggressively non-literary play, a glossary of 1920's slang recited in a mangy hotel-lobby. It deals with a single aspect of the pipe-dream syndrome—the I-thou relationship of dreamer and listener. The dreamer cannot quite believe his own story until someone else has heard it, nodded, said "Is that so." After that the dream enters the world of fact: it has gained, so to speak, a witness.

The action of *Hughie* consists of a drunken horse-player floundering round and round the elevator-cage, looking for a witness to his dreams. He had a listener once and they were happy together, giving birth to host of little pseudo-events, but that listener has recently died; and now the dreamer must woo himself a new one.

Like a man who always marries the same girl, Erie Smith, the dreaming horse-player, always falls for the same kind of listener; he is a push-over for night clerks. Hughie, his dream dream-listener, was a night clerk at this same hotel; and now Erie is trying to court his replacement.

This in itself tells us a good deal about Erie's character. A night-clerk in this kind of hotel is the listening equivalent of a prostitute. He is paid to sit there and take it; in fact, he is literally a captive audience, because he works in a cage. Erie Smith cannot find a listener on the open-market. He probably could not even keep a bartender at his end of the bar. His partner must virtually be strapped down.

In courting an audience, Erie Smith's "line" consists in reminiscing about his former one, Hughie. There was a *real* listener, boy; and as Erie describes the dreams he told to Hughie, and Hughie's superb reactions to them, we realize that the witness has actually been absorbed into the dream. Erie Smith is boasting, lying, about having been listened to; he dreams about the act of being heard.

As to his new prospect, Hughie's replacement: this fellow may be consigned to a cage, but his favors are not so easily won. As a professional solitary, he is accustomed to being his own listener. He talks to himself in a bemused kind of way of the possibility of making more noise than the garbagemen make in the morning, or of burning down the *whole* city, cement and all. This is narcissistic, closed-circuit listening, a heck of a thing to come across at three in the morning.

But Smith does not give up, and finally he succeeds in making a freak connection. His soliloquy happens to mesh at one point with the night-clerk's interior monologue. The name of Arnold Rothstein comes up. Rothstein was a celebrity of his time—and even then (the play takes place in 1928) celebrities were the stuff that dreams were made on. On the understanding that they are talking about Rothstein, and nothing but Rothstein, the new night-clerk consents to listen.

What follows is as tragic, on a small scale, as anything in O'Neill. Erie Smith is perfectly satisfied to have a listener on these terms; he acts as if he had made a conquest. And we suddenly see how little he asks of his listeners—the merest appearance of acquiescence will do, Smith will supply the rest. The night-clerk remains fast in his narcissistic slumbers, but Smith's fantasies of gambling and wenching have inserted themselves into these, by virtue of the Rothstein connection.

And from Erie Smith's zest in this new affair, we gather not only that there is a new Hughie in the making, but the converse, that the old Hughie was probably no better that the new one. Although death has transformed him into the perfect listener, he probably listened in his day just as perfunctorily as his successor does now. Smith has already observed several similarities between them, particularly their unmistakable "night-clerkness"—a quality, it appears of patience and passivity, of simply being there.

In other words, the I-thou of pipe-dream listening is among the most corrupt of relationships. The listener is allowed to think his own thoughts. Like the witness to a legal deed, he is required to provide only superficial assent. It may be wondered why he is needed at all: but Erie Smith is a gambler, not a night-clerk, he needs the appearance of action, of something happening. He has not yet sunk into the torpor of his victims, the self-absorbed listeners of the world.

Unfortunately, Jason Robards doesn't get anything like full mileage out of or into Erie Smith. He doesn't seem observant enough to be a really first-rate actor. His frenzied pirrouettings around the lobby are no substitute for drunken dither. He looks as if he is about to plunge up the stairs or out into the street; even when he drops his key, he is much too decisive about it.

It may be that José Quintero the director was trying to inject some spurious action into this splendidly static situation; if so, he has been unfair to drunks. The drunk who wants to make just one more point before going to bed should *teeter* more than Mr. Robards does.

Mr. Robards is not a very accomplished actor (his finest scene, in *Long Day's Journey Into Night*, was played seated) at the best of times, but he makes a few amends in the important final scenes where voice and baleful glee—his specialties—are the order of the day. Jack Dodson is properly glassy-eyed as the night-clerk.

Several critics have questioned whether *Hughie* is a play at all. But O'Neill, by the end of his career, was so total a dramatist that he could mount a complete drama in a ten-minute speech. The one-hour length of *Hughie* is more than enough to make it the most interesting play of the season. (At the Royale)

Commonweal, January, 15, 1965.

Theatre: O'Neill's *More Stately Mansions* Opens

Clive Barnes

Of all the great playwrights, Eugene O'Neill is the most banal. Even in his best plays he is likely to drop through into booby traps of cliché, and in his worst plays, melodrama, like poverty, is always with us. He wrote and rewrote. His plays were torn to pieces by himself. But his greatness was in a view of the dramatic epic so clear that few playwrights in this century could rival him. He dared legions, and was magnificently unprepared for the littleness of technique.

One presumes that *More Stately Mansions*, given its New York premiere at the Broadhurst Theater last night, was his final play. Or might have been his final play had he ever finished it or authorized its performance. What is being given at the Broadhurst is a curious thing indeed.

It is an abridgement of a play by O'Neill that O'Neill not only failed to finish, but which he specifically wished to die with him. One of his last acts, in that ironic hotel room where he died, was to tear up the only surviving copy of the manuscript. As Barbara Gelb, O'Neill's co-biographer has told, *More Stately Mansions* was first finished in Sweden by a Swedish director, but this present version is the work of the Broadway director José Quintero. Mr. Quintero should have had the honesty to accept his role in the program.

Merely to present this as the "American premiere" (they mean New York but conveniently chose to disregard out-of-town previews) of a play by Eugene O'Neill is offensively ingenuous, when it is no such thing. What we have here is José Quintero's adaptation and completion of a play by O'Neill that O'Neill in all sincerity destroyed. O'Neill was right.

The play was originally one of O'Neill's grand schemes and epic gestures, part of a cycle designed to show the triumph of American materialism over its

More Stately Mansions

touch of poetry and, on another level, to explain those curious relationships (well, perhaps not so curious) with his family that were somewhere the diesel fuel for his remarkable creative engine.

In its unfinished, raw and tortured state, it does, in my view, O'Neill's memory a disservice. With friends like Mr. José Quintero, the shade of O'Neill might think he needs no enemies, and being his own worst enemy was the privilege O'Neill always retained for himself.

The story takes place in Massachusetts between 1832 and 1841. Two women are fighting, with genteel bloodiness, for the love of a man. They are his wife and his mother, and oddly enough (yet not oddly at all if you examine the psychology) they have a great deal in common, and, in their ways, love each other. The man is worthless—a victim presenting himself to matriarchy for the most beneficial castration he can obtain.

The play is full of symbols, of gardens and summer houses, and phrases lost in the far blue yonder. Some of the dramatic technique is deplorable, with soliloquies shooting out of people's heads like the bubbles over characters in a cartoon, and windy phrases pouring forth, such as "nothing is natural not even nature."

But even seen through a glass darkly here are some of the great O'Neill themes. The man at the mercy of the woman he unwittingly crucifies, and all the bizarrely convoluting human relationships O'Neill thinks of as family. And then again his view, seen at a different level, of America, an epic theme of decline and fall, of greed and ruthlessness. Here, I suspect, the two levels of O'Neill, the national and personal, were intended to combine. In this version of the play they do not.

Looking at O'Neill now, it seems that his career was a long day's journey into a very special kind of epic theatre. At his much-praised height he had the impudence and guts to challenge *Elektra*, at the end, disregarded and underestimated, he was reduced to tearing up plays in a dead hotel room. Yet it was toward the end that he found his real greatness, and there are passages in *More Stately Mansions* that make you wonder what kind of play he might have written had he written it.

Here might have been the fusion between the national epic and personal monologue that could have sealed O'Neill's vision of the raw fantasies of the soul. Mr. Quintero has done the playwright enormous service in the past, and for this the world is grateful. But what he has attempted now—and he can reflect on this without pain—is a task that was beyond O'Neill himself.

Possibly where we might have hoped for more from Mr. Quintero was in the performances. These waver disturbingly. Ingrid Bergman, returning to the Broadway stage, is a woman so beautiful that she is herself a work of art. But as an actress she is less perfect, and cast as one of O'Neill's archetypal mother figures she seemed strangely gauche. She trades heavily on her natural charm and, in a sense, her very real inner goodliness (Miss Bergman only has to enter a stage—or, I am sure, a room—and any man with any blood or courtesy in him automatically starts to get up from his seat) but makes less of the strangely disparate character of Deborah Harford than you might have hoped.

Her partner in the feminine tourney is Colleen Dewhurst, with a voice like an ice pick and the looks of a hungry immigrant. She eats up her part as if it were breakfast, and contrives to give the reality—a mixture of pain, pathos and honesty—that O'Neill had sketched in. This was a fine performance, finer perhaps than Arthur Hill as the boy-husband, who had the cards stacked against him by the play, and never found his way out to a winning hand. But once again Mr. Quintero's somewhat mannered direction helped little.

There is little more to say. Praise for the settings of Ben Edwards, the costumes of Jane Greenwood and the lighting by John Harvey, all of which added to a production that had more of the look and feel of dramatic poetry than is the custom. But when all was said and done, I left the Broadhurst in sadness—sadness for what had been done, and what might be thought to have been done.

New York Times, November 1, 1967

The Stage: Unfinished Mansions

John Simon

The question "Who was the greatest American dramatist?" must be answered with a paraphrase from Gide, "Eugene O'Neill, alas." After some lively seafaring plays, O'Neill underwent a land change, and produced a string of celebrated bores. The strangely unhappy interlude lasted as long as a typical O'Neill play seems to, but at the end of it emerged two masterpieces of American and world theater, *The Iceman Cometh* and *Long Day's Journey Into Night*. *More Stately Mansions* is O'Neill's last, unfinished play, part of a contemplated cycle of 11. Dissatisfied, O'Neill himself tore up what he took to be the only manuscript; unfortunately, another survived. Now, if an author like Franz Kafka wants his work destroyed after his death, it is good to override the wishes of such a self-doubting, self-tormented genius. But when so self-esteeming, megalomaniacal a writer as O'Neill wanted something of his destroyed, I think it is safe to assume that he was right.

More Stately Mansions picks up the story of Sara Melody where it left off in *A Touch of the Poet*. She has married the rich mother's boy Simon Harford, and now this tough Boston-Irish lass has to battle it out for complete control of her husband with his devious, infantile, semi-dementedly scheming mother, Deborah. The main plot concerns the tooth-and-claw struggle of these women, who sometimes join in an unholy cabal, while the puerile but sneaky Simon sides up now with one, now with the other. The subplot involves the cancerously growing family business, of which Simon is the nominal, Sara the actual head. Somehow the internecine family and the grasping business are supposed to merge into a colossal image of America racing into materialism, but neither part of the play can stand on its own feet, and, together, they fall like a pair of drunks trying to prop up each other. The business plot is treated in a sketchy, manipulative way; the family infighting is merely a self-contradictory scheme for—and sometimes travesty of—what works so beautifully in *Long Day's Journey Into Night*. The motivations of the main characters are a maze of inconsistencies, and sniveling Simon hardly justifies all that matriarchal machiavellianism.

The last scene of the play, which had already seemed interminable, is a stultifying unmerrygoround of instant reversals of position, lightning arbitrariness and thunderous absurdity. It is like a season in the booby-hatch compressed into—I don't know how long, for my sense of time was blotted out by the sense of suffocation. Here O'Neill may be less to blame than the three men, including the director, who cut and rearranged the manuscript. Actually, the feeling here is not of something vast being pared down, but something so incomplete that every inferior, scratched-out reading had to be reinserted to eke out an evening. I felt inside an echo chamber in which the same speeches often reverberated ad nauseam.

Among the principals, Colleen Dewhurst as Sara manages to keep her chin above the torrents of the tempest in a mudpuddle, but Arthur Hill's genuine and Ingrid Bergman's spurious talents are submerged. Miss Bergman's acting is an anthology of attitudes, and a slender little volume it is. Additional harm is done by José Quintero's pretentiously inept staging. He keeps most of the action downstage, with the characters striking two-dimensional postures in front of Ben Edwards' shabby sets, and often sitting down on the very steps leading into the auditorium. This provides the already sinking feeling engendered by the play with an objective correlative. From supporting actors, Quintero elicits nothing like performances: Fred Stewart's windy lawyer and Lawrence Linville's stuffy younger brother are mirthless caricatures. Linville, moreover, is made to walk backwards much of the time, as if a crabbed person had to walk like a crab.

As I suggested Ben Edwards' sets are not of the sort worth framing by the actors. A specialist in the limited range from shabby gentility to abject dilapidation, Edwards has turned the rich Harford house and office not into a stately mansion but an old, moss-covered manse, complete with peeling wallpaper. And John Harvey's oblique lighting, going in for vesperal ambers, merely underlines the overstatements. Only Jane Greenwood's costumes are thoughtful and handsome.

In *Long Day's Journey* the characters keep offending one another, then promptly and profusely apologizing. But in that excellent play one is barely conscious of such iteration. Here, however, I kept my flagging spirits alive by keeping score: I counted 24 immediate apologies. But no amount of them would excuse this play. Yet there must be something, if not affecting, at least infectious about it—never in all my theatergoing have I heard an audience cough so much and so loud. But what rises from the ashes of the manuscript of *More Stately Mansions* is not a phoenix, only a turkey. *(At the Broadhurst)*

Commonweal, December 8, 1967.

The Brothel in O'Neill's *Mansions*

Jere Real

The successful staging in 1968 in both Los Angeles and New York of a major production of the Eugene O'Neill drama, *More Stately Mansions*, demands that some detailed critical analysis other than newspaper reviews at last be paid this play, the opinion of Mr. Robert Brustein and others notwithstanding. In his discussion of O'Neill's play in *The Theatre of Revolt*, Brustein, at that time theater critic of *New Republic*, dismissed *More Stately Mansions* with a footnote. The play was, he wrote, "sadly marred and incomplete." It was, in his view, "a regression, a throwback to an earlier stage of O'Neill's development." Had the play been destroyed as O'Neill specifically directed before his death, its loss would have been negligible.[1] In general, Mr. Brustein's appraisal is accurate; but the play has hovered about like a specter of O'Neill's that would not go away. It was produced first by the Swedish Royal Dramatic Theatre. A greatly revised text was published in 1964; and now a major production employing the talents of Ingrid Bergman, Arthur Hill, and Colleen Dewhurst has been mounted in the United States. Detailed analysis, incomplete and marred as the play well may be, seems justified.

Although *More Stately Mansions* was the last full-length O'Neill drama to be published, it actually was written before the great introspective play, *Long Day's Journey Into Night* and *The Iceman Cometh*, that were the masterful achievement of the playwright's final productive years. The writing of *More Stately Mansions* occupied part of O'Neill's writing schedule from 1935 to 1938. The play was to have been fourth[2] in O'Neill's massive nine-play cycle, *A Tale of Possessors Self-Dispossessed*, an historical saga of several generations of an American family who are corrupted by their material success. The revised typescript of the play inadvertently escaped burning by O'Neill and his wife, Carlotta, when the first two plays in the cycle were so destroyed. That script, in a collection of O'Neill papers at Yale University, was revised into an acting version by Karl Ragnar Gierow for the first production of the play in Sweden. In their definitive biography of O'Neill, Arthur and Barbara Gelb describe *More Stately Mansions*[3] as "five times the length of a conventional play." Both the Gierow version used by the Swedish Royal Dramatic Theatre and the recent New York stage version adapted by José Quintero were substantially abbreviated versions of the play.

In plot, the drama continues the story of several characters introduced by O'Neill in *A Touch of the Poet*, the third play in his cycle, and relates the continuing conflict between two women, Sara Melody Harford and Deborah Harford, who try to dominate Deborah's poetically-inclined son, Simon. Simon, at the conclusion of *A Touch of the Poet*, was to marry Sara; and following the marriage, he has abandoned gradually his artistic ambitions and assumed the aggressive mercantile attitude he previously despised in his father. His mother is frustrated both in her marriage and in her loss of Simon. She borders on insanity at the opening of the fourth play and lapses periodically into fantasy, envisioning herself as a mistress to a French king at Versailles. Temporarily, she is jarred back to reality when her husband's death leaves her in a financial crisis. To survive, she seeks *rapprochment* with Simon and his wife, Sara. Simon agrees to assume control of the family's business fortunes and through shrewd manipulation grows ever more successful. Deborah and Sara temporarily abrogate their competition for Simon with Deborah satisfying her selfish desires by dominating the Harford grandchildren. (This temporary armistice between Deborah and Sara takes place over a ten-year period in one of those typically long O'Neill temporal leaps). During these years, Simon grows increasingly restive with his business career: he has, like most O'Neill heroes since *Beyond the Horizon*, "a touch of the poet" he cannot lose. Similarly, he is obsessively disturbed by his growing alienation from both his wife and mother. He decides to bring his wife into his business activities paying her for their renewed "love" by turning over portions of the business empire to her. Simultaneously, he seeks to recreate the idyllic, though strange, childhood relationship he had with his mother in her bizarre, stylized garden of meditation. His actions provoke a new mother-wife conflict. The result is that Deborah goes mad, Simon reverts to infantilism, and Sara is left with a husband that she only can "mother" as she might a demented child.[4]

It is possible to draw from all of these machinations the conclusion that O'Neill simply was engaging in another exercise in Oedipal conflict[5]. While such aspects of O'Neill's own life always are relevant to any critical approach to his plays, there is, however, another more important thematic structure developed in *More Stately Mansions*; it is the theme of mankind's universal prostitution, that is to say, the human capacity to bargain away those very qualities that grant individuals that elusive distinction, humanity. (One must specifically differentiate at this pint between this general "prostitution" of humanity—O'Neill's view of man's inevitable self-debasement—and the more conventional sexual prostitution found in O'Neill plays, although, logically enough, the latter may serve to symbolize the former. The female prostitute character frequently is found in O'Neill plays, usually in romantically naive and generally sympathetic interpretations. One need only recall Anna in *Anna Christie*. Female prostitutes were not immoral creatures in O'Neill.[6] Usually, some abstract quantity, i.e., Fate or society, victimized the whore.) O'Neill, however, did find an immorality inherent in man's inability to deal with other human beings either emotionally or intellectually; and he despaired of individual's seeming incapability of resolving such alienation. In O'Neill's view, man invariably "sells out," bargains himself away morally for some material gain. Such universal "prostitution" is the primary theme he develops in *More Stately Mansions*. So it is that physical, emotional, and moral prostitution become a controlling metaphor in both the character's dialogue and in their relationsips with each other in the drama.

O'Neill's remarks in 1937 reveal that he personally held such a pessimistic view of human nature at the time he was engaged in writing this play. Commenting on an essay comparing the excesses of the French and Russian revolution that had been sent to him by Barrett Clark, O'Neill wrote:

> The last...sounds pessimistic...whereas I feel full of hope these days. For, noting the way the world wags, I am sure that Man has definitely decided to destroy himself and this seems to me the only truly wise decision he has ever made![7]

Another indication of the playwright's increasing pessimism during the period came early on 1939 in a comment he wrote to George Jean Nathan about a propagandistic play of Sean O'Casey. O'Neill lamented Casey's venture into political reform and said:

> the one reform worth cheering for is the Second Flood, and that the interesting thing about people is the obvious fact that they don't really want to be saved—the tragic idiotic ambition for self-destruction in them.[8]

When he made these last gloomy predictions, O'Neill had just completed the writing of *More Stately Mansions*. The playwright's personal pessimism easily can be compared to Simon's statement to Sara in the final scene of Act I of the play. The couple are discussing Simon's earlier aspiration to write a Rousseauistic plan for a "greedless Utopia," a project Simon has now abandoned. Simon tells his wife that he has burned his manuscript and continues:

> No, all you have to do is read your daily newspaper and see what man is doing with himself. There's the book that ought to be written—a frank study of the true nature of man as he really is and not as he pretends to himself to be—a courageous facing of the truth about him—and in the end, a daring assertion that what he is, no matter how it shocks our sentimental moral and religious delusions about him, is good because it is true, and should, in a world of facts, become the foundation of a new morality which would destroy all our present hypocritical pretenses and virtuous lies about ourselves. By God, it's a fascinating idea. I've half a mind to try it!"[9]

It is reasonable to believe that O'Neill well may have been thinking of his own cycle when he wrote Simon's literary musings in this scene. Simon, however, reverts from such impractical thoughts back to devising new methods for making money. In a final reflection on the duality of his desires, he says:

> What a damned fool man can make of himself. Keep on deliberately denying what he knows himself to be fact, and encourage a continual conflict in his mind, so that he lives split into opposites and divided against himself! (I, iii, p. 49)

The condition described by Simon is the state of the drama's three principal characters. Each of them fluctuates constantly between the good and evil instincts in their nature: Simon has conflicting desires about business and artistic pursuits as well as an ambivalent attitude toward his wife and mother; Sara has an irreconcilable desire for wealth and power and the overwhelming attraction of her love for her husband; and Deborah struggles to control Simon while trying to retain dominion of his household through her rapport with Sara. But in each conflict, the character succumbs to his worst desires and prostitutes himself to a selfish possessiveness.

The prostitution motif thus pervades the play in both action and dialogue. At the beginning (I, i), Deborah in a half-demented state, sees herself as the mistress of a French king. Her vision, however, is not merely sexual. She also sees herself as the power behind the throne, as one "who uses love, but loves only herself." (I, i, 13) Deborah's own marriage to Simon's father is empty and frustrating; she feels she has prostituted herself. Later, following Simon's marriage, Deborah speaks of her marriage and describes "Age and Ugliness" as "elderly suitors for my body":

> And every night they have lain in bed with me. Oh, yes, indeed! I have disciplined my will to be possessed by facts—like a whore in a brothel! (I, ii, 29)

She views Sara, the woman her son has married, as a "vulgar, common slut." (I, i, 21) Indeed, Sara did prostitute her love for Simon to opportunistic selfishness when she gave herself to him at the end of *A Touch of the Poet* in order to force him to marry her. Her marriage to Simon forces him into a business career rather than into writing. He discards his literary ambitions both for his wife and for wealth. Even Deborah's reconciliation with the couple takes on the aspect of a "bargain." In effect, she sells herself to them in return for the capital Simon can bring into the floundering family business after his father's death.

After that reconciliation, Simon is divorced increasingly from any emotional involvement with his wife; the new Sara-Deborah alliance excludes him. He then proposes that this wife become his mistress. She enters business partnership with him and begins to sell him her love in return for vast portions of his commercial empire. Shortly before Sara arrives at his office and agrees to his plan, Simon tells his brother:

> If you ever fall in love, Joel, take my advice and do not marry. Keep your love your mistress with no right of ownership except what she earns day by day, what she can make you pay for possession. Love should be a deal forever incomplete, never finally settled, with each party continually raising the bids, but neither one concluding a final role. Yes, my advice to you would be to shun marriage and keep a whore instead! (III, i, 72)

When Sara agrees to the arrangement her husband has formulated, Simon once more can make love to her. Their love becomes a mercantile bargain; rather than being based on mutual respect and sacrifice, marital love is based on the profit motive of prostitution. Sara's ready acceptance of Simon's plan furthers the play's dramatic irony. Simon evolved the new arrangement with his wife after he became unable to differentiate clearly in his own mind the personage of his wife and mother. Yet, in her new role as "mistress" to a commercial "king of America," Sara actually resembles Deborah and her fantasies as mistress to a French king more than ever. Explaining their new relationship, Simon tells Sara: "Here you are yourself, my wife, my partner—my mistress, too, I hope." (II, i, 5) He continues:

> Yes, you will have to learn to be shameless here. You will have to deal daily with the greedy fact of life as it really lives. You will have to strip life naked, and face it. And accept it as truth. (II, i, 91)

The new family arrangement initiates Simon's ultimate downfall. Sara comes to control the business, while Simon spends more time with his mother in her garden trying to recapture the childhood relationship he had with her.

Love as a merchandisable object also is reflected again in another scene at

Simon's office (III, i) where Simon makes Sara humiliate a banker who has been financially destroyed by their firm. The banker, initially proud, soon prostitutes himself by accepting a job Sara offers him with the attached condition that he be totally obedient. Sara tells the banker that he will be paid enough to "provide very moderate comfort for your family, and so continue to purchase, in part at least, their former love and respect." (III, i, 154)

As the struggle for possession of Simon by Sara and Deborah moves to its conclusion, O'Neill builds the prostitution motif to its final development. Simon goes to his mother's garden and demands that, together, they enter the mysterious summer house. Throughout the play, this summer house has been a symbol of their earlier relationship, of the tranquility offered by an escape into the past, and of the relief offered by complete fantasy or insanity. After hesitation, they are about to enter the house when Sara suddenly appears in the garden. Simon immediately challenges her: "How dare you trespass here? Do you think my mother's garden is a brothel?" (III, ii, 186) The garden is, indeed, a brothel; everyone present has prostituted themselves. In this final confrontation, Deborah and Sara haggle over Simon like fishwives at a market. Each tries to prove her superior love for Simon by showing greater sacrifice, but in so doing, their sacrifice takes on the character of bids for possession of the man. Deborah seemingly makes the greater sacrifice by entering the summer house—lapsing into total fantasy—alone. Her victory is an uncertain one, however, since Sara leads Simon away. As Deborah emerges from the summer house, the drama has come full circle. The mother again envisions herself as the "mistress" of an emperor, humanity has been perverted by the desire to possess. Simon, in a child-like trance, sees his wife as his "mother." Even Sara's final plea that she deliberately wreck the business empire is undercut by her practical consideration for salvaging large amounts of money on which they can live.

It is impossible to speculate on the form this play might have had if O'Neill had completed it. The drama has glaring inadequacies, in characterization, dialogue, and motivation, that might have been resolved by O'Neill's usually extensive revision. The published version retains many of the melodramatic elements that characterized many of the author's early works. In technique too, *More Stately Mansions* recalls earlier works. For example, the living room scene (II, iii) with Simon, Sara, and Deborah speaking their thoughts aloud is merely a diminutive version of Act Six of *Strange Interlude*. In spite of the embryonic nature of the work and the derivative nature of its style and technique form earlier O'Neill plays, *More Stately Mansions* was given a highly unified thematic form by its author. The recurring references in both dialogue and in the development of the characters' actions all support the premise that man prostitutes himself for material gain, even to the point of treating human relationships as property to be possessed. And if the theme was not fully realized in the essentially unfinished *More Stately Mansions*, O'Neill did carry his pessimistic vision to fruition in his later masterpieces.

NOTES

1. Robert Brustein, *The Theatre of Revolt* (Boston: Little, Brown & Company, 1962), p. 359.

2. In the nine-play cycle envisioned by O'Neill, *More Stately Mansions* was to be the fourth play following *A Touch of the Poet*. Later O'Neill decided that the first two plays of the cycle were too long and should be divided into two plays each. Such a division would have made *A Touch of the Poet* the fifth play and *More Stately Mansions* the sixth play in an eleven-play cycle. Some critics use the later numbering system in referring to the sequence of the cycle plays.

3. Arthur and Barbara Gelb, *O'Neill* (New York: Harper & Brother, 1962), p. 938.

4. Eugene O'Neill, *More Stately Mansions*, edited by Donald Gallup (New York: Yale University Press, 1964), pp. vii-xii. I am indebted to Mr. Gallup's prefatory note for information about Karl Gierow's acting version of the play. I have used Mr. Gallup's edition for my analysis.

5. Murray Hartman, "The Skeltons in O'Neill's Mansions," *Drama Survey*, V (Winter, 1966-67), pp. 276-279.

6. Gelb, *O'Neill*, pp. 125-127.

7. *Ibid.*, p. 824.

8. *Ibid.*, p. 830.

9. O'Neill, *More Stately Mansions*, Act I, scene iii, p. 47. All further quotations from the play are included and cited in the text.

Modern Drama, 11 (Spring 1970): 383-389.

4
Thematic Analysis

The Idea of Puritanism in the Plays of Eugene O'Neill

Stephen L. Fluckiger

    From almost the beginning of his career, critics have used the word "puritanism" to describe an important element in Eugene O'Neill's work. As early as 1921, shortly after *Diff'rent* had come to Broadway, Heywood Broun called O'Neill "a new Puritan of the theatre." Four years later Louis Broomfield described *Desire Under the Elms* as the "best analysis of witch-burning Puritans yet done," surpassing even *The Scarlet Letter*. And as recently as 1972, Harold Clurman in his *Nation* "Theatre" column describes the effect of O'Neill's puritanism" on *Mourning Becomes Electra*.[1] Apart from these fundamental kinds of observations, however, very little has been done to define the precise nature of O'Neill's "puritanism," his relationship and debt (if it exists) to New England's early theocracy and the effect of these factors on particular plays. William Shurr identified a possible cause for this oversight when he stated, "What the authors produced depended on the materials at hand, and finally historical criticism must assert itself to determine as precisely as possible what, indeed, was available."[2] In light of the historical techniques increasingly employed by Americanists and other scholars, it is not unlikely that in the near future examinations of O'Neill's reading and background will produce a reliable study of "American" elements that influenced the formation of O'Neill's art. Even without a "definitive" collection of such facts, many of O'Neill's familiar statements about the purpose of the theatre and internal evidence from some of the plays themselves, particularly *Desire Under the Elms*, reveal the considerable impact of Puritan ideas on America's greatest dramatist.

In placing Eugene O'Neill in the mainstream of America's literary tradition, John Henry Raleigh made this significant statement: "What O'Neill did then in *Dynamo* was to repeat in miniature the evolution from Cotton Mather to Henry Adams: from thunderas the rumblings of God and lightenings as His flashing (Act I) to the crooning, awesome dynamo, with the power and significatory of mysterious moral or religious meaning (Act III)."[3] In the final, ironic conclusion of *Dynamo*, O'Neill's undercutting of the literary tradition which Raleigh describes closely resembles Melville's treatment of New England's mores in *Pierre*. O'Neill's experience with what Raleigh calls the "nineteenth century brand" of "New England Puritanism" helps to explain the affinities that exist between these two American artists: similar backgrounds and temperaments produced similar responses to the vestiges of Puritanism that each confronted in his society. Shaped to a degree by Puritan force, Melville and O'Neill never completely freed themselves from its influence. After the manner of the early Americans, both writers present characters that become mere "abstractions, types, practically allegorical figures," "Puritan" in their lack of depth and substance. At the same time, responding to the multiplicity of modern life, O'Neill and Melville produced "insuperably complex multicharacters."[4] The dichotomy represented by these two methods of characterization reflects the ambivalence Melville and O'Neill display in their writing vis à vis Puritanism: averse to its content, the two are nevertheless in many ways indebted (however indirectly) to its habits of mind in the shaping of their literary forms and in the definition of their artistic visions.

Melville and O'Neill are related in other important respects. Through temperament and training, both developed deeply religious sensibilities, both rejected their early beliefs in later life, and both engaged in life-long searches for alternative forms of faith. One of the critical events of O'Neill's life which also figures prominently in his art was his refusal at age fourteen to continue attending church with his father, the culminating act in a steady three-year erosion in his faith.[5] A religious bias continued to inform the development of his aesthetic, however. At one point he declared, "I am interested only in the relation between man and God." The responsibility of the playwright, he believed, was "to dig at the roots of the sickness of today" which was caused by "the death of the old God."[6] The "death of God" as O'Neill understood it had serious implications for modern man. Devoid of intrinsic value, life must be redeemed by extrinsic systems. Kenneth Macgowan, a close friend, laid down O'Neill's emerging creed in these terms: the theatre is a "place for an instinctive expression of godhead.... The problem is to find a way to express the religious spirit independent of the church."[7] When asked to define the purpose of the theatre, O'Neill echoed Macgowan: "The theatre should give us what the church no longer gives us—a meaning."[8] O'Neill's search for meaning led him through numerous volumes of classical as well as modern thought: the ancient dramatists (Euripides, particularly), Racine, Ibsen, and Shaw provided models and materials for his creative imagination; Nietzsche and August Strindberg appealed to him particularly because they "offered a religion and an aesthetic, a mythology and a psychology."[9] But as with Herman Melville's

Calvinism, and like his Irish Catholic contemporary, James Joyce, O'Neill inevitably returned after all his searching to his beginnings, those crucial years between 1895 and 1902 (ages seven to fourteen). His mind like Stephen Dedalus' was "supersaturated with the religion" which he abandoned.[10] Even more than Joyce, however, O'Neill's "rigid Christian exile" at the Academy of Mount St. Vincent left a lasting impression on his mind.[11] In its severity and rigorous religiosity, O'Neill's boarding school experience produced memories and a sensibility highly attuned to the idea of American Puritanism.

In addition to its affinities to his early Catholic training, New England Puritanism provided a ready source of stock settings and character types which O'Neill repeatedly drew upon. As late as 1935 O'Neill set out to develop a cycle of plays dealing with approximately two centuries of New England history.[12] From *Diff'rent*, written in 1920, to *A Moon for the Misbegotten*, completed in 1943, O'Neill maintained a career-long fascination with the New England milieu. The spare meticulousness characteristic of Puritan life provided an ideal atmosphere for O'Neill's thematic comments on early twentieth-century ideas of propriety. *Diff'rent*, for example, opens on a small, spare parlor pervaded by "an aspect of scrupulous neatness." "In the center of the room there is a clumsy, marble-topped table. On the table, a large china lamp, a bulky Bible with a brass clasp, and several books that look suspiciously like cheap novels."[13] The juxtaposition of the bible with "cheap novels" indicates the kind of skeptical scrutiny traditional values undergo in the course of the play. As Timo Tiusanen observes, "it is the parlor itself, with the portraits on the walls, with the Bible on the table, with the joyless furniture, that makes Emma 'a Puritan maiden'." A product of her New England environment, she self-righteously repudiates her bridegroom, Caleb Williams, because of a transgression he had committed in the distant past. The relation continues in a sterile, fruitless manner for thirty years, culminating in what seem to be inevitable suicides.[14] In *Mourning Becomes Electra*, Christine, the mistress of the Mannon mansion, characterizes her house in terms similar to O'Neill's opening description of Emma Crosby's parlor in *Diff'rent*: "Each time I come back after being away," she says, nodding "scornfully toward the house," "it appears more like a sepulchre! The 'whited' one of the Bible—pagan temple front stuck like a mask on Puritan gray ugliness."[15] Christine's reference to death touches on the essence of O'Neill's presentation of Puritanism, a disease which desiccates the inner life while preserving outward appearances. Eventually it corrupts everything beautiful or alive: "What are you moongazing at" Christine asks her daughter. "Puritan maidens shouldn't peer too inquisitively at Spring? Isn't beauty an abomination and love a vile thing?" Dion's split personality in *The Great God Brown* dramatizes the horror of this kind of life. The repressed half of his self declares:

> Wakeup! Time to get up! Time to exist! Time for school! Time to learn! Learn to pretend! Cover your nakedness! Learn to Sin! Learn to keep step! Join the procession! Great Pan is dead! Be ashamed![16]

The mask from behind which Dion speaks in this scene succinctly epitomizes the stultifying uniformity required of his "Puritan" existence. As in *Diff'rent* and *Electra*, O'Neill repeatedly associates a New England setting with denial and repression, from Emma Crosby's parlor to the Mannon house, from the "despondent," stifling sitting room in the second act of *Beyond the Horizon* to the "neglected" tavern of *A Touch of the Poet*.[17]

O'Neill reveals his attitudes toward Puritanism through rhetorical as well as "scenic" imagery. Altogether "Puritan" or "Puritanical" are used six times in the plays. Invariably, the words appear in a context of "bitter mockery." In *The Iceman Cometh* Willie jestingly sings,

> "Oh, come up," she cried, "my sailor lad,
> And you and I'll agree,
> And I'll show you the prettiest *(Rap, rap, rap)*
> That you ever did see."

The "good woman" referred to in the song, according to Willie, displays an archetypally "lewd Puritan touch."[18] Other usages of the term are equally sarcastic: "In brief, Mike is a New England Irish Catholic Puritan, grade B," one character says in *Moon for the Misbegotten*; "It must be their damned Puritan background," says another in *A Touch of the Poet*. When not used in jest, "Puritan" connotes something sinister, almost threatening, as in this line from *More Stately Mansions*: "His whole character has something aridly prim and Puritanical about it."[19] Implicit in these statements is a sentiment O'Neill expressed in note #5 of *Mourning Becomes Electra*: "Puritan conviction of man born to sin and punishment—Orestes' furies within him, his conscience."[20] Sin, punishment, and death epitomize for O'Neill the essence of Puritanism. Life is overshadowed by death, living supplanted by guilt-ridden impotency. Ezra Mannon, a symbol of death-in-life, becomes O'Neill's emblematic Puritan: "His movements are exact and wooden and he has a mannerism of standing and sitting in stiff, poised attitudes that suggest the statues of military heroes. When he speaks, his deep voice has a hollow repressed quality, as if he were continually withholding emotion from it."[21] The senseless deaths of Emma and her fiance, for example, highlight the empty futility of the Crosby value system. Likewise, Lavinia's final imprisonment dramatically and emotionally consummates the self-destructive tendency implicit in the Mannon tradition.

These black elements are sometimes offset, however, by glimmers of redemptive light in the form of "conversion" experiences.[22] Ironically, the same tradition that teaches the depravity of man provides the means for man's rebirth; despair and hope come from the same source. This pattern agrees with O'Neill's method (the supernatural element removed, however): consigned to a meaningless existence, modern man must create order and purpose through his own efforts. With this kind of belief, it seems natural to expect that in the midst of a debilitating environment certain characters will strive for fulfillment. Rarely do humans triumph absolutely. In some of the less renowned plays, *Days Without End*, for example, a human will succeed unequivocally. John Loving emerges whole from a divided self to declare in a final, ecstatic exclamation, "I know! Love lives forever! Death is dead!...Life laughs with God's love again! Life laughs with

Puritanism 267

love!"[23] In his greatest plays, however, such moments either exist only symbolically or in substantially subdued forms; the redemptive exclamations become barely audible whispers. Ezra expresses a desire upon returning from the war, for example, to escape the cycle of death, unhappiness and barrenness in his own life and in his relationship with his wife. Constant exposure to death had lowered him to depths from which only hope or oblivion could emerge:

> It was seeing death all the time in this war got me to thinking these things. Death was so common, it didn't mean anything. That freed me to think of life. Queer, isn't it? Death made me think of life. Before that life had only made me think of death!
>
> Christine. (*without opening her eyes*) Why are you talking of death?
>
> Mannon. That's always been the Mannons' way of thinking. They went to the white meeting-house on Sabbaths and meditated on death. Life was a dying. Being born was starting to die. Death was being born. (*Shaking his head with a dogged bewilderment*) How in hell people ever got such notions! That white meeting-house. It stuck in my mind—clean-scrubbed and whitewashed—a temple of death! (82)

On seeing the white walls of the meeting-house splattered with blood, Ezra comes to realize religion's meaninglessness, the emptiness of his own life, and the "wall hiding [him and his wife] from each other!" (83). But his confession appears to serve no purpose. The change of heart experienced at war only hastens his destruction. "I hoped my homecoming would mark a new beginning—new love between us! I told you my secret feelings. I tore my insides out for you—thinking you'd understand!" (92). Instead, his rebirth only intensifies Christine's murderous feelings. But despite its ultimate futility, Ezra Mannon's resolution to work toward a "new beginning" a "new love" establishes the possibility for hope in a dead world.

The precedent for this kind of conversion experience appears as early as *Beyond the Horizon*. Robert, in the last stages of his sickness, rebukes his brother for his self-betrayal: "You're the deepest-dyed failure of the three [of us], Andy."[24] Then he adds a lesson learned from his own experience: "You'll be punished. You'll have to suffer to win back—" Unable to finish his sentence, the reader nevertheless gathers from the Biblical, even Puritan, context of Rob's words their intent. A few lines later he completes the thought: "Only through contact with suffering, Andy, will you—awaken" (153). As he dies, the admonition is repeated: "Remember, Andy—only through sacrifice..." (163). The sentiment expressed in these lines appears frequently in the Bible, from Isaiah's exclamation, "Awake, awake, put on strength, O arm of the LORD" (Isa. 51:9) to Paul's familiar exhortation, "If we suffer, we shall also reign with him" (I Tim. 2:12) or Peter's declaration that "Ye also...are built up...an holy priesthood to offer up spiritual sacrifices" (I Peter 2:5). The concepts Robert exemplifies and expresses are common to the Christian tradition. The repeated emphasis on punishment and suffering, however, typify O'Neill's use of Puritan motifs. Through his failure and pain, Robert achieves a vision and understanding that previously was inaccessible. The pattern of spiteful recriminations and tentative reconciliations in *Long Day's*

Journey Into Night also faintly resembles the Puritan cycle of self-abasement and divine acceptance. The closing scenes of the play are representative. After a particularly stinging insult about their Mother, Edmund punches his brother in the face. "Thanks Kid," Jamie ashamed mutters, "Glad you did. My dirty tongue. Like to cut it out."[25] Through similar repeated confrontations, the common despair over wife and mother brings a measure of empathy to the male members of the Tyrone family.

Such intimations of a better existence as many of the plays present are achieved only at a tremendous cost in human happiness. No play illustrates this better, perhaps, than *Desire Under the Elms*. One of the most "Puritan" of O'Neill's plays, the New England setting and tradition provide a context as important as the Greek elements that have traditionally been recognized as controlling the play's structure and plot.[26] Edger Racey noted that O'Neill also employed Biblical imagery, grafting "a religious symbology, almost an iconography" over the tragedy.[27] But he fails to account for the important role of Puritanism in shaping the action and themes of the play and in mediating between the setting, the characters' language, and the biblical imagery.[28] The play is set specifically "in newEngland, in the year 1850" and although O'Neill never mentions any specific religious context, Ephraim and his sons instinctively adopt a Biblical idiom: "Honor thy father!" Eben ironically chuckles, adding, "I pray he's died (2016).[29] In their belated rebuke, Simeon and Peter fall back on a conditioned response: "Ye'd oughtn't t' said that, Eben." " 'Twa'n't righteous." Their righteousness clearly consists more of mechanical, stock responses than of any personal religious sentiment. To Eben's denunciation of his sonship Simeon "dryly" replies: "Ye'd not let no one else say that about yer Maw! Ha!" (2017). When attempting to fathom their father's obsession for work, Simeon immediately falls back on a mystical, religious explanation: "It's somethin'—drivin' him—t' drive us!" "Whaal-I hold him t' jedgement!" Eben automatically responds. Then, as if thinking about the implications of his half-brother's remark, he asks, "Somethin'! What's somethin'?" But understanding of supernatural phenomenon lies well beyond Simeon's ken: "Dunno," he can only stupidly reply. But Eben, always self-consciously aware of the good and the evil inherent in his heritage (the ability to perceive and understand the hypocriticalness of his father's Puritanism, and of his own, is inherited from his "soft," empathetic mother) sees beneath the self-righteous "work ethic" that produced the farm. The "somethin'" driving Ephraim Cabot also drives Simeon and Peter to California—materialistic lust. The tension created by Eben's adversary relationship to the Puritanism in his own nature and in the environment that surrounds him is completely absent from the make up of his half-brothers. As true, full-blooded heirs of that tradition they accept and wear their hypocrisy completely without self-knowledge. Wholly instinctive, their response to life ("We'll maybe make 'em pay a hair for a hair!" [2017]) resembles Ephraim's dogmatic nearsightedness that fails to see in the tragedy that finally engulfs him any personal implication—only "the hand of God."

Ephraim's myopia, hardness, and pride not only indicate O'Neill's attitude towards Puritanism but contribute to the play's dramatic and thematic action. The old farmer's near blindness echoes a familiar Biblical concept portrayed in Jesus' condemnation of the Pharisees: "For judgment I am come into the world, that they which see not might see; and that they which see might be made blind" (John 9:39). "Made blind" by his exclusive singlemindedness, Ephraim displays many of the characteristics of the Pharisees and lawyers who in a spirit of self-righteousness put on an appearance of propriety only to cloak their greed and pride. (Cf. Luke 11:37:54) Leaving the farm to seek a wife, Ephraim justifies his physical lust—"I been hearin' the hens cluckin' an' the roosters crowin' all the durn day. I been listenin' t' the cows lowin' an' everythin' alse kicken' up till I can't stand it no more. It's spring an' I'm feelin' damned"—by declaring, "Now I'm ridin' out t' learn God's message t' me in the spring, like the prophets done" (2018). Later Ephraim omits altogether his feelings about "spring" and being "damned" when recounting the story of his "call" to Abbie. Still feeling a need to legitimize and justify his lust, he again utilizes Biblical imagery as a facade, reciting "with strange passion," "Yew air my Rose o' Sharon! Yer eyes air like..." Ephraim constantly identifies himself with Biblical prophets—Abraham ("It'd be the blessing' o' God, Abbie—the blessin' o' God A'mighty on me—in my old age"), Jacob (" 'An' Godhearkened unto Rachel'! An' God hearkened unto Abbie!" [2028]), Samuel ("God A'mighty, call from the dark!"), John the Baptist ("This spring the call come—the voice o' God cryin' in my wilderness"), and Peter ("God's hard, not easy! God's in the stones! Build my church on a rock—out o' stones an' I'll be in them!" [2029]). Ephraim's method of self-characterization resembles the seventeenth-century Puritan penchant for "plebeian" typologyzing, identifying events in Puritan history with Old Testament types as exemplified in the writings of Cotton Mather, Samuel Sewall, Thomas Hooker, Edward Johnson, and others.

In order to identify himself with the past, as we have seen, Ephraim liberally adapts the facts of his religious tradition to fit his distorted perceptions. He constantly emphasizes the severity, the iron will displayed, for example, by a figure like John Endicott as portrayed in Hawthorne's sketch, "Endicott and the Red Cross." Eben describes the Puritan's sternness while rebuking his father's furious cursing: "Yew 'n yewr God! Allus cussin' folks—allus naggin' em!" (2025). Characteristically, Ephraim is too wrapt up in himself to hear. "God o' the old! God o' the lonesome!" he cries. Cabot's constant worship of a God of vengeance and wrath amounts ultimately to merely a vindication of his own ego. His denial of human relationships leads to isolation, another characteristic of the life of the covenant Israelites which the Puritans emulated. "They's no peace in houses, they's no rest livin' with folks. Somethin's always livin' with ye" (2035). Facing down the whole community, Ephraim denounces with ministerial passion every person: "Ye're a sickly generation! Yer hearts air pink, not red! Yer veins is full o' mud an' water! I be the on'y man in the country! Whoop! See that! I'm a Injun! I've killed Injuns in the West afore ye was born...." The scene in the kitchen where Ephraim delivers his "sermon" brings to mind the famous generational conflict in the history of the early New England theocracy. By analogy to the early settlers, Ephraim rejects the newer generation as weak and unworthy of the privileges which he had to earn through his monumental efforts. In fact, Ephraim's claims to strength and endurance are constantly borne out through the play. In the climactic struggle with Eben outside the house, "the old man's concentrated strength is too much" for the son (2036). In order to gain his strength, however, Ephraim must exorcise all compassion, empathy, and humility.

Following the "God o' the old," Ephraim "growed hard." The harder he becomes, the more his pride grows. "When ye kin make corn sprout out o' stones, God's livin' in yew!" (2028). "I'd made thin's grow out o' nothin'—like the will o' God, like the servant o' His hand" (2029). "No, by God, I hain't easy!" (2036). His repeated blasphemy indicates the magnitude of his pride. As with Oedipus, however, the object of his pride, the productivity of the farm, becomes the means of his punishment. Alone, having finally driven away all human companionship, Cabot remains a prisoner of the land he so long coveted.

While severely critical, O'Neill's attitude toward the play's protagonist is not entirely condemnatory. It was of Ephraim, not Eben, that O'Neill observed, "He's so autobiographical."[30] While his fate is just, there is something admirable in Ephraim's single-minded dedication, in his implicit faith:

> God's hard, not easy!...I kin hear his voice warnin' me agen to be hard an' stay on my farm. I kin see his hand usin' Eben t' steal t' keep me from weakness. I kin feel I be in the palm o' His hand, His fingers guiden' me....It's a-goin' t' be lonesomer now than ever it war afore—an I'm gittin' old, Lord—ripe on the bough....(*Then stiffening*) Waal—what d'ye want? God's lonesome, hain't He? God's hard an' lonesome! (2041)

Like the Bundrens in *As I Lay Dying*, who view their hardships in carrying Addie's corpse to the Jefferson cemetery as signs of God's favor, Ephraim sees his trial as a confirmation of his way of life. Cabot's attitude also resembles the comments made by seventeenth-century Puritans in similar situations. Of her suffering at the hands of the Indians, Mary Rowlandson proclaimed, "The Lord hereby would make us the more to acknowledge His hand and to see that our help is always in Him." "God was with me in a wonderful manner, carrying me along and bearing up my spirit [so] that it did not quite fail."[31] The will to endure, the ability to see beyond life's reversals, to maintain faith in spite of suffering represent traits that O'Neill found lacking in many of the religions of his day.

Far more impressive than Ephraim's endurance, however, is Eben's act of self-sacrifice, an act that surpasses his father's Old Testament faith as far as Paul's doctrine of charity excels the principles of faith and hope. Significantly, Eben's dramatic reversal also resembles a conversion experience:

> I was waiting. I got to thinkin' o' yew. I got to thinkin' how I'd loved ye. It hurt like somethin' was bustin' in my chest an' head. I got t' cryin'. I knowed sudden I loved ye yet, an' allus would love ye! (2040)

Eben's "sudden" knowledge enables him to pay the ultimate penalty—"prison 'r death 'r hell 'r anythin'!" The play ends on a hopeful note in spite of the severity of their doom:

> ABBIE: Wait. (*Turns to EBEN*) I love ye, Eben.
>
> EBEN: I love ye, Abbie. (*They kiss. The three men grin and shuffle embarrassedly. EBEN takes ABBIE'S hand. They go out the door in rear, the men following, and come*

Puritanism 271

from the house, walking hand in hand to the gate. EBEN stops there and points to the sunrise sky) Sun's a-rizin'. Purty hain't it?

ABBIE: Ay-eh. (*They both stand for a moment looking up raptly in attitudes strangely aloof and devout.*) (2041)

Eben and Abbie's love has restored the true spirit of piety (faith, hope and charity) to the world.

NOTES

1. Heywood Broun, "*Diff'rent* Comes to Broadway at the Selwyn," *New York World*, 1 February 1921; Louis Broomfield, "The New Yorker," *Bookman* 60 (Jan., 1925), 621; Harold Clurman, *Nation* 215 (4 December 1972), 572-73. The citations are taken from Jordan Y. Miller's *Eugene O'Neill and the American Critic* (Archon Books, 1973), pp. 285, 272, and 424.

2. William H. Shurr, "Typology and Historical Criticism of the American Renaissance," *Emerson Society Quarterly* XX (1974), pp. 60-61.

3. *The Plays of Eugene O'Neill* (Carbondale, Illinois, 1965), p. 251. See the entire chapter, pp. 243-285, wherein Raleigh relates O'Neill to as diverse a span of writers as Richard Henry Dana, Henry Adams, Emerson, Thoreau, Whitman, Poe, Hawthorne, Melville, Twain, and Henry James.

4. Raleigh, pp. 20, 255.

5. Louis Sheaffer, *O'Neill: Son and Playwright* (Boston 1969), pp. 76-89.

6. Cited in *The Intimate Notebooks of George Jean Nathan* (New York, 1932), p. 180 in Edwin A. Engel's "Ideas in the Plays of Eugene O'Neill," John Gassner, ed., *Ideas in the Drama* (New York, 1964), p. 103.

7. *The Theatre of Tomorrow* (New York, 1921), pp. 177, 264-265. Cited in Engel, p. 103.

8. Cleanth Brooks, R.W.B. Lewis, Robert Penn Warren, *American Literature: The Makers and the Making* (New York, 1973), Vol. II, p. 2014.

9. Engel, pp. 105-106.

10. James Joyce, *A Portrait of the Artist as a Young Man* (Penguin Books, 1976), p. 240. Cf. Sheaffer, p. 434.

11. Sheaffer, p. 64.

12. For a full treatment of "A Tale of Possessors Self-Dispossessed," O'Neill's abortive cycle of plays, see John J. Fitzgerald, "The Bitter Harvest of O'Neill's Projected Cycle," *New England Quarterly* XL (September, 1967), 364-374.

13. *Diff'rent* (New York, 1925), p. 183.

14. *O'Neill's Scenic Images* (Princeton, 1968), p. 90.

15. *Mourning Becomes Electra* (New York, 1931), p. 31.

16. Cited in Sophus Keith Winther, *Eugene O'Neill: A Critical Study* (New York, 1961), pp. 45-46. See the entire discussion, "Anathema of Puritanism," pp. 43-53.

17. Tiusanen, pp. 89, 228-237, 322.

18. *The Iceman Cometh* (Random House, 1946), p. 40.

19. The above examples are cited in J. Russell Reaver, *An O'Neill Concordance* (Detroit, 1969), Vol. III, p. 1263.

20. Cited in Winther, p. 178.

21. Cited in Tiusanen, p. 230. For a view of the causes of O'Neill's sometimes bitter anti-Puritanism, see Camillo Pellizzi, "Irish-Catholic Anti-Puritan," in *O'Neill and His Plays: Four Decades of Criticism*, eds. Oscar Cargill, N. Bryllion Fagin, and William J. Fisher (New York University Press, 1961), pp. 353-357.

22. Engel, p. 104.

23. *Days Without End* (Random House, 1934), p. 157.

24. *Beyond the Horizon* (New York, 1921), p. 152.

25. *Long Day's Journey Into Night* (New Haven, 1955), p. 162.

26. Jay Ronald Neyers ("O'Neill's Use of the Phedre Legend in *Desire Under the Elms*," *Revue de Literature Comparee* XLI [January-March, 1967], 120-125) and Edgar F. Racey, Jr., ("Myth as Tragic Structure in *Desire Under the Elms*" in *O'Neill: A Collection of Critical Essays*, ed. John Gassner [Englewood Cliffs, New Jersey, 1964], pp. 57-61) examine the classical background of the play, including O'Neill's use of the Phedre legend by Racine and Euripides, the Oedipal theme in *Electra* and also Euripides' *Hypolytus*.

27. Racey, p. 57.

28. Egil Tornqvist, in "Jesus and Judas: On Biblical Allusions in O'Neill's Plays," *Etudes Anglaises* XXIV (January-March, 1971), 41-49, states that the purpose of Biblical allusions is "to indicate a discrepancy between the biblical (con) text on the one hand and the nature, aim or situation of the characters on the other" (41). But he only salutorily links these discrepancies with O'Neill's use of a Puritan ideal. Notably, one critic has discussed the connection between O'Neill's use of Biblical images and Puritanism: Peter L. Hays, "Biblical Perversions in *Desire Under the Elms*," *Modern Drama* XI (February, 1969), 423-428. He contends that *Desire* perhaps is not *controlled* but nonetheless "shaped" by this idea: the perversion of the Puritan religion "cripples love and destroys men."

29. Page numbers follow Brooks, Lewis and Warren's reprint of the text.

30. Brooks, Lewis, and Warren, p. 2015.

31. *The Narrative of the Captivity and Restoration of Mrs. Mary Rowlandson*, in Charles H. Lincoln, ed., *Narratives of the Indian Wars* (New York, 1913), pp. 113, 115.

Renascence, 30 (Spring 1978): 152-162.

Freedom and Fixity in the Plays of Eugene O'Neill

Linda Ben-Zvi

One of the constant poles in O'Neill's plays is this desire for freedom, a word that has particular significance when related to the O'Neill canon. In fact, the first four definitions of "freedom" in the *OED* seem specifically written with O'Neill in mind: "exemption or release from slavery or imprisonment; liberation from the bondage of sin (figurative); the quality of being free or noble; and the state of being able to act without hindrance or restraint." O'Neill constantly creates personae who long to escape the imprisonment they feel within the microcosmic world of the family and the macrocosmic world of twentieth-century materialistic society; who feel the weight of sin, and desire surcease from its burden; who seek if not nobility at least a life of purpose; and who yearn to be unhindered and unrestrained.

If freedom, then, is a constant theme in O'Neill works, it is set against an antithetical theme also at work in the shaping of an O'Neill play; the tendency toward and the desire for fixity. I choose that word for more than its euphonious pairing with freedom; it too seems peculiarly appropriate for particular tendencies in O'Neill's writing. The word originally comes from physics where it refers to the property of enduring heat without volitalization or evaporation. It also refers to the condition of not being liable to displacement or change, the desire for stability or permanence in situation. One has only to think of O'Neill's characters, some of whom are literally exposed to the heat of a fiery furnace, others to the hell and furnaces of the mind, to see the connections and the significance of the word in O'Neill's writing. Characters may quest after new experiences, seeking freedom from society and family; but at the same time almost all desire the very thing they are denying; fixity, home, "stability or permanence in situation." The pull between these two seemingly dichotomous poles creates the tensions and provides the imagery in many of O'Neill's plays, both in his early and later periods.

O'Neill's earliest successes were his Glencairn cycle plays, works deriving from his time at sea. Like the poem "Free," written, O'Neill said, "on a deep-sea barque in the days of Real Romance,"[1] they offer scenes of actual sea life, with characters shaped by the men O'Neill met and settings he knew. The fictional steamer *Glencairn* is seen at anchor off an island in the West Indies in *The Moon of the Caribees*, midway on a voyage between New York and England in *Bound East for Cardiff*, somewhere in the Atlantic in *In the Zone*. Yet despite the sea locales and the freedom such images should convey, there is something peculiar about O'Neill's depiction of the sea in these works. Rather than vast, open horizons, sea spume, the unleashed fury and power of nature—those things he experienced directly and read about in Conrad and London—O'Neill creates a very different world on the stage. In none of the plays is an expanse of sea shown. Instead the playing spaces tend to be closed, cramped quarters, small crowded bunks, foreshortened areas. In *Bound East for Cardiff* and *In the Zone*, action is confined to the forecastle. While *The Moon of the Caribees* is set on deck, only a brief strip of it is seen, and the action always seems to take place below, out of sight, again in the closed space of the forecastle—the sailor's home. Throughout that play, almost like a litany, Bella keeps reminding the men, "Into the forecastle boys." And in other early one act plays such as *Ile* and *Where the Cross is Made*, there are also severely restricted areas: Captain Keeney's cabin on board the steam whaling ship *Atlantic Queen* is a "small, square compartment about eight feet high";[2] the pseudo-"cabin" of Captain Bartlett is "a room erected as a lookout post at the top of his house."[3]

Instead of concentrating on openness, O'Neill limits the stage spaces in his sea plays to room-like, womb-like enclosures, which inhabitants accept without question, as an alternative to life on land. *The Glencairn* seems to provide less freedom than fixity, less openness than enclosure, in short a surrogate home and family replacing those left behind.

Set on the sea, yet mirroring the confines of home, O'Neill's early sea plays attest to the tensions created by the dual desires for freedom and fixity. The same dichotomy is repeated in O'Neill's first produced full-length work, *Beyond the Horizon*. Rather than having one actor experience the pull between travel and home, O'Neill creates a dual personae: Robert and Andrew Mayo. It is Robert who dreams of distant seas and curses the hills that confine him: "They're like the walls of a narrow prison yard shutting me in from all the freedom and wonder of life," he says.[4] "What I want to do now is keep moving so that I won't take root in any one place" (p.9). He readily admits the source of his romantic visions:

> ...beauty of the far off and unknown, the mystery and spell of the East, which lures me in the books I've read, the need of the freedom of great wide spaces, the joy of wandering on and on—in quest of the secret which is hidden over there (p.18).

The very generality of the speech should be an indication that Robert is pursuing some elusive, youthful fancy, which O'Neill somewhat deprecates by the inflated language he gives his protagonist. However, it is more likely that the author, thirty at the time of the composition, still shares with the speaker the vague longings that he expressed ten years earlier in "Free."

Beyond the Horizon was begun in 1918. About that time, O'Neill entered in his notebook this speech to be used in Act II of "Chris Christopherson," the earlier version of *Anna Christie*:

> No ties, no responsibilities—no guilty feeling, like the sea —always moving, never staying, never held by anything—never giving a damn—making the world part of you, not being a grain of sand carried, buried and lost and held back by other grains. Not American, Swede—but citizen of the sea which belongs to no one. Not a wife, marriage, an anchor but women of all lands and races—Woman! You might convert me.[5]

In the speech O'Neill again invokes the sea as the source of freedom, the same escape that Robert seeks. There is no depreciation of the desire in the words. What is present, however, is the parallel guilt and weight of responsibilities such an attitude evokes. Also expressed is an alternative means of freedom: women, quickly appended to "Woman!"— capital W, exclamation point—the singular subsuming all women, but clearly not "wife," who seems associated with what the speaker seeks to escape.[6]

In *Beyond the Horizon*, O'Neill explores a similar desire for escape and generalized love as expressed by Robert, who through his marriage to Ruth gives up his dream of flight. At the same time, O'Neill creates the contrary situation through the dual persona Andrew: the brother forced out of his secure world because he is spurned by Ruth, and who becomes an involuntary exile, never enjoying the world he sees because of the shadow of the world he has left. In this play, more than any other in the O'Neill canon, the stark pull between freedom and fixity is described, with neither alternative offering the hoped-for release and assuagement.

Robert never does leave home; he marries a woman (not Woman!). Andrew goes to sea, has women, but never the Woman! Tragedy ensues from both experiences. Seen in isolation, *Beyond the Horizon* might be interpreted as ironic, promising a happy ending if only the dreamer Robert had left and the man of the earth Andrew had remained. But placed in the context of other O'Neill plays, it is clear that no such easy solution is possible for any one individual, because the struggle dichotomized in this play is actually the dual struggle played out in the mind of each character, a struggle that allows no resolution in the O'Neill canon.

The tensions caused by this schism are manifested in the stage setting of the early sea plays; they become even more pronounced in the following plays where the contrary pulls become the central thematic concerns. In almost all O'Neill's works, when characters do actually get "beyond the horizon," what they find is far less than what they expected, and what they create are substitutes for the past. Rather than revel in rootlessness, most actually hold with tenacity to their surrogate homes.

The best example of freedom of sea life metamorphosing into fixity of home is found in the *The Harry Ape*, where Yank ridicules the idea of home while indicating how he has made a new home of his furnace world.

> Dis is home see? What d'yuh want with home? (*Proudly*) I runned away from mine when I was a kid. On'y too glad to beat it, dat was me. Home was lickings for me, dat's all.[7]

The "it" to which he now proudly boasts connection is not the sea, the horizon, or even freedom; it is the narrow, womb-like world below deck that he controls, and the men who now constitute the only family he has. When Mildred appears to dislodge him from this edenic, albeit horrifc, world, Yank suffers a second displacement. Adrift in an alien world, he cannot feel the freedom of rootlessness about which Robert speaks in *Beyond the Horizon* because his real desire is not to travel forth but to remain in place: his place. Only at the end of the play, in the death-hold of the ape, does Yank perhaps find what has eluded him. O'Neill closes the play by suggesting, "And perhaps, the Hairy Ape at last belongs" (p. 232). O'Neill does not say that Yank is free but rather that he may belong—in death.

As O'Neill got older the absorption with freedom in his plays became greater yet the need for fixity more pervasive. Running through the cycle plays of possessors self-dispossessed—as well as in the late, great plays—*The Iceman Cometh, Long Day's Journey into Night*, and *A Moon for the Misbegotten*—is the recognition that freedom, if possible at all, comes not from flight but from return, not in a promising future but in a redeemed past, not in life but in death. "There is no present or future—only the past happening over and over again—now, "James Tyrone says in *A Moon for the Misbegotten* while he rests in the arms of Josie Hogan.[8] His embedded monologue that constitutes the major section of the play traces a movement not outward—westward—but eastward, back to the home with the body of his mother, the mother he has irrevocably lost. Mary Tyrone makes a similar discovery in *Long Day's Journey into Night*: "The past is the present, isn't it? It's the future, too. We all try to lie out of that but life won't let us."[9] Her own growing obliteration of the present, through the fog of morphine, gradually allows her to sink into a yesterday, beyond the touch of those with whom she shares her present life: she is another irrevocably lost mother. Con Melody, early in Act II of *A Touch of the Poet* echoes the same thought: "no future but the past."[10] And in *The Iceman Cometh* Hickey appears, selling forgetfulness of past and future, but the habitue's of Harry Hope's bar reject his pitch. They know that the only thingleft for them is a commitment to the pipedreams shaped by the past.

If there is no future, if the past is all, the notion of escape into some new realm, a freedom in the unknown, is also precluded. And in fact, repeatedly in the later plays, O'Neill has characters specifically talk about freedom, but usually as a sorry substitute for the homes they have lost. One of the most direct examples of the pervasiveness of the desire for home against the freedom of flight appears in the opening scene of the 1931 fragment *The Calms of Capricorn*, where the freed slave Cato remarks:

> Freedom! I've had about all I want of it. Just the same old work, no freedom from that. Sure I earn a few dollars each month but I spend it all on whiskey and gambling and I'm broke the next day, so what good is it?[11]

He goes on to yearn for the past and home, even a slave home: "I wish I was back in Georgia. What I'd give for some corn pone and chitlins. That was the life" (p.5).

Cato is middle-aged and one might assume that freedom has lost some of its appeal to him; yet even among the young in this play freedom is seen as something less than desirable. Ethan, another young man who seeks a life on the sea, begins by recognizing the limitations of his quest:

> To me the sea meant freedom from all land values, but I find myself still enslaved by them, always obeying orders. And I feel a love for the sea and hate it for that very reason. I want to break away, to experience all the freedom of the spirit. (p.14)

Ethan, while disillusioned about the escape the sea might promise, does not actually yearn for home—and for a specific reason: he brings his family with him on board his ship the *Dream of the West*.

Other characters in the later plays leave their homes and families only to find that in adulthood they still yearn for their original fixity and for those from whom they have never psychically separated, most often the mother. Progressively in these later plays the exile seeks the woman, a combination mother/lover who becomes surrogate for the sea and freedom, and at the same time symbol for the fixity of home and love. Ethan refers to the sea as "a woman of all moods for all men, and all seductive and evil—devil mother or wife or mistress or daughter or waterfront drab" (p.15). By focusing more directly on the apotheosized female and equating her with the sea, rather than seeing her as another option promising freedom, as in the "Chris Christopherson" speech, O'Neill seems to indicate that the earlier desire for freedom through a sea change is impossible to achieve, that the only freedom lies ultimately in return to the past, and to the mother.

Perhaps the best example of this recognition comes in *More Stately Mansions*. In this play Simon Harford, the unseen suitor of *A Touch of the Poet*, is now married to Sara, Con Melody's daughter. There is no talk of fleeing or the sea. Act I finds him not only a husband but already a father, pursuing a life detached from his mother Deborah. Yet as the play progresses, it becomes clear that the son has never really left the world of his mother and that he still yearns to return to her: to the literal confines of her garden, to the symbolic world of childhood, the prelapsarian state before Sara, sexuality, and the adult world intervened. He admits to Deborah that "I began to remember lately—and long for this garden...this safe haven, where we could repose our souls in fantasy—evade, escape, forget, rest in peace!"[12] What he realizes is, "I have become so weary of what they call life beyond the wall, mother" (p. 103). Reshaping Robert's cry of thirty years earlier in *Beyond the Horizon*, Simon recognizes, as the younger hero did not, that life beyond walls or hills may offer no more and in fact much less than life at home. It is interesting to place these two plays in apposition because there is much in Simon's character that brings to mind the dual personae Robert and Andrew. Simon speaks of being "split into opposites and divided against himself. All in the name of freedom. As if at the end of every dream of liberty one did not find the slave, oneself, to whom oneself, the master is enslaved" (p. 49). Rather than the dual image of the man who would go and the man who would stay, O'Neill presents in the later play one character with a dual self, desiring both movement toward individualism and personal freedom and a commensurate movement back to infancy, mother and primal home. "Oh if you knew how desperately I long to escape her and become again only your son," (p. 178) Simon tells his mother, about his wife Sara.

His reverie of the past is intertwined with his memory of the fairytale of his youth, in which a king through "the evil magic of a beautiful enchantress, had been dispossessed of his realm and banished to wander over the world, a homeless, unhappy outcast" (p.110). The language is important. Movement outward, away from home no longer has even the pretense of adventure, of a search for freedom; it is clearly seen as dispossession, banishment: punishment wreaked by the enchantress—the evil mother. Dispelling the stated title of the cycle, "A Tale of Possessors Self Dispossessed," O'Neill makes clear that the figure in the tale has no volition; he has been acted upon, dispossesed by the mother.

Yet as Simon continues, there is a coda to the tale: a possibility of opening a door and returning to his kingdom. But the enchantresses warns, "If you dare to open the door you may discover this is no longer your old happy realm but a barren desert, where it is always night, haunted by terrible ghosts and ruled over by a hideous old witch, who wishes to destroy your claim to her realm, and the moment you cross the threshold she will tear you to pieces and devour you" (p. 111). The mother in this speech is seen as the malevolent force that keeps the child at bay, and time the trickster that makes of enchantresses hideous old witches. But even more revealing is O'Neill's method of presenting the desire for fixity: in a fairy tale, a fiction within the fiction of his play, even further removed from any possibility of realization, a story alive only in the mind of a grown man who retells it to the initial storyteller—the mother.

Simon concludes his tale by moaning, "So he remained for the rest of his life standing before the door, and became a beggar, whining for alms from all who passed by" (p. 111). The figure in the tale does not leave, nor does he seek a surrogate home on sea or land as earlier characters did when home was lost to them or they to home. Instead he remains a beggar at the door awaiting the hoped-for return to the safety and surety of home, the return to a past that probably existed only in the fairy tale recounted.

The play, however, does not end with Simon replicating the position of his fictive character. Instead he settles for what so many other O'Neill characters in the later plays must choose as substitute for the world they cannot recapture: marriage. He returns to Sara, and conjugal love; however, instead of the duality of wife/mother that had pulled at the hero throughout the play, O'Neill offers the conciliatory image of wife *as* mother, Sara embodying the maternal spirit of Deborah, offering solace in arms that Simon can enter.

The same image of mother/lover is repeated in O'Neill's last play *A Moon for the Misbegotten* where Josie embraces the sleeping James Tyrone, becoming at least until sunrise the mother he cannot reclaim. Yet for Tyrone, there is not the saving grace of sexual love; he is too lost for such healing restoration. Instead for him the playwright offers a more lasting freedom: death.

Throughout O'Neill's writings, in early as well as late plays, death has been seen as the ultimate freedom, and possibly the ultimate return to security and home. The sea offered only temporary respite; the mother was impossible to obtain and finally could be approached only through surrogate plural forms of woman. Death promises if not freedom at least surcease. Yank seems to achieve release at the end of *The Hairy Ape*, as had the earlier avatar Yank at the end of *Bound East for Cardiff*. Those who do not actually die often imagine death as a freedom for themselves. Nina Leeds, having given up the quest for happiness through men, muses about death: "I'm so contentedly weary with life."[13] Lavinia talks of dying within the all-consuming Mannon walls where "I'll live alone with the dead, and keep their secrets, and let them hound me, until the curse is paid out and the last Mannon is let die!"[14]

The most famous character who voices the hoped-for freedom that death may bring is probably Edmund Tyrone in *Long Day's Journey*. Like Simon in *More Stately Mansions*, he too yearns for a reclaiming of a lost realm and a lost mother. He has sought freedom on the sea, and in part he has been successful. But it is not the success that Robert might have envisioned in *Beyond the Horizon*. What he explains in his famous speech is not the thrill of rootlessness but the nonbeing of total immersion, a loss of self, that the sea provides, and finally a recognition that "for a moment I lost myself—actually lost my life. I was set free!" (p. 153). Yet the experience is momentary, Edmund continues: "Then the hand lets the veil fall and you are alone, lost in the fog again, and you stumble on toward nowhere, for no good reason!" (p. 153). The end of his reverie lies in the recognition that the speaker is one "who must always be a little in love with death!" (p. 154). The words are spoken as the lost mother is heard moving, alone, out of reach above.

A discussion of the pull between freedom and fixity and of the growing tendency of later O'Neill characters to shun the traditional notions of freedom for the desired freedom of home restored, or death, besides offering a way of describing the tensions within an O'Neill play, allows for some observations about O'Neill's writing in general. First, it cannot easily be subsumed under those designations for American writing that blithely divide the world by gender: males desiring freedom and females supporting fixity. The myth of American males seeking escape—down the Mississippi out of the reaches of a Widow Douglas who would civilize, away from the hands of a fair young thing who would tame and marry, the Leslie Fiedler paradigm[15]—falls apart when applied to O'Neill's works (and I suspect does not hold unqualified for other male writers either). In O'Neill's writing the tendency of the male characters is more consistently for fixity and security than for questing, despite their avowed disclaimers to the contrary. The need for roots seems to be a more pervasive need than for flight.[16]

Second, it helps explain O'Neill's depictions of and attitudes toward women, a troubling topic. As much as O'Neill desires to break with home and free himself from the confines of place, his stronger desire is to reconnect with that figure most identified with the past: the mother. It is she who becomes the dispossessor requiring the exile of the child, and it is she who is the illusory center the exile seeks. Women, as O'Neill wrote in his "Chris Christopherson" fragment, become substitutes for the mother, who remains an irretrievably lost figure, marking an irretrievably lost home. O'Neill continually replays this Freudian schism between mother and son. What may make this juncture so pronounced in his work is his own autobiographical struggles with his mother, Ella Quinlan O'Neill, whose addiction created a premature rupture that was thrust upon the playwright. The sea, escape, and marriage never seem to offer sufficient compensation for the lost home. And the mother—and all women—remain in O'Neill's works hated for the primal betrayal and desired for the primal recompense—that is never sufficient.

In this discussion I have focused—as O'Neill does—on the male persona. A question should be asked about the pull between freedom and fixity for female characters in O'Neill's writings, who should seek such return, since they too are separated from the mother and must leave the primal home. It is a question that male writers don't often ask. Harold Pinter—a playwright strikingly like O'Neill in his obsessive preoccupation with home and security—attempts to introduce the topic in his 1978 play *Betrayal*, when he has one character remark: "It's also true that nobody talks much about the girl babies leaving the womb." When his male friend responds, "I am prepared to do so," we find that the willingness leads nowhere since the speaker has nothing to say.[17]

O'Neill, too, usually has nothing to say about the commensurate difficulties of his female characters because his plays—like those of Pinter—are so concerned with the male experience, where women become auxiliary and usually adversarial: enchantresses or wicked witches, lovers or mothers, but always those figures against whom the male characters must seek freedom or toward whom they must seek redress and solace.

A brief glance at these women indicates that they have an easier time adjusting to the world outside the home than the men. Often practical, self-assured, and resourceful—usually cunning—they seem less tortured and more able to adjust to life "beyond the wall." Sara Melody is a survivor; so are Christine Mannon, and Josie Hogan. Anna Christie, at her first smell of sea air, goes through a change, one unimpeded by any fears of "dat ole davil."[18] At the end of the play, she does not return to the primal home, as Simon Harford desires; she creates her own, and she tells Matt and her father that it will be "a regular place for you two to come to" (p. 158). Lavinia Mannon, when she makes her sea voyage leaves her New England home and haunted memories behind:

> I loved those Islands. They finished setting me free. There was something there mysterious and beautiful—a good spirit—of love—coming out of the island and sea. It made me forget death." (p. 212)

Unlike her brother Orin, who voluntarily seeks the shelter of home and the mother he has lost, Lavinia struggles against the doom of the Mannon family. Even Nina Leeds, who ends in the comforting arms of a surrogate father, does so after seeking life through other men, none substitutes for the parent but substitutes for the lover. While she is the female figure placed most directly at the center of an O'Neill play, she is unlike his male personae, in her clear eschewing of place. If anything, she actively seeks escape from the confines of her father's house and more specifically his library—the demarcated "home" of this play. In one of her early reveries in Act One she thinks: "Now that's said...I'm going...never come back...oh, how I loathe this room!..." Nine acts later she may return to the same claustrophobic world through the agency of the surrogate father Marsden, but her return seems to her more like the promise of death than of hoped-for life, as it seems for O'Neill's male figures. In the course of the play she does not yearn for a return to the parent or to the familial home, as male characters so often do.

O'Neill has none of these women approximate the struggles of his male characters. It is only in the depiction of certain maternal figures that he sensitively explores some of the same tensions that his males experience. Two examples suffice. Deborah Harford and Mary Tyrone are both created primarily to fulfill the roles of mothers for lost sons. However, O'Neill depicts something of Deborah's own longings for freedom and flight: in her fantasy world in her garden, a Versailles of the mind, where she as courtesan walks with King Louie, or awaits Lord Napoleon. He also explores briefly her loneliness, and her fear of ageing, insanity, and death. And he touches on her need for self-possession against the encroachment of the son: "You were such a stubborn greedy little boy. I could feel your grasping fingers groping toward every secret, private corner of my soul" (p.

184). Yet it is apparent that Deborah and her personal wants and fears are of importance only in so far as they affect Simon. Her individuation is significant since it becomes the source for his own obsessive need for love. He says, "I have never forgotten the anguished sense of being suddenly betrayed, of being wounded and deserted and left alone in a life in which there was no security or faith or love but only danger and suspicion and devouring greed! By God, I hated you then! I wished you dead! I wished I had never been born!" (p. 184).

The words of the son are re-echoed in most of O'Neill's plays, most forcefully in *Long Day's Journey Into Night*. In that work, again O'Neill makes some effort to have his mother figure, Mary Tyrone, tell of her own needs for home, friends, purpose, and love. She becomes the woman most nearly identified with the dualities of the male personae. She too lives in a world where the present is overshadowed by the past. In her case, the desired freedom from home is achieved not through a sea trip but through the variant acceptable for O'Neill's women: marriage, in this instance to the dashing James Tyrone. Yet the ensuing freedom from the past is countered by her yearning for return to childhood, and love, not of mother, but of mother church and the mothers of the church. The last words of the play are her soliloquy about her own search for freedom and her desired return to the fixity of home and youth. Yet again her litany is spoken against the refrain of the last male words just sounded: a recrimination implicit in the Swinburne poem Jamie recites:

> Let us go hence, go hence; she will not see.
> Sing all once more together; surely she,
> She too, remembering days and words that were,
> Will turn a little toward us sighing; but we,
> We are hence, we are gone, as though we had not been there.
> Nay, and though all men seeing had pity on me,
> She would not see. (p. 174)

While the poem can be read as an acknowledgement of the shared pain that both sexes experience, the emphasis in the lines and in the play is on the woman's denial of "pity on me," pity on the sons and husband who need her.

In O'Neill's plays, though the duality of freedom and fixity can be found in the lives of both women and men, it is the male experiences of exile and return—to the mother—that is the dominant theme told and retold, unresolved and unresolvable as it was in the life of O'Neill.[19]

NOTES

1. Sheaffer, *Son and Playwright*, p. 164.

2. *Ile*, in *The Plays of Eugene O'Neill* (New York, 1955), p. 535.

3. *Where the Cross is Made*, Ibid., p. 555.

4. Eugene O'Neill, *Beyond the Horizon* (New York, 1925), p. 72. All further references to this play will appear in the text.

5. *Eugene O'Neill at Work*, ed. and annotated by Virginia Floyd (New York, 1981), p. 25.

6. This speech was written just after O'Neill entered into marriage with Agnes Boulton, and may reflect his own ambivilance between freedom and fixity and the confines of marriage.

7. Eugene O'Neill, *The Hairy Ape* in *Anna Christie, The Emperor Jones, The Hairy Ape* (New York, 1972), pp. 170-171.

8. Eugene O'Neill, *A Moon for the Misbegotten* (New York, 1974), pp. 82-83.

9. Eugene O'Neill, *Long Day's Journey into Night* (New Haven, 1977), p. 87.

10. Eugene O'Neill, *A Touch of the Poet* (New Haven, 1957), p. 63.

11. Eugene O'Neill, *The Calms of Capricorn* (New Haven, 1981). p. 5. Further references to the play appear in the text.

12. Eugene O'Neill, *More Stately Mansions* (New Haven, 1964), p. 103. Further references to the play appear in the text.

13. Eugene O'Neill, *Strange Interlude* (New York, 1959), p. 222.

14. Eugene O'Neill, *Mourning Becomes Electra* (New York, 1959), p. 376.

15. Leslie Fiedler, *Love and Death in the American Novel* (New York, 1966).

16. When O'Neill was asked to cite his reason for the demise of America, he noted the society's failure to "set down roots." Interestingly, his friend and colleague Susan Glaspell, when posing the same question in her play *Inheritors*, has her persona Madeline say, "It got set too soon." For the male writer, O'Neill, fixity seems the higher good, at least for society; for the woman writer, Glaspell, fixity is what impinges on the freedom of her female personae and, therefore, she sees any roots as restrictive for her woman—and for the health of society in general.

17. Harold Pinter, *Betrayal* (London, 1978), pp. 63-64. It is interesting to note that when Pinter wrote the screenplay for *Betrayal* some years later, he changed this wording, omitting even the promise of explanation. After noting that girl babies "don't make such a fuss about it" [leaving the womb], one character asks, "Why do you think that is?" and the other responds, "I have no answer." "Do you think it has anything to do with the differences between sexes?" the former posits, to which he receives the reply, "Good God you're right. That must be it."

18. *Anna Christie*, ed. cit., p. 670.

19. A version of this paper was presented at the conference "Eugene O'Neill: The Later Years," sponsored by the Eugene O'Neill Society, in May 1986.

Modern Drama, 30 (March 1988): 16-27.

O'Neill's Many Mothers: Mary Tyrone, Josie Hogan, and Their Antecedents

Judith E. Barlow

Eugene O'Neill is rightly praised as a theatrical innovator and experimenter, a writer who helped bring life to an American drama largely dominated by formulaic comedies and melodramas, stock characters and stale ideas. Yet in at least one way O'Neill remained traditional and conservative. His depiction of women only rarely strays from the narrow limits of the conventional male view prevalent in Western culture and literature, or in fact from much of the Catholic ethos with which he grew up. For the most part O'Neill's female character's are perceived from outside, from a masculine perspective that wishfully invests them with powerful maternal desires or condemns them for the lack of such feelings. If O'Neill seems daring in his often sympathetic portraits of prostitutes, this is because to him the distinction between virgin and whore is less important than the division between those women who "mother" men and those women who do not.

In the majority of O'Neill's plays his heroes seek union with a motherly woman,[1] and frequently their search is successful: many of his female characters do love children, even though those children are more often forty than four. Indeed, one may make two generalizations: "motherliness" in O'Neill's world has little to do with biology or sexuality; his maternal characters are as likely to be whores, virgins, or childless wives as they are to be biological parents, while those they mother are usually adults and nearly always male. Further, what largely determines not only the male characters' attitudes toward the women but the playwright's attitude as well is the extent to which they fulfill the maternal function: O'Neill is by no means identical with these male figures, whose flaws he readily exposes; to assume that he simply speaks through them is to underestimate his artistic powers and deny the complexity of his vision. Nevertheless, O'Neill's apotheosizing of the maternal female character is unquestionably a dominant motif throughout his canon.

"Motherly" may be defined, for O'Neill, in very traditional terms: nurturing, caring for, and protecting others; being willing to subordinate one's own dreams and concerns to the loved one's desires; and being willing to forgive any and all transgressions. A women who has these qualities still may not succeed in bringing peace and happiness to herself and her men, but failure in any of these categories invites both authorial censure and tragic consequences.

The number of women in the O'Neill canon who regard their husbands or lovers with maternal solicitude is legion and encompasses such diverse figures as the earth-mother whore Cybel in *The Great God Brown* and Madeline Arnold in *Strange Interlude*—the latter a woman who, at the advanced age of nineteen, has "*a distinct maternal older feeling in her attitude toward*" her fiancé Gordon.[2] "My son," "my boy," "my poor little boy" or "my child" are terms uttered, at various times, by Hazel Niles in *Mourning Becomes Electra*, Abbie Putnam in *Desire Under the Elms*, Miriam in *Lazarus Laughed*, Nina Leeds in *Strange Interlude*, and Eleanor Cape in *Welded*; in none of these cases are they referring to children. Margaret in *The Great God Brown* considers her husband the eldest of her sons, an attitude she shares with Sara Harford in *More Stately Mansions*. One of the most amazing love scenes in American drama shows Abbie Putnam wooing Eben Cabot with "*a horribly frank mixture of lust and mother love*" (NP, 178). She kisses him passionately as she promises to replace his dead parent. Saintly Eileen Carmody, the eighteen-year-old tuberculosis victim in *The Straw*, views her siblings as her "babies," and on her deathbed she responds with "*motherly, self-forgetting solicitude*"[3] when told that the man she loves is ill. And these female characters are not scorning their husbands' and lovers' childishness: their remarks are made affectionately or, at most, with indulgent pity.

When we look at actual biological mothers, we find that a woman's failure as a mother often grows from the same roots as her failure as wife and lover. A list of the "failed mothers" in O'Neill's canon would be long. The still-born infant in *Before Breakfast*, one of a large group of dead children in O'Neill's plays, symbolizes Mrs. Rowland's inability to nurture either husband or child. The "breakfast" she prepares for her spouse—equal helpings of mockery, recrimination, and self-pity—proves lethal. Ruth Mayo in *Beyond the Horizon* attempts to subordinate Robert's dreams of adventure to her vision of rural domestic bliss. While Ruth is victim as well as victimizer, her inability to appreciate her husband's dreams is mirrored in her casual attitude toward their daughter, who is far more attached to Robert than to her. In short order, Robert follows the baby girl to the grave. The unseen Rosa Parritt in *The Iceman Cometh*, faithful to neither lover nor son, attempts to impose her ideals of revolutionary conduct on them. The lover escapes into alcoholic scepticism but the son retaliates with betrayal, creating a burden of guilt that he can assuage only by suicide. Ella Downey in *All God's Chillun Got Wings* cannot protect her infant from death nor support her husband's dreams of becoming a lawyer. Unable to forgive her husband for the "sin" of being black, Ella—in an O'Neillian role-reversal—winds up as the mad "child" cared for by the self-sacrificing "Uncle Jim."

Conversely, the "good mother's" maternal ministrations extend to husband and offspring alike. The most obvious example, of course, is the idealized Essie Miller in *Ah, Wilderness!* Essie feeds and nurses her husband and children, appears to have no ambitions beyond her family's physical and emotional health, and makes certain that their punishments are light even when they transgress the moral code she upholds.[4] Her greatest betrayal is serving her husband the bluefish he erroneously believes has a "peculiar oil" that poisons him. Another "good mother," this one pathetic rather than comic, is Nora Melody in *A Touch of the Poet*. Priding herself on being "the only one in the world...nivir sneers at his dreams,"[5] Nora declares that she has "no pride at all" (LP, 257) except in her self-sacrificing love for Con. She subordinates her own desires to Con's wishes and, while her primary allegiance is to the husband she comforts "*as if he were a sick child*" (LP, 246), she still finds time to minister to her daughter Sara.

Mary Tyrone's dilemma is that she has found herself in an O'Neill play. Like most of O'Neill's male characters, her husband and sons demand of her that triumvirate of virtues which Essie and Nora possess: nurturance, forgiveness, and renunciation of her dreams for theirs. Insofar as she fails in these obligations, both her family and the playwright condemn her; insofar as O'Neill reveals her suffering, her self-condemnation, and even the impossibility of most women's satisfying all of these demands, he asks us to pity and sympathize with her.

Ironically, since O'Neill's male characters are generally appalled by the notion that their female parents could be sexual beings, the biological mothers are in their eyes automatically tainted. The obviously demented Reuben Light of *Dynamo* isn't alone in his anguish over maternal sexuality. Jamie Tyrone not only replaces his mother with a maternal prostitute, he identifies Mary's addiction with promiscuity: "I'd never dreamed before that any women but whores took dope!"[6] It doesn't take a psychoanalyst to see that his mother's sexuality is nearly as disturbing to him as is her drug-taking. One source of his antagonism toward Edmund is surely that this much younger brother proves Mary's continued intimacy with the father, Jamie's past—and present—rival.

Caught in a further double-bind that the childless "mothers" never face, Mary long ago had to choose between going on tour with the husband who wanted her and staying behind with her children. When the baby dies, she castigates herself as an unfit parent (much as O'Neill himself often uses dead children to symbolize—and punish—weak mothers). The physical and emotional pain attendant on bearing and caring for children, and the guilt that accrues when one cannot protect them, become too much for her; she retreats into drugs after the birth of Edmund and later refuses to acknowledge that he has a potentially lethal illness. Mary is trapped in a no-win situation: to admit the gravity of Edmund's illness is to face the guilt—reasonable or not—of having once again failed to protect a child. To retreat into drugs is to bear the guilt of abandoning her family. Jamie most of all, but Edmund and Tyrone as well, condemn her for this abandonment, her inability to nurture. It may well be that Mary's refusal to eat, although partly a result of the drugs and perhaps a touch of vanity, symbolizes her refusal to be the mother her men seek. O'Neill's most motherly characters—Essie Miller, Sara Harford, Nora Melody, Josie Hogan, Mrs. Fife, Cybel—have the ample maternal figure, including the large comforting breasts, that Mary is anxious to avoid. In the last moments of the play, Edmund makes
a final attempt to appeal to her by blurting out the truth about his illness. She rejects this request for maternal solicitude with an emphatic "No!"

Nor is Mary willing to forgive the men their transgressions, as the ideal O'Neill woman must. When Mary tells Tyrone that she cannot forget, "but I forgive" (*Long Day's*, 114), we know that she is being less than truthful. Her repeated recitations of Tyrone's failures, dating back to a drunken honeymoon night some thirty-five years earlier, are evidence of this; to forgive yet never forget is not to forgive at all.

Further, Mary cannot entirely forget the dreams she once had that conflicted with her desire to be a wife and mother. Tyrone evidently resents her claims that she could have been a concert pianist or a nun. He attributes her reveries about a musical career to the "flattering" of nuns who know nothing of such things (*Long Day's*, 138). And it must be added that the playwright also gives us no cause to credit Mary's claims to musical prowess; while Tyrone's beautiful voice and carriage remind us of the great actor he might have been, all we witness of Mary's talent is the "*stiff-fingered groping*" (*Long Day's*, 170) of an aging arthritic.

Edmund mourns with his father the loss of Tyrone's chance to be a great thespian; Mary's dream of a musical career is taken seriously by no one but Mary herself.

The playwright gives at least a little more credence to Mary's second dream, the one she considers "the more beautiful": to become a nun (*Long Day's* 104). Although Tyrone dismisses this out of hand as "the worst" delusion (*Long Day's*, 138), the opening stage directions tell us that Mary's "*most appealing quality is the simple, unaffected charm of a shy convent-girl youthfulness she has never lost—an innate unworldly innocence* (*Long Day's*, 13). Had Mary remained virginal, she would have faced none of the troubles she laments throughout *Long Day's Journey Into Night*. On the other hand, of course, there would also have been no family—a family that despite everything loves her as she, despite everything, loves them. Mary Tyrone is finally neither mother nor virgin, and in this lies much of the tragedy of the Tyrone family. The men demand that she be a mother—in all senses of the word—but she cannot and will not fulfill that role. Even in her drugged stupor, however, she cannot regain the virginal innocence for which she so desperately yearns.

Moreover, Mary's nostalgia obscures the fact that virginity and innocence are not inherently valuable in O'Neill's world. On the other hand, O'Neill sometimes reserves his worst punishments for those women, like Christine Mannon and Ada Fife, who are sexually promiscuous.[7] There is at least a little bit of the playwright himself in *Mourning Becomes Electra*'s Peter Niles, who flees in "*horrified repulsion*" when Lavinia Mannon claims that she has been a native's "fancy woman" (*NP*, 866). On the other hand, however, the purest woman is not necessarily the best: motherly (and largely sexless) prostitutes like Cybel fare better in O'Neill's world than do repressed and censorious virgins. Virginity is a virtue only when it is coupled with the very same maternal qualities demanded of wives and female parents.

Diff'rent is usually treated as a rather naïve Freudian case study, and surely there is merit to this interpretation: having denied her sexual drive its "natural" outlet through marriage to Caleb, Emma Crosby's repressed feelings later emerge in a grotesque desire for his despicable nephew Benny. Looked at another way, however, Emma's failure is a failure of the cardinal feminine virtue of forgiveness; her "crime" goes back beyond Freud to the double standard. In expecting Caleb to be as pure and virginal as she, she is going against nature, society, and the conservative O'Neillian code which holds up different sexual standards for men and women. Benny may be twenty-seven years younger than she, but Emma is right in vehemently denying Caleb's claim that she has been like "a mother" to the young man (*SSP*, 246). There is little in her actions that fits into O'Neill's constellation of maternal characteristics; her refusal to put concern for Caleb above concern for herself, and her selfish desire to mold him into her ideal of what a man should be, destroys them both.

Lily Miller in *Ah, Wilderness!* is a more appealing figure than Emma Crosby. She too lacks the important quality of forgiveness, although Sid's escapades—consorting with "tarts," habitual drunkenness, inability to hold a job—are more reprehensible than Caleb's single fall from grace. Moreover, O'Neill grants Lily the qualities of protectiveness and nurturance that Emma lacks: she freely admits that she feels like a mother to her niece, nephews and students, and she soothes the remorseful Sid "*as if he were a little boy*" (LP, 86). Essie accurately observes that Lily "seems to get some queer satisfaction out of fussing over him like a hen that's hatched a duck" (LP, 124). Lily's unwillingness to accept Sid as he is causes both of them pain, but insofar as this virgin possesses some of the maternal characteristics Emma Crosby lacks, she is a far less negative—and less severely punished—figure than her coldly Puritanical predecessor.

One might say that Lily is a sort of intermediary figure between Emma Crosby and Josie Hogan. It would be more accurate, however, to say that Josie combines all of the maternal, feminine virtues that the male characters have been seeking throughout the O'Neill canon. Just as Mary Tyrone is neither mother nor virgin, so Josie Hogan is both, and O'Neill portrays her as the most positive female character in his plays. Josie is more sorely tried than Essie Miller, but she is also less slavishly servile and pitiable than Nora Melody. Although Josie is herself a virgin, she is willing to accept and forgive Jim Tyrone's sexual excesses. Interestingly, the word "different" occurs half a dozen times in the last acts of *A Moon for the Misbegotten*. Yet while O'Neill asks us to view Emma Crosby's demand that Caleb be "different"—purer than other men—as a foolish and destructive ideal, Jim's insistence that this might be "different" from all his previous nights and that Josie be "different" from the whores he has known is a painfully heart-felt request which we understand and to which Josie nobly accedes.

Unlike Mary Tyrone, Josie is willing to be silent so that others might speak. Disturbed by his drugged mother's recriminations, Edmund begs Mary: "For God's sake, stop talking" (*Long Day's*, 74). Jim Tyrone repeatedly asks Josie not to talk that "raw stuff." One wonders whether the men are disturbed only by *what* the women are saying, or by the fact that they are speaking at all. The Tyrone men want a listener who will sympathize with their dreams and commiserate with them for their failures. The morphine turns Mary loquacious instead, and the men themselves—particularly Edmund—must fill the role of auditor for each other. "Yea, though we sang as angels in her ear,/She would not hear," Jamie quotes maudlinly in the final moments of the drama (*Long Day's*, 173). Josie, by contrast, stills her own voice, abstains from the liquor that might (like Mary's morphine) free her tongue, and accepts the role of listener to Jim's tale of woe—a double role because she also stands for his deceased mother as well. Indeed, the identification between the two is an ominous metaphor for Josie's renunciation of self: she symbolically merges not only with another woman, but with a woman who is dead.

Just as Josie accepts the role of confessor that Mary refuses, so too she accepts, scarcely seems to notice, the physical and social limitations against which her predecessor chafes. Doris Nelson accurately observes that Eugene O'Neill's male characters are given mobility while his female characters are confined to a single domestic place.[8] This is certainly true of Mary Tyrone; friendless and alienated, during the course of the play she manages only a short car trip to buy the drugs that will lock her even deeper in her private world. Mary yearns for escape from her home, in part because this seemingly female domestic territory includes no women confidants. She wishes "there was a friend's house where" she could "laugh and gossip awhile" as she did in her convent days (*Long Day's*, 85-

86). Mary finally becomes so desperate for female companionship—for someone to listen to *her* story—that she bribes the servant with drinks to spend a few minutes with her.

Josie Hogan's boundaries are larger: the farm on which she toils, though meagre, is physically less confining than the Tyrone house. Her world, however, is even more relentlessly masculine than Mary's. Having grown up the only girl in a houseful of brothers, she has apparently never had—nor does she desire—female friendship. In fact, of course, the desire for female companions would be largely futile in O'Neill's dramatic universe: celebrations of various kinds of male bonding may be found from the early sea plays to the late works, but it is a rare female character who has a woman friend or sister. Josie never seriously expresses a wish to leave the confines of the farm except in the company of Jim Tyrone.[9] Like such characters as Margaret, Abbie Putnam, and Princess Kukachin before her, she isc content to define herself in terms of men or to let them define not only the world in which she lives but the world of her imagination. Even Josie's fantasies of being promiscuous, unacceptable as they are to Jim Tyrone and to the conventional code of female morality, are ultimately forgivable because they revolve around her desire to "give" herself to men. By contrast, Mary's dreams of a convent life take her away from the male-defined realm she resents. For all these reasons, Josie does not evoke in the male characters who love her the level of guilt and anxiety a restless Mary does.

O'Neill creates Josie as a woman who has nurtured and protected a succession of men of all ages: her younger brothers, her father, and of course Jim Tyrone. Josie is acutely self-conscious about her large size, which she believes makes her unattractive to men. What she discovers is that her ample figure, symbol of her maternal nature, is precisely what Jim—like so many other O'Neill men—desires. While Mary Tyrone neither cooks nor willingly eats, Josie raises the very food she prepares. Whether boiling eggs for Jim or preparing her father's supper, she is the source of physical as well as emotional nourishment.

Josie freely sacrifices her own dream—sexual union and possible marriage with Jim—to his desire that she be the chaste figure to whom he can confess his sins and from whom he can receive at least absolution if not a renewed will to live. Josie suffers for her self-abnegation, the loss of her dream, yet her consolation (like Nora Melody's) is that she has comforted the man she loves. "I want you to remember my love for you gave you peace for awhile" (LP, 407) she tells Jim. For O'Neill's perfect mother, the act of giving solace is its own reward.

It is not surprising that for the Catholic O'Neill the perfect woman is a motherly virgin. The long Pieta pose that opens Act Four clearly links Josie with the Virgin Mary and echoes a series of briefer but similar tableaux in his earlier plays: Abbie holding Eben in the last scene of *Desire Under the Elms*, Cybel comforting a dying Billy in *The Great God Brown*, Sara cradling Simon in the Epilogue to *More Stately Mansions*.[10] Josie, the heroine of O'Neill's last completed play, may be seen as his final forgiveness of women, the final demonstration of his ability to envision a positive feminine force. Nevertheless, the very conservative terms in which this goodness is cast—nurturance, forgiveness, self-sacrifice, chastity—testify to the parochial view of woman as mother that pervades his canon.[11]

O'Neill, of course, is by no means alone. The most famous fiction writers of his generation—F. Scott Fitzgerald, Ernest Hemingway, and William Faulkner—offer strikingly similar pictures. As James Tuttleton notes, all of these novelists "seem to have had greatest sympathy with the prevailing stereotype of the 'womanly woman,' the woman with an old-fashioned sense of her role as life-giving, nourishing, life-sustaining presence ministering to her husband or family."[12] O'Neill's final female character is last seen entering her home, saying a benediction for her lover as she prepares to cook breakfast for her father.

O'Neill's portrait of Mary Tyrone is invested with a good deal of sympathy; more sinned against than sinning, she has suffered from her own and others' mistakes, as well as from circumstances beyond anyone's control. And when he draws a woman who chafes at the overwhelming demands placed upon her, who imagines—albeit in a drug fantasy—a world in which she would have a story separate from that written for her by her male kin, O'Neill goes beyond his other creations: Mary is his most complex and theatrically powerful stage woman. Coupled with his sympathy and understanding for Mary, however, are anger and resentment—present not only in *Journey*'s male characters but in the playwright himself, who comprehends but cannot entirely forgive her for refusing to live up to his vision of maternal femininity. No such ambiguity surrounds Josie Hogan. Josie stands as the saviour for whom nearly all O'Neill's heroes search. She also stands as the narrowly-defined feminine ideal against which the other women characters, including Mary Tyrone, are measured and found wanting.

NOTES

1. Travis Bogard discusses "the dual wife-mother character" in the introduction to *The Later Plays of Eugene O'Neill* (New York: Random House, 1967), xv-xvi, and "the search for the surrogate mother" in *Contour in Time* (New York: Oxford University Press, 1972), 436-40. See also Doris V. Falk, *Eugene O'Neill and the Tragic Tension* (New Brunswick, N.J.: Rutgers UP, 1958), 76.

2. Eugene O'Neill, *Strange Interlude*, in *Nine Plays by Eugene O'Neill* (1932; New York: Random House, 1941), 666. Cited in the text as NP.

3. _____, *The Straw*, in *Six Short Plays of Eugene O'Neill* (New York: Random House, 1951), 122. Cited in the text as SSP.

4. Trudy Drucker aptly dubs Essie Miller "a *Ladies'-Home-Journal*-wife-and-mother." See "Sexuality as Destiny: The Shadow Lives of O'Neill's Women," *The Eugene O'Neill Newsletter* 6.2 (1982): 9.

5. Eugene O'Neill, *A Touch of the Poet*, in *The Later Plays of Eugene O'Neill* 228. Cited in the text as LP.

6. _____, *Long Day's Journey Into Night* (New Haven: Yale University Press, 1956), 163. Cited in the text as *Long Day's*.

7. Drucker, pp. 8-9, makes a similar point and also discusses O'Neill's harsh treatment of virgins.

8. Doris Nelson, "O'Neill's Women," *The Eugene O'Neill Newsletter* 6.2 (1982): 6.

9. Josie's threat to leave the farm is intended to scare and punish her father. Unlike her brothers, she is content to stay and work the land rather than seek new opportunities elsewhere.

10. The unpublished Epilogue is in the Eugene O'Neill Collection, Collection of American Literature, Beinecke Library, Yale University.

11. Although her approach is different from mine in several ways, and her conclusion more tentative, Doris Nelson also finds that O'Neill presents "a somewhat limited view of half the human race" (7).

12. James W. Tuttleton, "'Combat in the Erogenous Zone': Women in the American Novel between the Two World Wars," *What Manner of Woman: Essays on English and American Life and Literature*, ed. Marlene Springer (New York: New York University Press, 1977), 292.

Perspectives on O'Neill: New Essays. Ed. Shyamal Bagchee. Victoria, British Columbia: University of Victoria, 1988, 7-16.

An O'Neill Chronology

June 14, 1877   James O'Neill, Sr. marries Ella Quinlan.

September 10, 1878   James O'Neill, Jr. born.

Fall 1883   Edmund O'Neill born.

March 4, 1885   Edmund O'Neill dies.

October 16, 1888   Eugene O'Neill born (hereinafter O'Neill).

December 28, 1888   Carlotta Monterey born.

October 2, 1909   O'Neill marries Kathleen Jenkins.

May 5, 1910   Eugene O'Neill, Jr. born.

August 1912   O'Neill begins work for the *New London Telegraph*.

October 11, 1912   Kathleen Jenkins O'Neill divorces O'Neill.

December 9, 1912   O'Neill departs for state sanitarium at Shelton, Conneticut.

December 24, 1912   O'Neill arrives at Gaylord Farm Sanitarium, Wallingford, Conneticut.

June 3, 1913	O'Neill discharged from Gaylord Farm.
July 16, 1914	O'Neill requests admission to George Pierce Baker's English 47 class at Harvard.
Summer 1915	Provincetown Players present its first bill on Cape Cod (officially organized as a theatre during the Summer of 1916).
Summer 1916	Provincetown Players produce *Bound East for Cardiff* (1913/14)* and *Thirst* (1913/14) at Wharf Theatre on Cape Cod.
November 3, 1916	*Bound East for Cardiff* opens at Playwright's Theatre in Greenwich Village.
December 1, 1916	*Before Breakfast* (1916/17) opens at Playwrights' Theatre.
January 5, 1917	*Fog* (1913/14) opens at Playwrights' Theatre.
February 16, 1917	*The Sniper* (1915) opens at Playwrights' Theatre.
October 31, 1917	*In the Zone* (1916/17) opens at Comedy Theatre.
November 2, 1917	*The Long Voyage Home* (1916/17) opens at Playwrights' Theatre.
November 30, 1917	*Ile* (1916/17) opens at Playwrights' Theatre.
April 12, 1918	O'Neill marries Agnes Boulton.
April 26, 1918	*The Rope* (1918) opens at Playwrights' Theatre.
November 22, 1918	*Where the Cross is Made* (1918) opens at Playwrights Theatre.
December 20, 1918	*The Moon of the Caribbees* (1916/17) opens at Playwights' Theatre.
October 30, 1919	Shane O'Neill born.
October 31, 1919	*The Dreamy Kid* (1918) opens at Playwrights' Theatre.

February 2, 1920	*Beyond the Horizon* (1918) opens at Morosco Theatre.
March 8, 1920	*Chris Christopherson* (1919) opens at Apollo Theatre in Atlantic City, New Jersey.
June 3, 1920	Pulitzer Prize awarded to *Beyond the Horizon*.
August 10, 1920	James O'Neill, Sr. dies.
November 3, 1920	*The Emperor Jones* (1920) opens at Playwrights' Theatre.
December 27, 1920	*Diff'rent* (1920) opens at Playwrights' Theatre.
June 1, 1921	*Gold* (1920) opens at Frazee Theatre.
November 10, 1921	*The Straw* (1918/19) opens at Greenwich Village Theatre.
November 10, 1921	*Anna Christie* (1920) opens at Vanderbilt Theatre.
February 28, 1922	Ella Quinlan O'Neill dies.
March 4, 1922	*The First Man* (1921) opens at Neighborhood Playhouse.
March 9, 1922	*The Hairy Ape* (1921) opens at Playwrights' Theatre.
May 21, 1922	Pulitzer Prize awarded to *Anna Christie*.
November 8, 1923	James O'Neill, Jr. dies.
November 8, 1923	Kenneth Macgowan becomes Director of Production for Provincetown Playhouse, previously Playwrights' Theatre, effectively bringing to an end the Provincetown Players.
March 17, 1924	*Welded* (1922/23) opens at 39th St. Theatre.
May 15, 1924	*All God's Chillun Got Wings* (1923) opens at Provincetown Playhouse.
November 11, 1924	*Desire Under the Elms* (1924) opens at Greenwich Village Theatre.

January 23, 1926	*The Great God Brown* (1925) opens at Greenwich Village Theatre.
May 14, 1926	Oona O'Neill born.
January 9, 1928	*Marco Millions* (1923/25) opens at Guild Theatre.
January 30, 1928	*Strange Interlude* (1926/27) opens at John Golden Theatre.
April 9, 1928	*Lazarus Laughed* opens at Pasadena Community Playhouse, Pasadena, California.
May 8, 1928	Pulitzer Prize awarded to *Strange Interlude*.
February 11, 1929	*Dynamo* (1928) opens at Martin Beck Theatre.
July 1, 1929	Agnes Boulton O'Neill files for divorce.
July 22, 1929	O'Neill marries Carlotta Monterey.
October 26, 1931	*Mourning Becomes Electra* (1929-31) opens at Guild Theatre.
October 2, 1933	*Ah, Wilderness* (1932) opens at Guild Theatre.
January 8, 1934	*Days Without End* (1932/33) opens at Guild Theatre.
November 12, 1936	Nobel Prize awarded to O'Neill.
October 9, 1946	*The Iceman Cometh* (1939) opens at Martin Beck Theatre.
September 25, 1950	Eugene O'Neill, Jr. dies.
November 27, 1953	O'Neill dies.
November 7, 1956	*Long Day's Journey Into Night* (1939-41) opens at Helen Hayes Theatre.
May 2, 1957	*A Moon for the Misbegotten* (1943) opens at Bijou Theatre.
October 2, 1958	*A Touch of the Poet* (1935-42) opens at Helen Hayes Theatre.

Chronology

December 22, 1964   *Hughie* (1941/42) opens at Royale Theatre.

October 31, 1967   *More Stately Mansions* (unfinished) opens at Broadhurst Theatre.

November 18, 1970   Carlotta Monterey O'Neill dies.

* Dates in parenthesis indicate year(s) of composition.

Selected Bibliography

BOOKS

Ahuja, Chapman. *Tragedy, Modern Temper and O'Neill*. Atlantic Highlands, N.J.: Humanities, 1983.
Alexander, Doris. *The Tempering of Eugene O'Neill*. New York: Harcourt, Brace and World, 1962.
Atkinson, Jennifer McCabe. *Eugene O'Neill: A Descriptive Bibliography*. Pittsburgh: University of Pittsburgh Press, 1974.**
Barlow, Judith E. *Final Acts: The Creation of Three Late O'Neill Plays*. Athens: University of Georgia Press, 1985.
Berlin, Normand. *Eugene O'Neill*. New York: St. Martin's Press, 1988.
Bloom, Harold. *Eugene O'Neill's* Long Day's Journey Into Night. New York: Chelsea House, 1988.
____. Eugene O'Neill's *The Iceman Cometh*. New York: Chelsea House, 1987.
Bogard, Travis. *Contour in Time: The Plays of Eugene O'Neill*. Fair Lawn, N.J.: Oxford University Press, 1972.
____. *The Eugene O'Neill Songbook*. Ann Arbor, Michigan/London: UMI Research Press, 1988.**
____ and Jackson Bryer, eds. *Selected Letters of Eugene O'Neill*. New Haven: Yale University Press, 1988.**
____. *The Later Plays of Eugene O'Neill*. New York: Random House, 1967.
____, ed. *The Unknown O'Neill: Unpublished and Unfamiliar Writings of Eugene O'Neill*. New Haven: Yale University Press, 1988.**
Boulton, Agnes. *Part of a Long Story*. Garden City: Doubleday, 1958.
Bowen, Crosswell and Shane O'Neill. *The Curse of the Misbegotten: A Tale of the House of O'Neill*. New York: McGraw-Hill, 1959.

Bryer, Jackson, ed. *The Theatre We Worked For: The Letters of Eugene O'Neill to Kenneth Macgowan*. New Haven and London: Yale University Press, 1982.**

___. *The Merrill Checklist of Eugene O'Neill*. Columbus, Ohio: Merrill, 1971.**

Cargill, Oscar, N. Bryllion Fagan and William J. Fisher, eds. *O'Neill and His Plays: Four Decades of Criticism*. New York: New York University Press, 1961.*

Carpenter, Frederic I. *Eugene O'Neill*. New York: Twane Publishers, 1979.

Chabrowe, Leonard. *Ritual and Pathos: The Theatre of O'Neill*. Lewisburg, Pa.: Bucknell Univeristy Press, 1976; London: Associated University Presses, 1976.

Chothia, Jean. *Forging a Language: A Study of the Plays of Eugene O'Neill*. Cambridge, Eng.: Cambridge University Press, 1979.

Clark, Barrett H. *Eugene O'Neill*. New York: Robert M. McBride, 1927.

___. *Eugene O'Neill: The Man and His Plays*. New York: Dover Publications, 1947.

___ and Ralph Sanborn, eds. *A Bibliography of the Works of Eugene O'Neill Together with the Collected Poems of Eugene O'Neill*. London: Benjamin Blom, 1965.**

Commins, Dorothy, ed. *Love and Admiration and Respect: The O'Neill-Commins Correspondence*. Durham, N.C.: Duke University Press, 1986.**

Cronin, Harry C. *Eugene O'Neill, Irish and American: A Study in Cultural Context*. Salem, N.H.: Ayer Co. Publishers, 1976.

Deutsch, Helen, and Stella Hanau. *The Provincetown, A Story of the Theatre, 1915-1929*. New York: Farrar and Rinehart, 1931.

Engel, Edwin A. *The Haunted Heroes of Eugene O'Neill*. Cambridge, Mass.: Harvard University Press, 1953.

Estrin, Mark W., ed. *Conversations with Eugene O'Neill*. Oxford, Miss.: University Press of Mississippi, 1990.**

Falk, Doris V. *Eugene O'Neill and the Tragic Tension: An Interpretive Study of the Plays*. New Brunswick, N.J.: Rutgers University Press, 1958.

Floyd, Virginia, ed. *Eugene O'Neill at Work: Newly Released Ideas for Plays*. New York: Frederick Ungar, 1981.**

___, ed. *Eugene O'Neill: A World View*. New York: Frederick Ungar, 1979.*

___. *The Plays of Eugene O'Neill: A New Assessment*. New York: Frederick Ungar, 1984.

Frazer, Winifred D. *Love as Death in* The Iceman Cometh: *A Modern Treatment of an Ancient Theme*. Gainesville: University of Florida Press, 1967.

___. *E.G. and E.G.O.: Emma Goldman and* The Iceman Cometh. Gainesville: Florida University Press, 1974.

Frenz, Horst. *Eugene O'Neill*. New York: Frederick Ungar, 1971.

___. Frenz, Horst, and Susan Tuck, eds. *Eugene O'Neill's Critics: Voices from Abroad*. Carbondale, Ill.: Southern Illinois University Press, 1984.*

Gallop, Donald, ed. *Eugene O'Neill: Work Diary (1924-1943)*. 2 vols. New Haven, Conn.: Yale University Library, 1981.**

Gassner, John. *Eugene O'Neill*. Minneapolis: University of Minnesota Press, 1965.
___, ed. *O'Neill: A Collection of Critical Essays*. Englewood Cliffs, N.J.: Prentice Hall, 1964.*
Geddes, Virgil. *The Melodramadness of Eugene O'Neill*. The Brookfield Pamphlets, No. 4, Brookfield, Conn.: The Brookfield Players, 1934; Folcroft, PA: Folcraft, 1973; Norwood, PA: Norwood, 1977.
Gelb, Arthur and Barbara. *O'Neill*. New York: Harper and Row, 1962; 1987.
Glaspell, Susan. *The Road to the Temple*. London: Benn, 1926; New York: Frederick A. Stokes, 1927.
Goyal, Bhagwat S. *The Strategy of Survival: Human Significance of O'Neill's Plays*. Ghazibad [India]: Vimal, Prakashon, 1975.
Griffen, Earnest G., ed. *Eugene O'Neill: A Collection of Criticism*. New York: McGraw-Hill, 1976.*
Hinden, Michael. Long Day's Journey Into Night: *Native Eloquence*. Boston: G.K. Hall, 1990.
Josephson, Lennart. *A Role: O'Neill's Cornelius Melody*. Stockholm, Sweden: Almqvist and Wiksell International, 1977; Atlantic Highlands, N.J.: Humanities Press, 1978.
Kobernick, Mark. *Semiotics of Drama and the Style of Eugene O'Neill*. Amsterdam: Benjamins, 1989.
Leech, Clifford. *Eugene O'Neill*. London: Oliver & Boyd, 1963; Grove Press, 1963.
Liu, Haiping and Lowell Swortzell, eds. *Eugene O'Neill in China: An International Centenary Celebration*. Westport, Conn.: Greenwood Press, 1992.
Long, Chester Clayton. *The Role of Nemesis in the Structure of Selected Plays by Eugene O'Neill*. The Hague: Mouton, 1968.
McDonough, Edwin J. *Quintero Directs O'Neill*. Chicago: A Cappella Books, 1991.**
Manheim, Michael. *Eugene O'Neill's New Language of Kinship*. Syracuse: Syracuse University Press, 1982.
Martine, James J., ed. *Critical Essays on Eugene O'Neill*. Boston: G.K. Hall, 1984.*
Maufort, Marc. *Songs of American Experience: The Vision of O'Neill and Melville*. New York: Peter Lang, 1990.
___. *Eugene O'Neill and the Emergence of American Drama*. Atlantic Highlands, N.J.: Humanities Press, 1989.
Miller, Jordan Y. *Eugene O'Neill and the American Critic: A Summary and Biographical Checklist*. 2nd ed. Hamden, Conn.: Archon Books, 1973.**
___, ed. *Playwright's Progress: O'Neill and the Critics*. Chicago: Scott, Foresman, 1965.*
Moorton, Richard F., Jr., ed. *Eugene O'Neill's Century: Centennial Views on America's Foremost Tragic Dramatist*. Westport, Conn.: Greenwood Press, 1991.*
Orlandello, John. *O'Neill on Film*. Rutherford, N.J.: Fairleigh Dickenson, 1982.
Porter, Laurin R. *The Banished Prince: Time, Memory, and Ritual in the Late Plays of Eugene O'Neill*. Ann Arbor, Mich./London: UMI Research Press, 1988.
Prasad, Hari M. *The Dramatic Art of Eugene O'Neill*. New York: Advent, 1987.

Raleigh, John Henry. *The Plays of Eugene O'Neill.* Carbondale, Ill.: Southern Illinois University Press, 1965.
___, ed. The Iceman Cometh: *A Collection of Critical Essays.* Englewood Cliffs, N.J.: Prentice-Hall, 1968.*
Ranald, Margaret L. *The Eugene O'Neill Companion.* Westport, Conn.: Greenwood Press, 1984.**
Reaves, J. Russell. *An O'Neill Concordance.* Detroit: Gale, 1969.**
Robinson, James A. *Eugene O'Neill and Oriental Thought: A Divided Vision.* Carbondale, Ill.: Southern Illinois University Press, 1982.
Sarlos, Robert Karoly. *Jig Cook and the Provincetown Players.* Amherst, Mass.: University of Massachusetts Press, 1982.
Scheibler, Rolf. *The Late Plays of Eugene O'Neill.* Bern, Switzerland: Francke Verlag, 1970.
Sheaffer, Louis. *O'Neill: Son and Artist.* Boston: Little, Brown, 1973.
___. *O'Neill: Son and Playwright.* Boston: Little, Brown, 1968.
Shipley, Joseph J. *The Art of Eugene O'Neill.* Seattle: University of Washington Chapbooks, University of Washington Bookstore, 1928.
Sinha, C.P. *Eugene O'Neill's Tragic Vision.* Atlantic Highlands, N.J.: Humanities, 1981.
Skinner, Richard Dana. *Eugene O'Neill: A Poet's Quest.* New York: Longmans Green, 1935; Revised ed. New York: Russell & Russell, 1964.
Smith, Madeline and Richard Eaton. *Eugene O'Neill: An Annotated Bibliography.* Hamden, Conn.: Garland, 1988.**
Stroupe, John, ed. *Critical Approaches to O'Neill.* New York: AMS Press, 1988.*
Tiusanen, Timo. *O'Neill's Scenic Images.* Princeton: Princeton University Press, 1968.
Tornqvist, Egil. *A Drama of Souls: O'Neill's Studies in Supernaturalistic Technique.* New Haven, Conn.: Yale University Press, 1969.
Vena, Gary. *O'Neill's* The Iceman Cometh: *Reconstructing the Premiere.* Ann Arbor, Mich./London: UMI Research Press, 1988.**
Wainscott, Ronald H. *Staging O'Neill: The Experimental Years, 1920-1934.* New Haven and London: Yale University Press, 1988.**
Winther, Sophus Keith. *Eugene O'Neill: A Critical Study.* New York: Russell and Russell, 1961.

SCHOLARLY ARTICLES

Adler, Jacob H. "The Worth of *Ah, Wilderness!*" *Modern Drama* 3 (December 1960): 280-288.
Adler, Thomas P. "'Through a Glass Darkly': O'Neill's Esthetic Theory as Seen through His Writer Characters." *Arizona Quarterly* 32 (1976): 171-183.
___. "A Cabin in the Woods, a Summerhouse in a Garden: Closure and Enclosure in O'Neill's *More Stately Mansions.*" *Eugene O'Neill Newsletter* 9 (Summer/Fall 1985): 23-27.

Selected Bibliography

Alexander, Doris M. "Captain Brandt and Captain Brassbound: The Origin of an O'Neill Character." *Modern Langauage Notes* 74 (April 1959): 306-310.
___. "Eugene O'Neill: The Hound of Heaven and the Hell Hole." *Modern Language Quarterly* 20 (December 1959): 307-314.
___. "Eugene O'Neill as Social Critic." *American Quarterly* 6 (Winter 1954): 349-363.
___. "Hugo of *The Iceman Cometh*: Realism and O'Neill." *American Quarterly* 5 (Winter 1953): 357-366.
___. "*Lazarus Laughed* and Buddha." *Modern Language Quarterly* 17 (December 1956): 357-365.
___. "The Missing Half of *Hughie*." *The Drama Review* 11 (Summer 1967): 125-126.
___. "Psychological Fate in *Mourning Becomes Electra*." *PMLA* 68 (December 1953): 923-934.
Alvis, John. "On the American Line: O'Neill's *Mourning Becomes Electra* and the Principles of the Founding." *Southern Review* 22 (January 1986): 69-85.
Andreach, Robert J. "O'Neill's Use of Dante in *The Fountain* and *The Hairy Ape*." *Modern Drama* 10 (May 1967): 48-56.
___. "O'Neill's Women in *The Iceman Cometh*." *Renascence* 18 (Winter 1966): 89-98.
Antush, John V. "Eugene O'Neill: Modern and Postmodern." *The Eugene O'Neill Review* 13 (Spring 1989): 14-27.
Arestad, Sverre. "*The Iceman Cometh* and *The Wild Duck*." *Scandinavian Studies* 20 (February 1948): 1-11.
Asselineau, Roger. "*Mourning Becomes Electra* as a Tragedy." *Modern Drama* 1 (December 1958): 143-150.
Bab, Julius. "Eugene O'Neill--As Europe Sees America's Foremost Playwright." *Theatre Guild Magazine* 9 (November 1931): 11-15.
Barlow, Judith E. "*Long Day's Journey Into Night*: From Early Notes to Finished Play." *Modern Drama* 22 (March 1979): 19-28.
Baum, Bernard. "*Tempest* and *Hairy Ape*: The Literary Incarnation of Mythos." *Modern Language Quarterly* 14 (September 1953): 258-273.
Ben-Zvi, Linda. "*Exiles, The Great God Brown*, and the Specter of Nietzsche." *Modern Drama* 24 (September 1981): 251-269.
Bentley, Eric. "Trying to Like O'Neill." *Kenyon Review* 14 (July 1952): 476-492.
Berlin, Normand. "The Beckettian O'Neill." *Modern Drama* 31 (March 1988): 28-34.
___. "Ghosts of the Past: O'Neill and Hamlet." *Massachusetts Review* 20 (Summer 1979): 312-323.
___. "O'Neill the Novelist." *Modern Drama* 34 (March 1991): 49-58.
___. "O'Neill's Shakespeare." *Eugene O'Neill Review* 13 (Spring 1989): 5-13.
Bermel, Albert. "O'Neill's Funny Valentine." *Eugene O'Neill Newsletter* 12 (Summer-Fall 1988): 18-22.
Black, Stephen A. "Letting the Dead Be Dead: A Reinterpretation of *A Moon for the Misbegotten*." *Modern Drama* 29 (December 1986): 544-555.

___. "O'Neill's Dramatic Process." *American Literature* 59 (March 1987): 58-70.
___. "War among the Tyrones." *Eugene O'Neill Newsletter* 11 (Summer/Fall 1987): 29-31.
Bloom, Steven F. "The Role of Drinking and Alcoholism in O'Neill's Late Plays." *Eugene O'Neill Newsletter* 8 (Spring 1984): 22-27.
Bower, Martha. "The Cycle Women and Carlotta Monterey O'Neill." *Eugene O'Neill Newsletter* 10 (Summer/Fall 1986): 25-29.
Brashear, William R. "The Wisdom of Silenus in O'Neill's Iceman." *American Literature* 36 (May 1964): 180-188.
Butler, Robert. Artifice and Art: Words in *The Iceman Cometh* and *Hughie*." *Eugene O'Neill Newsletter* 5 (Spring 1981): 3-6.
___. "Eugene O'Neill and the Orient: A Forward Glance." *Eugene O'Neill Review* 13 (Spring 1989): 27-28.
Cardullo, Bert. "The Function of Simon Harford in *A Touch of the Poet*." *Eugene O'Neill Newsletter* 8 (Spring 1984): 27-28.
Carpenter, Frederic I. "The Enduring O'Neill: The Early Plays." *Eugene O'Neill Newsletter* 1 (May 1977): 1-3.
Cate, Hollis L. "Ephraim Cabot: O'Neill's Spontaneous Poet." *Markham Review* 2 (May 1971): 115-117.
Chabrowe, Leonard. " Dionysus in *The Iceman Cometh*." *Modern Drama* 4 (February 1962): 377-388.
Chaitin, Norman C. "The Power of Daring." *Modern Drama* 3 (December 1960): 231-261.
Chioles, John. "Aeschylus and O'Neill: A Phenomenological View." *Comparative Drama* 14 (Summer 1980): 159-187.
Cohn, Ruby. "Absurdity in English: Joyce and O'Neill." *Comparative Drama* 3 (Fall 1969): 156-161.
Corey, James. "O'Neill's *The Emperor Jones*." *American Notes and Queries* 12 (1974): 156-157.
Costello, Donald P. "Forgiveness in O'Neill." *Modern Drama* 34 (December 1991): 499-512.
Cunningham, Frank R. "'Authentic Tidings of Invisible Things': Beyond James Robinson's *Eugene O'Neill and Oriental Thought*." *Eugene O'Neill Review* 13 (Spring 1989): 29-39.
___. "*Lazaurus Laughed*: A Study in O'Neill's Romanticism." *Studies in the Twentieth Century* 15 (1975): 51-75.
Dahlstrom, Carl. "*Dynamo* and *Lazarus Laughed*: Some Limitations." *Modern Drama* 3 (December 1960): 224-230.
Day, Cyrus. "*Amor Fati*: O'Neill's Lazarus as Superman and Savior." *Modern Drama* 3 (December 1960): 297-305.
Dickinson, Hugh. "Eugene O'Neill: Anatomy of a Trilogy." *Drama Critique* 10 (Winter 1967): 44-56.
___. "Eugene O'Neill: Fate as Form." *Drama Critique* 10 (Spring 1967): 78-85.
Doyle, Louis F. "The Myth of Eugene O'Neill." *Renascence* 17 (Winter 1964): 59-62.

Drucker, Trudy. "Sexuality as Destiny: The Shadow Lives of O'Neill's Women." *Eugene O'Neill Newsletter* 6 (Summer/Fall 1982): 7-10.
Driver, Tom. "On the Late Plays of Eugene O'Neill." *Tulane Drama Review* 3 (December 1958): 8-20.
Eisen, K. "'The Writing on the Wall': Novelization and the Critique of History In *The Iceman Cometh*." *Modern Drama* 34 (March 1991): 59-73.
Engel, Edwin A. "Eugene O'Neill's *Long Day's Journey Into Night*." *Michigan Alumni Quarterly* 63 (1957): 348-354.
___. "O'Neill, 1960." *Modern Drama* 3 (December 1960): 348-354.
Fagin, N. Bryllion. "Eugene O'Neill." *Antioch Review* 14 (March 1954): 14-26.
Fambrough, Preston. "The Tragic Cosmology of O'Neill's *Desire Under the Elms*." *Eugene O'Neill Newsletter* 10 (Summer/Fall 1986): 25-29.
Fieldman, R. "Longing for Death in O'Neill's *Strange Interlude* and *Mourning Becomes Electra*." *Literature and Psychology* 31 (1981): 39-48.
Fiet, L.A. "O'Neill's Modification of Traditional American Themes in *A Touch of the Poet*." *Educational Theatre Journal* 27 (December 1975): 508-515.
Fitzgerald, John J. "The Bitter Harvest of O'Neill's Projected Cycle." *New England Quarterly* 40 (September 1967): 364-374.
___. "Guilt and Redemption in O'Neill's Last Play: A Study of *A Moon for the Misbegotten*." *Texas Quarterly* 9 (Spring 1966): 146-158.
Fleisher, Frederic. "Strindberg and O'Neill." *Symposium* 10 (Spring 1956): 84-93.
Flory, Claude R. "Notes on the Antecedents of *Anna Christie*." *PMLA* 86 (January 1971): 77-83.
Floyd, Virginia. "The Search for Self in *The Hairy Ape*: An Exercise in Futility?" *Eugene O'Neill Newsletter* 1 (Winter 1978): 4-7.
Frazer, Winifred. "King Lear and Hickey: Bridegroom and Iceman." *Modern Drama* 15 (December 1972): 267-277.
___. "Revolution in *The Iceman Cometh*." *Modern Drama* 22 (March 1979): 1-8.
Frenz, Horst. "*Marco Millions*: O'Neill's Chinese Experience and Chinese Drama." *Comparative Literary Studies* 18 (September 1981): 362-367.
___, and Martin Mueller. "More Shakespeare and Less Aeschylus in Eugene O'Neill's *Mourning Becomes Electra*." *American Literature* 38 (March 1966): 85-100.
Fuchs, E. "O'Neill's Poet: Touched by Ibsen." *Educational Theatre Journal* 30 (December 1978): 513-516.
Gabbard, L.P. "At the Zoo: From O'Neill to Albee." *Modern Drama* 19 (December 1976): 365-374.
Garvey, S.H. "The Origins of the O'Neill Renaissance: A History of the 1956 Productions of *The Iceman Cometh* and *A Long Day's Journey Into Night*." *Theatre Survey* 29 (May 1988): 51-68.
Gassner, John. "Eugene O'Neill: The Course of a Modern Dramatist." *Critique: Critical Review of Theatre Arts* 1 (February 1958): 5-14.
___. "Homage to Eugene O'Neill." *Theatre Time* 3 (Summer 1951): 17-21.
Gierow, Karl-Ragner. "Eugene O'Neill's Posthumous Plays." *World Theatre* 7 (Spring 1958): 46-52.

Granger, Bruce Ingham. "Illusion and Reality in Eugene O'Neill." *Modern Language Notes* 73 (March 1958): 179-186.
Grimm, R. "A Note on O'Neill, Nietzche, and Naturalism: *Long Day's Journey Into Night* in European Perspective." *Modern Drama* 26 (September 1983): 331-334.
Hartman, Murray. "*Desire Under the Elms* in the Light of Strindberg's Influence." *American Literature* 33 (November 1961): 360-369.
___. "Strindberg and O'Neill." *Educational Theatre Journal* 18 (October 1966): 216-223.
Hawley, William. "*The Iceman Cometh* and the Critics--1946, 1956, 1973." *Eugene O'Neill Newsletter* 9 (Winter 1985): 5-9.
Haywood, Ira N. "Strindberg's Influence on Eugene O'Neill." *Poet Lore* 39 (Winter 1928): 596-604.
Highsmith, James. "The Cornell Letters: Eugene O'Neill on His Craftmanship to George Jean Nathan." *Modern Drama* 15 (May 1972): 68-88.
Hill, Philip G. "A New Look at Mary Cavan Tyrone." *Southern Theatre*. 21.1 (1977): 11-17.
Hinden, Michael. "Desire and Forgiveness: O'Neill's Diptych." *Comparative Drama* 14 (Fall 1980): 240-250.
___. "Liking O'Neill." *Forum* 2.3 (1973): 59-66.
___. "The Transitional Nature of *All God's Chillun Got Wings*." *Eugene O'Neill Newsletter* 4 (May-September 1980): 3-5.
___. "When Playwrights Talk to God: Peter Shaffer and the Legacy of O'Neill." *Comparative Drama* 16 (Spring 1982): 49-63.
Hornby, Richard. "O'Neill's Metadrama." *Eugene O'Neill Newsletter* 12 (Summer/Fall 1988): 13-18.
Jackson, Esther M. "O'Neill the Humanist." *Eugene O'Neill Newsletter* 1 (September 1977): 1-4.
Jenckes, Norma. "O'Neill's Use of Irish-Yankee Stereotypes in *A Touch of the Poet*." *Eugene O'Neill Newsletter* 9 (Summer/Fall 1985): 34-38.
Jiji, Vera. "Reviewers Responses to the Early Plays of Eugene O'Neill: A Study in Influence." *Theatre Survey* 29 (May 1988): 69-80.
Josephs, Lois S. "The Women of Eugene O'Neill: Sex Role Stereotypes." *Ball State University Forum* 14.3 (1973): 3-8.
Kalson, A.E. and L.M. Schwerdt. "Eternal Recurrence and the Shaping of O'Neill's Dramatic Structures." *Comparative Drama* 24 (Summer 1990): 133-150.
Kaufman, R.J. "On the Supression of Modern Classic Style." *Modern Drama* 2 (February 1960): 358-369.
Keane, Christopher. "Blake and O'Neill: A Prophecy." *Blake Studies* 2 (Spring 1970): 23-24.
Kennedy, J.D. "O'Neill's Lavinia Mannon and the Dickinson Legend." *American Literature* 49 (March 1977): 108-113.
Krutch, Joseph Wood. "Eugene O'Neill's Claim to Greatness." *New York Times Book Review*, September 22, 1957: 1.

Selected Bibliography

___. "Eugene O'Neill, the Lonely Revolutionary." *Theatre Arts* 36 (April 1952): 29-30.
___. "O'Neill's Tragic Sense." *American Scholar* 16 (Summer 1947): 283-290.
Labelle, Maurice M. "Dionysus and Despair: The Influence of Nietzsche upon O'Neill's Drama." *Educational Theatre Journal* 25: 436-442.
Lai, S. "Mysticism and Noh in O'Neill." *Theatre Journal* 35 (March 1983): 74-87.
Lecky, Eleazer. "*Ghosts* and *Mourning Becomes Electra*: Two Versions." *Arizona Quarterly* 13 (Winter 1957): 320-338.
Lee, Robert C. "Eugene O'Neill's Remembrance: The Past is Present." *Arizona Quarterly* 23 (Winter 1967): 293-305.
___. "Evangelism and Anarchy in *The Iceman Cometh*." *Modern Drama* 12 (September 1969): 173-186.
___. "The Lonely Dreams." *Modern Drama* 9 (September 1966): 127-135.
Levitt, H. N. "Comedy in the Plays of Eugene O'Neill." *Players Magazine* 51 (Fall 1976): 92-95.
Lewis, W.B. "O'Neill and Hauptmann: A Study in Mutual Admiration." *Comparative Literary Studies* 22 (Summer 1985): 231-243.
McAleer, John J. "Christ Symbolism in *Anna Christie*." *Modern Drama* 4 (February 1962): 389-396.
McDermott, Dana S. "Robert Edmond Jones and Eugene O'Neill: Two American Visionaries." *Eugene O'Neill Newsletter* 8 (Spring 1984): 3-10.
McDonald, David. "The Phenomenology of the Glance in *Long Day's Journey Into Night*." *Theatre Journal* 31 (October 1979): 343-356.
McDonough, Carole, and Brian McDonough. "*Mourning Becomes Electra*: A Study of the Conflict between Puritanism and Paganism." *English Review* 3: 6-19.
McLaughlin, Bruce W. "*Strange Interlude* and *The Divine Comedy*." *Theatre Journal* [Albany] 12.2 (1973).
Mandl, Bette. "Family Ties: Landscape and Gender in *Desire Under the Elms*." *Eugene O'Neill Newsletter* 11 (Summer/Fall 1987): 19-23.
___. "Wrestling with the Angel in the House." *Eugene O'Neill Newsletter* 12 (Winter 1988): 19-23.
Manheim, Michael. "Eugene O'Neill: America's National Playwright." *Eugene O'Neill Newsletter* 9 (Summer/Fall 1985): 17-23.
___. "O'Neill's Transcendence of Melodrama in *A Touch of the Poet* and *A Moon for the Misbegotten*." *Comparative Drama* 16 (Fall 1982): 238-250.
Massa, A. "Intention and Effect in *The Hairy Ape*." *Modern Drama* 31 (March 1988): 81-90.
Metzger, Deena P. "Variations on a Theme: A Study of *Exiles* by James and *The Great God Brown* by Eugene O'Neill." *Modern Drama* 8 (September 1965): 174-184.
Moleski, J. "Eugene O'Neill and the Cruelty of Theatre." *Comparative Drama* 15 (Winter 81/82): 327-342.
Moorton, R.F. "The Author as Oedipus in *Mourning Becomes Electra* and *Long Day's Journey Into Night*." *Papers on Language and Literature* 25 (Summer 1989): 304-325.

Murphy, Brenda. "O'Neill's Realism: A Structural Approach." *Eugene O'Neill Newsletter* 8 (Summer/Fall 1983): 3-6.
Muchnic, Helen. "Circe's Swine: Plays by Gorki and O'Neill." *Comparative Literature* 3 (Spring 1951): 119-128.
Nelson, Doris. "O Neill's Women." *Eugene O'Neill Newsletter* 6 (Summer/Fall 1982): 3-7.
Nethercoat, Arthur H. "Madness in the Plays of Eugene O'Neill." *Modern Drama* 18 (September 1975): 259-279.
____. "O'Neill's More Stately Mansions." *Educational Theatre Journal* 27 (May 1975): 161-169.
____. "The Psychoanalyzing of Eugene O'Neill." *Modern Drama* 3 (December 1960): 242-256.
____. "The Psychoanalyzing of Eugene O'Neill: Postscript." *Modern Drama* 8 (September 1965): 150-155.
Nolan, Patrick, J. "*The Emperor Jones*: A Jungian View of the Origin of Fear in the Black Race." *Eugene O'Neill Newsletter* 4 (May-September 1980): 6-9.
Oliver, R.W. "From the Exotic to the Real: The Evolution of Black Characterization in Three Plays by Eugene O'Neill." *Forum* 13 (1976): 56-71.
O'Neill, Joseph P., S. J. "The Tragic Theory of Eugene O'Neill." *Texas Studies in Literature and Language* 4 (Winter 1963): 481-493.
O'Neill, M.C. "Confession as Artifice in the Plays of Eugene O'Neill." *Renascence* 39 (Spring 1987): 430-441.
Pallette, Drew B. "O'Neill's *A Touch of the Poet* and His Other Lost Plays." *Arizona Quarterly* 13 (Winter 1957): 308-319.
____. "O'Neill and the Comic Spirit." *Modern Drama* 3 (December 1960): 273-279.
Pommer, Henry F. "The Mysticism of Eugene O'Neill." *Modern Drama* 9 (May 1966): 26-39.
Pond, Gloria Dribble. "A Family Disease." *Eugene O'Neill Newsletter* 9 (Spring 1985): 12-14.
Porter, Laurin R. "*The Iceman Cometh* as Crossroad in O'Neill's Long Journey." *Modern Drama* 31 (March 1988): 16-27.
____. "Bakhtin's Chronatope: *A Touch of the Poet* and *More Stately Mansions*." *Modern Drama* 34 (September 1991): 369-382.
Presley, D.E. "O'Neill's Iceman: Another Meaning." *American Literature* 42 (November 1970): 387-388.
Quinn, Arthur Hobson. "The American Spirit in Comedy and Tragedy." *English Journal* 13 (January 1924): 1-10.
____. "Eugene O'Neill, Poet and Mystic." *Scribner's* 80 (October 1926): 368-372.
Quinn, James P. "*The Iceman Cometh*: O'Neill's Long Day's Journey into Adolescence." *Journal of Popular Culture* 6 (Summer 1972): 171-177.
Quintero, José. "Postscript to a Journey." *Theatre Arts* 41 (April 1957): 27-29.
Raleigh, John Henry. "O'Neill's Long Day's Journey and New England Irish-Catholicism." *Partisan Review* 26 (Fall 1959): 573-592.
____. "Strindberg in Andrew Jackson's America." *Clio* 13 (Fall 1983): 1-15.

Ready, R. "The Play of the Misbegotten." *Modern Drama* 31 (March 1988): 81-90.
Regenbaum, Shelly. "Wrestling with God: Old Testament Themes in *Beyond the Horizon*." *Eugene O'Neill Newsletter* 8 (Summer/Fall 1984): 13-14
Reinhardt, Nancy. "Formal Patterns in *The Iceman Cometh*." 16 (September 1973): 119-127.
Robinson, James A. "Convergences and Divergences: Father and Son in *A Touch of the Poet* and *The Iceman Cometh*." *American Literature* 59 (October 1987): 323-340.
____. "Ghost Stories: Iceman's Absent Women and Mary Tyrone." *Eugene O'Neill Newsletter* 12 (Winter 1988): 14-19.
____. O'Neill's Grotesque Dancers." *Modern Drama* 19 (December 1976): 341-349.
____. "Taoism and O'Neill's *Marco Millions*." *Comparative Drama* 14 (Fall 1980): 251-262.
Rosen, Kenneth M. "O'Neill's Brown and Wilde's Gray." *Modern Drama* 13 (February 1971): 347-355.
Rothenberg, Albert. "Autobiographical Drama: Strindberg and O'Neill." *Literature and Psychology* 17 (1967): 95-114.
Roy, Emil. "The Archetypal Unity of Eugene O'Neill's Drama." *Comparative Drama* 3 (Winter 1969/70): 263-274.
____. "*The Iceman Cometh* as Myth and Realism." *Journal of Popular Culture* 2 (Fall 1968): 399-313.
____. "Tragic Tension in *Beyond the Horizon*." *Ball State University Forum* 8 (Winter 1967): 74-79.
Rust, R. Dilworth. "The Unity of O'Neill's *S.S. Glencairn*." *American Literature* 37 (November 1965): 280-290.
Scheick, W.J. "Ending of O'Neill's *Beyond the Horizon*." *Modern Drama* 19 (December 1976): 365-374.
Scrimgeour, J.R. "From Loving to the Misbegotten: Despair in the Drama of Eugene O'Neill." *Modern Drama* 29 (March 1977): 37-53.
Selmon M. "Past, Present and Future Converged: The Place of *More Stately Mansions* in the Eugene O'Neill Canon." *Modern Drama* 20 (December
Shaughnessy, Edward P. "Eugene O'Neill: The Development of the Negro Portraiture." *MELUS* 11.2 (1984): 87-91.
1985): 553-562.
Shawcross, John T. "The Road to Ruin: The Beginnings of O'Neill's Long Day's Journey." *Modern Drama* 3 (December 1960): 289-296.
Sogiuzzo, A. Richard. "The Uses of the Mask in *The Great God Brown* and *Six Characters in Search of an Author*." *Educational Theatre Journal* 18 (October 1966): 224-229.
Stafford, John. "Mourning Becomes America." *Texas Studies in Literature and Language* 3 (Winter 1962): 549-556.
Stamm, Rudolf. "Eugene O'Neill's *The Iceman Cometh*." *Scandinavian Studies* 29 (1948): 138-145.
Straumann, Heinrich. "The Philosophical Background of the Modern American Drama." *English Studies* 2 (June 1944): 5-78.

Stroupe, John H. "Abandonment of Ritual: Jean Anouilh and Eugene O'Neill." *Renascence* 28 (Spring 1976): 147-154.

___. "*Marco Millions* and O'Neill's Two Part Two-Play Form." *Modern Drama* 13 (February 1971): 382-392.

___. "O'Neill's *Marco Millions*: A Road to Xanadu." *Modern Drama* 12 (February 1970): 377-382.

Tornquist, Egil. "Ibsen and O'Neill: A Study of Influence." *Scandinavian Studies* 37 (August 1965): 211-235.

___. "Jesus and Judas: On Biblical Allusions in O'Neill's Plays." *Etudes Anglaises* 24 (1971): 41-49.

___. "*Miss Julie* and O'Neill." *Modern Drama* 19 (December 1976): 351-364.

___. "O'Neill's Lazarus: Dionysus and Christ." *American Literature* 41 (January 1970): 543-554.

Trilling, Lionel. Eugene O'Neill, a Revaluation." *New Republic* September 23, 1936: 176-179.

Tuck, Susan. "O'Neill and Frank Wedekind." *Eugene O'Neill Newsletter* 6 (Spring 1982): 29-35; (Summer/Fall 1982): 17-21.

Vena, Gary. "Chipping at the *Iceman*: The Text and the 1946 Theatre Guild Production." *Eugene O'Neill Newsletter* 9 (Winter 1985): 11-17.

___. "Congruency and Coincidence in O'Casey's *Juno* and O'Neill's *Journey*." *English Studies* 68 (June 1987): 249-263.

___. "The Role of the Prostitute in the Plays of O'Neill." *Drama Critique* 10 (Fall 1967): 129-137; 11 (Winter 1968): 9-14; 11 (Spring 1968): 82-88.

Voelker, P. "Eugene O'Neill's Aesthetic of the Drama." *Modern Drama* 21 (March 1978): 87-99.

Waith, Eugene M. "Eugene O'Neill: An Exercise in Unmasking." *Educational Theatre Journal* 13 (October 1961): 182-191.

Waterstradt, Jean Ann. "Another View of Ephraim Cabot: A Footnote to *Desire Under the Elms*." *Eugene O'Neill Newsletter* 9 (Summer/Fall 1985): 27-31.

Weiss, A. Samuel. "O'Neill, Nietzche, and Cows." *Modern Drama* 34 (December 1991): 494-498.

Weissman, Philip. "Conscious and Unconscious Autobiography in the Dramas of Eugene O'Neill." *Journal of the American Psychoanalytic Association* 5 (July 1957): 432-460.

Winther, Sophus Keith. "*Desire Under the Elms*: A Modern Tragedy." *Modern Drama* 3 (December 1960): 326-332.

___. "Eugene O'Neill: The Dreamer Confronts His Dream." *Arizona Quarterly* 21 (Autumn 1965): 221-273.

___. "*The Iceman Cometh*: A Study in Technique." *Arizona Quarterly* 3 (Winter 1947): 293-300.

___. O'Neill's Tragic Themes: *Long Day's Journey*." *Arizona Quarterly* 13 (Winter 1957): 295-307.

___. "Strindberg and O'Neill: A Study of Influence." *Scandinavian Studies* 31 (August 1959): 103-120.

Whitman, Robert F. "O'Neill's Search for a Language of the Theatre." *Quarterly Journal of Speech* 46 (April 1960): 153-170.
Wright, Robert C. "O'Neill's Universalizing Technique in *The Iceman Cometh*." *Modern Drama* 8 (May 1965): 1-11.
Young, William. "Mother and Daughter in *Mourning Becomes Electra*." *Eugene O'Neill Newsletter* 6 (Summer/Fall 1982): 15-17.
Zapf, H. "O'Neill's *Hairy Ape* and the Reversal of Hegelian Dialectics." *Modern Drama* 31 (March 1988): 81-90.

* Critical anthologies containing essays not listed in this bibliography.
** Bibliographies or collections of O'Neill's non-dramatic writings.

Index

A

Actors Studio, 117
Adler, Alfred, 62
Aeschylus, 127, 135
Ah, Wilderness!, 149, 150, 152-158, 160, 169, 170, 212, 213, 284, 286
Aldredge, Tom, 120, 184
Alexander, Arthur, 122
Alexander, Doris M., 105, 137
All God's Chillun Got Wings, 5, 60, 61, 65-70, 73, 77, 89, 284
American Literature, 115,
American Mercury, 58, 126
American Spectator, 92,
Anathema! Litanies of Negation, 105
Anders, Glenn, 102, 118, 124
Anderson, Erville, 16
Anderson, John, 150
Anna Christie, 4, 27-30, 34, 43, 53, 57, 124, 166, 168, 176, 257, 274
Antoine, Andre, 56,
Antony and Cleopatra, 55
Aristophanes, 33
Arnold, Edward, 16
Ashley, Arthur, 19
As I Lay Dying, 270
As You Like It, 227

Atkinson, J. Brooks, 2, 5, 99, 126, 175, 195
Auden, W.H., 45,
Autobiographical content, 3, 4, 193-199, 220, 221

B

Baker, Lee, 131
The Banished Prince, 250
Barlow, Judith, 6
Bannon, Ian, 221
Barnes, Clive, 183, 199, 252
Barnes, Howard, 173
Barton, Bruce, 191
Barton, James, 173, 191
Beckett, Samuel, 193
Before Breakfast, 17, 283
Belasco, David, 13, 58, 231
Ben-Ami, Jacob, 58
Benchley, Robert, 3, 5, 129,175
Bennett, Richard, 16
Bentley, Eric, 2, 138, 197, 216
Ben-Zvi, Linda, 6, 272
Bergman, Ingrid, 253, 255, 256
Betrayal, 279
Beyond the Horizon, 14-20, 26, 34, 167, 257, 265, 267, 273-275, 277, 278, 283
Beyond the Pleasure Principle, 112
Biberpelz, 76

Big Grand Opus, 125
Biographical criticism, 6
Birth of a Nation, 70
The Birth of Tragedy, 88-93, 96
Blair, Eugenie, 29
Blair, Mary, 26, 59
Blake, Edmund, 93
Blake, William, 93
Bloom, Steven F., 200
Bogard, Travis, 184, 187
Book of Revelations, 105
Booth, Edwin, 211
Bound East for Cardiff, 10, 12, 14, 35, 273, 278
Bowen, Croswell, 143
Brady, Alice, 128, 130, 133
Braithwaite, William Stanley, 69
The Bridegroom Cometh, 179
Brooklyn Academy of Music, 198
Broomfield, Louis, 263
Broun, Heywood, 9, 263
Brown, Arvin, 160, 196, 197
Brown, Gilmore, 105, 121, 122
Brustein, Robert, 3, 191, 250, 256
Brydon, W.B., 217
Burt, Frederic, 40
Byron, George Gordon, 243

C

Cagney, Jeanne, 174
Caldwell, Zoe, 198, 212
The Call, 166
The Calms of Capricorn, 276
Cannon, Glenn, 214
Capalbo, Carmen, 214-216
Carb, David, 122
Carey, Harry, 151
Cargill, Oscar, 68, 89
Carpenter, Frederic, 152, 222
Castellun, Maida, 27
Catholic World, 150
Chalmers, Thomas, 131
Chalzel, Leo, 174
Chapman, John, 233
Chekhov, Anton, 197
"Childe Harold", 243, 246
Choephoroi, 135
Chothia, Jean, 5, 221
"Chris Christopherson", 274, 276, 279
Chris, 14, 34
Christian Century, 112, 165
Christian, Robert, 72

Circle in the Square Theatre, 71, 73, 160, 175, 183, 191, 216, 217
Clancy, Deidre, 119
Clark, Barrett H., 3, 4, 12, 53, 67, 81, 89, 102, 105, 142, 257
Clurman, Harold, 36, 87, 217, 233, 236, 263
Cohan, George M., 149, 151
Cohn, Ruby, 153
Colbert, Claudette, 124
Collins, Russell, 173
Comedy Theatre, 12
Commager, Henry Steele, 218
Commonweal, 84, 216, 252, 255
Comparative criticism, 6,
Comparative Drama, 148
Condon, Eva, 40
The Connection, 193
Conrad, Joseph, 65,
Conway, Kevin, 198
Cook, Elisha, 150
Cook, George Cram, 73
Cornford, F.M., 96
Corrigan, Emmett, 19
The Count of Monte Cristo, 3, 175
Cox, Brian, 120
Crabtree, Paul, 173
Croft, Paddy, 197
Culbertson, Ernest, 69
Curley, James Michael, 205
Cusack, Cyril, 214, 216, 217

D

Dance of Death, 57
Dancy, Virginia, 197
Day, Cyrus, 88, 177, 188
Days Without End, 2, 161, 163, 166, 170, 178, 231, 266
Death of a Salesman, 45, 192
de Beauvoir, Simone, 185, 187
De Casseres, Benjamin, 88, 105, 142
Desire Under the Elms, 73, 74, 77, 81, 90, 167, 195, 263, 267, 283, 288
Dewhurst, Colleen, 160, 212, 218, 219, 221, 221, 254-256
Diff'rent, 25, 26, 43, 167, 263-265, 286
Digges, Dudley, 124, 173, 174, 191
Dillman, Bradford, 194, 195
Dodson, Jack, 252
The Doll's House, 29
Donley, Robert, 37
Don Quixote, 45

Index

Dostoievsky, Fedor, 174
Dowling, Eddie, 172, 174
Doyle, David N., 206
Drama, 83, 105
The Dramatic Moment, 216
The Dreamy Kid, 15, 66, 67
Drucker, Trudy, 6
Duncan, Augustin, 39
Dunham, Clark, 184
Dynamo, 2, 105, 122-126, 161, 169, 231, 263, 284

E

Eastman, Fred, 162
Edwards, Ben, 37, 192, 213, 220, 254, 255
Eliade, Mircea, 46
Eldridge, Florence, 193, 195, 200
Electra, 75, 130, 135
Eliot, T.S., 63, 96
Ellis, Charles, 26
Emigrants and Exiles, 204
The Emperor Jones, 19, 20, 22, 23, 25, 26, 42, 44, 45, 48, 50, 53, 56, 59-61, 66-70, 89, 124, 125, 206
"Endicott and the Red Cross", 269
Engel, Edwin, 153
Eugene O'Neill Newsletter, 120, 190, 203
Euripides, 127, 135, 264
Everyman, 83
Expressionism, 60

F

Falk, Doris, 6
Fareleigh, Margaret, 11
The Father, 57, 129
Faulkner, William, 288
Faust, 103, 162
Field, Betty, 118, 236
Fielder, Leslie, 279
Firkens, O.W., 19
The First Man, 39, 40, 53, 57, 126
Fisher, Jules, 184
Fitzgerald, F. Scott, 44, 288
Fitzgerald, Geraldine, 197, 199, 212, 237
Flanders, Edward, 219
Fluckiger, Stephen L., 263
Fog, 166
Fonda, Jane, 118
Fontanne, Lynn, 19, 101, 102, 118
Forging a Language, 5, 221
Foster, Gloria, 200
The Fountain, 81, 82, 90, 100, 181

Francis-James, Peter, 200
Frank, Waldo, 179
Frazer, Winifred, 30, 186
Freeman, 57
Freeman, Al Jr., 200
Freud, Sigmund, 105, 112, 113, 179, 134-136
The Future of an Illusion, 151, 180

G

Gallagher, Peter, 203
Galsworthy, John, 12, 60
Gassner, John, 3, 110
Gaul, George, 124
Gazzara, Ben, 118, 186, 123
Gelb, Arthur and Barbara, 6, 31, 252, 256
Gelber, Jack, 193
Gentry, Minnie, 72
Gibbs, Wolcott, 197
Gierow, Karl Ragner, 256
Gilbert, Ruth, 174
Gillett, Peter J., 61
Gillmore, Margalo, 38
Gilpen, Charles S., 21, 22
Glaspell, Susan, 27
Glover, John, 88
Gold, 4, 26, 167
Golden, Annie, 160
Goncourt, Edmond and Jules, 55
Gorki, Maxim, 28, 171, 175, 179, 183
Great Gatsby, 47
The Great God Brown, 32, 83, 85-87, 89, 93, 96, 103, 121, 124, 136, 166, 168, 182, 231, 265, 283, 288
Greek tragedy, 75, 76, 126-129
Greene, James, 191
Greenwich Village Theatre, 10, 12, 13, 73, 75, 81, 89
Greenwood, Jane, 192, 254, 255
Grey, Katherine, 38
Gulliver's Travels, 45
Gwillim, Jack, 184

H

Hack, Keith, 118
The Hairy Ape, 31, 34, 41-45, 48, 51, 53, 56, 60, 61, 73, 77, 82, 89, 93, 124, 149, 166, 169, 275, 278
Halbwachs, Maurice, 206
Hale, Louise Closser, 16
Hamilton, G.V., 138

Hamlet, 56, 222
Hammond, Percy, 40, 100
Hampton, Mary, 19
Harrigan, William, 84, 86
Harwood, Harry, 38
Harvey, John, 254, 255
The Haunted, 139
Hauptmann, Gerhart, 55, 56, 60, 76
Hawthorne, Nathaniel, 269
Hays, David, 196
Hayes, Helen, 234-236
Hayes, Peter L., 77
Hayes, Richard, 214
Hazeldine, James, 120
Hearn, George, 160
Heart of Darkness, 65
Helburn, Theresa, 223
Hemingway, Earnest, 47, 288
Henry IV, 222, 230
Hepburn, Katharine, 119, 202
Higgins, Michael, 184
Hill, Arthur, 254-256
Hiller, Wendy, 213, 216-218
Hinden, Michael, 88
Hingle, Pat, 118
Historical scholarship, 6
Hofmannstahl, Hugo von, 53, 75
Hogarth, Leona, 84, 86
Hooker, Thomas, 269
Hopkins, Arthur, 28
Hornby, Richard, 229
Horne, Geoffrey, 118
Hughes, Barnard, 191
Hughie, 250, 252
The Hunted, 140, 145
Huston, Walter, 74, 76
Hyman, Earle, 200

I

Ibsen, Henrik, 54, 56, 167, 175, 179, 197, 264
Ibsen, John Duffy, 206
The Iceman Cometh, 2, 3, 32, 61, 68, 77, 91, 171-186, 189, 191-193, 195, 206, 219, 226, 229, 233-235, 237, 254-256, 265, 275, 284
Ile, 12, 13, 35, 167, 273
The Importance of Being Earnest, 227
In the Zone, 12, 13, 14, 166, 273
It Can Not Be Had, 125

J

Jackson, Glenda, 119
James, Henry, 234
Jane Eyre, 185
Jefferson, Joseph, 149
Jens, Salome, 217, 218
Jerusalem, 93
Johnson, Edward, 269
Jones, Henry Arthur, 161
Jones, James Earl, 184
Jones, John Christopher, 191
Jones, Robert Edmond, 23, 29, 73, 75, 81, 84, 86, 92, 127, 128, 130, 131, 172, 174
Jory, Victor, 122
Joy, Nicholas, 173, 174
Joyce, James, 264

K

Kalem, T.E., 236,
Keane, Doris, 58
Keith, Robert, 84, 86
Kennedy Center, 198
Kerr, Walter, 6, 193
Kilty, Jerome, 221
King Lear, 21
Kim, Willa, 203
Kreymborg, Alfred, 16
Kroll, Jack, 197
Kruger, Otto, 38
Krutch, Joseph Wood, 3, 5, 73, 81, 105, 114, 131, 152

L

Language, 2-5, 54, 76, 81-83, 172, 183, 214-216
Larimore, Earle, 118, 128, 131, 162
Lawrence, D.H., 95
Lazarus Laughed, 90, 97, 105, 120, 121, 166, 231, 283
LeGallienne, Eva, 151
Lemmon, Jack, 201
Leopard's Spots, 70
Leslie, Bethel, 201, 202
Lewis, Sinclair, 99
Levaux, David, 221
Levine, Michael, 119
Lewis, Sinclair, 60
Lewisohn, Ludwig, 4, 26
Little Johnny Jones, 149

Index

Lindsay, Vachel, 65
Linville, Lawrence, 255
Lithgow, John, 37
Lockhart, Gene, 150
Long Day's Journey Into Night, 2, 4, 6, 23, 31, 91, 152, 157, 160, 175, 176, 183, 193-200, 202-205, 210, 212-214, 219, 220, 229, 233, 234, 237, 243, 252, 254-256, 267, 275, 278, 280, 285, 289
The Long Voyage Home, 13, 35
The Long Way Home, 12
Loraine, Robert, 162
Lord of the Flies, 62
Lord, Pauline, 28, 29, 37
Lovell, John, Jr., 68
The Lower Depths, 28, 171, 179, 183, 191

M

Macaulay, Joseph, 11
Macfie, Jane, 160, 213
Macgowan, Kenneth, 22, 93, 138
MacKeller, Helen, 16
Malraux, André, 182
Mandl, Bette, 6, 184
Manheim, Michael, 6
Mann, Theodore, 184
March, Fredric, 194-196, 212
Marco Millions, 77, 90, 99, 100, 102, 105, 109, 110, 149, 168
Marcuse, Herbert, 50
Marion, George, 29
Markey, Enid, 151
Markham, Marcella, 174
Marquis, Marjorie, 150
Marriot, John, 173
Marshall, E.G., 173
Masks, 75-76, 83-87
Mason, Benedict, 119
The Masses, 166
Mather, Cotton, 269
McCarthy, Mary, 2, 214, 216
McClain, John, 213
McCrane, Paul, 191
McKoy, Samantha, 200
McMartin, John, 88
Mellon, Thomas, 204
Meltzer, Harold, 11
Melville, Herman, 264
Mencken, H.L., 167
The Metaphysics of Love and the Sexes, 106
Millay, Edna St. Vincent, 22

Miller, Arthur, 45, 177
Miller, Jonathan, 200, 202, 203
Miller, Kerby, 204, 205
Ming Cho Lee, 72
The Miracle, 121
Mitzel, Max, 16
Modern Drama, 36, 81, 99, 160, 182, 212, 261, 282
Moeller, Philip, 102, 128, 130, 131
Moffatt, Donald, 191
A Moon for the Misbegotten, 4, 183, 206, 213-217, 219, 220-222, 227, 231, 264, 266, 275, 278, 286
The Moon of the Caribbees, 12, 66, 67, 82, 90, 273
Moore, Dennie, 151
More Stately Mansions, 91, 238, 242, 248, 252-257, 260, 266, 276, 278, 283, 288
Moriarity, Michael, 198
Morris, Mary, 74, 76
Motherhood, 282-289
Motley, 196
Mourning Becomes Electra, 3, 5, 90, 126, 127, 129-138, 142, 146, 169, 175, 181, 195, 231, 263, 265, 283, 286
Mower, Margaret, 39,
Muchnic, Helen, 186
Musser, Tharon, 196
Mythological themes, 22-30

N

Nathan, George Jean, 2, 57, 125, 143, 161, 167, 222, 258
Nation, 27, 37, 74, 88, 133, 236, 263
Native Son, 69
Naturalism, 60
Naughton, James, 197
Nazimova, Alla, 128, 130, 133
Neighborhood Playhouse, 39
Nelligan, Kate, 220, 221
Nelson, Doris, 6, 287
Nelson, Richard, 203
Newsweek, 199
New Republic, 18, 43, 53, 61, 76, 87, 170, 193, 256
New York Call, 29,
New York Daily News, 73, 234
New York Drama Mirror, 10, 19
New York Evening Post, 16
New York Globe and Commercial Advertiser, 11
New York Herald, 40, 102

New York Herald Tribune, 174, 194
New York Journal American, 151, 214
New York Magazine, 161, 213, 221
New York Post, 59, 118, 173, 200
New York Sun, 14, 38
New York Times, 15, 24, 26, 30, 100, 122, 129, 176, 184, 196, 254
New York Tribune, 10, 41
New Yorker, 131, 197
Nichols, Dudley, 186, 188
Nietzche, Friedrich, 88, 89, 91, 93, 95, 96, 106, 264
No Exit, 186
Nugent, S. Georgia, 134

O

O'Casey, Sean, 237, 258
Old Times, 209
Oliver, Edith, 196
Olivier, Laurence, 199
O'Neill, Carlotta Monterey, 143, 198, 256
O'Neill, Edmond, 205
O'Neill, Ella Quinlan, 205, 279
O'Neill, James, 3, 129, 175, 205
O'Neill, James, Jr. (Jamie), 198, 228
Orestia, 135, 234

P

Page, Geraldine, 118
Paradise Lost, 47
Parritt, Dan, 174
Parsifal, 103
Pasadena Community Playhouse, 120
Passing of the Third Floor, 179
Pedi, Tom, 173, 174
Petherbridge, Edward, 120
Phoenix Repertory Company, 87
Pichel, Irving, 122
Pierre, 269
Pinter, Harold, 209, 279
Pirandello, Luigi, 222, 230
Pitkin, William, 214
Porter, Laurin, 238
Portman, Eric, 233, 235, 236
Powers, Eugene, 40
Powers, Tom, 118
Priest, Jimmy, 176
Prince, Harold, 88
Prince, William, 118, 151
Prometheus Unbound, 93
Proust, Marcel, 207, 210

Provincetown Players, 10, 14, 20, 22, 23, 25, 60,
Provincetown Playhouse, 23, 167
Provincetown Theatre, 40, 58,
Pulitzer Prize 3, 4
Puritanism, 263-270

Q

Quintero, José, 37, 117, 175, 191, 192, 194, 195, 212, 220, 237, 252, 253, 255, 256
Quinn, Arthur Hobson, 3

R

R.M.L., 75
Racey, Edgar, 267
Racine, Jean, 264
Raleigh, John Henry, 3, 152, 185, 188, 203, 263
Rattigan, Terence, 236
Real, Jere, 256
Reid, Carl Benton, 173, 174
Reinhardt, Max, 53, 121
Rememberance of Things Past, 207
Religious themes, 161-165, 161, 177-182
Renascence, 272
A Research in Marriage, 138
Rhys, Jean, 185
Richardson, Ralph, 199, 236
Riders to the Sea, 28, 33
Ritual, 36-45, 234-247
Ridges, Stanley, 162
Robbins, Carrie F., 184
Ridge, Lola, 16
Robards, Jason, 160, 191, 194-196, 198, 212, 219, 221, 237, 251
Robeson, Paul, 23, 159
Robinson, Edward Arlington, 79, 149
Robinson, James A., 221
Rogers, John, 19
The Rope, 11, 12, 14, 77
Rosencrantz and Guildenstern Are Dead, 222
Ross, Katherine, 194, 196
Der Rote Hahn, 76
Rowlandson, Mary, 270
Roy, Emil, 44
Royle, Selena, 162
The Rubaiyat of Omar Khayyam, 153
Ryan, Mitchell, 217
Ryan, Robert, 197, 199

Index

S

S.S. Glencairn, 73, 166
Saint Joan, 45
Sampson Agonistes, 50
Sardou, Victorien, 56
Saroyan, William, 171
Sbarge, Raphael, 161
The Scarlet Letter, 263
Schopenhauer, Arthur, 89, 91, 105-107, 109, 110, 112-115
Scott, Campbell, 71, 72, 212
Scott, George C.,
Scribe, Augustin, 56
Sea Mother's Son, 31
The Second Sex, 185
Sedgwick, Kyra, 160
Servant in the House, 179
Servitude, 92
Sewall, Samuel, 269
Sexual themes, 105-115, 134-145
The Shadow of the Glen, 28
Shakespeare, William, 54, 55, 223
Shanewise, Lenore, 122
Shannon, Frank, 29
Shaw, George Bernard, 45, 264
Shawcross, John T., 152
Sheed, Wilfrid, 250
Shelley, Percy, 93
Shepard, Sam, 221
Sherwin, Louis, 10
Sheaffer, Louis, 6, 152, 187, 222
Sheridan, Jamey, 160, 213
Sherwood, Robert, 161
Shoemaker, Ann, 84, 86
Shurr, William, 263
Sights and Spectacles, 216
Simon, John, 160, 212, 220, 254
Simonson, Lee, 124
Six Characters in Search of an Author, 222
Skelton, Thomas R., 192
Skinner, Richard Dana, 83
Skybell, Steven, 160
Sophocles, 127, 135
Spacey, Kevin, 202, 203
Stanhope, Frederick, 19
Stanley, Kim, 234-236
Stevens, Morton L., 174
Stewart, Fred, 255
Stoppard, Tom, 230
Straiges, Tony, 203

Strange Interlude, 5, 100-106, 108, 109, 112-115, 117, 118, 119, 123, 125, 128, 169, 181, 207, 231, 260, 283
The Straw, 29, 37, 124, 166, 168, 283
A Streetcar Named Desire, 47, 235
Strindberg, August, 5, 54, 55, 57, 88, 105, 175, 197, 209, 237, 264
The Sun Also Rises, 47
Sunday, Billy, 191
Supernaturalism, 5
Swedish Royal Dramatic Theatre, 256
Synge, John Millington, 33

T

A Tale of Possessors Self-Dispossessed, 256, 257
Tamarkin, Nicholas, 160
The Tempest, 223
Theatre Arts Magazine, 12
Theatre Guild, 101, 128, 130, 149, 150, 162, 167, 173, 191, 217
The Theatre of Revolt, 250-256
Thomas, Vickie, 72
Throckmorton, Cleon, 23
Thus Spoke Zarathustra, 88, 91
Thirst, 14, 62, 66, 69
Thoreau, Henry David, 100
Tibbett, Lawrence, 68
Tidblad, Inga, 212
Time, 238
The Time of Your Life, 171
Tiusanen, Timo, 224, 265
Tone, Franchot, 118, 214, 216, 217
A Touch of the Poet, 154, 206, 221, 229, 223, 234, 236, 238, 243, 254, 259, 265, 266, 275, 276, 284
Towse, J. Rankin, 15
Trilling, Lionel, 48, 165, 215
Tully, Tom, 151
Tuttleton, James, 288

U

Ulysses, 210
Ullman, Liv, 37

V

Vahey, Brian, 221
Van Devere, Trish, 72
Van Laan, Thomas F., 152

Van Rensselaer Wyatt, Euphemia, 149
Vanity Fair, 162
Vatic, 119
Vidal, Gore, 234,
Vogue, 12, 125, 217
Vonnegut, Marjorie, 40

W

Waith, Eugene, 95
Walker, Kathryn, 237, 238
Wallace, Ronald, 197
Warren, George C., 120
The Wasteland, 96
Washington Square Players, 10, 13, 167
Watt, Douglas, 71
Watts, Richard, 117, 171
The Web, 90
Webb, Elmon, 197
Die Weber, 76
Weekly Review, 22
Weiss, Marc B., 221
Welch, Mary, 69
Welded, 2, 57, 58, 61, 126, 161, 168, 283
Wenger, John, 11
West, Anthony, 216
Westley, Helen, 102, 123, 124
What Is Wrong With Marriage?, 138
Where the Cross Is Made, 14, 181, 273
Wide Sargasso Sea, 185
The Wild Duck, 56, 179, 191
Wilkens, Frederick C., 118
Williams, Tennessee, 47, 235
Wilson, Dore, 122
Wilson, Edmond, 5, 60
Wilson, Elizabeth, 160
Without Ending of Days, 125
Wolfe, Thomas, 234
Wolheim, Louis, 40, 43
Women in O'Neill, 184-190, 208-211, 279-289
Woodson, William, 214
Woolf, S.J., 177
Woollcott, Alexander, 4, 14, 25, 29
Wright, Richard, 69, 70

Y

Young, Stark, 41, 58, 60, 85

Z

Zipprodt, Patricia, 72

About the Editor

JOHN H. HOUCHIN is currently Assistant Professor of Theater at Southern Illinois University at Carbondale. His articles have appeared in the *Dictionary of Stage Directors* (Greenwood Press) and *The Drama Review*.

PS
3529
.N5
Z62728
1993